THE ROOTES STORY

VOLUME 2: THE CHRYSLER YEARS

THE ROOTES STORY

VOLUME 2: THE CHRYSLER YEARS

GEOFF CARVERHILL FOREWORD BY NICK ROOTES

THE CROWOOD PRESS

First published in 2023 by
The Crowood Press Ltd
Ramsbury, Marlborough
Wiltshire SN8 2HR

enquiries@crowood.com

www.crowood.com

British Library Cataloguing-in-Publication Data
A catalogue record for this book is available from the British Library.

ISBN 978 0 7198 4178 1

Frontispiece: Geoffrey Rootes – second Lord Rootes.

Typeset by Simon and Sons
Cover design by Blue Sunflower Creative; layout and artwork by Ryan Lambie and Geoff Carverhill
Printed and bound in India by Replika Press Pvt Ltd

CONTENTS

FOREWORD

In this second volume of the Rootes Story, Geoff Carverhill reveals how the family business adapted to develop innovative new cars suited to the post-war era. Times were changing and car manufacturers had to change rapidly to meet buyer expectations. Rootes Group rose to the challenge in the 1960s and '70s with new models, underpinned by a competitions department that achieved outstanding rallying successes. However, against a background of industrial unrest, funding challenges and political interference, the going was getting tougher by the year.

Geoff paints a vivid picture of the period. Through meticulous research and interviews with people who worked for Rootes, he takes the reader on a journey that starts post war and which travels through the take-over by Chrysler, culminating in Chrysler UK's absorption into the Peugeot Group. It's a journey with many twists and turns, including strikes, political interventions, transatlantic culture clashes and, of course, the development of some remarkable cars that remain much loved to this day.

As I was a teenager in the Sixties, my own recollection of the period is of being fortunate enough to travel in some wonderful cars that included every type of Humber and, not forgetting, a memorable 120mph test drive in a Sunbeam Tiger prototype with my father, Geoffrey Rootes, at the wheel. I also got to drive my very own Sunbeam Stiletto, followed by an H120 Sunbeam Rapier. Little did I realise, while I was enjoying myself, just how difficult it must have been for my father, who steered the business through the most turbulent of times and the handover to Chrysler.

I'm immensely grateful to Geoff Carverhill for revealing the full story. It takes tenacity to write a book of such breadth and depth. I believe it will be of great interest, not just to Rootes car enthusiasts, but also to anyone who wants to understand how the motor industry evolved post war through the Sixties and beyond.

Nick Rootes
3rd Lord Rootes

INTRODUCTION AND ACKNOWLEDGEMENTS

In May 2013, shortly after I had been commissioned by Crowood to write *The Rootes Story*, I was invited by James Spencer of the Rootes Archive Centre to the 50th Anniversary of the launch of the Hillman Imp. The event took place at the site of the Rootes Scotland factory at Linwood, where the Imp was made, and would be the start of a re-appraisal of a company I thought I knew about. I got to talk, first hand, to people who worked at Linwood all those years ago. On the bus trip from Glasgow Central station to Linwood the warmth and sense of humour of those on board put a big smile on my face, and I have not forgotten it. The experience made me to take a fresh look at Rootes, and dispel some myths about the company as well as eliminate some popular misconceptions, not just about Linwood but about the whole of the Rootes organization.

Although this volume of The Rootes Story has presented numerous challenges, due to the convoluted and complex nature of the Rootes Group's activities from the 1960s onwards, it has brought some remarkable rewards, in as much as I have got to meet some of my childhood motorsport heroes: the late Sir Stirling Moss, whom I interviewed for Volume 1; wonderful Rosemary Smith; the late Paddy Hopkirk; Peter Procter and the late Andrew Cowan.

I feel privileged to have met and interviewed many ex-Rootes employees, pupils and apprentices, some of whom occupied senior management positions at Rootes and subsequently, Chrysler UK. Without their valuable input, this particular volume would not have been possible; it is after all, their story.

During one of the lockdown periods that took over our lives during the Covid pandemic, I was very pleased to be able to facilitate a reunion of four ex-Rootes pupils who were trainees together, but who hadn't met for sixty years! I had received an email from Patrick Cook, now resident in Florida, who had helped run Rootes Venezuela during the Sixties. He had bought a copy of Volume 1 of

The Rootes Story and had read comments by Kit Foster, Peter S. Badenoch, who now resides in Windsor, Ontario and Tom Cotton and asked me to put him in touch with them. They all duly met up by the wonders of email and Zoom! I was also able to put Patrick in touch with another ex-Rootes Venezuela colleague, Geoff Parr. My thanks to them for sharing their Rootes 'export' experiences.

Other ex-Rootes personnel also made some valuable contributions: Richard Guy; Scott Glover; Duncan Robertson; Stuart Mitchell; William Stuart; Anthony Stevens; Arthur Long; Geoff Wells; Mike Andrews; Ray Davies; Richard Avery; Ken Foxon; Keith Cockell; Phil Anslow; David Wells; Andy Kirkman; Martin Newbould; Douglas Field; Mike Jones; Bill Papworth; George B. Heath; John Haviland; Nigel Hughes; Alan Horsfall; Bill Blanch; Colin Valentine; Dave Edwards; David Lloyd; Owen Swinerd; Gordon Jarvis; John Harris; Wynne Mitchell; Leon Gibbs; Rodney Cane, Keith Cockell and Ron Roscoe. Thanks to all for your time and in some cases for lending me valuable photographs to reproduce in the book.

Other equally important 'thank yous' include those directly or indirectly associated with Rootes: Clive Harrington, for sharing his photographs and his father's experiences as managing director of Thomas Harrington Ltd, the famous coachbuilders in Worthing, Sussex; Nicholas Webster (and Clive Harrington) for the potted history of Thomas Harrington Ltd; Kit Spackman, of Pressed Steel Ltd; Tim Ware, son of Peter Ware, for his father's biography and family photographs and Paul Easter, ex-BMC works rally driver, for loaning his valuable Kodachrome transparencies of the London-Sydney Marathon. Andy Bye and all at the Rootes Archive Centre have provided information and photographs, as have Coventry Archives at the Herbert Art Gallery & Museum in Coventry – thanks to Damien Kimberley and Victoria Northridge.

Without the one marque car clubs, books like this would be much more difficult to create, so thanks to all who provided photographs from club archives and who diligently checked text for factual accuracy: Graham Vickery of the Sunbeam Tiger Club, Stephen Lewis of the Post Vintage Humber Car Club; Andy Goldsmith of the Sunbeam Alpine Owners Club; David Freeth, Nigel Hughes and Bob Marsden of the Singer Owners Club; Ray Sellars of Hillman Owners Club and writer and historian Bill Munro, for everything Carbodies.

Last but not least, to the Rootes family, the late Tim Rootes for his sense of humour and insightful knowledge of his father's and his uncle's company – Sir Reginald Rootes and Lord Rootes. To Nick Rootes, who has been very supportive throughout and who allowed me to spend a very enjoyable few days going through his family archives – I feel privileged to have been allowed to do

so. Bill Rootes, son of Brian Rootes, gave some insightful recollections from his father's and Bill's own experiences while working for Rootes.

Thanks also to the staff at Crowood, for their patience and tolerance, and one very important person, without whom I would not have finished this book, had it not been for her encouragement and support – my wife Sue.

Thank you one and all.

This book is dedicated to Peter Procter and Andrew Cowan, two 'team mates' and gentlemen of Rootes motorsport.

**Geoff Carverhill – the end bar stool, The Royal Oak, Cogenhoe, Northampton.
September, 2022**

CHAPTER 1

EMPIRE-BUILDING

'I don't mind what I sell, provided it's British!'
— William Rootes Snr

The rolling countryside of the Weald of Kent, in the south-east of England, with its leafy lanes and picture postcard villages, seems an unlikely backdrop to inspire a young lad to embrace late nineteenth-century England's still new phenomenon – the motor car. However, it did, and within twenty-five years, William Rootes would witness the start of what would become, under the stewardship of his two sons, William and Reginald, one of Britain's largest and most important motor vehicle manufacturing concerns.

William Rootes was born in Goudhurst, Kent, in 1869. His father, Edward, ran a small general engineering business in the village repairing agricultural machinery and, at twelve years of age, William joined his father helping

out in his engineering workshop. By 1895, William had opened his own cycle shop in Goudhurst, was married, and had had a son, William Edward, born in 1894. His second son, Reginald Claud, was born in 1896.

William's cycle business was successful enough for the family to move to nearby Hawkhurst around 1901, where he had acquired a shop, showroom and workshop premises in which to sell and service bicycles and motor-cycles; however, very soon, the motor car bug, which had initially been sparked following a visit to the 1895 Horseless Carriage Exhibition at Tunbridge Wells, would take precedent over bicycles and motorcycles. In 1907, William formed the Rootes Motor Agency, with prominent names such as Darracq, Humber, Swift, Vauxhall

A well-known photograph of the Wm. Rootes' motor depot and showroom at 7, Station Road, Hawkhurst, Kent.

NICK ROOTES

MOTOR CARS.

WILLIAM ROOTES,
ENGINEER.

HAWKHURST, Kent.

TELEGRAMS : ROOTES, HAWKHURST.
TELEPHONE : No. 8, HAWKHURST.

The front cover of one of
Wm. Rootes' first motor
car catalogues, c. 1908.
NICK ROOTES

and De Dion forming part of the roster. WR, as William Rootes became known locally, built up a profitable business in Hawkhurst, and his eldest son Billy started to take a lot of interest in all things mechanical, as his father had with Billy's grandfather. Billy was a quick learner and an astute young man, but proved to be a source of concern to his father, who was worried about his son's academic abilities. So, at the age of sixteen Billy was sent as an apprentice to the Singer Motor Company in Coventry to see if his technical abilities would be more impressive than his academic abilities. In the event, they were – Billy Rootes proved an exemplary student and, as he matured, would also turn out to be a very competent salesman. Reggie, on the other hand, filled the academic role with ease, and upon leaving Cranbrook School, joined the Admiralty, having passed the First Class Civil Service Examination.

Apprentices at Singer
Motor Company in
Coventry. Billy Rootes,
aged 16, is seated in the
front row, third from the
left. NICK ROOTES

By 1913, with William Rootes and son Billy now in business together, larger premises were acquired in Maidstone to cope with an increase in motor car sales and servicing. With the outbreak of the First World War, Billy joined the Royal Naval Volunteer Reserve, leaving his father to run the business. In 1916, Billy married Nora Press; the following year he and his father formed Rootes Ltd, and had acquired the old tannery in Maidstone, which was converted to the Len Engineering Works, to start the first aero engine repair business. The aero engine contract came as a result of Billy being sent to Clément Talbot in London, while in the RNVR to oversee aero engine production, during which time he highlighted a need, in order to prevent unnecessary wastage, to recondition and repair aero engines, rather than build new ones. Billy was demobilised towards the end of 1917 and seconded to carry out the reconditioning of the aero engines, which took place at Rootes Maidstone. This saved the Air Ministry a colossal amount of money, and clearly demonstrated Billy's commercially aware methodology. During this period he had persuaded his brother Reggie to give up a promising career in the civil service and join the family business. In 1920, Billy and Reggie were made joint managing directors of Rootes Ltd. The company would go from strength to strength following the end of the war, enabling William Rootes Snr to retire in 1924.

By the early 1920s, Rootes Ltd had secured numerous motor agencies, including Austin, Singer, Humber, Wolseley, Bean and Ford. Many of Britain's motor manufacturers were turning to Rootes to sell and distribute their cars and trucks, and by the mid-1920s, they would be the largest motor distributors in Britain.

Family life was also taking shape for the brothers. In 1917, Billy and Nora had their first son, William Geoffrey (known as Geoffrey). Two years later, Brian Gordon was born. Both sons would eventually play important roles in the development of the business. Reggie had also married, in 1922, to Joyce Bensted. They had a son, Timothy David, in 1925, and he too would join Geoffrey and Brian as part of the Rootes dynasty.

At its peak as a motor distribution company in the mid-1920s, the Rootes organisation was exporting around 3,000 vehicles a year, especially to Empire countries such as India, which was to prove a valuable territory for Rootes products. Rootes had become a key supplier to the British Raj, and one of Rootes' prominent customers, the Jam Sahib of Nawangar, is rumoured to have had 157 cars; no doubt a substantial proportion of which were supplied by Rootes Ltd. The Jam Sahib would later offer his hospitality to Billy Rootes when he visited India with his son Geoffrey in 1936. Australia and New Zealand were other dominion territories that were well represented by Rootes products, as well as principal European,

The offices, workshops and showrooms of Rootes Ltd, Len Engineering Works, Mill Street, Maidstone in 1934.

ROOTES ARCHIVE CENTRE TRUST

South American and Far East locations. In 1931, Reginald Rootes founded Rootes Argentina, based in Buenos Aires.

The 'most palatial hotel in India' was accommodation for Geoffrey Rootes and his father on their trip around the world in 1936. The Viceroy's Palace in New Delhi was a 340-room residence of the Viceroy of India, then Lord Willingdon. Designed by Edwin Lutyens, the building took seventeen years to complete. NICK ROOTES

THE ACQUISITION TRAIL

Being well connected was essential to the success of Rootes as a sales and distribution business, but the Rootes brothers felt they needed to have more control over the motor companies they were representing, which meant one thing – manufacturing. One fast track to owning a manufacturer was through acquisition, and the first of these came in 1925 when they acquired the old-established coachbuilding concern, Thrupp & Maberly of Cricklewood, north-west London. The following year, Rootes moved into Devonshire House, Piccadilly, a prestigious set of offices and showrooms in Mayfair, London, which would become their headquarters and export division offices for the next four decades.

'Rootes' London Headquarters, Devonshire House, Piccadilly.
ROOTES ARCHIVE CENTRE TRUST

A Sunbeam Talbot 4-Litre Saloon on the Thrupp & Maberly stand at the 1938 Earls Court Motor Show. COVENTRY ARCHIVES

During the mid-1920s, Rootes had made an unsuccessful attempt to acquire the Wolverhampton-based company Clyno, so instead turned their attention to Humber in Coventry, which proved to be the door that would lead to the Rootes brothers' manufacturing aspirations becoming a reality. In 1926, Humber had acquired Luton-based bus and lorry manufacturer Commercial Cars Ltd, and it was felt by the Humber chairman Col. J.A. Cole that the acquisition of neighbouring car manufacturer Hillman would enable the necessary economies of scale for Humber to continue as a profitable manufacturing concern. Rootes, meanwhile, had become minority shareholders of Humber and through their association with and assistance of the Prudential Assurance Company were able in 1928, to acquire an interest in Hillman. By 1932, Rootes had acquired a controlling interest in Humber Ltd, which included Hillman and Commer, as the Luton company was now known.

The Humber-Hillman-Commer Combine gave Rootes the impetus to start to compete with the 'big boys' of British motor manufacturing – Austin, Morris, Ford, Wolseley, Rover and Standard – but manufacturing was of little value if the manufacturer could not sell its products, and one of the reasons that Rootes had been so successful as a sales organisation was its dealer network. During the early 1920s, in order to sell and distribute their vehicles, they had set out to acquire strategic dealerships and dealer networks: Tom Garner in Manchester; Robins & Day; and the Canterbury Motor Company in Kent. The biggest coup, however, came in 1923, when Rootes gained control of the George Heath & Company chain of twenty main dealers and forty smaller regional dealerships.

Manufacturing acquisition didn't stop with Humber. In 1934, with a name change to Rootes Securities Ltd the previous year, they took over the Huddersfield-based company Karrier Motors, who had made their name building municipal vehicles, coaches and buses. In 1935,

Karrier production was transferred down to the Commer Cars factory at Luton. This period demonstrated the pace at which the Rootes brothers went about seeking out companies to buy, and by the latter part of the Thirties, Rootes were a force to be reckoned with and considered to be an important part of Britain's motor manufacturing scene.

In 1935, Humber, Hillman, Commer and Karrier, plus Thrupp & Maberly, were to be joined by Sunbeam and Talbot. With the demise of the Sunbeam-Talbot-Darracq Combine in January 1934, the company that Billy Rootes had been seconded to during his time in the RNVR, Clément Talbot, became part of the Rootes Group in 1934. The Sunbeam Motor Car Company of Wolverhampton would become part of the Group in 1935. By 1938, both companies would be rationalised to become Sunbeam-Talbot Ltd. During this period, most of the body panels were supplied by Pressed Steel Ltd, in Oxford, so when Rootes became aware that British Light Steel Pressings Ltd, in Acton, West London, which was contained within the STD Combine, was up for grabs, they were only too keen to acquire the firm as an additional source for metal pressings and body panels. Rootes acquired BLSP in 1937. Another piece in the manufacturing jigsaw had been fitted.

A Karrier RSC Sweeper-Collector in Luton, 1937, two years after the Karrier factory at Huddersfield was closed to concentrate production on both Commer and Karrier vehicles at Luton.

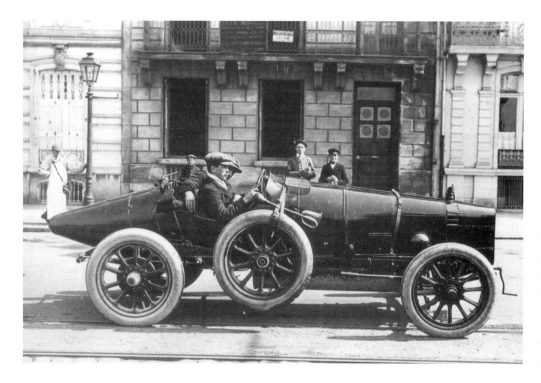

One of the famous marques acquired by Rootes in 1935 was Sunbeam. Racing driver Kenelm Lee Guiness won the Thierry Prize for regularity of running, in the Coupé de l'Auto at Boulogne on 21 September 1913. His Sunbeam was the only car to complete the course without a stop.

COVENTRY ARCHIVES

HILLMAN CARS — FINEST VALUE FOR MONEY

HILLMAN MINX

"A Good Car Made Better" is the Hillman Minx for 1934. The latest developments in design and augmented equipment have been added to Minx roominess and reliability without increase in price.

Family Saloon £159.

The light car with the looks and performance of a "big car."

An advertisement in the December 1933 edition of *Autocar* for the 1934 Hillman Minx. Introduced in 1932, the Minx would become one of the most famous ever British family cars and would evolve and endure for thirty-eight years.

BUILDING THE FUTURE

The early Thirties saw the introduction of the first Rootes-influenced cars. In 1931, the Hillman Wizard made its entrance at a banquet at London's Royal Albert Hall, but despite the showbiz-style launch and publicity that surrounded the Wizard, it turned out not to be a commercial success. However, the next car to be introduced by Rootes, in 1932 certainly was! It was the Hillman Minx and would be the mainstay of their light car range for generations to come. Rootes would continue to update existing models and introduce new ones during the Thirties. In 1932, the first completely new Humber – the 'Twelve' – was launched; in 1935, the Snipe, which was completely redesigned and featured the Dynamax 4.1 litre 6-cylinder engine and a new type of independent front suspension. Known as 'Evenkeel', it was a similar set up to GM's 'Knee-action' system, which utilised upper and lower pivoting wishbones with coil springs. In 1939, Rootes produced the first integral-bodied Minx, but imminent war with Germany would put a stop to any further product development until 1946.

A brochure illustration for the 1936 Humber 12 Vogue, designed in collaboration with Paris fashion designer Capt. Molyneux. POST VINTAGE HUMBER CAR CLUB

WAR YEARS

The role that Rootes, and particularly Billy Rootes played during the Second World War cannot be underestimated. In early 1936, Rootes were approached by the Air Ministry to participate in the British shadow factory scheme to build duplicate factories in the 'shadow' of existing motor industry plants, which would allow quicker transference of production to war matériel and in particular, aircraft.

The 'Balkan Adventure'. Rootes became past masters at creating publicity opportunities for their products. In 1936, *Daily Mail* motoring correspondent W.A. McKenzie took a Humber Snipe on a gruelling 2,000-mile journey from England to Istanbul, Turkey. On the return journey, he raced the famous Orient Express train back to Dover. The '36 Snipe is pictured in Istanbul. ROOTES ARCHIVE CENTRE TRUST

During the war, at a new shadow factory at Ryton and at Speke, near Liverpool, Rootes built one out of every seven bomber aircraft built in the UK. The aircraft Rootes were tasked with building was the Bristol Blenheim bomber and, later in the war, a smaller quantity of Beaufighters. Nearly 3,000 bombers were built by Rootes, as well as ten million aero engine spares for Rolls-Royce, and overhauling 25,000 Rolls-Royce and Bristol aero engines. Statistics for war matériel produced at other Rootes plants is equally impressive. According to War Office records it was estimated that the Rootes Group supplied sixty per cent of all armoured cars, thirty-five per cent of all scout cars and eleven per cent of the national output of wheeled vehicles, including Humber staff cars and Commer Q4 4-ton general

utility trucks. By 1944 the Commer-Karrier factory at Luton had produced 31,268 vehicles towards the war effort.

The 'Blitz' on London and other major towns and cities during 1940 had caused serious damage and killed many, but the raid on Coventry was particularly devastating.

The Coventry Mark 1 Armoured Car was developed towards the end of the Second World War as a joint venture between Humber, Commer and Daimler. It entered service in 1944 but was predominantly used by the French in Indo-China after the war.

Coventry literally glowed from the fires caused by the bombing. The Humber plant at Stoke was badly hit during the raids, as was Number 1 Shadow Factory at Stoke, but escaped serious damage.

The contribution made by Rootes during the war did not go unnoticed; in 1942, Billy Rootes received a knighthood for his efforts and unceasing dedication to the production of vehicles and aircraft for the war effort.

POST-WAR AND THE SELLER'S MARKET

The mood of post-war Britain was entirely different to that at the outbreak of war. The noted historian L.C.B. Seaman described the change of mood when *'the British people passed a vote of no confidence in the past, and proclaimed a quiet, determined wish for a social revolution.'* In the General Election of July, 1945, the Labour party, under leader Clement Attlee scored a landslide victory, defeating Winston Churchill's Conservative Party and the Liberal Party. The sweeping social changes set out by Atlee's Labour government would form an economic blueprint for Britain for the next twenty-five years; a mixed economy model that would be endorsed by future Tory as well as Labour governments.

Billy Rootes (seated on floor) with wife Nora and eldest son Brian, relaxing in their garden at Stype Grange, near Hungerford, Berkshire.
NICK ROOTES

Britain's motor manufacturing sector shrugged its shoulders with the news and got on with the job of re-organising its factories and changing back to civilian production, knowing that they were entering a marketplace of pent-up demand for passenger cars and commercial vehicles – a seller's market. Rootes wasted no time in re-aligning its products for post-war production, as well as rationalising its models and product ranges.

Rootes had always intended to model their business on the American motor manufacturers, in particular General Motors. Now with Sunbeam-Talbot in the range and a new version of the Talbot 10 and 2-litre models, Rootes could offer a genuine range of cars for specific market segments: Hillman – small, practical family cars; Sunbeam-Talbot – cars for the sporting motorist; and Humber – luxury cars for the middle and upper classes. Commer and Karrier commercial vehicles also started to wear product segment hats: Commer – vans and trucks for general commercial and private coach operators; and Karrier – municipal and specialised commercial vehicles.

The late Forties and Fifties would prove a boom time for the motor industry, despite having to endure the frustration of government intervention in the form of steel and raw material allocation being based on a targeted export sales figure. Initially, at least fifty per cent of production would be for export, as part of the government's 'Export or Die' strategy, which meant that a thriving market in second-hand cars would develop until the early 1950s when new cars would, once again, find a place in British showrooms and the domestic market. However, a 'Catch 22' situation developed in that some manufacturers, Jaguar and Standard, for example, could not always get hold of sufficient supplies of fuel or raw materials in order to build the required amount of cars to meet the export quotas! It was a vicious circle, but one that Rootes seemed to circumvent – possibly because they had allocated most of their production for export.

Billy Rootes was in fact an enthusiastic export promoter, and duly exceeded the quotas, as he saw exports as an essential part of the future growth and survival plan for Rootes, as well as for Britain. He would become chairman of the Dollar Exports Council in 1951. Reginald Rootes was also knighted for his services to the motor industry and the war effort in 1946. Later that year, Rootes acquired the first of their many overseas manufacturing plants, at Fisherman's Bend, Port Melbourne, Australia. A close relationship with Todd Motors in New Zealand had existed since 1936, where Hillman and Humber cars and Commer trucks were sold, and this loyal relationship would carry on for years to come. Sir Reginald had looked after North American export sales until Brian Rootes took over in 1947 and, by

1950, Brian had started to establish a dealer network in North America, with a showroom headquarters in Park Avenue, New York and a service depot in Long Island City. Rootes Motors (Canada) Ltd had been formed in 1947 by a Canadian lawyer/businessman, Robert J.Fennell, who had got to know the Rootes brothers before the war. By 1954, Rootes were exporting to 132 countries, including locations in Ireland, Europe, North Africa, the Middle East, Far East and South, East and West Africa.

A late-Thirties Commer 'N' Series poses outside the van owners' shop in the West Kensington area of London.
CHAS K. BOWERS & SON

A Commer LN5 forward control coach from 1938/9.

In 1949, Rootes established Automobile Products of India, to build CKD cars and trucks. This continued until 1956, when the Indian government insisted on more local component manufacture, a situation which was replicated with Isuzu in Japan, who had built Minx saloons under licence since 1953. The assembly of Japanese Minx saloons would continue until the early Sixties, but Japanese industry would eventually overtake and force out foreign manufacturers, as Japan started to acquire a new confidence in car designing and building.

As the post-war period rolled on into the 1950s and 1960s, it became apparent that British governments of the day would use motor manufacturing as a barometer of the nation's wealth, and would use the industry to suit its own given agenda. Both Labour and Conservative governments for the next twenty years would get embroiled in the functioning of the motor industry, to the industry's ultimate detriment. From the outset, as economics historians David Thoms and Tom Donnelly point out in their appraisal of Coventry's motor manufacturing scene during the post-war period, the *'fiscal and monetary policies [of successive governments] served to create an uneven pattern of domestic consumer demand.'* This situation may have been acceptable if you were building washing machines, but the complexities surrounding designing, building and selling motor cars would not withstand such interventions over a long period of time. Rootes, as well as BMC and Standard-Triumph, would all be forced to relocate some of their production to unemployment hotspots, which as far as Rootes was concerned, would prove to be a significant nail in the coffin of their eventual demise, but for the time being, the economic upwave was here, and it looked like it was here to stay!

HUMBER – BY ROYAL APPOINTMENT

In 1934, Humber was granted a Royal Warrant by The Prince of Wales. He continued to be a loyal and enthusiastic customer of Rootes, except for a brief diversion to Buick in 1936, when he ordered two very special Canadian-built McLaughlin-Buick Limousines from the London General Motors agent Lendrum & Hartman. It is thought that Wallace Simpson used her Buick to make her flight to Cannes, in the South of France, and Edward too used his Buick, although the couple would be seen travelling by Buick or Humber during this period in the South of France!

From correspondence held by the Rootes family, what is certain is that Billy Rootes gave Edward his full co-operation during this time; a personal handwritten letter from Billy Rootes, dated 11 December 1936, the day of the King's abdication, to Edward's Assistant Private Secretary, Sir Godfrey Thomas, stated that:

> *'I have arranged for Vallet and my car to be at Buckingham Palace at 5.30 this evening, the registered number being CVH 193.*
>
> *'If any further assistance is required, please do not hesitate to call upon me … and that anything which you may desire in the way of transport, should be supplied immediately.*
>
> *'I feel that I must say how very grieved and upset I am at the terribly anxious time through which His Majesty is now passing. If you have an opportunity, will you please convey to His Majesty my respectful sympathy.*
>
> *(Signed) Billy.'*

On 1 January 1937, a telegram was received at Billy's home, Stype Grange, from Triesting, Austria, stating, *'Many thanks your good wishes – Edward.'*

Edward, now the Duke of Windsor, would continue to use Rootes vehicles, adding numerous Hillman and Humber cars to his fleet, and Billy Rootes always reciprocated Edward's patronage, which was remembered by ex-Rootes, Devonshire House employee, John Haviland: *'You always knew when the Duke of Windsor was visiting London, because a Burgundy Humber Pullman, and chauffeur, would be outside Claridges.'*

In the post-war years, Humber would continue to receive Royal patronage. During the Fifties, Humber Pullman Limousines, as well as Humber Super Snipes, would be the official cars supplied for the Queen and Duke of Edinburgh for state occasions and Royal Tours.

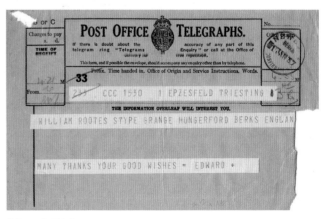

A 'special' telegram. NICK ROOTES

Princess Elizabeth in the Humber Pullman Landaulette, as part of her tour of Norwich during the 1951 Festival of Britain celebrations. COVENTRY ARCHIVES

Her Majesty the Queen passing out of Pussellawa Resthouse, halfway stop to Nuwara Eliya to Kandy, on the 1954 Royal Tour of Ceylon (now Sri Lanka) in one of the four Humber Cabriolets, specially converted from Super Snipe Mark IV Saloons, by H.J. Mulliner of London.

COVENTRY ARCHIVES

STREAMSTYLE SUNBEAM TALBOTS, A NEW HAWK AND THE MAGNIFICENT MINX

In June 1948, the Rootes Group launched the first of its completely new post-war models – the Sunbeam Talbot 80 and 90 Saloon and Drophead Coupé. Dubbed as 'Streamstyle' Sunbeam-Talbots by Rootes marketing, they would replace the old 10 and 2-litre models.

The styling was created in conjunction with Loewy International, the London office of Raymond Loewy's industrial design company, as were new integral-bodied versions of the Hillman Minx and Humber Hawk that were unveiled at the Earl's Court Motor Show in October 1948.

As with all Rootes cars of the time, the need to wait for the end of a model year was ignored and detail changes came into being almost as soon as the cars were launched. The Sunbeam Talbot models and the Hillman Minx and Humber Hawk would continue to receive ongoing 'improvements' such as increased power output, better braking systems and improved lighting.

The new Sunbeam-Talbot 80 and 90 sold well in domestic and for export markets. In September 1950, the 80 model was discontinued and the 90 replaced by a 90 Mark II version. In 1952, a further revised version, the 90 Mark IIA, was offered. This model would remain until 1954, when the Talbot name was dropped and would be known as the Sunbeam Mark III. This would coincide with the launch of a new two-seater sports model, the Sunbeam Alpine.

The debut of new 'streamstyled' Sunbeam Talbot 80 and 90 models at the 1948 Earl's Court Motor Show. LEON GIBBS ARCHIVES

EVOLUTION OF POST-WAR HUMBERS

1947 Super Snipe. COVENTRY ARCHIVES

1951 Hawk Mark IV. LEON GIBBS ARCHIVE

1953 Super Snipe Mark IV. LEON GIBBS ARCHIVE

1958 Super Snipe Series 1 Estate. POST-VINTAGE HUMBER CAR CLUB

Stirling Moss rounds a hairpin bend on the 1954 Alpine Rally. He came third in class and won a gold cup for three consecutive unpenalised runs. COVENTRY ARCHIVES

Sheila Van Damm in the Sunbeam Mark III at the start of her last Monte Carlo Rally in 1956. COVENTRY ARCHIVES

In 1947, Norman Garrad, Sunbeam-Talbot's sales manager, had the idea of forming a works competition department. Garrad was a firm believer that competition 'improved the breed'. By 1948, a budget was granted for Garrad to pursue his idea, and the Rootes competition department was born. It would turn out to be a very successful venture, as well as being the first factory-sponsored works competition department to be formed by a major British manufacturer. Significant names from the world of racing, such as Stirling Moss and Mike Hawthorn, joined soon-to-be household names in the world of international rallying like Sheila Van Damm, Peter Harper, George Murray-Frame and George Hartwell.

Garrad was ahead of his time in creating the Rootes 'works' team. As well as having opportunities to rapidly improve the technical specifications of production cars, Garrad was very aware of the numerous valuable publicity opportunities that could be gained through competition success.

1953 Sunbeam Alpine Mark 1, finished in Sapphire Blue with Light Fawn leather interior, the same colour combination as the Alpine featured in the movie *To Catch A Thief*, **starring Cary Grant and Grace Kelly. Owner: Nick Rootes.**

AUDAX AND THE SERIES HUMBERS

Development of new Rootes car models continued at a pace during the mid- to late Fifties, and in 1953, Rootes renewed their agreement with the Loewy organization to help with a new range of cars – codenamed 'Audax'. This range was the culmination of the Rootes brothers' manufacturing ambition, which was to build cars on the American principle of utilising a commonality of components, sheet metalwork and platforms, and be spread across several product ranges. In 1955, forty five years after a young Billy Rootes had been apprenticed at Singer Motors Ltd, Rootes acquired the company, and it would prove an ideal contender for Audax. Also in '55, Rootes added Hills Precision Die Castings Ltd to their list of companies to make components such as door handles, badges and headlight bezels.

The first car to be launched under the Audax banner was the Sunbeam Rapier. Inspired by Raymond Loewy's 1953 Studebaker Starliner, the Rapier made its debut in October 1955, followed in May 1956 by the Hillman Minx Saloon. An upmarket version of the Minx would complete the passenger car line-up in September 1956 – the Singer Gazelle. The first of the new-style Hillman Husky Series 1 Estate Cars, to replace the original Mark 1 model, would appear in January 1958 which, minus side windows, would also be sold as the Commer Cob van. During this period, the commercial vehicle division of Commer-Karrier was just as busy as the car divisions and proving to be very successful with their heavy goods vehicle ranges. In 1955, they relocated production from Luton to a brand new site at Dunstable. They were now capable of offering a commercial vehicle payload range from

Ronnie Adams and John Boyes in a Humber Super Snipe Series 1, as it fords a river in March 1959 during the Coronation Safari Rally. Paddy Hopkirk and Ronnie Dalton were team mates in the same event, driving a Hillman Husky. COVENTRY ARCHIVES

EVOLUTION OF POST-WAR HILLMAN MINX SALOONS

1949 Mark IV.

1953 Mark VI (21st Anniversary). COVENTRY ARCHIVES

1954-56 Mark VIII. COVENTRY ARCHIVES

1958 Series III Special.

7-cwt vans to 12-ton trucks. In 1956, a new range of 10- and 12-ton Commer tractor units was launched, utilising their revolutionary TS3 diesel engine, a 3-cylinder, horizontally opposed-piston two-stroke unit which was built by Tilling-Stevens of Maidstone, another company that had come into the Rootes Group fold in 1951.

By the mid-Fifties, the Humber range was starting to look its age, and in 1957, a new-look Humber Hawk was launched. The lower-profile body shell was to be shared by the 6-cylinder Super Snipe, introduced in 1958. Both featured Loewy-inspired styling clues, as well as some from GM's 1955 'Motorama' cars such as the Chevrolet Bel-Air.

In 1959, the icing on the cake for Rootes was the launch of an entirely new version of the Alpine. The new Sunbeam Alpine Series I utilised the floorpan from the Hillman Husky – but otherwise it really was completely new and the handsome little two-seater sports car would quickly prove be a prime source of revenue for Rootes in domestic and the all-important American export markets.

In 1959, the Rootes Group was at its peak; Sir William was made Baron Rootes of Ramsbury, and they could feel justifiably proud of the fact that they had achieved an immense amount in terms of their ambitions in the motor manufacturing game, but the

Sheila Van Damm with one of the girls from her father's famous club, The Windmill, showing off the new 1958 Sunbeam Rapier Series 2 Convertible in London.

future for the company would prove much more challenging, as domestic and foreign competition increased and markets changed.

Rootes Maidstone, May 1950. ROOTES ARCHIVE CENTRE TRUST

An array of Rootes cars in the service department of Rootes' London Service Station, Ladbroke Hall, c. 1958.

Tilling-Stevens Ltd at Maidstone was acquired by Rootes in 1950 and this was where the development and manufacture of the TS3 opposed piston 2-stroke diesel engine took place. Two Hillman Minx cars, a Humber Hawk, a Commer Van and an Austin A135 Princess for good measure, are conveniently parked outside the factory in this mid-Fifties publicity shot.

NICK ROOTES

CHAPTER 2

SWINGING UNEASILY
INTO THE SIXTIES

'The Rootes [brothers] were superb salesmen. They built Rootes up to be a world vehicle maker. But salesmen live in the deal today; they are not very good at planning for the future. The Sixties became a buyer's market and without a new range of cars in the pipeline things started to go wrong!'

— Anthony Stevens – Rootes Product
Planning Manager

As the new decade dawned, it was becoming clear that the 1960s would be like no other decade before it. The seller's market for cars was now turning into a buyer's market, as product availability improved, more models were being introduced and European car manufacturers who had recovered from the disruption of the Second World War, were now offering cars for the British market that were serious considerations for new car buyers. For the first time since the war, buyers were being lured away from home-grown products by a Volkswagen, Renault, Simca, Peugeot or Fiat.

However, the boom did have a slow start, as Britain hit a recession in 1960; sales of cars were generally down, and the regulatory policy that successive governments had imposed on the motor manufacturing industry had not allowed the industry to plan for any kind of realistic long-term growth, and taxation policy had one of the

most de-stabilising effects on sales and profit margins. Since purchase tax had been introduced, the rates of the tax had yo-yo'd up and down from the sublime to the ridiculous. This, combined with a 'stop-go' policy of hire purchase restrictions being lifted or put in place, added further instability into the market; 1960 was a 'stop' year. The following year also saw a slump in sales and in July '61, it was reported that the Chancellor of the Exchequer, Mr Selwyn Lloyd, would increase purchase tax from fifty per cent to fifty-five per cent. Following the announcement, Geoffrey Rootes, who had been speaking at a ceremony introducing the new Singer range, within minutes of the Chancellor's announcements, commented:

> *'We in the Rootes Group strongly believe in holding down costs and prices at the present time and our spirit is one of willing co-operation with the Chancellor in the need to strengthen the nation's economy. On the other hand, we must warn him of further restricting our home market. This is a time to expand in business, not to contract, and there is a limit to the number of times the motor industry can be used as a safety valve to control spending at home.'*

He went on to state the need for a sound home market, emphasising that it had been the motor industry that had been the main earner of foreign currency, and warning that *the goose cannot go on laying the golden eggs if it is not allowed to exercise on its home range.*

The comments were picked up by *Autocar* magazine and duly reported under the headline *'Chancellor "Regulates" instead of accelerating the motor industry'*, but the government was again using the motor manufacturing

A brochure cover for the 1960 Hillman Minx Series IIIA.

industry to balance its books and the statement fell on deaf ears.

Serious though these policies seemed at the time, the future interventionist policies of the 1960s and 1970s governments would prove to be even bigger 'spanners in the works' than any of the regulatory policies of the 1950s.

Buyers of Rootes cars during this period would in general be more concerned about the car's ability to get to and from work of a week day, and to be able to reliably and comfortably transport a family and a boot full of associated clobber to and from Skegness for a fortnight's holiday,

George Hartwell's palatial new dealership premises in Holdenhurst Road, Bournmouth in the late Fifties. Although Commer was sold alongside Hillman, Humber and Sunbeam, it took a while longer for the Singer name to appear on Rootes main dealerships as Singer still had their own national dealer network. ROOTES ARCHIVE CENTRE TRUST

An airbrushed publicity shot for the Hillman Husky Series II, *c.* 1960. ROOTES ARCHIVE CENTRE TRUST

or maybe to the golf club at weekends. Despite the reputation Rootes had gained during the Fifties in rallying, cars like the Hillman Minx were not considered by prospective buyers for their 0–60 mph times. One such owner who required a reliable workhorse, and who remembers it as being *'one of the best cars we ever had'* was Ian Hammerton, who regularly took his wife and three children on holiday from west Kent to the Netherlands in a Hillman Minx Series IIIB Estate. Although it was reasonably economical, the performance is best summed up by his son Mike, who was out in the Minx one day with his Dad, and wondered about the performance capabilities of the car: *'I said to Dad, "See how fast it can go, Dad!" and told him to floor it! He did, and then I realised that was how he drove it all the time!!'*

Rootes products in the early Sixties appealed predominantly to middle-class buyers – the same market segment that had been the prime purchasers of motor cars in the Fifties. With full employment across much of Britain, especially in the south east, that market was changing fast, and it was being changed by younger buyers who had the money to buy a car, but, with the exception of the stunning new Sunbeam Alpine Sports Car, Rootes had little to offer this burgeoning new youth market. The Audax models – the Minx, Gazelle and Rapier, although still good sellers and excellent cars, had been around for five years, but now there was the BMC Morris Mini Minor and Austin Seven to contend with, as well as the Triumph Herald and the new Ford Anglia 105E. Rootes was still three years away from the launch of their new small car, the Hillman Imp, of which development had at least been officially announced to the public. The Humber Hawk and Super Snipe models had already been out of the box for a couple of years in 1960 and their appeal was limited to the professional middle and upper-middle class motorist, a market which, in Sixties Britain, was shrinking. The Super Snipe had, however, been given a very neat front end makeover for 1960, in the form of twin headlamps and a thin-barred wraparound grille, which transformed and modernised the look of Super Snipe very effectively. In this respect, it was good for another five years and this would at least guarantee its future as a high-end luxury car.

The dilemma that the Rootes Group found itself in at the start of the Sixties was one of having to respond to rapid changes in market conditions, a task that with their relatively limited financial resources was not going to be easy. Despite the introduction, and success, of the Audax range, Rootes had failed to achieve the economies of scale required in order to provide profit levels that would enable re-investment in plant and up-to-date production methods. Also, since going public in 1949, they

A Humber Hawk Series 2 photographed on Epsom Downs.
POST VINTAQE HUMBER CAR CLUB

Henry Korman of the BBC French service, recording his impressions of the 1960 Earl's Court Motor Show on the Humber stand. COVENTRY ARCHIVES

penniless in London during the Fifties and by the early Sixties was well on his way to becoming a millionaire. Stephen rented some run-down shop units near Regent Street and, starting with 'His Clothes', turned them into

One of the Rootes Group's publicity stunts in 1960 was in presenting a new Sunbeam Alpine to singer and actor Sammy Davis Jnr., who had just finished a three-week visit to Britain, which included a series of hectic one-nighters as well as appearing at the Royal Command Performance at the London Palladium.

Police were called in to control crowds as Rootes personnel pushed the car, wrapped in polythene and tied with a wide red ribbon to the stage door of the 'Pigalle Theatre' in London's Piccadilly, where Sammy had been appearing in cabaret.

The Alpine was a 'bon voyage' gift from night club owner Al Burnett. Registered SD50, it was shipped by Rootes to the United States for Sammy's personal use. COVENTRY ARCHIVES

had pursued a policy of high dividends to shareholders, a factor which also impacted on profit levels, but loyalty to shareholders has always been a business priority for Rootes. They did, however, benefit from having a healthy liquidity position.

A new youth culture was starting to change life in early Sixties Britain. It brought a social change to the country that would hit the British establishment like a freight train. It changed the course, and image, of post-war Britain and ushered in the Swinging Sixties. Fashion and pop music joined forces to create an environment that would establish opportunities for young, up-and-coming entrepreneurs. They were tapping into and capturing the youth market in any way they could. A young Glaswegian named John Stephen had arrived

colourful clothes boutiques, in what would become the epicentre of Swinging London – Carnaby Street; Mary Quant added her unique design style to female fashions and photographer David Bailey captured it all on film. During the second half of the Sixties, Mod fashion and music 'iconistas' such as The Kinks, The Small Faces and The Rolling Stones would all be regular visitors.

Another entrepreneur who, for a brief time, added a new look to London's streets, was Michael Gotla, boss of London motor dealer Welbeck Motors. Gotla had identified a loophole in the law concerning the operation of taxi-cabs. If a taxi-cab was 'pre-booked', in the same way as a traditional private hire car service, he could compete with traditional black cabs with a cheaper alternative. In July 1961, the minicab hit London's streets when Gotla put two-hundred red Renault Dauphine 4-door saloon cars into service. He also extended his new minicab service to Greater London, where there were fewer black cabs operating. Bold though his idea was, it didn't last long and, by late 1962, the Dauphines were finding new homes on used car forecourts. Although Austin held the black 'Hackney' cab market with its Carbodies purpose-built FX4 cabs, for private hire operators, who were confined generally to airport and station runs, weddings, or where people wanted a one-off chauffeur service, the Humber Hawk, with its excellent build quality, comfort and reliability had established itself as the hire car operator's favourite.

Car manufacturers who had the resources to be able to respond to the rapid changes in trends during this period,

would take advantage of the burgeoning new youth market, and Ford were certainly in a position to dominate. Although their new Consul Classic and the sleek two-door hardtop version of the Classic, the Capri, were slow to capture volume sales, it would be the next model introduction from Ford that would set the bar for the rest of the industry to jump. Launched in 1962, the Cortina was a straightforward, comfortable, stylish family car with saloon and estate car variants and a price tag that wouldn't break the bank, and Ford marketing took every opportunity to make the new Cortina look 'chic'!

Despite a limited product range, Rootes made a good job of updating and improving its models, without the need for substantial body re-working. The Hillman Minx was in its Series IIIA form by 1960, with a new grille and rolled over rear wings, which was also a design feature of the Singer Gazelle. The Minx, Gazelle and the Sunbeam Rapier got a close ratio four-speed gearbox with a floor-mounted gearshift and a hypoid rear axle, replacing the old spiral-bevel type. The Gazelle reverted to a single carburettor in Series IIIB form, replacing the twin Zenith downdraught carbs that had been fitted on the IIIA. The last change to the range of Audax models was... yes, you guessed it, the Series IIIC, with a more powerful 1592cc engine to replace the 1494cc unit. They would be marketed as Minx 1600 and Gazelle 1600. Both continued to have convertible and estate car versions available as Series IIIC models, but these versions would be discontinued in the summer of 1962 to make way for the new Super Minx and Singer Vogue models.

A quartet of Hawks surround an Austin A60 Cambridge. Baldry's Taxis of Wellingborough, Northamptonshire, ran a fleet of Humber Hawks as their preferred chauffeur car throughout the Sixties. REX BALDRY

A Singer Gazelle Series IIIA Estate.

SINGER OWNERS CLUB

Hillman Minx 1600 (Series IIIC) Saloon.

ROOTES ARCHIVE CENTRE TRUST

The Series II Alpine, with 1.6-litre power, making its Continental debut at the Paris Motor Show.

ROOTES ARCHIVE CENTRE TRUST

A 1961 American dealership promotion for the Alpine and other Rootes products. ROOTES ARCHIVE CENTRE TRUST

All of these frantic model designation changes, sometimes only a few months after the announcement of a model revision, came at a cost, not only in terms of re-tooling and parts listings, but to the levels of management and the workforce who were being asked to make the changes. At dealership level, it would be highly likely to find even the most conscientious parts manager scouring the local papers for any vacancies at a local Ford dealer! That is how it was at Rootes during this period, but this approach to engineering clearly had to change, as works director Bill Hancock became very aware:

> 'The Rootes brothers, always giving preference to sales demands, were continually changing policies of design, varieties and quantities, and this put a heavy strain on labour relations. But with the systems that I adopted there was no real labour unrest up to the time I retired from Rootes.'

The Sunbeam Rapier Series III was launched in late 1959, with bright new two-tone exterior colours and co-ordinated interior trim packages, including a revised dash layout with wood grain trim. A number of technical improvements, exclusive to the Rapier, included disc brakes and an aluminium cylinder head for the 1494cc engine. These changes, together with minor external appearance alterations, were carried through to the Series IIIA in 1961 when it was fitted with the 1592cc

The Sunbeam Rapier Series IIIA was the last Rapier model to be made available as a convertible. This 1963 version, finished in its unique special order Singer colour combination of Maroon and Cavalry Beige, is seen photographed at one of Rootes publicity department's favourite photo locations – Bosham in Hampshire. Owner: Mike Biddulph.

The Supreme *Sunbeam Rapier*
NOW WITH LARGER 1·6 LITRE ENGINE

Evocative early Sixties brochure artwork for the Sunbeam Rapier.

engine. In 1960, the Sunbeam Alpine also received the 1592cc engine and thus became the Series II model.

The Alpine was still very much ahead of the game, competition-wise, both in North America and in Britain. Despite BMC dumping the old 'frogeye' Sprite and replacing it with a new model in 1961, together with an MG Midget version, the Alpine had refinements that were still missing in Austin-Healey, MG and Triumph sports cars of the time – wind-up windows! The Alpine was also one of the only sports cars on the market that a six-foot tall driver could get in, drive in comfort, and get out of with ease!

THE 'OLD GUARD' RETIRES

Since the formation of Rootes Motors Ltd in 1949, to replace the old Rootes Securities Ltd, which had been formed in 1933, the Rootes family had held virtually all of the senior management positions. In 1960, Lord Rootes remained chairman with Sir Reginald as deputy chairman. Lord Rootes' eldest son Geoffrey had been appointed managing director of the manufacturing divisions of Rootes Motors Ltd in 1960, as well as chairman of the Society of Motor Manufacturers and Traders. Brian Rootes had returned from the United States in 1956 to become managing director of the sales division of Rootes Motors Ltd. Sir Reginald's son Timothy was appointed a director of Rootes Ltd, a subsidiary company that had been formed in 1933 to carry on the distribution and servicing of the products of the Rootes Group. He was also made joint managing director of Humber Ltd.

In 1960, there were some significant changes in senior management – as members of the 'old guard' who had made valuable contributions to the Rootes Group's success were now retiring.

Bill Hancock, as works director and general manager, had served a total of just under twenty years at Rootes in two chunks. Firstly, from 1935, when he joined Rootes from Daimler as works manager of Humber in Coventry, and secondly, when he was brought back at the instigation of the Rootes brothers in 1948, from Rubery Owen, which he had joined in 1942. In 1958, Hancock had been awarded the OBE for his services to the Midlands motor industries. During his time at Rootes he had been a positive force in labour relations and in increasing production efficiency at Coventry.

Hancock's replacement was Bill Garner, who had been general manager of the Rootes Diesel Engine Division at Tilling-Stevens Maidstone since 1952, and according to

Hancock, it was *'a good move, as Garner was a good works man and a good controller of labour, but he also did what he was told policy-wise!'*

Bernard (B.B.) Winter also retired in 1960 as director of engineering at Rootes. His thirty-six years of continuous service to Rootes started in 1923, when he joined Rootes as a service representative and subsequently service manager of Humber-Hillman at Coventry. He became chief engineer of Humber Ltd in 1935 and was appointed director of engineering in 1938. Winter was known as a 'belt and braces' engineer; he would never embrace anything too advanced or unusual, although his support for the radically different 3-cylinder, 2-stroke horizontally-opposed diesel engine developed by Commer, still seems at odds with his otherwise conservative approach to engineering.

Winter's replacement as director of engineering was forty-two year old Peter Ware, who was anything but conservative, and who had adopted a forward-thinking, inventive, but practical approach to engineering. It was as an artist that allowed him to provide a good visual basis to illustrate his ideas. His father, Sidney Ware, was chief engineer at Straker-Squire and had been an influence on the young Peter Ware, but it was as a protégé of Sir Roy Fedden, when he joined the Bristol Aeroplane Company in 1940 as an engineer, that he started to hone his flair for innovation and invention in engineering.

Prior to BAC, Ware had joined Dartmouth Royal Naval College as a thirteen-year-old cadet, and successfully passed out to go to the Royal Naval Engineering College at Keyham. After a brief spell as an engineering officer, he was invalided out of the Royal Navy in 1938 with TB, joined a second time, but was invalided out again, after serving on an armed merchant cruiser which played a deadly cat and mouse game with the German pocket battleship *Graf Spey*.

In 1942, Ware was made technical assistant to Roy Fedden (who was knighted in 1942), and much of Ware's work was directed towards developing ever-higher power outputs from the Bristol sleeve-valve engines which ultimately allowed bombers to increase flight ceilings by 10,000 feet and out of flak range. Later, after Fedden had left BAC, he worked with Fedden on alternative power plants for motor torpedo boats and improving their performance. After the war, he joined Sir Roy Fedden in his newly-formed motor car company, which had been set up to develop some very adventurous designs, and although none made it to production stage, this experience had proved valuable, having learnt a great deal from Fedden, whom he rated highly as a talented engineer. Ware then moved on to work for Leyland,

CAV and Dowty, where he succeeded in turning their Fuel Systems Division round from a loss to a £¼ million profit in the first year, but he felt that his face didn't fit, so returned to CAV Electrical as chief engineer, from where he was headhunted by Rootes, following a recommendation by none other than Sir Roy Fedden. He joined Rootes in 1958, and was made director of engineering in 1959. As a marketing-led company, Rootes were becoming all too aware of their engineering shortcomings, and the initial brief to Peter Ware from the Rootes brothers was to strengthen the company's engineering capability, a task that as far as he was concerned was well overdue. Ware brought a number of competent engineers with him to help him address some of the fundamental problems as he sought to improve ride and handling characteristics across the range. They included David Hodkin from E.R.A. and Peter Wilson, who would become chief experimental engineer.

The third member of the 'old guard' to retire was Geoffrey Cozens, managing director of Commer-Karrier in Luton since 1937. Cozens was responsible for successfully integrating the Commer and Karrier product ranges during the late Thirties, hence the company became known as Commer-Karrier, as well as overseeing the transfer of main production from Luton to Dunstable in 1955. He had continued to build on the successes of the Rootes commercial vehicle products, making the division a profitable part of the Rootes Group, and a market leader in the specialist municipal vehicle sector. His place was taken by forty-year-old Rex Watson Lee, initially as director and general manager; it was not until 1962 that he would be appointed managing director of Commer Cars Ltd.

Rex Watson Lee had a distinguished war record which earned him an MBE. He joined Rootes in 1948 as a student, working in the foundry, but his relationship with the Rootes family went back beyond that. During the war Geoffrey Rootes and Rex Watson Lee, as fellow officers, became good friends. They met up again after the war at Humber, and Watson Lee became his personal assistant. In 1956, Watson Lee became managing director of the Rootes parts division when the truck and car parts divisions were merged.

LABOUR RELATIONS IN THE MOTOR INDUSTRY

Many of the major problems facing the British motor industry during the 1960s came about as a result of a combination of historical and political occurrences.

For medium-sized companies like Rootes and other Coventry-based companies like Standard-Triumph, the 'stop-go' taxation policy of the late 1950s was making it extremely difficult for companies to carry out any kind of meaningful forward planning. In a 'stop' year, there would be inevitable layoffs, which would spike the guns of the trade unions, resulting in unwanted industrial action. Growing stocks of unsold vehicles during the sales slump of 1960 compounded production problems for Standard-Triumph, resulting in 1,700 being made redundant and a three-day working week. Rootes were able to meet demand and continue with some kind of equilibrium which did not affect their labour relations to any great extent.

A historical issue that had been inherited from the post-war Labour government was that they had allowed numerous trade unions to represent various different trades in car factories, instead of one union representing the total workforce, as was the case in America, in which the United Auto Workers would negotiate with management on behalf of all workers. Similarly, in Germany, one union, the IG Metall (Industriegewerkschaft Metall) would represent all trades in all of the German car factories. The presence of a multitude of different unions in British factories encouraged demarcation and the piece-work pay structures that had been put in place during the post-war period to increase efficiency, had the effect of stifling innovation in production methods and resistance to new types of labour-saving machinery.

The Coventry 'Gang System' and Ryton – the self-governing republic

In Coventry, most car factories had developed variants of the piece-work model with the adoption of the 'Gang System' of payment by results, in which a group of workers would work together to achieve their bonuses, based on the output performance of the 'Gang' and organised by union shop stewards. This had the effect of allowing management to give away shop floor operational responsibility so that the vacuum in management hierarchy was effectively filled by shop stewards, who assumed a kind of quasi-managerial position within the company. There is no evidence to suggest that this system did not work, however, except that when measured day work was introduced much later, although it took control away from shop stewards, management was ill-prepared to reassume shop floor

Ryton – the self-governing republic. A Sunbeam Rapier convertible on the assembly line at Ryton in November 1961.
COVENTRY ARCHIVES

and production responsibility, in particular with regard to quality control and line planning. At Rootes, according to Thoms and Donnelly in their detailed analysis of Coventry motor manufacturing:

> 'The shop floor and the gangs came to be organized by the stewards who exercised a high level of control over the booking in of work and the pace and loading levels of the track, so that by 1960 Ryton was said to be virtually a self-governing republic. Providing the system and cars left the factory in the required numbers, Rootes management appears to have been unconcerned about its own withdrawal from the shop floor.'

Apart from a few minor skirmishes during the Fifties and early Sixties, the Rootes Group had achieved a relatively stable labour relations record. The Rootes brothers clearly valued their workforce: it was not uncommon for Lord Rootes to be seen talking to one of the workers on the shop floor during one of his walkabouts. He had a genuine interest in people and had a brilliant memory, often remembering workers' first names and their personal family situations.

The effects of the Acton strike

Both the Coventry plants were felt to be important cogs in the Rootes machine, so it was perhaps not too surprising that when industrial relations within the group did break down it was at one of the Group's satellite plants that was operating 'outside the gaze' of the Rootes brothers, and not a Coventry plant. On 6 September 1961, when 1,000 workers walked out of the plant at British Light Steel Pressings in Acton, it caused a prolonged and bitter thirteen-week strike, and one which would place the Rootes Group in a dire financial position.

Trouble at the Acton plant had been brewing during the previous eighteen months with numerous stoppages and unofficial strikes, but most of these were petty squabbles of short duration. The 1961 dispute, which started to rear its head in August '61, was different. The strike was over feared redundancies at the plant. New car sales had slumped during the year and Rootes had been stock-piling components at Acton. Militant members of the Acton workforce called for an unofficial strike until the management would declare 'no redundancy', and start negotiating on a shorter working week and work-sharing. A similar scheme had been started at Thrupp & Maberly, Rootes' coachbuilding concern, in October 1960. The

A Commer delivery truck attempting to collect or deliver parts at the BLSP factory during the strike.

principal products supplied by BLSP at that time were bodies for the Humber Hawk and Super Snipe, panels for the Karrier Bantam and cabs for the Commer forward control series. It virtually halted Rootes car production around mid-October and had similar consequences for Commer-Karrier.

The Rootes management was not prepared to enter into any agreements at this point in time. Lord Rootes

The British Light Steel Pressings plant at Acton, photographed during the Fifties. The main building is in Warple Way, which is about a third up on the right of the picture. Acton Vale runs along the left. Most of this gaggle of industrial buildings were inherited by Rootes from the Talbot and Darracq coachbuilding concern during the Thirties.

NICK ROOTES

was of the opinion that to give in to the troublemakers at Acton would set a precedent for the motor industry, and the management, in effect, dug their heels in. Lord Rootes was not alone in his feeling about the situation, as he had wide support from the motor industry in general. The Acton plant had gained a reputation for having a militant workforce with a number of 'agitators'. Furthermore, neither the main engineering union nor the skilled workforce supported the strike.

Rootes had made a stand against unconstitutional action, but the cost to the company was immense – £3 million in lost profits, and guaranteed wage payments to the Coventry plants in the earlier stages of the strike cost around half-a-million pounds. At the end of this long, drawn-out battle, there were no winners – only losers. Rootes lost production as well as badly needed profit, and striking workers lost their jobs.

Following the resumption of production, Lord Rootes made an announcement to the press in December 1961, expressing his gratitude to *'the thousands of our employees who remained loyal to us throughout the dispute, even though it caused them and their families hardship'*.

The Rootes coffers had been seriously depleted, and the strike changed the direction of the organization. It could not have come at a worse time, with the development of the Hillman Imp and the replacements for the Audax range. The 1961 sales slump also compounded the problem and figures released in November 1961 showed profits at their year-end, in July 1961, as being virtually sliced in half – to £2,911,652 from £5,863,852 the previous year. But the real seriousness of the Rootes group's financial problems was not revealed until 1962. Their profits had been wiped out, with record losses of £2 million, and although 1963 did see a significant clawing back of profit, to just under £200,000, it was still not enough. The following year, Rootes, for the first time in its history, would be selling a significant portion of its shareholding, to the Chrysler Corporation of America, in order to stay in business.

The Rootes family had felt at the time that the strike was due to Communist influence and immediately called for a personnel list to be drawn up of all Communist Party sympathisers employed at their plants. The damage had, however, already been done. Reflecting on the whole episode years later, Geoffrey Rootes stated in his memoir: *'We stood out as a matter of principle against Communist infiltration and influence, but in retrospect we might have been better to compromise to some extent.'*

Early in 1962, with New Year celebrations still ringing in their ears, the Rootes board decided that a plan had to be put in place to ensure future continuity of supply of panels and bodies. During November and December 1961, they had approached both Pressed Steel at Cowley and GKN Sankey at Wellington, Shropshire, to discuss the viability of either company being an alternative supplier to BLSP. A confidential draft report was prepared by Mr A.L. Goate, of the Rootes finance department at Devonshire House, on 2 January 1962, regarding the feasibility of sourcing alternative suppliers to replace BLSP production and the possibility of completely closing down and selling off both BLSP and Thrupp & Maberly.

There were a great many factors involved in such a move, and while the initial attraction of cost-savings in transport, the elimination of continuous investment in plant and machinery and an injection of capital from the sale of the leasehold of the properties, negative factors included de-commissioning and transferring machinery and plant to a new supplier, as well as the cost of redundancy and severance payments to workers at the plants.

Lord Rootes responded initially to the draft report in a memo to the other members of the board on 4 January 1962:

> *'Following our conversation yesterday, I attach a copy of the rough notes prepared by Mr Goate yesterday on BLSP and Thrupp & Maberly. With regard to the change-over period arising from our discussion at lunch yesterday and the subsequent discussion with Mr Goate and Mr Shrigley, [general manager of BLSP] we rather changed our views to those expressed in the notes … My own feeling is that you [Geoffrey] and Brian made a very valid point in suggesting that we should not approach the BLSP position with labour until after the Motor Show, say at the beginning of November 1962.'*

Lord Rootes continued his comments on timing, the difficulty of building up sufficient stocks to cover the change-over period to the new supplier and played 'Devil's Advocate' by highlighting the advantages of selling off Thrupp & Maberly against any possible future profit from the plant. Rootes Properties Ltd owned the leaseholds to both BLSP and Thrupp & Maberly:

> *'In the past, as you are aware, we have made fairly substantial profits … but as you said yourself yesterday, it seems doubtful that with the range of bodies we are now intending to build there, we shall be able to operate the plant economically and cover our overheads.*
>
> *'We could deal with both factories more or less in parallel in the autumn of 1962. This has the obvious disadvantage*

that we are facing two lots of trouble at the same time and risking labour ganging together to resist the closing down of the factories.

'On the other hand, it has the advantage that we get the whole operation out of the way during the winter of 1962/3 and start off with a clean policy of concentration of manufacture thereafter. Also it might be easier to handle from a public relations aspect.'

A detailed final report was prepared by Mr Goate and was presented to the board on 7 March 1962. Ongoing negotiations between both parties continued, during which time the manufacture of the Commer QX cab was moved to Sankey. Although prices quoted to Rootes for building light car sets and Humber bodies from Sankey were lower than Pressed Steel, the Rootes board were concerned about Sankey's lack of experience in building large unitary construction bodies in quantity. They were more experienced in commercial vehicle cab bodies, so the QX and its replacements, the C and V Series, seemed obvious choices for Sankey to build. Also, an integral part of any agreement with Rootes was that any new supplier should take over all of the BLSP tools, jigs, presses and tool room equipment, something that Sankey's were reluctant to do.

Although Pressed Steel were more of a known quantity to Rootes, and they had offered the use of a new premises at Theale, near Reading, Berkshire, to accommodate the new Rootes work, their higher quoted prices and their reluctance to fit in with Rootes' planned timing of closures left the Rootes board with an unresolved quandary. The net result was that although a decision had been made that no other new Humber bodies would be built at BLSP, both British Light Steel Pressings and Thrupp & Maberly would, for the time being, remain part of the Rootes Group.

SUPER MINX, VOGUE, SCEPTRE – DESIGN AND DEVELOPMENT

Towards the end of the Fifties, it was clear that the replacements for the Audax range were overdue, and so the brief went out for a replacement range of cars.

Initially, a Minx, Gazelle and Rapier IV were the new models that Ted White and his styling team at Humber Road were challenged with creating, utilising existing engines, transmissions and running gear. The result, however, was not quite what Rootes management had in mind. It was to be the last major styling brief that Ted White and Ted Green – 'the 'Two Teds' – as they had

become known, would be involved in. They had created a new saloon and an estate car variant for Hillman and Singer, with a convertible body for both in the pipeline. When the time came for the first finished full-size styling proposal to be shown to Lord Rootes, he was less then pleased with the result. Bill Papworth, who later joined Rootes from Ford, was told this story some time after the event by Ted White and Peter Ware:

'Reggie was taking more of the action during the development of the Super Minx. The procedure for the final sign-off was taking the full-size model out of the studio, down in the lift and onto the recreation ground, covered up and everyone would gather round. This was Reggie's day, but Billy was invited, and rolled up with his chauffeur in his Pullman, tottered across and walked round the Super Minx with not a word. He [just] turned to Reggie and said, "You must have eyes in your arse!" ... walked back to his car and drove away.'

Timothy Rootes, Sir Reginald's son, had a less dramatic reaction to the new car, but was equally disappointed:

'Geoffrey and I were asked to view the full-size wooden car outside – painted with chrome and styling embellishments. I had a genuine feeling of disappointment when the Super Minx was submitted. We had a rather conservative body engineer, who was no doubt sound and cost-conscious, but he lacked flair and foresight.'

The styling department at Rootes was in a state of flux in 1961, and it is important to put the background to the situation in the styling department during this time into context.

This three-quarter front view of the new Minx shows one of the original examples of front-end treatment that was not approved of by Lord Rootes. COVENTRY ARCHIVES

A Rapier IV prototype mock-up on the roof of the Stoke Styling Studio. POST VINTAGE HUMBER CAR CLUB

In the viewing studio at Stoke, a full-scale model clearly still intended as a Rapier. POST VINTAGE HUMBER CAR CLUB

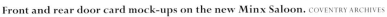

Front and rear door card mock-ups on the new Minx Saloon. COVENTRY ARCHIVES

Both Ted White and his assistant Ted Green had scored many successes over a long period of time with Rootes, but were a different breed of stylist to the new incumbents that had been joining Rootes since the late Fifties. The 'Two Teds' were always smartly dressed in dark suits, whereas newer members of the styling team were, as Roy Axe explains in his memoir:

'… in full art school regalia, which at the time was a combination of sports jackets, drainpipe trousers and "brothel creeper" shoes … These people, with their art school backgrounds were as alike as chalk and cheese compared with the "Two Teds". As a result, there were two camps, and neither had a lot of respect for [each] other.'

Roy Axe had joined Rootes in 1953 as an apprentice body engineer and would rise through the ranks to take on senior styling responsibilities for Rootes. By 1961, he was working with some influential and talented stylists, such as William Towns and Rex Fleming. Bob Saward and Tom Firth came from Ford and all of these stylists would in time stamp their identity on future Rootes models. As Roy Axe explains:

'What Bob Saward and Tom Firth brought from Ford was … much more sophisticated sketching techniques that were in use by Ford at the time. Most of the sketch work was done by crayon, on rough art paper, and often coloured paper. Bob and Tom had some good advanced techniques, which we all quickly embraced, and which improved our sketch techniques considerably.

'There was Ron Wisdom, who was one of the real characters of the place and who was capable of some very fine design ideas but was something of a loner … In addition, there was a man called Howard Beasley, who was something of a renegade; he seemed to do more modelling work than sketching, but I have seen him do some wild sketches too … Ted White saw him as an enemy in the camp and quite a disruptive one.'

With a styling dilemma surrounding the new designs, a change of plan was quickly instigated. Also, the new car at the time of the initial showing was probably still being called a 'Minx'; the 'Super Minx' name came shortly afterwards. Several factors were now important considerations, not least that of cost. Both the Singer and the Hillman versions would prove to be significantly more expensive cars to produce than the Minx and Gazelle and they also looked much bigger than their predecessors. In Ted White's defence, they were only marginally bigger – 1¾ inches (44.15mm) longer and 1½ inches (37.9mm) wider. White had actually created a roomier

car by extending the wheelbase and shortening the rear overhang. By lowering the overall height slightly, these factors combined to give the impression of a much larger car than was actually the case. Time, or rather lack of it, was another consideration if a 1961 introduction was to be achieved. The new Minx was sent back to the drawing board for styling changes, and a decision was made to bring out the new range as additional models alongside re-skinned versions of the Minx and Gazelle. The new models would be known as the Hillman Super Minx and the Singer Vogue. The Rapier would, for the time being, remain in the Rootes line-up with only detail changes. The Super Minx would ultimately emerge with a cleaner front end with a large stainless horizontally-barred grille flanked by single headlamps with sidelamp 'eyebrows' positioned above each headlamp in the front wings. Tom Firth was responsible for the re-design of the Super Minx. As the Singer styling had already been approved, it was presumably ready to go before the Super Minx, and in July 1961, with little fanfare other than the usual motoring and national press reviews, the Singer Vogue Saloon became the first of the new models to be introduced.

In October 1961, the Super Minx Saloon was launched at the Paris Motor Show. Both the Vogue and the Super Minx were well received by the press. Autocar magazine was complimentary, but not gushing in its appraisal of both models. Pitched against competitors' models in Autocar, the Vogue measured up remarkably well and in some ways much better. It offered a more powerful engine than the Ford Consul 375, Austin A55 and Vauxhall Victor, but was heavier than all except the Consul, and showed comparable interior space and comfort to all of the others, but… all of these comparable models would soon be up for replacement – the Vogue and the Super Minx were only just starting out.

With production of the Super Minx and Vogue well underway by 1962, the next task for Rootes was to add more models to the new product range and offer a new model to replace the Sunbeam Rapier.

In February 1962, production started on a Vogue Estate. However, due to lack of space at any of Rootes' production facilities, the Vogue Estate body shells were built by Carbodies in Coventry, who were already building estate car versions of the Humber Hawk and Super Snipe. In 1961, they had won an IBCAM (Institute of British Carriage and Automobile Manufacturers) gold medal at the Earl's Court Motor Show for their Super Snipe Estate. The Vogue Estate, several years later,

Once the Gazelle had become a Vogue, it was intended that a Convertible would accompany saloon and estate car versions. But in the end, only the Hillman version made it as a 'drop top'.
COVENTRY ARCHIVES

What turned out to be the Vogue Estate started out as a Gazelle. COVENTRY ARCHIVES

would win a silver IBCAM medal for Carbodies in the utility coachwork class.

Initially, both the Vogue and big Humber estates were built at the old Singer factory in Birmingham and then production was transferred to Carbodies, as Bill Lucas, works manager at Carbodies explained in an interview with historian Bill Munro:

> 'The Singer estate was converted at Holyhead Road from a saloon. It provided a turnover to keep a nucleus of skilled men at Carbodies. They were two tone [and a] trouble to paint. They introduced metallics ... You never knew what was coming out of the oven. In one place we got a lovely metallic colour and in other places it was patchy. We [often] had to flat it down and do it again.'

Bill Lucas had left Carbodies in 1954 after the BSA takeover of the company and joined Airflow Streamlines in Northampton as Works Manager, which is how the Hawk and Super Snipe prototype work came to be done by the Northampton firm. He returned to Carbodies in 1961. Due to the Vogue Estate taking up production space at Carbodies' main site at Holyhead Road, Lucas had to find additional space for the big Humber estates to be finished:

> 'BLSP did the saloon. They sent the shell with the roof cut off to Singer at Birmingham. I did the first ten prototypes at Airflow Streamlines ... We'd got so much work on [at Carbodies] ... I heard that Baginton airport [near Coventry] was going to be let out into factory units ... I wanted the

Members of the press evaluating the new Hillman Super Minx Saloon during its introduction on 2 October 1961 in Paris.
COVENTRY ARCHIVES

SINGER VOGUE MARK I (1961) SPECIFICATIONS

Body style
Four-door, four/five-seater saloon, unitary construction

Engine
4 cylinder, overhead valve, pushrod; three-bearing crankshaft

Power output:	1592cc (97.2cu in) developing 62bhp (net) at 4,400rpm
Bore and Stroke:	81.5 x 76.2mm (3.21 x 3.00in)
Compression ratio:	8.3:1 (7.8 or 6.9:1 optional)*
Torque:	85.8lb ft at 3,000rpm*
Fuel pump type:	AC mechanical
Carburettor:	Solex 32 PBIS downdraught*
Cooling system:	Water – pump and fan

Transmission
Four-speed gearbox with synchromesh on top, third and second gears. Centre floor gear change. (Column change lever available – export only)

Clutch:	Borg & Beck 8in (203mm) single dry plate type. Hydraulic operation.
Gear Ratios:	Top 4.22:1; Third 5.88:1; Second 9.04:1; First 14.13:1; Reverse 17.9:1. With Laycock overdrive: Overdrive Top 3.57:1; Top 4.44:1; Overdrive Third 4.97:1; Third 6.19:1; Second 9.51:1; First 14.87; Reverse 18.84:1*
Final drive:	Hypoid bevel type. Final drive ratio 4.22 (without overdrive) 4.44 (with overdrive)*

Electrical and Lighting

Ignition:	Coil and distributor with alternator. 12-volt, 38-amp Lucas battery*
Lighting:	Dual headlamps with dipped (outer) and main beam. Floor-mounted dipswitch. Front side light unit with flashing indicator; Rear lamps – amber flashing indicator, reflector, tail/stop lamp
Instruments:	Speedometer including mileage and trip recorder, water temperature gauge, oil pressure gauge, fuel gauge, ammeter, warning lights for main beam, ignition and flashing indicators

1961 Singer Vogue Mark 1 Saloon. ROOTES ARCHIVE CENTRE TRUST

Standard equipment:	Two-speed self-parking windscreen wipers; heater and ventilation system; Tudor screenwasher; clock; padded interior sunvisors; overriders; childproof door locks; boot floor mat. Tool kit, pillar jack and starting handle

Suspension and Wheels

Front:	Independent with wishbones, coil springs, double-acting telescopic shock absorbers. Torsion bar stabiliser
Rear:	Semi-elliptic leaf springs, double-acting telescopic shock absorbers
Wheels and Tyres:	13in (330.2mm) pressed steel wheels. Chrome hubcaps, stainless trim rings. Dunlop 5.90 x 13 tyres
Steering:	Burman recirculating ball type
Brakes:	Lockheed hydraulic with 9in (228.6mm) diameter, 1.75in (44.4mm) wide drums front and rear. Handbrake mounted at the side of the driver's seat operates mechanically on the rear wheels

Dimensions

Overall length:	13ft 9¼in (4,197mm)
Overall width:	5ft 2¼in (1,581mm)
Overall height:	4ft 10¼in (1,479mm)
Ground clearance:	6½in (165mm)
Track:	Front: 4ft 3½in* (1,302mm)
	Rear: 4 ft ½in* (1,232 mm)
Wheelbase:	8ft 5in* (2,565mm)
Turning circle:	36ft* (10.97m)
Fuel tank capacity:	11 gallons* (50 litres)
Unladen weight:	(with 5 gals fuel) 2,429lb* (1,102kg)

Performance

0–30 mph:	6.0 secs*
0–60 mph:	20.9 secs*
Top speed:	82–87mph (approx)*

Colours

Single tones:

** Saloon only   ***Estate Car only

Lake Blue with Lake Blue upholstery
Biarritz Blue with Blue upholstery**
Smoke Green with Green upholstery**
Foam White with Scarlet upholstery**
Maroon with Beige upholstery**
Embassy Black with Bright Red upholstery**
Silver Grey Metallic with Scarlet upholstery**
Sapphire Blue Metallic with Blue upholstery**
Dawn Mist with Bright Red upholstery
Charcoal with Bright Red upholstery***

Two tones: (Body colour / Roof colour / upholstery)
Lake Blue / Foam White with Lake Blue upholstery
Biarritz Blue / Windsor Blue with Blue upholstery**
Smoke Green / Sage Green with Green upholstery
Foam White / Pippin Red with Scarlet upholstery**
Maroon / Cavalry Beige with Beige upholstery**
Dawn Mist / Charcoal with Bright Red upholstery
Charcoal / Windsor Blue with Blue upholstery***

Optional Extras and Accessories

Smiths Radiomobile, Pye or Ecko radio; Smiths Easidrive automatic transmission; Laycock-de Normanville overdrive; Reutter individual front seats; safety belts; whitewall tyres; wing mirrors, clock

Price:

Saloon: £655 (Basic)*; Estate Car £730 (Basic)*

Model Variants:

Estate Car (introduced May '62)

Significance:

First of the 'Super Minx' style of Rootes cars to be launched

All data Rootes Motors Ltd except *Autocar* – July and September 1961

LAKE BLUE/FOAM WHITE

SMOKE GREEN/SAGE GREEN

Vogue Erwin Wasey swatches. ROOTES ARCHIVE CENTRE TRUST

Hillman Super Minx Estate. ROOTES ARCHIVE CENTRE TRUST

Hillman Super Minx Convertible. ROOTES ARCHIVE CENTRE TRUST

part where the bombers were flown in for repair. We got it before the rates for the property were decided. Eric Blackburn [works engineer] laid the track … [and then] we put the stoving oven in.'

The press tools and jigs for the Humber estate panels had been transferred from Singer to Holyhead Road, where the body shells were assembled and painted. From Baginton the finished bodies were then shipped to Rootes at Humber Road for final assembly.

For the rest of the Super Minx and Vogue range, Rootes still relied on Pressed Steel at Cowley. In May 1962, Estate Car versions of Vogue and Super Minx became available. In June, a convertible Hillman version was added, but no Singer version.

Kit Spackman was a Research & Development apprentice, test technician and subsequently a test engineer at Pressed Steel from 1962 when the new models were being built, and had first-hand knowledge of the Super Minx and Vogue:

'The Super Minx Estate was built at Cowley. The whole Super Minx production line was in R Building at Pressed Steel and ran on parallel tracks, each track for a particular model … there were two for Super Minx saloons, one for Vogue saloons and one for Super Minx Estates … The saloons were assembled on the line and the last job was to put the doors on, then the conveyor would lift the body up and whizz it over the road to the paint shop.

The Super Minx convertibles were built in a separate section and not on a track like the other models and were very much "hand built" items, with a special crew of assembly guys who certainly let you know they were special … I built some of them myself because when the holiday came up they didn't quite

know what to do with me. The line wasn't working as they were changing over to the next model and the foreman said, "Make yourself useful", so I said, "I don't know what to do." He asked me what I was doing last time and I told him I was making the crossmembers for the bottom of the Super Minx Convertibles. He said, "Can you build a whole Super Minx body?" I said, "I dunno!" I built four or five of them in a couple of weeks. I remember they had huge doors!'

In the late summer of 1962, the Vogue Mark 1 evolved into the Vogue Mark II. A Super Minx Mark II followed on in October. Most of the changes were made across the range. Individual front seats replaced the bench seats, although the Super Minx received a plainer 'tuck and roll' style of upholstery and would no longer be available in a two-tone scheme. The petrol tank on both models was moved to the nearside wing of the boot to increase storage capacity and disc brakes up front replaced drum brakes. Borg-Warner 35 Automatic transmission replaced the Smiths Easidrive system, twin reversing lamps and amber front indicators were standard on the Vogue; Super Minx carried on until October '64 and the Mark III before it was allowed to have combined amber flashing indicators and sidelights at the front. Both versions were visually unchanged, with the exception of a lack of a chrome strip on the bonnet of the Vogue.

At the end of 1964, Rootes decided to discontinue production of the Super Minx Convertible. What Rootes designers had achieved with this handsome convertible was a unique hood design: the Super Minx was the only British-built volume production convertible to feature a full-length American-style cantilevered one-piece hood that covered a full four-seater body, a feature that was probably overlooked at the time, and has been since forgotten. Unfortunately, what Rootes failed

Comedy actor Mario Fabrizi collects his new Hillman Super Minx from Ilford, Essex, Rootes dealer Ray Powell Ltd. GRAHAM GRIMBLE

New **HILLMAN
SUPER MINX** CONVERTIBLE

to achieve was enough profitable sales to make the car viable beyond 1964.

If the replacement for the Minx and Gazelle was initially a disappointment, the model that was being developed to replace the Rapier was not. It may have taken longer in development, but Rootes management wanted a stylish 4-door sports saloon, built on the same Super Minx floorpan and utilising the same, or similar, mechanicals – and that is what they got. During its development period, the Rapier replacement was certainly known as the 'Sunbeam Mark 1, four-door Saloon' and is mentioned several times in memos from Lord Rootes to the rest of the board when the BLSP and Thrupp & Maberly viability studies were being carried out. Prototype versions carried RAP 1, RAP2 and RAP 3 codes. In its final version, the car was still known as the Rapier four-door Saloon, but right at the last minute it was changed and became the Humber Sceptre. The Sceptre debuted in February 1963 and the Rapier continued as Series IV, with revised interior appointments, an increase in power and a front end makeover that gave it a cleaner look.

When *Motor* magazine road tested the new Sceptre in June 1963, they acknowledged Rootes' success in

'combining sporting and luxury characteristics within compact dimensions … fast, stable, sturdy, notably comfortable and very well equipped, the Humber Sceptre is tempting value at under £1,000.'

Other 'Marks' of Super Minx, Vogue and Sceptre would continue, alongside Minx, Gazelle and Rapier, and although the models would give Rootes some extra sales that might have otherwise gone to the Vauxhall Victor, Ford Corsair or BMC Farina, the ranges still did not give them appropriate economies of scale to make sufficient profits. With the retention of the term 'Series', confusion also reigned as to what the correct terms for the new Super Minx family should be. Officially, the cars were 'Mark' but 'Series' was printed on the cover of the Mark 1 Vogue owner's manual as well as some later publications. Vehicle Identification Schedules published by Rootes, however, state 'Mark'. Peter Ware made it quite clear in a conversation with Nigel Hughes, who went on to work for a brief time at Chrysler UK, that Rootes had always intended the Super Minx, Vogue and Sceptre to be 'Mark', in order to avoid confusion with 'Series', and this was confirmed later in correspondence with Hughes from Geoffrey Rootes, who was by then the second Lord Rootes.

HUMBER SCEPTRE MARK I (1963) SPECIFICATIONS

Body style
Four-door, four/five-seater saloon, unitary construction

Engine
4 cylinder, overhead valve, pushrod; three-bearing crankshaft

Power output:	1592cc (97.2cu in) developing 80bhp (net) 85.5bhp (gross) at 5,200rpm
Bore and Stroke:	81.5 x 76.2mm (3.21 x 3.00in)
Compression ratio:	9.1:1
Torque:	91lb ft at 3,500rpm.
Fuel pump type:	AC mechanical
Carburettor:	Zenith 36WIA3 twin downdraught carburettors. Light alloy induction manifold
Cooling system:	Water – centrifugal pump and fan

Transmission
Four-speed gearbox with synchromesh on top, third and second gears. Centre floor-mounted gear lever. Laycock-de Normanville overdrive on third and top, with self-cancelling switch

Clutch:	Borg & Beck 8 in. (203mm) Hydraulic single dry plate type
Gear Ratios:	Top 4.22:1; Overdrive Top 3.389:1; Third 5.887:1; Overdrive Third 4.717:1; Second 9.038:1; First 14.128:1; Reverse 17.896:1
Final drive:	Hypoid bevel type. Final drive ratio: 4.22:1.

Electrical and Lighting

Ignition:	Coil and distributor with dynamo. Lucas 12-volt, 38-amp battery*
Lighting:	Dual headlamps with dipped and main beam. Floor-mounted dip switch. Front side light unit with flashing indicator. Rear lamp clusters with amber flashing indicator, reflector, tail/stop lamp. Separate reversing lamps
Instruments:	Speedometer with mileage and trip recorder; rev. counter; clock; water temperature gauge; ammeter, fuel and oil gauges; warning lights for headlight main beam, ignition, flashing indicators and overdrive; headlamp flasher
Standard equipment:	Two-speed self-parking windscreen wipers; heater and ventilation system; Tudor screen washer; fully reclining front seats; cigarette lighter; padded interior sunvisors; overriders; childproof door locks; boot floor carpet. Tool kit, pillar jack and starting handle*

1964 Humber Sceptre Mark 1.

Suspension and Wheels

Front:	Independent coil springs with Armstrong double-acting hydraulic telescopic shock absorbers with wishbones. Anti-roll bar. No grease points
Rear:	Semi-elliptic leaf springs, Armstrong double-acting hydraulic telescopic shock absorbers
Wheels and Tyres:	13in (330.2mm) pressed steel wheels. Chrome hubcaps, stainless trim rings Dunlop C41 6.00 x 13 tubeless tyres
Steering:	Burman recirculating ball type
Brakes:	Lockheed 9¾in (247.7mm) vacuum servo-assisted front discs; 9in (228.6mm) drums on rear. Handbrake mounted at the side of driver's seat operates mechanically on rear wheels

Dimensions

Overall length:	13ft 9½in (4,197.4mm)
Overall width:	5ft 3¼in (1,607mm)
Overall height:	4ft 9in (1,448mm)
Ground clearance:	6½in (165mm)
Track:	Front: 4ft 3¼in* (1,302mm) Rear: 4 ft½in* (1,232mm)
Wheelbase:	8ft 5in* (2,565mm)
Turning circle:	36ft* (10.97m)
Fuel tank capacity:	10.5 gallons (47.7 litres)
Unladen weight:	(with 5 gallons fuel) 21½cwt* (1092kg)

Performance

0-30 mph:	5.5 secs.*
0-60 mph:	18.2 secs.*
Top speed:	85–90 mph (approx)*
Fuel consumption:	24 mpg at average 50mph

Colours (**1964 m-y)
Single tones:
Quartz Blue Metallic with Azure Blue upholstery
Bronze Metallic with Rich Beige upholstery
Solent Blue Metallic with Pearl Grey upholstery
Pippin Red with Regency Beige (or Black**) upholstery
Goodwood Green Metallic with Black upholstery**
Autumn Gold Metallic with Black upholstery**
Royal Blue Metallic with Blue upholstery**

A rear three-quarter artist's impression from the 'new Humber Sceptre' brochure. POST VINTAGE HUMBER CAR CLUB

Two tones: (Body colour / Roof and boot colour)

Velvet Green / Sage Green with Green upholstery
Quartz Blue Metallic / Moonstone with Azure Blue upholstery
Solent Blue Metallic / Moonstone with Pearl Grey upholstery
Pippin Red / Pearl Grey with Regency Beige upholstery
Moonstone / Quartz Blue Metallic with Azure Blue upholstery

Optional Extras
Smiths Radiomobile, Pye or Ecko radio; safety belts;
whitewall tyres; wing mirrors

Price: £825 (Basic)

Model Variants: None

Significance: Rootes' entry into the 'compact luxury sports saloon' market
All data Rootes Motors Ltd except *Motor* July 1963

NEW HUMBER SCEPTRE
A SUPERBLY EQUIPPED SPORTS SALOON

The Sceptre brochure featured high-quality artwork to depict the new model. POST VINTAGE HUMBER CAR CLUB

A Humber Sceptre Mark 1 and a Vauxhall Victor taking part in the popular, annual Mobil Economy Run in 1964.

SUNBEAM VENEZIA

The creation of the Sunbeam Venezia Superleggera, like the Trojan horse at the gates of Troy, seemed like a good idea at the time. At best, it was a glorious folly – at its worst, a commercial flop and a financial disaster for one of Italy's most prominent specialist coachbuilding firms. But the Venezia deserves its rightful place in automotive history as a worthy example of Anglo-Italian engineering and design. The highly competitive sports touring car segment at that time already had contenders fighting it out in the form of the Alfa Romeo 2600 Spyder and the Lancia Flaminia. Both used Touring Superleggera Milano to add flair and style to the look of their cars, as did Aston Martin, Lamborghini and Maserati.

Rootes' involvement with Touring of Milan goes back to 1959, following the introduction of the

Sunbeam Alpine. Project engineer Alec Caine had approached Touring to see if they could come up with some modifications on future versions of the Alpines. They provided a number of solutions for Rootes which would find their way into subsequent Alpines. Development of the Venezia seemed a logical progression from the agreement that Rootes had entered into with Touring in October 1961 for them to assemble Super Minx Saloons and Alpines, to be sold through Rootes Italia. Utilising off the shelf parts such as the radiator grille from the Sunbeam Rapier, headlight surrounds from the Sceptre and the tail lamp unit from the Super Minx, all Touring had to do was to create a glamorous and stylish two-door 2+2 sports saloon body that would fit with Humber Sceptre floorpan and running gear, and that is what they did!

Carrozzeria Touring was run by Carlo Felice Bianchi Anderloni, who had taken over from his father in 1948. Touring had developed a specialised method of building aluminium over steel bodies. Aluminium body panels were attached to a tubular steel skeleton which enabled an aerodynamic and ultra-lightweight design, known as Superleggera.

Someone who knows the inside story of the Venezia is Kit Power, who joined Rootes as a management trainee in 1957 and was sent to work at Devonshire House when he was given the opportunity to go to Milan:

'After I'd worked in London for about a couple of years, they asked me if I would go out to Italy and become the number two to George Carless, who was the general manager of Rootes Italia. I spent about two years in Milan and that was a very interesting exercise because it was before [we joined] the Common Market ... and Rootes had the idea to assemble cars within the Common Market and thereby avoid import duties and so on.

'So an arrangement was made with Touring of Milan, whose main business was building aluminium bodies for Aston Martin [Alfa Romeo and Lancia]. But they wanted volume and they had built a new factory [at Nova Milanese] and they wanted to fill it, so a scheme was arranged where they would assemble the Sunbeam Alpine and the Rootes Italia company would market that in Italy ... then assembling the Hillman Super Minx as well. In the course of all that, the suggestion came up ... that they would build a Touring aluminium body on a Humber Sceptre [chassis], and we [Rootes Italia] would market it as a sports coupé. That was duly done and the Sunbeam Venezia was the result.'

According to historians John Neal and Alain Thirion, the idea of building a sports saloon specifically aimed at the Italian market originated from George Carless in the spring of 1960. He put the proposal to Brian Rootes, who thought it a good idea, as did Sr Anderloni, who needed volume production for his new factory, which was due to open in 1962.

Design and prototypes

In 1961, Touring commenced work on the design of the car, which bore a resemblance to Lancia and Maserati models that were being built at the time by Touring. The principal draughtsmen on the project, according to Neal and Thirion, were Frederico Formenti and Aquilino Gilardi. It was apparently George Carless who chose the name Venezia.

Lord Rootes, having been shown a 1:10 scale model of the Venezia, gave approval for a prototype to be built. It was fitted to a Super Minx floorpan (which was identical to the Sceptre floorpan), and modifications were made to the seating and dashboard, but no engine was installed. In mid-1962, it was sent back to England and was approved for production by Touring. The prototype was subjected to months of testing by Rootes, who then made their own modifications and fitted a 1592cc Rootes engine with a single twin-choke Solex carburettor and a four-speed gearbox.

Debut in Venice

The car was announced in Milan on 9 September 1963 and officially launched three days later in St Mark's Square, Venice – where else? It arrived by gondola through the city's canals in order to get to St Mark's. The occasion was attended by local dignitaries and it was well received by the press. The ever-irreverent Doug Blain, then writing in *Small Car* magazine, commented: *'The major impression is one of confident sophistication...'* and described it as *'a sort of Rapier with the edges knocked off and an added touch of flair!'*

Kit Foster saw the project through to the end:

'It was never a great commercial success, particularly as Lancia had launched their two-door Sports Coupe – the Flaminia – and the Sunbeam name wasn't really known in Italy. Because our numbers were rather small, the price was

awfully high, so in the end, we only built just over 200 of them [although another estimate states that only about 145 were built]. The last ones [in 1966] were in fact, sold in France and in Belgium, as well as in Italy [and Spain]. They never brought any back to the UK ... except for one – mine, which was right-hand-drive ... and the prototype was right-hand-drive.'

The Venezia may have sold more units if it had been given the option of a more powerful engine, but it also had the additional baggage of little or no development money. Speculation abounded that Brian Rootes' car was a special V8 version, but according to his son Bill was *'probably the one he gave me – dark blue with red trim. It didn't have a V8 engine, although that might have been nice!'*

Time had run out for any development of the Venezia and its demise was not all Rootes nor all Touring's fault. A strike at Touring's factory in 1963 did a lot to weaken the Italian company's finances, but it was changes to Italian taxation on big-engined cars which meant that the contracts between Lamborghini and Maserati were no longer forthcoming. By March 1965, the company had gone into receivership and by the end of 1966, Touring Superleggera Milano had ceased trading.

The Sunbeam Venezia Superleggera gained first prize in the Gran Turismo class for cars up to 1800cc in the Concours D'Elegance in Florence, 30 and 31 May 1964. COVENTRY ARCHIVES

As for Kit Foster – he went back to Rootes' export office at Halkin House in London as manager of the Overseas Shipping Department. Shortly after Touring went into administration, George Carless went on to run Rootes Bahamas and Rootes Italia was closed down.

COMMER-KARRIER – PROFITABLE INNOVATION

If the Rootes car divisions were struggling to maintain profitability during the early Sixties, then Commer-Karrier, the Rootes Group's commercial vehicle division, under managing director Rex Watson Lee, was going from strength to strength, and contributing significantly to the Rootes balance sheet.

By 1963, Commer-Karrier had scored a hat trick in successful new model introductions. In January 1960, Rootes entered the competitive, but lucrative, 15 cwt van market with the Commer 1500 ¾-ton van range. In 1961, the Walk-thru, a high-capacity, easy access, door-to-door delivery van was launched and in 1962, the C and V Series of medium and heavy goods trucks to replace the successful, but ageing QX models, became available.

The Commer 1500 ¾-ton van was designed and built by Pressed Steel at Cowley. The clean, uncluttered lines of the new van made it one of the most modern-looking, forward-control vans available, in a market that

These Rootes publicity shots of the Venezia show the Touring Superleggera styling off to good effect. SUNBEAM ALPINE OWNERS CLUB

THOMAS HARRINGTON LTD

In 1897 Thomas Harrington started building light horse-drawn passenger wagonettes, flys and landaus at his premises in Church Street, Brighton. Within three years the original works was expanded and new showrooms were acquired in King Street. The increasing popularity of the motor car meant that this became the mainstay of the business, alongside commercial vehicle bodywork.

Unlike many, Harrington adapted well when standardisation of body designs by private car manufacturers in the 1920s caused the decline of that part of activities. What work there was tended to be for bespoke chassis such as Bentley or Bugatti and this perhaps led to the upmarket image that Harrington continued to foster throughout their existence. In fact, cars continued to be a feature of Harrington work right up to the end of the company, but they were very much the minority. Production of luxury coach and bus bodies became the major occupation of the firm, with commercial vehicle bodies a smaller but significant proportion of the output.

In 1930 a purpose-built factory known as Sackville Works was constructed at Old Shoreham Road, Hove. The site area always limited production to approximately 200 vehicles a year and would be one, although not the main reason, that Harringtons eventually ceased trading.

During the Second World War, Harringtons built new or repaired damaged vehicles for supply to the armed forces. Part of the works was converted to manufacture air frame components and prototype aircraft components. Harringtons became skilled in the techniques of light aluminium alloy construction, which were incorporated into post-war coach production.

During the 1950s, a greater use of fibreglass was successfully applied to their products, thus saving on the costly panel beating process. By the early Sixties, when the success of the Cavalier coach was resulting in batches of large orders, the limitations imposed by the factory size were

The distinctive artwork of George Bishop; a 1952 Harrington 33-seat saloon coach on a Commer Avenger chassis.

becoming more and more apparent and Harrington once again turned to the car side of their business in an attempt to maximise production area. This prompted the production of a series of fibreglass fastback 'GT' coachbuilt conversions, designed to convert a drophead style sports tourer into a fixed-head coupé. Base vehicles were the Sunbeam Alpine and Triumph TR4. The Sunbeam Harrington Alpine, based on the Series II Alpine, was introduced in March 1961. A Series C, based on the Series III Alpine replaced it and the last Harrington Alpine model, the Series D, being based on the Series IV. About 110 Harrington Alpines in total were made, of which only a handful were Series C or D models.

Sunbeam Harrington Le Mans brochure. CLIVE HARRINGTON

Fibreglass was also extensively used in the PSV conversions to the early models of Commer 1500 twelve-seater minibus, which were particularly successful. For the purchaser, the attraction of this was that although the conversion cost more than the standard minibus, full PSV-specification vehicles were exempt from purchase tax and this helped make the project viable.

Harrington bodywork, along with Beadle, Duple and Plaxtons, became a notable supplier of high-quality coachwork for the Commer Avenger.

An ardent fan of the special-bodied Alpines from Worthing. The Duke of Gloucester with his Harrington Le Mans Alpine. CLIVE HARRINGTON

Harrington had always been a family firm. Ernest G. Harrington and Thomas R. Harrington (the sons of the founder, Thomas) were joint managing director and chairman until 1960. Clifford Harrington, who had been a joint director since the Fifties in charge of coach building, was keen to embrace the best continental influences and was the prime mover behind the styling of the Cavalier and Grenadier coaches. However it was clear that things had to change. The bespoke work that had 'filled in space' around the coach production was beginning to dry up.

Harrington had been a Rootes agent since the Thirties, the car dealership side of the business being run separately from showrooms in Hove and Worthing. In 1961, Rootes asked Harringtons to make a lighter and more aerodynamic Alpine in order to reduce drag and enable a higher top speed in track racing. This they did by creating a completely new nose cone in light aluminium, with a Harrington-style

fixed-head roofline. The unique car, driven by Peter Harper and Peter Procter, won the coveted 'Index of Thermal Efficiency' in the 1961 Le Mans 24 hour race. The following year, two Alpines, with Harrington-modified 'Kamm-tails' and removable hardtops were entered at Le Mans. Although the Harrington modifications worked well, the cars suffered from engine and transmission problems; the highest placed Alpine finished in fifteenth position, driven by Harper and Procter.

In October 1961 at the Earl's Court Motor Show, and in response to Rootes' race success at Le Mans, Harrington

The Harrington Alpine Coupé, number 34, during practice at the 1961 Le Mans. *Left to right*: **Peter Procter; Peter Harper; Norman Garrad and David Hodkin, talking to Paddy Hopkirk, who drove Harrington Alpine number 35 with Peter Jopp.** CLIVE HARRINGTON

The Harrington Rootes showroom at Worthing, Sussex, in 1948. CLIVE HARRINGTON

Paddy Hopkirk pushes on through the 'esses' in the 1962 Le Mans race. PETER PROCTER

(continued overleaf)

launched a new model, the Sunbeam Harrington Le Mans. As with their other coachbuilt conversion it too was based on the Series II Alpine, but was produced as an official Rootes model, and marketed by Rootes through their worldwide dealer network. Around 260 of the Harrington Le Mans models were built and production ceased with the run out of the Series II Alpine in February 1963.

During this period, the Rootes family had seen Thos. Harrington Ltd as a worthwhile investment, and had been

Smiles all round! The launch of the Sunbeam Harrington Le Mans at the 1961 Earl's Court Motor Show. *Left to right*: **Gordon Harrington (in dark suit); Clifford Harrington; Brian Rootes; HRH Princess Alexandra; Donald (later Lord) Stokes. George Hartwell can be seen in between Brian Rootes and her Royal Highness.** CLIVE HARRINGTON

buying into the business through their Robins & Day chain of car dealerships. By 1961, Robins & Day had gained a majority shareholding in Thos. Harrington Ltd. The company therefore did not become part of the Rootes Group, but a wholly owned subsidiary of Robins & Day Ltd.

As far as the Harrington family was concerned this should have provided a steady stream of specialist work from Rootes companies and potential for cash injection. Sadly, this was not to be the case. Later there were some changes in management when George Hartwell came in as managing director and in November 1962, Desmond Rootes came on to the board as director of motor trading. Clifford Harrington resigned from the board and left the firm in October 1962. Gordon H. Harrington took his place as general manager, manufacturing. At the same time Geoffrey Harrington was appointed to the Board as sales manager, manufacturing division.

The conversions on the Commer minibus kept the Rootes connection ticking over until near the end and in fact after the closure of Sackville works, the fibreglass conversions continued to be produced at Rootes Maidstone although no longer badged as Harringtons.

By the mid-Sixties, the firm was in a deadlock situation. As far as coaches were concerned no money was made available to develop new models, even though preliminary plans had been made for a replacement for the Cavalier/Grenadier range. The Crusader IV had seen a return to composite construction in order to reduce costs. It was also quite clear that the bespoke method of production that had served Harrington so well on its small site could no longer be made cost effective. Geoffrey Harrington resigned in April 1965. During 1965, coach-building activities were discontinued. The Harrington name continued as a retailer of motor cars.

Clifford Harrington (*left*) and Gordon Harrington on the Downs, with the new Sunbeam Harrington Le Mans. CLIVE HARRINGTON

Commer Avenger Harrington Contender Mark IV, 41-seat integral coach, fitted with a Rootes TS3 diesel engine.

had been dominated by vans such as the Ford Thames, Austin/Morris J2-M16 and the Standard Atlas.

The Commer van, however, had an edge! It was available in no fewer than sixteen standard versions: panel van with hinged or sliding doors; two pick-ups; a light bus version; a dropsider; a high top van; and countless other bodies such as a milk float, security van or mobile shop which would be built by specialized outside bodybuilders. One of the most popular conversions was as a motor caravan by Martin Walter Ltd – the Dormobile Coaster. With its side-hinged rising roof, it was possible to convert a Commer bus into a fully fitted out two- or four-berth camper van. Coachbuilt versions followed: the Jennings Roadranger and the Bluebird Highwayman, which turned out to be one of the most successful van conversions after Bluebird Caravans Ltd transferred production from the BMC J2 chassis to the Commer 1500. With the success of the Commer Highwayman, by 1964, Rootes agreed to drop its own version by Rootes Maidstone, in order to concentrate on supplying base vehicles for Bluebird.

The key to the versatility of the new van range was in the construction of the underframe. A flat platform unitary type sub-assembly offered the necessary strength and rigidity to enable numerous types of standard and coachbuilt bodywork. In true Rootes form, many mechanical components were straight out of the Rootes parts bin. As well as the Hillman 1494cc 4-cylinder engine and four-speed gearbox, the back axle and prop shaft was Humber Hawk and the independent front suspension comprised of a front crossmember from the Sunbeam Alpine and Humber Hawk wishbones.

The ¾-ton van range would go on to have an incredibly long production life of twenty-three years. The 1500

One of the most popular motorhome combinations during the 1960s was the Bluebird Highwayman fitted on a Commer 1500 Series 2 chassis. MARTIN WATTS

Calthorpe carried out the camper bodywork conversion on this 1961 Commer Series 1¾ ton (1500) bus. MARTIN WATTS

Commer 7 ton Mk.III (QX) Forward Control dropsider, delivered in January 1960 by Rootes Maidstone.

¾-ton van range was supplemented in November 1962 by a larger capacity 1 ton 2500 model, now with twenty-one different body versions. In 1971 both the 1500 and 2500 versions were joined by an intermediate 2000 version, all of which were available with a Borg Warner 35 automatic gearbox option. Ultimately it would end up as the Dodge Spacevan, after a production life of nearly three decades, with virtually no major design changes.

The Commer Walk-Thru was launched at the Commercial Motor Show in October 1961. The uniqueness of the Walk-thru in early-Sixties Britain was that it did not fit exactly into any given market segment in Britain. Instead, it created its own market segment, based on existing vehicles in use in North America — that of a basic, no-frills, cheap to run, easy access, multi-drop, door-to-door delivery van.

COMMER 1500 ¾-TON VAN (1960) SPECIFICATIONS

Vehicle description
Unitary construction forward control panel van

Engine – Petrol
4 cylinder, overhead valve – pushrod operated; three-bearing crankshaft; three-bearing camshaft

Power output:	1494cc (91.2cu in) developing 52bhp (gross) at 4,500rpm
Bore and Stroke:	79 x 76.2mm
Compression ratio:	7.0:1
Torque:	76lb ft (10.51 kg m) at 2,200rpm
Fuel pump type:	AC mechanical
Carburettor:	Solex downdraught
Cooling system:	Water – pump and fan

Transmission
Four-speed gearbox with synchromesh on top, third and second gears. Gear lever mounted centrally on toeboard

Clutch:	Borg and Beck 8in (203mm) single dry-plate type
Gear Ratios:	Top Direct; Third 1.52:1; Second 2.34:1; First 4.08:1
Prop shaft/Rear axle:	2in (50mm) Hardy Spicer propeller shaft; Semi-floating hypoid-bevel type. Standard rear axle ratio: 5.125:1 (Optional ratio: 5.625:1)

Electrical and Lighting

Ignition:	Coil and distributor with dynamo; 12-volt, 38-amp Lucas battery
Lighting:	Two Lucas sealed-beam headlamps. Dipped beam controlled by foot-operated dip switch. Separate combined side lamp / turn signal unit. Rear lamp cluster incorporates tail, brake, amber turn signal indicator, reflector; rear number plate light; interior light. Two single speed windscreen wipers. Two spoke steering wheel with centre horn push with indicator 'stalk' switch mounted on the steering column
Instruments:	Speedometer, lights and windscreen wiper switches; oil, generator warning and flashing indicator lights

General Equipment:	Interior mirror; two exterior rear view mirrors. Ventilating system. Tool kit including jack and wheelbrace

Suspension and Wheels

Front:	Independent coil springs and wishbones with anti-roll bar and telescopic hydraulic dampers
Rear:	Semi-elliptic underslung leaf springs
Wheels and Tyres:	15in pressed steel wheels. Chrome hubcaps. Dunlop 6.00/6.40-15 (6 ply) tubeless tyres
Steering:	'Cam Gears' cam and peg unit with 17 to 1 ratio.
Brakes:	Lockheed hydraulic four wheel system, with two leading shoe on front wheels, leading and trailing on rear. Handbrake mounted at the side of driver's seat operates mechanically on rear wheels. Brake drum sizes: Front 10in diameter x 2¼in wide (254mm x 57.15mm). Rear 9in diameter x 1¾in wide (228.6mm x 44.45mm)

Dimensions and Payloads

Overall length:	14ft 0in (4,267mm)
Overall width:	6ft 1in (1,854mm)
Overall height:	6ft 7½in (954mm)

**Loading height
(standard tyres):** 23½in (597mm)

**Ground clearance
(minimum laden):** 7¼in (184mm)

Track: Front: 48in (1,219 mm) Rear:
55½in (1,410 mm)

Wheelbase: 7ft 6in (2,286 mm)

Turning circle: 36ft ** (1,097cm)

**Registration weight
(hinged door van):** 22cwt (petrol); 23¼cwt
(diesel)

**Maximum permissible
gross vehicle weight:** 41cwt (4,600lb) (2,087kg)

Internal van body space: 200cu ft (5.66cu m)

Fuel tank capacity: 9 gallons (40.91 litres)

Fuel consumption –

Petrol engine: 29.5mpg** (fully laden at
average speed of 31mph).

Diesel engine: 53.93mpg** (fully laden at
average speed 30.5mph)

Colours and Optional Extras

Primer or Toledo Red; April Yellow; Seacrest Green; Foam Grey; Wickham Blue. (Foam Grey available as a Duotone Colour on passenger models)

- *Passenger seat; *Centre seat (*Standard on passenger models); Floor protection strips; Rear quarter bumpers; Heater.
- Spare wheel, tyre and carrier; Optional tyres on goods models: 6.50/6.70-15-6 ply. Radiator thermometer (Passenger models)
- 4 cylinder, 1,621cc (99cu in) indirect injection overhead valve diesel engine (Perkins 'Four-99') developing 42.3bhp.

gross at 3,600rpm. (governed maximum). Torque 71lb ft (9.81kg m) at 2,250rpm

Price: £499 (Basic)

Model Variants: Chassis drive-away unit with hinged doors; Chassis cab drive-away unit with hinged doors; Van with hinged doors and extra side door; Van – sliding doors; Standard Pick-up; Canopy Pick-up; Standard Dropsider; High Top Van; Ambulance; Gown Van; Luton Van; Baker's Van; Bottle Float; Mobile Shop; Light Bus 12-seater; P.S.V. Bus 12-seater; Contractors Bus 14-seater; Station Wagon eight-seater; Caravan two berth or four berth

Significance: Rootes' entry into the volume production light-duty 15 cwt delivery van market

All data Commer Cars Ltd except ** *The Commercial Motor* – 8 January 1960 and 1 April 1960

Apart from a standard panel van, some of the different guises a Commer 1500 ¾ ton were available in were a Canopy Pickup; High Top Van and Luton Van. ROOTES ARCHIVE CENTRE TRUST

From 1965, the Commer 1500 Series III PA van (sliding door) with all-synchromesh gearbox.

Commer 1500 and 2500 Series brochure artwork.

The concept of the Walk-Thru came about following a series of trips made during the 1950s by Geoffrey Cozens and chief engineer A.J.Smith to America and Canada. Cozens had compiled a very detailed report on manufacturing techniques in North America, which included the design and manufacture of door-to-door delivery vans. Successful models by Dodge, Chevrolet and GMC were studied, as was a rather more specialized van from a small but significant independent called Divco. It was a combination of all of these vans that laid the framework for the Walk-Thru, and it was A.J.Smith who conceptualised the design for Commer to build. Designed 'in-house' at Luton, it was made available in 1½-, 2- and 3-ton versions with four-cylinder petrol and light-diesel engines in the 1½- and 2-ton models, and the light-six de-rated Humber Super Snipe petrol engine, which was available in all models. A Perkins diesel was optional. The basic van versions were offered on a variety of wheelbase lengths, as well as chassis/cab and chassis/front end versions, to facilitate various body options.

The Commer C and V Series truck range formed the third part of the Commer hat trick. The CA Series was the replacement for the QX model and was introduced in 1962, initially as an 8-tonner. It featured an entirely new cab, designed and built by GKN Sankey at their Hadley Castle Works, near Wellington, which

The sliding door version of the Commer Walk-Thru made an ideal airline equipment support van.

COMMER WALK-THRU 1½ TON VAN (1961) SPECIFICATIONS

Body style
Forward control panel van body – all-steel welded
construction – mounted on separate chassis

Engine – petrol
4 cylinder (4P.138) overhead valve; one piece cylinder block
and crankcase; 'Lo-ex' alloy pistons; three bearing camshaft;
three bearing crankshaft

Power output:	2266cc (138,27cu in) petrol engine developing 56bhp at 3,400rpm
Bore and Stroke:	81 x 110mm
Compression ratio:	6.25:1
Torque:	104lb ft at 1,600rpm
Fuel pump type:	AC mechanical
Carburettor:	Solex downdraught
Cooling system:	Water – pump and fan

Transmission
Four-speed synchromesh gearbox; centrally-positioned
floor-mounted lever

Clutch:	9in (228mm) Single Dry-plate type
Gear Ratios:	First: 5.77:1; Second: 3.029:1; Third: 1.703:1; Fourth Direct; Reverse: 6.985:1
Final drive:	Spiral bevel type; Axle ratio: 5.57:1

Electrical and Lighting

Ignition:	Coil and distributor with dynamo; 12-volt, 64-amp Lucas battery
Lighting:	Two Lucas sealed-beam headlamps and separate sidelights, column-mounted, lever type dip switch. Separate front and rear flashing indicators. Twin stop/tail lamps. Rear number plate lamp
Instruments:	Speedometer with oil pressure and main beam warning lights; starter, carburettor and hand throttle control; fuel gauge, choke and temperature gauge (petrol models) mounted in instrument panel located to the right of the steering column. Dual windscreen wipers – single speed

NEW COMMER 'WALK-THRU'
RANGE OF 1½ · 2 AND 3 TONNERS, PETROL OR DIESEL

The Commer Walk-thru brochure issued in September 1961
for the launch of the van range.

Suspension and Wheels

Front and Rear:	Semi-elliptic front and rear springs with double acting piston type hydraulic dampers
Chassis specification:	Ladder type frame construction with carbon manganese steel side members
Wheels and Tyres:	16in two-piece steel wheels, width 6.00G, offset 1.25, single rear. 7.50-16 (8 ply) tyres
Steering:	Cam and peg
Brakes:	Girling hydraulic two-leading-shoe on front wheels, leading/trailing shoes on rear. Mechanical handbrake to rear wheels operated from column-mounted lever

Dimensions and Payloads

Maximum Gross Vehicle Weight:	3.79 tons/8,500lb/3,850kg/76cwt
Complete dry vehicle weight:	40½cwt (approx)
Nominal payload rating:	1.5 tons/3,360lb/1,524kg
Internal van body space:	350 cubic feet (9.91cu m)
Overall length:	17ft 3¾in
Overall width:	6ft 9¼in
Overall height:	7ft 3½in (approx – laden)
Ground clearance:	7¾in
Track:	Front: 5ft 6½in Rear: 4ft 10½in

(continued overleaf)

Wheelbase:	10ft 3in/123in
Turning circle:	44ft
Fuel tank capacity:	10 gallons (45.4 litres)
Maximum speed:	55mph (88.5km/h)

Optional Extras – all models
Twin heaters and demisting equipment; Passenger seat; Rear quarter bumpers; Porous chrome cylinder bores (Van der Horst patent) for extended engine life

Engine options:
1: 4P.138 4 cylinder 2266cc petrol (as above)
2: 6P.181 6 cylinder 2965cc (180 cu. in.) petrol, developing 85bhp at 3,800rpm. Torque: 147lb ft at 1,400rpm.
3: 0.138 Diesel 4 cylinder 2260cc (137.89cu in) developing 56bhp at 3,000rpm. Torque: 100lb ft at 1,750 rpm.
4: Perkins 4.203, 4 cylinder 3330cc (203cu in) diesel, developing 63bhp at 2,600rpm. Torque: 142 lb ft at 1,350rpm

Prices: 1: £832; **2:** £890; **3:** £952; **4:** £998 (all prices are basic)

Model Variants: Chassis / Scuttle; Chassis and cab
Significance: First multi-stop, short haul, large capacity delivery van range of its kind in Britain
All data Commer Cars Ltd – September 1961

The Walk-thru chassis/cab versions utilised folding 'jack-knife' type doors, which were copied directly from the American Divco door-to-door multi-drop delivery van.

A 1962 Commer CA 8-ton platform lorry demonstrator, fitted with the Rootes TS3 opposed-piston two-stroke diesel engine.

had seen considerable expansion to take on additional automotive work. In 1961, GKN had established a new 'Commercial Cab Shop' to build the C Series cabs, as well as cabs for Leyland trucks.

As well as the 8-tonner, a new CA 7½-tonner was offered, and was built alongside existing QX 7-ton models, until new C-Series versions could be built

to replace old QX models. The C-Series trucks were offered with a choice of three wheelbases and petrol or TS3 diesel engine options. By 1963, the new Sankey cab was being fitted across the Commer-Karrier range, and the QX finally bowed out. The Commer VA 4-, 5-, 6- and 7-ton ranges filled in the gaps, along with corresponding Karrier Gamecock chassis, which included a municipal version with a seven-seat crew cab extension by Carbodies.

Although the VA utilised the same body as the CA, its appearance differed by only having single headlamps. It was available in three wheelbase versions, including a tipper, but the TS-3 diesel was not an option. Instead, either the Perkins 6.354 or 4-cylinder 4.236 became available towards the end of 1963 in the 4-tonner, as well as two 6-cylinder petrol engine options in 6-ton models.

In 1963, the CA became the CB, with only minor detail changes being made to specifications and appearance. The new maximum-gross class 14- and 16-ton Maxiload with its uprated TS-3 engine, also featured power-assisted steering and on the CC models, a full-air divided brake system to help cope with the increase in engine power and payload weight. The CC models also

A Commer V Series
airside service truck
and Sud Aviation
Caravelle airliner
of Air France at
Heathrow Airport in
the early Sixties.

A Karrier-
badged dropsider
demonstrator in
the grounds of the
Dunstable assembly
plant.

A Karrier-badged C Series
forward control chassis with
a Carbodies crew cab and
Binmaster tipping refuse body
with optional cab salvage rack.

20   COMMER VC.7 FORWARD CONTROL MODEL 141in. (3.581m) WHEELBASE

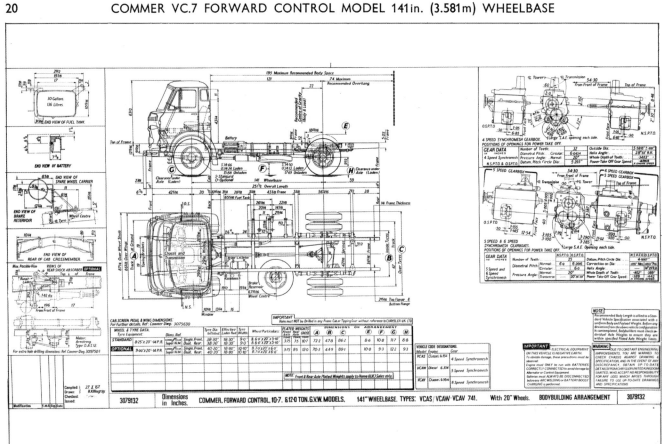

Vehicle bodybuilders drawings for the Commer VC7 Forward Control series.

Two hardworking Commer CC Maxiloads, c. 1965, operated by Granary Haulage of Burton-on-Trent. A change in 'Construction and Use Regulations' required manufacturers to quote Gross Vehicle Weights (GVW) of trucks rather than payload weight. To assist in coping with the ever-increasing power output demands and heavier gross and payload weights, a full-air divided brake system was a feature of the new CC Maxiload in 1964.

The showroom at Ryton, c.1962, showing the latest offerings from Rootes.

offered a further boosting of TS-3 power to 135bhp. As with the C Series, the V Series designation would change as detail changes were made; VA became VB in 1965 and subsequently VC.

The success of the new Commer-Karrier models came as a result of combined development of all of these van and truck ranges at the same time, so it was a very hectic period for the division. To cope with production demands, further work on the Dunstable assembly plant, the building of which had begun in 1953, was necessary. A new production line for the ¾-ton van was installed, which effectively doubled the output of vehicles being produced at Dunstable. It was the first Commer production line to adopt full-scale mass-production techniques.

Two separate production lines existed for assembly of medium and heavy goods vehicles. Each line ran nearly 500 feet in length; one for special purpose and municipal applications and the other for larger Commer and Karrier trucks. The factory received a final extension of 175,000 square feet to accommodate Walk-thru and remaining truck and van body production to be transferred from Luton to Dunstable.

Despite the traumatic events of 1961 at British Light Steel Pressings, the early Sixties represented the maintaining of the status quo for the Rootes Group. The family were still in control and they had cleverly created new models and updated their passenger car range without need for significant investment; something the Rootes brothers had become masters at over the years. Production at BLSP had returned to a more normal state, which meant that subtle updates to the big Humbers could be made in order to keep the designs fresh. In 1962, the Hawk Series III and Super Snipe Series IV were both given a new rear window shape and exterior trim changes, and became part of the range that featured the new Super Minx family. The Minx and Gazelle, now in Series V form, from late 1963, featured a new, flatter roofline and a rear window with less of a wraparound than the Series III models.

However, the commitment to the launch of Hillman Imp in 1963 and the ever-present shadow of a continuing lack of funds to enable future planning would mean that 1964 would be a year of many changes, and one that would signal the start of the most difficult phase in the history of the Rootes Group to date.

A fine car –
still further
improved

NEW HUMBER HAWK

A restyled rear window and stainless gutter trim were subtle changes on both Super Snipe Series IV and Hawk Series III saloons.

CHAPTER 3

THE SCOTTISH AFFAIR – THE IMP AND LINWOOD

'The Imp was a completely new car from the ground up and technically very difficult… The fact that it was done at all and so well and had such an influence on the world industry is a huge tribute to Rootes engineers and the Rootes team and the energy of the place.'

– Bill Papworth
– Rootes Product Planning Manager

The morning of Friday, 3 May 1963 was much like any other Friday morning for Malcolm Richardson as he went to open up his Rootes dealership in Rugby, Warwickshire, with one exception; they were participating in the launch of a brand new Rootes model. When he arrived, there were throngs of people outside, three deep, surrounding the showroom, all anxious to sneak a look at the new small car that the Rootes Group had been developing. In order to contain the anticipation of the excited throngs, Malcolm duly unlocked the doors, went inside and pulled the covers off the car that had been the talk of the motoring and national press for weeks – the new Hillman Imp.

This scene was replicated in Rootes showrooms all around the country. Getting the Imp to its launch date had been a long, difficult slog, with Rootes overcoming many obstacles on the way. The previous day, the brand new factory at Linwood near Paisley in Renfrewshire, Scotland, had been officially opened by HRH The Duke of Edinburgh, amid a pageant-like show that bore similar characteristics to the one that had seen the unveiling of the Hillman Wizard at London's Royal Albert Hall three decades earlier.

DESIGN AND DEVELOPMENT – APEX

The first official prototype of the Rootes Group's new small car was codenamed Apex. But it was not the first prototype small car idea that Rootes had played with. During the late Forties, Craig Miller, who was chief research engineer under B.B. Winter, designed a small Volkswagen-based twin-cylinder car which acquired the nickname 'Little Jim'. However, prototype stage was only as far as 'Little Jim' got.

The early Fifties was a fervent period for Rootes, with activities in their expanding global empire still focusing on growth through acquisition, as well as Lord Rootes' ambitions of creating multiple product ranges using a commonality of parts and components, so to concentrate limited financial resources on one model was probably very low down the 'To Do' list for Rootes. Commenting in 2013, on the allocation of development money, Timothy Rootes, Sir Reginald's son, made it quite clear that *'Billy was spending all of the development money on his precious Humbers, when he should have been putting it into a small car like the Imp!'*

However, in 1955, two designers working at Humber had come up with a concept for a small car that they thought would fit ideally into the Rootes product range.

One of the first publicity shots of the new Hillman Imp for the launch brochure.

Tim Fry and Mike Parkes then took their idea to their boss Bernard Winter, who agreed with their proposal and basically told them to *'get on with it!'* With the combination of youthful enthusiasm and a degree of naivety, the two designers set about creating a prototype. What they came up with was a very small, basic, but aerodynamic car that could seat four adults – just, and be cheap to run. Tim Fry styled the car and Villiers was instructed to build a 600cc twin-cylinder, air-cooled engine. A local Coventry firm, Bayton Sheet Metal, was commissioned to build the body. By late 1956, the car, which had earned the nickname 'The Slug', because of its rather dumpy looks, was ready to be presented to the Rootes Board. However, Villiers did not have an engine available, so a Citroën 2CV unit was used instead.

The Rootes management's reaction to 'The Slug' was lukewarm bordering on one of complete horror! It was not the kind of car that they wanted to associate themselves with, so 'The Slug' was sent to the styling department for a re-appraisal. Although the redesign was less utilitarian in appearance, it was made clear that a more conventional-looking car was what the Board had in mind.

What Parkes and Fry had done was to set their sights too low, and so they now were tasked with raising their aim, by creating a larger, better-engineered car that, although still fairly basic, would accommodate four adults comfortably, plus their luggage, and still be reasonably economical to run. They were also steadfast in their opinion that the car should be fun to drive. What they came up with was what came to be Rootes' first serious step towards creating a new small car – project Apex.

The first Apex prototype received a complete redesign, but still had the noisy twin-cylinder engine, and although it was a step in the right direction, the Rootes Board's enthusiasm for the new prototype was as underwhelming as ever, but it had at least been given the go-ahead. A new set of criteria was applied to Apex, and as it would be larger and more comfortable, it would need more power, so a four-cylinder water-cooled engine to replace the air-cooled twin was placed at the top of the list, making Apex more Austin A40 – less Goggomobil!

This new look at the Apex placed it in a different class to their original concept. Due to the impracticalities of putting a 4-cylinder, water-cooled unit in the front of a small car, Parkes and Fry decided on a rear engine configuration, in order to remove the need for prop-shafts that created unwanted passenger compartment intrusions. The constant velocity joints that would appear on the front-wheel-drive Mini was still an 'engineering unknown' as far as Rootes were concerned. The

The Apex prototype in 1956 with the Villiers 600cc flat-twin engine. COVENTRY ARCHIVES

engine and gearbox would have to be lightweight, and for this reason Mike Parkes considered aluminium alloy castings instead of traditional cast-iron. In the knowledge that Coventry Climax had gained a reputation for lightweight engines that would be the right size to power their car, Parkes duly contacted them, and they agreed to draw up some designs that might suit Rootes, based on their lightweight fire pump range. What Parkes had in mind was a version of the FWMA racing engine that Coventry Climax had produced in 1958. As this engine was an off-shoot of the fire pump range of engines, Parkes requested, and got, copies of the drawings for the 750cc FWA (Feather Weight Automobile) engine. The final version of the engine to be used in the Imp was developed from the lightweight fire pump engine, but was also closely related to the FWMA Formula One engine. It was decided that the engine/gearbox should be configured as a transaxle, but as Rootes had little experience with transaxles, the job was given to a talented young ex-Jaguar apprentice named Adrian 'Bill' West, who joined the team as transmission engineer. Other more specialist engineers with specific design strengths were coming on board: Bob Croft took charge of body engineering and Harry White was chief chassis engineer. Barbara Harris came in as draughtswoman.

The task of designing an engine that would be suitable for the car, utilising the Coventry Climax designs, was given to Leo Kuzmicki, a Polish ex-patriate who had settled in England after the war. He had gained a great deal of engineering experience on Norton motorcycle engines and the Vanwall Grand Prix racing engine. It had been hoped that three engine sizes would be possible for Apex: 800cc; 875cc; and 1000cc. In the event the team had to compromise on one size: 875cc.

A line-up of a rare group of talented individuals who helped make the Imp a reality. *Left to right*: Tim Fry; Bob Saward; Harry White; Leo Kuzmicki; Adrian 'Bill' West; Ken Sharp; Craig Miller; Peter Ware; Bob Croft.

One of the managers who would get close to Imp production was Scott Glover. As a young management trainee, he had worked as personal assistant to Peter Ware during the early stages of Imp development approval:

'There was a study group of three senior directors: Peter Ware, George Shrigley, who was manufacturing planning director at that time and Bill Bryant, who ran the plastics and die-casting business [Hills Precision]. They were sent to America to explore the feasibility of aluminium die-cast engines and so on …'

Ware, Shrigley and Bryant concentrated their efforts on the US outboard motor manufacturing sector that utilised the Doland Jarvis method of high-pressure aluminium die-casting, which was to prove a good solution for the gearbox castings and ancillaries, but not for the engine blocks. For this process they turned to a British company, Alumasc Ltd, of Burton Latimer in Northamptonshire. As their expertise was in thin-wall, low pressure die-casting of aluminium beer barrels, they were able to provide a solution to solving the problem of how to cast aluminium engine blocks with cast-iron liners in situ.

APEX TO IMP

By 1960, the Apex had been given a name – Imp, and the styling of the Imp, which was in its final stages in 1961, was down to Rootes stylist Bob Saward, who had created a functional and stylish three-box configuration, which included the opening rear window that as far as

Tim Fry was concerned, was a must. That feature was a first; the mini-hatchback had been born. Many references have been made about the Imp's similarity in appearance to the rear-engined Chevrolet Corvair, introduced in '59; but the Corvair and the Imp also shared the same neat crimped waistline with the German NSU Prinz 4, introduced in 1961.

Apex styling development from model to full-size mockup

⅜th Scale model.

BOB SAWARD COLLECTION – RICHARD SOZANSKI – IMP CLUB

First full-size mock up.

BOB SAWARD COLLECTION – RICHARD SOZANSKI – IMP CLUB

First modification.

BOB SAWARD COLLECTION – RICHARD SOZANSKI – IMP CLUB

Second modification.

BOB SAWARD COLLECTION – RICHARD SOZANSKI – IMP CLUB

Final viewing – Imp three-quarter front.

BOB SAWARD COLLECTION – RICHARD SOZANSKI – IMP CLUB

Third Modification.

BOB SAWARD COLLECTION – RICHARD SOZANSKI – IMP CLUB

Final viewing – Imp three-quarter rear.

BOB SAWARD COLLECTION – RICHARD SOZANSKI – IMP CLUB

With the departure of B.B. Winter into retirement and Peter Ware being made chief executive engineer, a new impetus was given to the project. Ware hastened the development of the Imp by being an enthusiastic supporter of the project. His close relationship with the development team, and his technical knowledge of the project enabled him to 'sell' some of the advanced technical aspects of the new car to the Board when any resistance to new design innovations was met.

After the Apex project had been given the go-ahead to be developed, Rootes had set about looking for somewhere for the new car to be built. Initially, it was intended to build a new assembly plant on land adjacent to the Ryton plant on the A45, but the government, under Prime Minister Harold Macmillan, refused to grant an industrial development certificate. A similar plan was put forward on land Rootes had acquired at Houghton Regis, next to the Commer-Karrier plant at Dunstable. That too was refused an industrial development certificate. So, in 1958, Rootes had started to look elsewhere, and encouraged by the promise of government money, they chose Scotland. Due to the close proximity of the Pressed Steel plant and a new strip mill at Ravenscraig, it

was decided that Linwood, near Paisley in Renfrewshire would be the most suitable location. There were 'fors' and 'againsts' in taking on such a risky venture. Labour was plentiful, but few available workers were skilled in the building of cars, and wages were significantly lower than in the Midlands.

The decision to go to Scotland was not one that Rootes arrived at overnight, and Harold Macmillan was certainly a major player in influencing the decision. The Conservative government had been successful in getting other major manufacturers to locate to Development Areas, i.e. unemployment hotspots. With significant financial inducements from the government in the form of grants and loans, Ford was persuaded to open a plant in Halewood, Standard-Triumph to Speke, near Liverpool and Vauxhall to Ellesmere Port. Only Rootes and BMC, who would build trucks at Bathgate, would locate to Scotland rather than Merseyside. It was also hoped that as manufacturers established plants in the North, they would be followed by sections of the automotive industry supplier base, but that did not materialise and suppliers kept their heels firmly dug in the Midlands.

This aerial photograph of the Ryton plant, viewed from the southern end, shows the area of land to the right of the A45 main road, which had been acquired by Rootes and was considered for building an assembly plant for the Imp, but the government refused to grant an industrial development certificate. NICK ROOTES

Prime Minister Harold Macmillan and Billy Rootes chatting at the Motor Show.

It is important to understand the effect that Macmillan had on the decision to build the Imp in Scotland, because in doing so it would change the future direction and profile of Rootes as a motor manufacturer. Harold Macmillan had become a friend of Billy Rootes and there was a mutual respect and trust between the two men. They had similar attitudes and interests; they were also the same age. As a parliamentary secretary to the Ministry of Supply during the war, it is highly likely that Billy Rootes and Macmillan's paths crossed regularly; both were working closely with Lord Beaverbrook at the time, and especially as Macmillan's role was to effect an increase in the quality and output of armoured vehicles, of which the Rootes Group was a major supplier.

Macmillan could be described as a 'socialist Conservative', supporting the Welfare State and Keynes' mixed-economy model that had been established under the Attlee government. As the Conservative MP for Stockton-on-Tees, he had been shocked by the poverty suffered by his working-class electorate. In the post-war period he became an expert on industrial policy and upon re-entering politics, following a brief period working for the family publishing company, he set about planning how his ambition of high or full employment could be realized. Following his defeat of Anthony Eden in 1957 and re-election in 1959, the motor industry would again be used as a pawn in a government game – a means to achieve Macmillan's aim to reduce the unemployment disparities of Britain.

Macmillan possessed a quiet and unflappable charm, which he no doubt used to convince Billy Rootes that they would be looked after and that the plan would benefit HM Government as well as the Rootes Group. Although Billy Rootes was no pushover as far as business negotiations were concerned, there was more than a degree of logic and sense attached to Macmillan's proposals. A visit to Rootes' estate at Ramsbury in November 1959 to shoot was, no doubt, used to consolidate plans, as by 1960, the decision was made to start producing the Imp in Scotland. On 30 September 1960, an official announcement was made to the public of the Rootes Group's intentions.

With the clock ticking, time was not a luxury that the Apex development team had, but as the team grew, the 'can do' attitude that exemplified Rootes came into its own. The atmosphere was a happy one, and one of constructive help in all directions, and much of this impetus had been down to Peter Ware. Everyone was committed to problem solving and being innovative, as Wynn Mitchell, who worked on Imp development at Ryton remembers:

'When I look back on it, working at Ryton on the Imp were my happiest working days. I worked in the drawing office … on transmissions. Mike Parkes was in the office, Tim Fry was in the office. Craig Miller was our boss at the time … He'd come in the morning, park his car by the gatehouse, go along the bottom corridor, put his head in every department,

Harold Macmillan visits Ramsbury, 21 November 1959. The Ramsbury shooting party, *left to right:* Sir Reginald Rootes; Lord Rockley; Lady Rockley; the Right Honourable Harold Macmillan; Lady Rootes; Lord Rootes; Loelia Duchess of Westminster; the Earl of Wilton; Colonel E.J.S.Ward; Geoffrey Rootes and Major Douglas Roberts. NICK ROOTES

[go] down to the bottom office where Ron Riddiford [workshop foreman, engineering] was in charge, chat to Ron, up the stairs along the top corridor, saying "Good morning" to everybody and … into his office. So every morning, he said "Good morning" to virtually everyone who worked in the place!

'We'd be there about quarter past eight in the morning just chatting. When half past eight came we'd just go to our desks and carry on and it was great. What I liked about those days was you'd draw something, go to the print room, get some prints off, take them downstairs [and] you'd say, "We want one of those" … Some weeks later, they'd say, "Those bits have come", or "That bracket has come" and you'd take it down to the bottom office to Ron Riddiford and say "I want this fitted to a car" and then … you'd go along and try it, you'd modify it. You drew it and you followed it all the way through. It was terrific … It was a lovely atmosphere to work in and we thought we were designing the best car the world had ever seen!'

During 1960, a small production engineering team under Tom Clay was put together to work alongside the design teams. Bill Bryant had been made director and general manager of the new company, Rootes (Scotland) Ltd, which was headed by Hon. Geoffrey Rootes, as managing director. Bryant had been in charge of Hills Precision Diecastings Ltd, the Rootes Group's plastics and die-casting division and it was felt that he was best placed to oversee the implementation of new die-cast plant at Linwood.

BUILDING THE LINWOOD PLANT AND EARLY PRODUCTION

In May 1961, construction of the main building on the 278-acre site commenced. The building contractors were the Glasgow-based Melville, Dundas and Whitson Ltd.

When the initial capital expenditure forecasts were made prior to 1960, it was realised at meetings held at Coventry that the project costs were escalating to a much higher level than predicted. Following his position as assistant to Peter Ware, Scott Glover was then asked to work as personal assistant to Bill Bryant. Scott was present at one of these difficult meetings:

'In late 1960, I do remember being asked to sit in on meetings to take minutes … The whole project was reckoned to cost £12 million. I remember there was a piece of paper Sir Reginald had written on – £4 million grant … £4 million loan … £4 million buildings…

'Before the final go-ahead was given, the production engineering team came up with estimates as to what the

The Rootes Linwood plant from the air shows how large the complex was in relation to the administration buildings at the front. The Pressed Steel plant is visible in the lower right-hand corner, showing the transporter bridge connecting it and the main plant. NICK ROOTES

tooling costs would be ... I think it was the end of 1960 or the beginning of '61, and there was a big meeting with Sir Reginald, Geoffrey, and I think financial people ... I was responsible for putting together the first Board report. [This was done] in conjunction with Bill Bryant as to where the project was. [The report] identified that the production engineering estimates were higher than the provisional ones that had been put together some months earlier by Bill Hancock and George Shrigley ... It was a real moment of truth because it clearly was pushing the figures higher than the already stretched finance capability.'

According to the figures quoted by David and Peter Henman in their detailed analysis of the Imp project, the investment in the project represented £22.5 million, of which £10 million would be provided by the government. Rootes had raised potential investment capital by selling off the 'Ordinary' shares in their subsidiary Rootes Acceptances Ltd for £3.5 million. In their annual financial report for the year ending 31 July 1959, the Group had made a record profit of £3.9 million, it stated that: *'Arrangements are in hand for the issue of a further £3.5 million Debenture Stock...'* Although Rootes' assets and the company's liquidity position was good, for the short and medium-term, Rootes Motors Ltd would be sailing close to the wind. However, Scott Glover has a very different view as to who financed what:

'Apart from development of the product and the salaries of the people establishing [it], there was very, very little Rootes money that went into it ... There was a government grant, a government loan and the factory was leased out to Rootes. [The project] didn't use Rootes money as capital.'

Despite Macmillan's assurances that the government would 'look after' Rootes, future profitability was clearly an essential factor in the Linwood gamble. This was also prior to the BLSP debacle that was about to kick off.

The project would, however, give employment to 4,000 workers at Rootes and 1,500 additional employees at the adjacent Pressed Steel factory, who would make the bodies. A modern car assembly block and the best quality factory machinery, with modern offices and the latest in computer technology went into the Linwood complex, as well as a separate die-casting plant. Scott Glover was appointed production control manager in mid-1961, and worked closely with John Adams, the systems manager, who between them instigated some very sophisticated computer systems, which was a result of Geoffrey Rootes' positive attitude during this period.

He constantly encouraged the management team to think outside the box and not implement ideas just because that was the way they had always done them at Coventry. This attitude was supported by Ken Gannay, the finance manager, as Scott Glover recalled in 2021:

'Our "Godfather" was Ken Gannay, the finance manager and he said, "Go and look at unusual places", so we went and looked at a raft of companies – computer companies, Marks & Spencer ... to try and get ideas. We then decided to develop production control and material control facilities based on an ICT 1301 computer, which was quite advanced in those days.'

The new computer system enabled them to control production and material flow from suppliers and within the plant. Scott Glover moved up to Linwood in 1962, and by the spring of '62 the main production buildings were built, with the whole factory complex nearing completion by the winter of '62. Production of cars would soon start in order to stockpile vehicles in readiness for the roll out to the dealers and the opening of the factory in May 1963. Meanwhile, the job of taking on a new labour force was implemented. Duncan Robertson was one of the many new local employees to work at Linwood and one of the few who received training at Coventry:

'I was interviewed at Canterbury Street, Birmingham and then I was interviewed at Linwood in the November of 1961. I started in February 1962 at Canterbury Street. I stayed at digs in Glencoe Street, Coventry. The package included a

The control console and electronic punch–card data processing system used to co-ordinate the flow of correct components to the assembly line.

free flight home when in Coventry. I then came back up on 5 April 1962 and started at Linwood.'

His description of the factory layout and production sequence:

'With the Imp it was all [assembled] in here, except the engine. The die-casting we cast for the gearbox, the machine shop machined the gearbox, and then sent it over to the other building to assemble it. Then they shipped it over to the UMB, the Unit Machine Building, who machined it and filled it with the gears. That in turn, came over [to] the assembly building to be linked up with engines that came up from Stoke.

'At the same time as they were building the buildings here, they were building the buildings opposite – "K" and "L" buildings. The "K" Building was known as the "Crazy K". "K" was welded sub-assemblies, and they passed them into "L" building [where] the body shell was completed [Pressed Steel Co]. From that section [they were moved] into another part of "L" building where they were painted. The painted bodies then came across the road on a conveyor belt, into the car assembly building where they were putting wheels, engine and gearbox – from underneath. That ran [to] the far end of the car assembly building and went into a rolling road.'

As a section leader of administration, Duncan Robertson was in charge of ordering and planning for the Engineering Department, which included controlling expenditure for engineering:

The Archdale Transfer Machines in the 'Unit Machine Shop', where suspension arms would be automatically passed through each of the eleven machining operations. UMB also housed machine tools and the heat treatment plant.

The line of bulk melting furnaces in the die-casting plant, capable of handling 3½ tons of aluminium an hour. The metal storage is immediately behind and consumption being approximately 100 tons per week.

The view down the main aisle of the Die-casting Plant showing the high-pressure die-casting machines in the foreground and the bulk melting furnaces on the left.

'The costs would be sent to Renfrew Airport [and] to Birmingham, for Geoffrey Rootes' approval within the week.'

As capital costs started to increase, so also did the variable costs, as another newly installed manager, Bill Papworth, discovered. His experience at Ford in product planning was now being put to the test at Rootes. Bill had been tasked with cost analysis on the Imp, as well as a proposed new medium-sized car based on the Imp – the Swallow. Bill describes his induction to the Rootes Group in November 1962:

'In '62 they'd just gutted out a lot of machine tools from the old Singer works ... I had been put into a department that was run by a chap called Cyril Weighell. He was a production engineer, involved in manufacturing technology – that was his speciality – very clever. Cyril had offices in the rump of this old Singer factory. I joined there in November. The factory was being gutted, the roof was caving in and water was coming into the factory floor. You walked out of the general offices and there were all the bolts out of the concrete floor where the machine tools had been, so you'd walk out of the general manager's office along the factory, then dive into another office. I was allocated a huge office with a tin desk, one chair, a filing cabinet. The cracks in the plaster and paint had been raked out and there was this wonderful 'art work' of pink plaster. I arrived, Cyril Weighell's secretary arrived with her little dog and showed me the office. Cyril arrived a little later and said, "Not quite sure what you do, but the family have got a meeting on 14 January and whatever you do, you should do it in preparation for this meeting."

'The Duke of Edinburgh was scheduled for the Imp launch on 3 May 1963, so one day under six months before the tape was cut, I was given this bare office, empty filing cabinet, one chair and told to "go and do what you do".

'So I found my way around, met people and talked with people. I made friends with a man called A.K. Meggitt, who was the Chief Accountant at Humber. Tim Rootes was head of the car division and he relied on Meggitt, who was very close with Shrigley, the Devonshire House accountant, one of the older gang, Billy's men. They were incredibly good, really.

'In early January 1962 I pulled together some staff and spent a lot of time with the engineers – the Hodkin brothers, Peter Ware, Harry Sheron and two really good Rootes servants, by that I mean really loyal people – W.S. [Stan] Taylor and Don Tyrell, who did the vehicle costing and investment costing.

'Between all these inputs and spending lots of time with Meggitt, the accountant, we put together a story pack in two documents – one which was narrative and the other spreadsheets. This looked at the Imp and the Swallow and it tried to reconcile them with the published accounts and this package was sent to the car division board a week before 14 January, so they convened at Ryton with Geoffrey in the chair, and all the Devonshire House people – George Shrigley and co, Meggitt, Peter Ware, Tim Rootes etc.

'I was put on the stand as their new toy, and we quickly homed in on one figure ... out of all of these documents, there was only one figure that was important, and it related to the Imp and it showed that the main proposed volume model – the Imp deluxe – not on it's export market, but on the domestic market, was priced to sell at £6 below its variable cost.

'The people who had taken the time to read the documents had drawn circles around this number ... and they, including Sir Reginald said they weren't used to seeing columns headed "pounds millions".

'This was 14 January, so not far away from [launch date] 3 May, and as the saying goes, "the shit hit the fan!" Geoffrey turned to Meggitt, the accountant, and said, "Meggitt, are these figures right?" There was a deathly hush – the whole room went quiet. Meggitt squirmed in his seat for a good few seconds until he said, "Yes, Mr Geoffrey." It became clear that they had walked themselves into really serious trouble!'

The contrasts between Ford and Rootes were stark and someone like Bill Papworth was ideally placed to realize that the Imp was under-funded and, because of time constraints, under-developed:

'The Imp was an all-new design, new body, new everything and technically quite advanced. Some would say going for the rear-engine thing was misguided, but okay, if it had been a front-engine design they'd still have had the same problems. The research and development budget within the Rootes engineering department, leaving aside production engineering, manufacturing investment was £530,000. When I left Ford about a year earlier, I was aware that the engineering development budget for the Escort was £2.3 million. It was the successor to the 105E Anglia, which had been quite an innovation compared to the previous Prefect. Essentially the same car with a new body, same engine, gearbox, a bit bigger and a bit fancier, the Escort was in effect a big facelift. The Imp was a completely new car from the ground up and technically very difficult – you cannot do it for £530,000! The fact that it was done at all and so well and had such an influence on the world industry is a huge tribute to Rootes engineers and the Rootes team and the energy of the place.'

Once production had started, more additional capital and variable costs were coming to light. The low-pressure die-cast aluminium process for the cylinder blocks was expensive, but that cost was a 'known'. The engine blocks had to be cast in Scotland, but due to a lack of engine build expertise in Scotland had to be sent to Ryton for assembly. After having the aluminium head fitted, which was manufactured by Aeroplane & Motor Aluminium Castings in Birmingham, they were sent back to Linwood for assembly in a car – a round trip of some 600 miles!

Painted bodies at Pressed Steel on the overhead conveyor to the Trim Shop. They would then be carried on the overhead track across the transporter bridge to the Car Assembly Block. ROOTES ARCHIVE CENTRE TRUST

Transaxle assembly, comprising engine, gearbox, final drive and rear suspension in the Unit Machine Shop, prior to being sent by overhead conveyor to the Car Assembly Block.

ROOTES ARCHIVE CENTRE TRUST

The main assembly conveyor track in the Car Assembly Block.

ROOTES ARCHIVE CENTRE TRUST

The 'Car finished conveyor' where cleaning and inspection were carried out and any necessary rectification highlighted.

ROOTES ARCHIVE CENTRE TRUST

Trains known as the 'Imp Specials' would ferry 100 cars at a time, four or five times a day to and from Linwood and Gosford Green near Coventry.

PROTOTYPE AND PRE-PRODUCTION TESTING

As building of the new factory had progressed, so production machinery needed to be installed and commissioned. But before that could happen, the Imp specification had to be finalized for production. Mike Parkes instigated a rigorous test programme, so that any faults or last-minute changes to specification could be made. In October 1961, Parkes took a prototype Imp on a 3,800 mile, fifteen-day tour around France and Spain. Accompanied by three development engineers and a Singer Gazelle full of spares as tender car, the Imp proved reliable, with no serious problems occurring. The old aero engine test house on the A45 at Ryton, which had originally been used as the development and test building, had a change of use to carry out solely rig testing for all product ranges, once Imp production at Linwood had been established. The Rootes Engineering function was then centralized at Stoke. Rig testing at Ryton on individual components from the Imp was followed by pre-production testing, which began in June 1962. Mike Parkes had arranged a series of tests, which began with a 5,000-mile test route around Europe that would throw European weather extremes at the test cars, going into France, Spain, Germany, the Swiss Alps and Austria. Next, a 10,000 miles in ten weeks series of tests in the south-west of Ireland, to prove suspension, brakes and body sealing. Another test, which was regularly made, was around the Scottish Highlands. A young trainee sales manager who was involved with these tests was Douglas Field:

'They wanted pupils and apprentices to drive the Imp proto-types up in Scotland. These were L1 and L2 ... handbuilt prototypes. There was a group of us based at Monroes of Invergordon, who were Rootes dealers, where the cars were housed. We had a team leader who organised our days and that was Mike Parkes.

'There was a group of five or six of us who used to drive these cars every day around an A9 circuit up to Wick and Thurso, across the Moors, 200 miles a day, seven days a week ... We also had a tender car following, in case we broke down. This was in the autumn of 1962.'

Duncan Robertson used to look after the allocation of test cars based at the factory:

'As I was section leader of administration, I had five Imps [allocated to me] at one time. I had a roster and the foreman would say, "Can I take a car out?" So what we did was we got the keys of the cars that the engineering department had maintained and at half past eight [08.30 am] in the morning said, "There's the keys, come back in at half past twelve [12.30 pm], put 150 miles on the clock." Then someone else would take it out at half past one [1.30 pm] – 150 miles – get it back by half past four [4.30 pm], and then at the weekend it was given to a manager who would take it out and come back on Monday with 300 miles on the clock, and every so often they would put 1,000 miles, 1,500 miles, 3,000 miles and then they would look at the engine to see if it had any faults.'

Cars were also tested in urban conditions – in Birmingham – 1,000 miles in three weeks. Eventually, cars were sent to export territories such as Kenya, North America and Scandinavia. At the end of the test programme, in February 1963, the Imps had proved their reliability, with a relatively small amount of problems, which the development team would try to rectify. But time had not been on the Imp's side, and several component failures, such as the water pump, problems of which had been reported by test drivers and in rig testing, were, for whatever reasons, not being addressed.

As much of the testing had been done with the cars being driven flat-out, and not enough testing done in ordinary traffic, with Mr Ordinary driving, serious faults would eventually come to light on production models, but the Duke of Edinburgh was coming, and all eyes and efforts were on the official opening of the factory.

As the great day approached, it was becoming clear to all concerned that more time was needed, not just to ensure quality consistency in final assembly, but in component manufacture, such as in the new die-casting plant. Bill Garner was responsible for the implementation of the die-casting plant, and although the main installation of the machines had gone well, the low-pressure casting of the cylinder blocks was taking longer to refine. Consistency was a problem and some of the castings were suffering from a degree of porosity. Peter Ware felt that another six months was needed in order to make sure everything worked well in production and with the Imp itself. Ware fought his case with Lord Rootes and other members of the family, but it was to no avail; the Duke of Edinburgh was booked and that was that ... and as Tom Cotton, another Rootes manager who would soon be Linwood bound, succinctly states, 'You couldn't turn round to The Duke of Edinburgh and say "Could you come back next week?"'

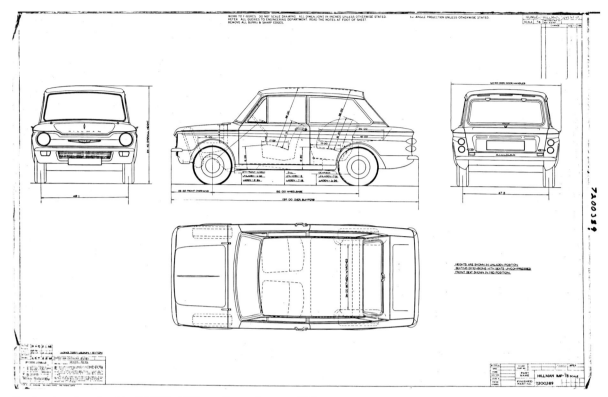

Production drawing No. 700289 – Hillman Imp – January 1963.

ROOTES ARCHIVE CENTRE TRUST

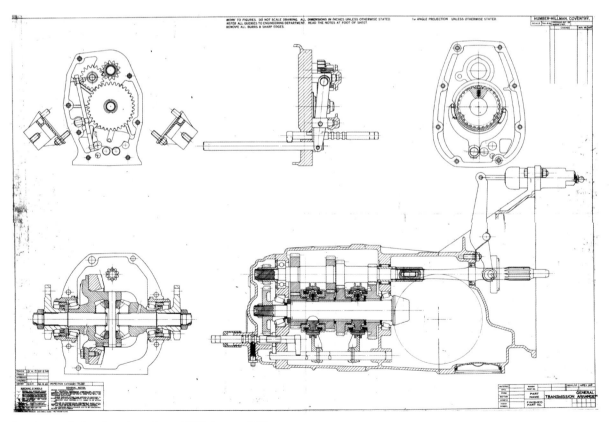

Imp transmission drawings, issued 25 February 1963. ROOTES ARCHIVE CENTRE TRUST

The foyer and entrance to the administration offices at Linwood, which also doubled as a display area for cars and products. ROOTES ARCHIVE CENTRE TRUST

Peter Ware and Lord Rootes explain the finer points of the new Imp, while the Duke of Edinburgh looks on in amusement. Geoffrey Rootes is on the extreme left of the group. TIM WARE

2 MAY 1963 – THE LINWOOD OPENING CEREMONY

The evening before the official opening of Linwood, Lord Rootes had arranged for the Duke of Edinburgh to stay at Glenalmond, his Scottish house in Perth, in readiness for a prompt start. On the morning of 2 May, Prince Philip duly arrived at Linwood in a chauffer-driven Humber Super Snipe and was greeted by Lord Rootes and Geoffrey Rootes. The Duke officially unveiled the ceremonial plaque at Linwood, and in typical Prince Philip fashion, in his own words, pronounced, *'It is with great pleasure that I open this thing … whatever it is…'*

A speech was made by Prince Philip, in which he referred to the efforts of *'the whole of the Clan Mac Rootes!'* Lord Rootes and Geoffrey Rootes responded. To the members of the press, invited civic guests, Rootes management and representatives of suppliers to Rootes, it was a great day for Linwood. A tour of inspection of the new factory was headed by Peter Ware. Although Ware lost his battle to delay the launch of the Imp, according to his son Tim, *'he did gain a small moral victory by wearing a naval veteran's tie at the launch which was duly noticed and appreciated by the Duke.'*

As the ceremony came to a close, the Duke of Edinburgh drove himself in a new Hillman Imp, accompanied by Lord Rootes and Geoffrey Rootes, back to Renfrew Airport. Prince Philip had clearly enjoyed the whole event, overstaying his visit by some considerable time. In his appreciation of the invitation, separate letters to Lord Rootes and Lady Rootes were sent by Rear Admiral, Sir Christopher Bonham-Carter, treasurer to the Duke of

The Duke of Edinburgh and his entourage on part of the factory tour, walking through the Unit Machine Building. COVENTRY ARCHIVES

The Duke inspects an Imp body on the overhead conveyor system during his walkabout of the factory. COVENTRY ARCHIVES

73

The Duke of Edinburgh watching Mr. J.P. Wilson carrying out the final test for an Imp at the end of the production line.

COVENTRY ARCHIVES

Lord Rootes and Geoffrey Rootes prepare the Duke of Edinburgh for his drive in the new Hillman Imp.

COVENTRY ARCHIVES

Edinburgh, and show the lengths Lord Rootes went to accommodate the Royal party:

> 'Dear Billy,
> The Duke of Edinburgh asks me to thank you for a very interesting day at Linwood. That he was more than ordinarily interested was pretty clear from the time he took! I hope this didn't disrupt other people's arrangements too much. It didn't really matter to us at all.
> 'It is terribly good of your wife to give me a week on the Inver. I will book rooms at Loch Inver ... Perhaps you could tell me who to contact there – ghillie, keeper or factor, to show me the river.
> 'We had a wonderful day at Benbecula. The weather came in absolutely perfect.
> Yours,
> Christopher'

The smiles and handshakes of 2 May, however, were quickly forgotten as the launch of the Imp and the job of building the new cars got under way. Within a short space of time, one problem compounded another. Apart from potential quality issues, such as poor build quality by a still inexperienced workforce, the dealerships were complaining about component failures from disgruntled customers. Problems with brakes, transmission and the automatic choke, as well as rear window leaks and head gasket failure ... the list goes on. In November 1963 it was decided that every second Imp off the line would get a full quality control inspection. This at least ensured that the Imps that did leave the factory were as good as they could be. But it didn't deal with the problems that hadn't

With the Rootes Linwood administration building in the background, the Duke of Edinburgh drives a Hillman Imp, with Lord Rootes and Geoffrey Rootes as passengers, back to Renfrew Airport. COVENTRY ARCHIVES

been ironed out during the Imp's all too short development period. So, in early 1964, one of the test cars was put back on the road with experienced test driver Alec Wise, with a challenge to put 100,000 miles on the car in twelve months. It was hoped that any problems would be quickly found and a plan could be instigated to put the problem right in production. They didn't have to wait

Imp tester Alec Wise in WHS171, during his marathon 120,000-mile test run takes a hairpin bend at speed on a road leading from Loch Long to Loch Lomond.

COVENTRY ARCHIVES

long! After only 15,110 miles the gearbox failed. A new gearbox was fitted and Alec Wise continued his marathon test, achieving 120,000 miles in total.

A number of problems had arisen with the transmission. Internal component failure, poor assembly and

MEET THE **NEW HILLMAN IMP**

AN INSPIRATION IN LIGHT CAR DESIGN

The 'New Hillman Imp' brochure cover for May 1963.

HILLMAN IMP MARK 1 (1963) SPECIFICATIONS

Hillman Imp Deluxe Mark 1.

Body style
Two-door, four-seater saloon, unitary construction, rear-mounted engine

Engine
4-cylinder, overhead camshaft, aluminium alloy die-cast block

Power output:	875cc (53.41cu in) developing 42bhp at 5,000rpm
Bore and Stroke:	68 x 60.375mm (2.677in x 2.377in)
Compression ratio:	10:1
Torque:	52lb ft at 2,800rpm.
Fuel pump type:	AC mechanical

Carburettor:	Solex 30 PIHT downdraught with automatic choke.
Cooling system:	Water – centrifugal pump and fan.

Transmission
4-speed all-synchromesh gearbox. Aluminium alloy die-cast gearbox casing. Centre floor gearchange

Clutch:	5½in (139 mm) Laycock diaphragm hydraulically operated
Overall Gear Ratios:	Top 4.138:1; Third 5.702:1; Second 8.905:1; First 16.595:1; Reverse 13.824:1;
Final drive:	Hypoid bevel drive through rubber and universal joint coupling shafts to rear wheels. Final drive ratio: 4.857:1

Electrical and Lighting

Ignition:	Coil and distributor. 12-volt Lucas battery
Lighting:	Sealed beam headlamps with main and dipped beam 'stalk' and headlamp flasher switch mounted on instrument binnacle. Front combined side light/amber flashing indicator light mounted below front bumper. Separate rear amber indicator and stop/tail lamps. Two oblong reflectors fitted above rear bumper. Interior light

Instruments: Speedometer, fuel gauge and warning lights for flashing indicators, oil pressure, headlamp main beam and ignition

Standard equipment: Self-parking windscreen wipers, driver's sun visor, Triplex 'zone toughened' windscreen

De luxe model only: Heating and ventilation system, screen washers, passenger's sun visor, four stowage pockets, swivelling front quarter lights, carpeting throughout

Suspension and Wheels

Front: Independent coil springs and swing axle. Grease points eliminated by use of rubber bushes. Telescopic shock absorbers.

Rear: Independent coil springs and trailing links on detachable sub-frames. Telescopic shock absorbers.

Wheels and Tyres: 12in (305mm) 5.50 x 12 Dunlop 'Gold Seal' C.41 tubless tyres. Pressed steel wheels. Chrome hubcaps

Steering: Rack and pinion

Brakes: Girling hydraulic 8in (203mm) drums on front and rear. Lining area 75sq in (483.87sq cm). Floor-mounted handbrake operated mechanically on rear wheels

Dimensions

Overall length: 11ft 7in (3,530mm)
Overall width: 5ft 0¼in (1,530mm)
Overall height: 4ft 6½in (1,378mm)
Ground clearance: 5½in (140mm) (laden); 6¼in (159mm) (unladen)
Track: Front: 4ft 1¼in (1,250mm)
Rear: 4ft 0in (1,219 mm)
Wheelbase: 6ft 10in (2,083mm)
Turning circle: 30ft 6in (929.6cm)

Fuel tank capacity: 6 Imperial gallons (27.28 litres)
Unladen (dry) weight: 1505lb (683kg)*

Performance

0–30: 5.4 seconds*
0–60: 23.0 seconds*
Top speed: 70mph (approx)*
Fuel consumption: 28–39 mpg* (US gallons)

A brochure illustration 'X-ray' view of the Imp.

Colours
Tartan Red with Beige upholstery
Loch Blue with Azure Blue upholstery
Foam White with Red upholstery
Balmoral Grey with Azure Blue upholstery
Skye Blue with Dark Blue upholstery
Embassy Black with Red upholstery
Glenalmond Green with Apple Green upholstery

Optional Extras
Smiths Radiomobile, Pye or Ecko radio; safety belts; whitewall tyres; Dunlop 'SP' tyres with wide rim wheels; wing mirrors; heater blower (De luxe model only)

Price: £532 (De luxe model)(Basic plus Purchase Tax)

Model Variants: None

Significance: Rootes entry into the small car market and their answer to the BMC Mini

All data Rootes Motors Ltd except *Car & Driver* magazine November 1963

Golf bags in here please! The May 1963 brochure showing the opening rear window feature of the Imp. The invention of the 'mini-hatchback'!

ROOTES *make motoring history with the new* HILLMAN IMP

Hillman Imp. An inspiration in light car design. Imp has a rear-mounted, aluminium die-cast, overhead camshaft engine . . . 875 cc giving 42 bhp, a comfortable 75 mph, and a touring fuel consumption of 40-45 mpg. Imp has independent suspension all round. Carries four with room to spare. Gives estate car convenience, generous luggage space. And Imp has no greasing points, is easy to service, slashes maintenance costs. Go Imp!

IMP SALOON £508.1.3 (£420, plus p.t. £88.1.3)

IMP DE LUXE with heater and unique 'thru-flow' ventilation, screen washers, opening quarter lights, four stowage pockets, fully carpeted floor, twin sun visors, headlamp flasher and safety belt anchor points all included: **£532.4.7** (£440 plus p.t. £92.4.7)

HILLMAN IMP

an inspiration in light car design
MAIN DEALERS
COVENTRY GARAGE
HOLYHEAD RD LIMITED **TELEPHONE 28581**

Printed at The Studio Press (Birmingham) Ltd., Elkington Street, Birmingham, 6.
Advertising Contractors   Spabas Ltd.. 44 Chandos Place, London, W.C.2.

Regional advertisements, such as this one from the Coventry Evening Telegraph, created a lot of interest in the new Imp.

The Imp being announced to the public at the Salon Internazionale Dell'Automobile, Turin in October 1963.

COVENTRY ARCHIVES

'People say it was under-developed, but it wasn't under-developed… we knew most of the things that were wrong with it, but there wasn't either the time or the money to do anything about it!'

faulty bearings were some of the issues, but another problem was the loss of oil caused by leakage through either the seals on the input shafts, bell housing or drive shaft seals, due to the excessive pressure build up in the gearbox. The solution was to fit an air vent on the end plate, and although the transmission problems were drastically reduced, the transaxle would remain a future 'Achilles Heel' of the Imp.

Peter Ware had campaigned for more pre-production development time, and he was not alone. David Lloyd was involved with early Imp development and would become manager of engine and transmission development in the early Seventies and then chief engineer under Peugeot. He felt that many of the early problems with the Imp could have been eliminated, given more time:

Another aspect to Imp foibles that Rootes hadn't bargained for was 'Mr and Mrs Ordinary' in their new Imps, poodling around towns and villages and getting stuck in traffic! This would be the most severe test of the Imp to date, and in many cases new customers ended up back at a Rootes dealership, less than happy with their new purchase. However, 'Mr Ordinary', who may have been a lifelong Minx owner, assumed that he could treat his Imp the same as his old Minx, but this was not the case. The misfortunes of the early production Imps were a combination of owners ignoring service bulletin advice, poor build quality and component failure.

By the spring of 1964, it was clear that the Rootes Group had been sitting on a warranty returns time bomb, and that something had to be done very quickly to make the Imp more reliable. The solution, which was the Mark 2 version, however, did not come quickly enough to prevent the new Rootes small car from gaining a reputation for

Early Mark 1 export Imps, dockside, awaiting shipment.

COVENTRY ARCHIVES

unreliability, from the press and public alike. Sales of the Imp were declining and the initial impetus and excitement had been lost. During 1964, a mighty effort on Rootes' part, in modifying the Imp specification and in getting a more consistent quality from Linwood production was achieved, and the result of the engineering staff efforts was – the Mark 2.

MANAGEMENT CHANGE – THE BIG SHAKE UP

In an effort to get Linwood running smoothly, rapid and constant changes of management occurred for at least a year after the Imp launch. June 1964 saw a significant shake up and Scott Glover witnessed the changes:

'Bill Bryant was ousted by the Board, along with Bill Carter [works director], and then George Cattell came in as director and general manager in the summer of 1964. The assembly manager George Minton was also removed and I was asked to be assembly manager and works manager under Alan Simpson, who had been machine shop manager but became works manager reporting directly to George Cattell.'

Cattell had been the Rootes Group's director of personnel, having joined them in 1961. Tom Cotton remembers him:

'George Cattell – straight as a die; you could trust him. He saw immediately there would be no safe future on any piece-

work, so he managed to introduce measured day work in all of the factories, which was quite an achievement.

'He had been Abdul Rahman's right-hand man in the creation of Malaysia [chief minister of Malaya, which became Malaysia in 1963].'

The measured day-work system introduced by Cattell at Linwood took some time for production workers who had been used to piece-work to get accustomed to, but in time, Cattell's plan started to show results. The main issues that needed to be addressed were, according to Scott Glover, assembly quality and productivity, and a solution to the issues came in the form of manning and running the assembly line in a properly 'man assigned' format, as drawn up by the works study department under Michael Hancock (son of Bill Hancock, the Rootes' works director during the Fifties). Scott Glover describes the process:

'This involved stopping the line for a couple of days – whilst every operator's job was outlined to him – and slowly restarting and building progressively up to the planned production rate. The work force was generally supportive, but by that time was getting more militant. And so the process took longer than planned, in order to try to foster joint involvement and participation. So many hours were spent in negotiations and discussions with trade union representatives. Clearly this process was very costly with so much production being lost, but Cattell was very supportive and involved us all far more than previously.'

A BBC Outside Broadcast unit at RAF Stanmore in January 1964, filming the television series *Know Your Car*, in which Anthony Marsh is talking about the new Hillman Imp.

COVENTRY ARCHIVES

In April 1965 it was announced that George Cattell would return to Coventry as managing director of Humber Ltd and that Bill Garner would take over Cattell's position at Linwood. Garner had been director and general manager of Humber Ltd and was an experienced factory manager of the 'old school' and continued to achieve the assembly quality and productivity plans that George Cattell had instigated.

MARK 2 AND SUPER IMP

In September 1965, the Hillman Imp Mark 2 was introduced, along with an upmarket Super Imp version. The basic Imp saloon model was discontinued. In the autumn of 1964, Rootes had introduced a plusher version of the Imp – the Singer Chamois, which also got the Mark 2 treatment. Also, as the Commer Cob car-derived van series was coming to an end, it was replaced by a Commer Imp van version.

The Imp Mark 2 Deluxe was everything the Mark 1 should have been, and more so. Apart from discreet little 'Mark 2' badges on the doors, externally it looked the same. Technically, a lot had changed and it was now a very good car. The automatic choke bit the dust very early on and was replaced by a manual choke even prior to the Mark 2 introduction. The innovative pneumatic throttle that was a Tim Fry idea for the Mark 1 was another component that worked during development testing, but which had failures in everyday use. The throttle linkage to the carburettor took the form of a diaphragm, which when compressed by the accel-

With the lowering of the pivot point on the front suspension to correct the camber on the front wheels, the Mark 2 lost the 'bow-legged' look of the Mark 1. The slightly fatter profile of radial tyres also helped improve the stance of the Mark 2.

erator pedal pushed a column of air through a pipe to a mechanism which opened (or closed) the throttle. But lost pressure due to leakage from the pipe would cause the throttle to be embarrassingly ineffective. Although not ideal, a conventional throttle cable was fitted as the solution.

One of the most consistent warranty claims was for head gasket failure. As the block tended to 'flex' after a relatively short period of time, the design was modified with strengthened webbing and stronger cylinder head bolts. The head also benefited from larger ports and larger inlet and exhaust valves as well as a new type of head gasket. The original clutch was also found to be wearing out too

The Super Imp debuted around the same time as the Mark 2.

1964 Singer Chamois.
SINGER OWNERS CLUB

The Commer Imp Van replaced the Minx-based Cob as the car-derived van option in the mid-Sixties.

quickly, so a larger 6¼-inch diameter clutch replaced the original 5½-inch version and a complete re-think of the water pump design solved another on-going warranty issue. The Mark 2 received many other modifications, to the body, cooling system, suspension, steering and brakes, but also to the interior: the parcel shelf received leathercloth covering, front and rear seats were more substantial, as well as more comfortable and two ashtrays were fitted in the rear. The Mark 2 models were also a great deal quieter, due to additional layers of sound deadening underseal. The stance of the Imp Mark 2 was also improved by lowering the pivot point on the front

suspension to correct the camber on the front wheels. The pivot point on the Mark 1 Imps was raised because the front side lights were apparently too low to meet regulations.

While it is difficult to refute the fact that there was a long list of technical problems with the Mark 1 Imp, the Mark 2 models were a vast improvement but, as Scott Glover says, '*Give a dog a bad name...*'

In the Imp's defence, when it comes to other small cars of the period, both the BMC Mini and the Triumph Herald suffered from quality issues in their early days – footwells and door bins filling with water at the slightest hint of rain would beleaguer early Mini owners, while the Herald would rattle its way around until Standard-Triumph could find a solution to the Herald's 'bolt-on panels' problem. Also, both the Herald and the Mini were loss-leaders. In 1962, Standard-Triumph lost £10 on every Herald sold and the Mini never made a profit for BMC in its early years. We may have forgiven the Mini and the Herald for their early quirks, but history, it seems, has been less forgiving of the Imp.

In 1965, the situation at Linwood improved as quality became more consistent and profitability increased. It had been a long trek for Rootes and the Imp and its derivatives would see another eleven years of production, but this was only the beginning of the Imp story and Linwood.

CHAPTER 4

COMPETITIONS IN
THE EARLY SIXTIES

'The Rootes mechanics were wonderful mechanics … wonderful – the best!'

Paddy Hopkirk – Rootes works rally driver

As soon as the new decade was underway, the Rootes Competition Department calendar was starting to look very full. Between January 1960 and the summer, Rootes works cars would compete in no fewer than five international rallies: the Monte Carlo Rally; the Circuit of Ireland; the Tulip Rally; the Acropolis Rally; and the French Alpine, achieving some impressive results, especially for the Sunbeam Rapier. The recently introduced Sunbeam Alpine would quickly make its name as a competitive circuit race car.

Rootes' works drivers Sheila Van Damm and Peter Harper take a publicity test drive in the new Sunbeam Rapier Series 1 in 1955. COVENTRY ARCHIVES

RAPIER – ROOTES'
COMPETITIONS 'MAINSTAY'

Since its introduction in 1955, the Sunbeam Rapier had become Norman Garrad's new weapon to enable his works drivers to use against competition from the BMC and Standard-Triumph works teams. During this period, Peter Harper was very much the 'golden boy' as far as

the works team at Rootes was concerned. His skill as a driver with Series I and Series II Rapiers had provided Rootes with more than respectable class and outright wins, making the BMC Riley 1.5 look quite pedestrian. A serious rally contender for the Rapier came in the form of the Volvo PV544, and there were numerous private entrants who chose the Volvo over a Rapier – both were well built, reliable and handled well, considering both were designed and built as family saloon cars. The Volvo had been a consideration for Peter Procter, who was looking at which car to buy as a privateer rally driver. At a meeting at the Motor Show in 1958 with Norman Garrad, he explained that he was going to buy a new car for rallying and didn't know whether to go for a Rapier or a Volvo! This was like the proverbial red rag to a bull as far as Garrad was concerned, who immediately offered him a well-prepared car to works competition standard if he chose a Rapier over a Volvo. The decision also led to him getting a works drive for Rootes. Procter did two rallies as a private entrant, the Tulip and the Alpine and then joined Peter Harper in the RAC Rally in 1959 for his first works drive.

Paddy Hopkirk was another ambitious young rally driver who would also join Rootes as a works driver, but Paddy's opportunity came about because of an impetuous mistake that led to him losing his drive with a rival team:

'I was driving for Standard-Triumph and I'd won an Alpine Cup and I was trying to get my second cup in a TR3 and I was driving up the Stelvio and I got a flat tyre on the way up, and I carried on to try and get to the top of the stage of the Stelvio, on time, and the engine overheated and we were forced to retire … Ken Richardson sacked me!

'So I did the Monte Carlo Rally with Les Leston, as a co-driver [in a Riley 1.5 in 1959] as I just wanted to stay

Bill Bleakley, co-driver to Jimmy Ray; Paddy Hopkirk; Jimmy Ray, who came second in class and Norman Garrad with three new Series III Sunbeam Rapiers prepared by Rootes Competitions Department for the Tulip Rally in 1960.
COVENTRY ARCHIVES

in the picture … I was walking through the bar of the Hermitage Hotel [at Monte Carlo] and Basil Cardew, the journalist from The Daily Express, *who I knew, said to Norman Garrad – they'd both had a few gin and tonics – "there was a young driver who's just been sacked by Triumph", and Norman Garrad called me over and said, "Would you like to do the Safari?" I nearly fell over … Mike Hawthorn had just been killed and was down to drive the car as a publicity stunt, so I got Mike's seat! I can't remember how many times I said, "Yes please sir" to Norman Garrad!'*

So, with Paddy Hopkirk on the team, who drove in The East African Coronation Safari Rally in 1959 in a Hillman Husky with Ronnie Dalton, the Rootes team were looking like serious contenders for future class wins in

Peter Procter driving his privately-entered Rapier in the 1959 Alpine Rally with Greg Wood and co-driver John Mennell, at the finish of the '59 Tulip Rally. PETER PROCTER

international rallies. But having two very talented and very ambitious drivers on the same team doesn't always bode well for harmonious team spirit, as Paddy quickly found out:

'*Peter Procter was with Peter Harper and Peter Harper was the works driver and the quickest driver and I hated him because he always beat me. We went on the Alpine Rally in the Rapier [1960]. I remember the mechanics – wonderful mechanics – they told us we mustn't go over, I think it was, 6,500 revs, and Peter Harper was behind me and he took a few seconds off me – I couldn't believe it!*

'*Well, Peter Procter was his co-driver, he'd had a row with Peter Harper … and he said, "Paddy, what revs are you using?" and I said, "6,500" and he said, "Try using 8,000!!"… and the next hill climb I tried using 8,000 and I took a few seconds off of Peter Harper – I was so pleased!*'

Although Peter Procter doesn't recall the incident he does confirm the rivalry between the two:

'*There was definitely a certain amount of animosity [between them] … They did have a very intense rivalry, and as I sat alongside Peter [Harper] I felt the brunt of it, and I tried to be the mediator. It was quite difficult. Peter was a great driver, but once or twice in the early days I remember having to bite my tongue … but eventually, I got the confidence to just be honest with him and shut him up on these things.*

'*The last event I did with him [Harper] was the Alpine … and Paddy beat us! … He got his own back on Peter.*'

Paddy Hopkirk and Jack Scott finished sixth overall in their Rapier in the 1960 Alpine Rally. COVENTRY ARCHIVES

The 1962 Monte Carlo Rally line-up of drivers and Rootes works Rapiers, *left to right:* Peter Harper; Peter Procter; Graham Robson, who partnered Procter; and Paddy Hopkirk with co-driver Jack Scott.

According to Procter, Norman Garrad knew what was going on but was reluctant to intervene, but also would not have wanted things to get out of hand. He knew he had star drivers in his team and if his plans worked out, he also knew they were capable of putting Rootes in the competition spotlight. He was right!

In 1959, Paddy Hopkirk, with co-driver Jack Scott in a Series II Rapier came third overall and first in class in the Alpine Rally. In 1960 the Rapier started scoring consistent class wins in virtually all international rallies: the Monte Carlo, with Peter Harper, partnered by Peter Procter, achieving class and fourth overall; Jimmy Ray scored a second in class in the Tulip Rally; and the Harper/Procter team came first in class in the Acropolis and the French Alpine, with Hopkirk second in class and Peter Jopp third in class in the Alpine. Hopkirk achieved a class win in a Rapier in the Silverstone Touring Car Race, but it was Harper who clinched the Class win at the Brands Hatch Touring Car Race, as well as the Inter-

national Compact Car Race at Riverside, California as a private entry.

By 1961, the Sunbeam Rapier was scoring class and outright wins in rallies and international races, and wins not just confined to the works team either: Ricardo Rodriguez won the Carrera Ciudad de Mexico in a Rapier and Dick Nash and Gene Hobbs took a Rapier to a convincing third overall in the SCCA 12-Hour Race at Marlboro, in America. In the Scottish Rally, John Melvin won outright in an Alpine, while Paddy Hopkirk came first overall in the Circuit of Ireland, a feat he would continue to repeat with monotonous regularity. In 1962, Rapier crews would bring back a total of nine awards after brilliant performances in the Monte Carlo Rally, which included a third overall for Hopkirk and Rootes being awarded the Charles Faroux manufacturer's team prize. Class wins for the Rapier also came in the Acropolis, several saloon car and touring car races, the prestigious Tour de France Automobile and the RAC Rally. In

Harper and Procter in the 1961 Alpine Rally. Sunbeam Rapiers finished 1-2-3 in class, despite snow and some of the most arduous stages of any Alpine to date, Paddy Hopkirk and Jack Scott finished third overall, beating Harper and Procter, who came fifth overall and Keith Ballisat and 'Tiny' Lewis, who were seventh overall. PETER PROCTER

Another arduous Alpine! The 1963 event saw the Rapier of Peter Procter and Adrian Boyd crash, after being the only Rapier in the top twenty of the fastest cars on Mont Ventoux. PETER PROCTER

Peter Procter and Rapier in the 1962 RAC Rally. PETER PROCTER

the Scottish Rally, a new name who was just starting to have success, and who would feature in future Rootes competition successes, was Andrew Cowan. As a private entry, Cowan would achieve first overall in a Rapier in the 1962 Scottish Rally.

THE SUNBEAM ALPINE
IN COMPETITION

The early sales promotions and publicity campaigns for the Alpine had been sufficient to give the car a high profile in both domestic and foreign markets, but once combined with Norman Garrad's efforts in competition, sales took off, especially in America.

Sales of Alpines were particularly brisk on the West Coast due to the promotional efforts of the Rootes' California representative, Henry Henkel. Unfortunately for Rootes, Henkel had other ideas as to where the money from deposits for Rootes cars should go, as Paddy Hopkirk found out after a trip to America in 1960. Paddy was competing at Riverside, California, along with Peter Harper, in the Compact Car Race and Henkel was assigned to look after them. Paddy remembers his encounter with Henkel well:

'The Rootes PR man in the States was a wonderful guy — or so it appeared — by the name of Henry Henkel. He took us down from the Mission Inn, where we were staying, to a beach resort called Salton Sea, where he and his beautiful wife were living ...

'About a year later, Henkel came to London and was visiting Lord Rootes in Park Lane on his way to Switzerland. He had a very large suitcase with him which was, as it turned out, full of cash, and he was on his way to place the money in a Swiss bank account. It came out later that it was the biggest swindle in the motor trade and involved the US auditors for Rootes. He had been selling cars to the dealers under HP agreements, but the cars were fictitious. Despite this, Henkel had the cheek to call in and stay with his boss, Lord Rootes — with the money with him in the suitcase!'

When and how Rootes found out about the scam is unclear, but no doubt the family would have made sure a tight lid was kept on this particular episode in Anglo-American relations.

From the point of view of competitive racing, 1961 was a good year for Rootes, and the Alpine was proving a worthy contender to take on the Abingdon MGs, as well as the more glamorous Alfas and occasionally Porsches in SCCA events in America. Immediately after the '61 Monte Carlo, in which Rune Backlund and Nils Falk repeated their class win of 1960, as part of a privately entered Swedish team of three Sunbeam Alpines, preparations were made by Norman Garrad for competing in the 1961 Sebring 12 hour Race, in Florida, in March. Despite Garrad organizing pit practices for the mechanics at Silverstone, and despite the Alpines being faster than the MGAs on actual race day, the inexperience of the Rootes mechanics in the pits was showing and the Abingdon crew's pit stops took a fraction of the time of Rootes' pit stops and subsequently were able to beat them. It was a disappointing result for Rootes, with

Testing the Alpine at Silverstone for the 1961 Sebring event. Front row: Norman Garrad; Peter Harper; Mike Parkes; Peter Procter and reserve driver Peter Bryant. Rear row: Rootes experimental department head Peter Wilson and Syd Henson from Ferodo. PETER PROCTER

Bill Buchman, seen here with his mechanic Doc Yant at Sebring in 1962 or '63, successfully raced an Alpine in SCCA events. He ran Buchman Motors in Sarasota, Florida and was the Rootes dealer for that area during the 1960s. Buchman switched to the Alpine in 1963 from a 1957 Alfa Romeo Guilietta Spider 1300. A.R. WOODS

Buchman, with independent mechanic Jack White, at W. Palm Beach, Florida, in September 1965. He had a lot of success in his Alpine and won the FP SE Championship in SCCA with it. He certainly earned enough National points to attend the first SCCA National Championship race in California at Riverside in 1964 and the next year at Daytona Beach. A.R. WOODS

Sebring, Florida – 12 hour Endurance Race, March 1961, *left to right:* Norman Garrad – Rootes Competitions manager; Peter Procter; Peter Harper, Ken Miles; Lew Spencer; Tom Payne, John Panks – Rootes Inc; Freddie Barrette, Joe Sheppard, Philippo Theodoli.

PETER PROCTER

3000RW, the Harrington Alpine Coupé, before the 1961 Le Mans race, with Norman Garrad and George Hartwell.

CLIVE HARRINGTON

The Harrington Alpine Coupé in action. CLIVE HARRINGTON

The starting grid of the 1961 24 hour Le Mans, showing the two new Alpines – 3001RW, the Hopkirk/Jopp entry and 3000RW, the Harper/Procter entry.

CLIVE HARRINGTON

Harper and Procter getting a class win, but only finishing seventeenth overall. The other Alpine, driven by Hopkirk and Jopp claimed fourth in class and finished thirty-fourth overall, after having a replacement head gasket fitted, in the pits – a task that few other teams would have even attempted!

In the 1961 French Alpine, Mary Handley-Page had also repeated a third in class position of 1960 in an Alpine, as well as a second Coup des Dames. In May came Scottish Rootes dealer John Melvin's outright win in the International Scottish Rally in his Alpine, followed by Peter Harper and Peter Procter winning the coveted 'Index of Thermal Efficiency' prize in their specially-built Harrington-bodied Alpine at the Le Mans 24 Hour Race in June '61. They finished sixteenth overall.

The event: 3000RW in the pits for refuelling and a nervous Jim Ashworth (hands in pockets) looks on as a mechanic re-fastens the bonnet catches. CLIVE HARRINGTON

On 14 October, at Riverside International Raceway, Jack Brabham entered a locally prepared Alpine in the three-hour Grand Prix d'Endurance race partnered with Stirling Moss, who drove for the final hour. Apart from an untidy start, which scared the hell out of Brabham, who was used to a more professional approach to racing than some of the moneyed privateers in Corvettes and Porsches, he found production sports car racing to be a *very comfortable way to go motor racing*. Brabham and Moss finished an impressive third overall and first in class.

In 1962, it was back to Sebring… Garrad was not going to let the disastrous result of 1961 dissuade him from upsetting the MGs from Abingdon. As in '61, Harper and Procter fielded the main Rootes works entry, number 41 and were backed up by some competent 'locals': Joe

Sheppard and Tom Payne in number 42 works Alpine and Ken Miles and Lew Spencer in the other, number 43. A fourth Alpine, a private entry, number 44, a Harrington Alpine driven by Theodolio and Barrette joined the works effort. The usual practice of 'dodgem' rides by a portion of the entrants was also standard practice at Sebring, as with other American circuits. On lap one, Peter Harper was side-swiped by Yenko's Corvette Sting Ray and Ken Miles' Alpine hit the OSCA driven by Denise McCluggage. Despite receiving extensive body damage to his Alpine, Harper beat the MGs and the Sting Ray of Yenko and between them Harper and Procter came fifteenth overall and third in class. The Alpine driven by Ken Miles and Lew Spencer retired with a broken engine but Tom Payne and Joe Sheppard limped home in thirty-second position.

In June 1962, the 24 Hour Le Mans Race beckoned its seductive hand again. With a degree of experience now, the Rootes Competition Department prepared three Alpines, one for Procter and Harper, one for Hopkirk and Jopp and the third as a spare. The bodywork was suitably modified by Harringtons to create a higher boot line and a squared off, or as Clive Harrington calls it, 'Kamm-tail' rear end. The cars were certainly faster than the '61 cars but suffered from mechanical problems: sticking throttles and overdrives giving up were just two problems that dogged both cars. However, the Hopkirk/ Jopp car retired after ten hours with engine failure, but the Harper/Procter car finished in fifteenth position and third in class. Respectable, if still a bit disappointing and their fuel consumption precluded them from an 'Index' prize. 1962 was a tougher race than '61 for the Rootes

Bruce McLaren was one of the Lew Spencer Team SCCA Alpine drivers, seen here in 1962 at Riverside. He finished seventh overall. The Alpine next to McLaren's, number 50, was driven by Ken Miles.

Loading the works Alpines on board the British Air Ferries freighters bound for Le Mans 1962. SUNBEAM ALPINE OWNERS CLUB

had earned Rootes a lot of competition accolades, but it was time for them to make way for the little Imp, a transition which would start to take place during 1964. American participants would continue to campaign the Alpine in racing: in 1963, Jerry Titus and Dave Jorden gained a third in class at Sebring and the Alpine of Paul and Alfonso Romero had an outright win in the Mexico Rally of 1962.

Meanwhile, Norman Garrad would, according to Rapier competition historian Tim Sutton, be *'eased into retirement against his wishes'*. Norman's son Lewis Garrad would take over the competitions department, but poli-

Group's 'dynamic duo', but they would have one more crack at Le Mans in '63. They were joined by new team mates at Le Mans, Keith Ballisat and Tiny Lewis. Both cars retired with engine failures, possibly as a result of the mechanics trying too hard to get the proverbial quart out of a pint pot with the little Rootes 1592cc engines. Following a less than successful outing for the Rootes Sunbeam Rapiers in the 1962 Acropolis Rally, Paddy Hopkirk decided to take up an offer from Stuart Turner to join the BMC Competition Department. All three of the Rapiers on the Acropolis had run their big-end bearings and Paddy, as a consequence, was out. While in Glyphada, he had a drive in Pat Moss' big Healey 3000, and that was it, Paddy was hooked!

Generally, both the Rapier and the Alpine had performed extremely well in rallying and racing and

For the 1963 Le Mans event, Harper and Procter drove 9201 RW, the number 33 Alpine that had experienced engine failure for Hopkirk and Jopp in the '62 event. Harper and Procter also had a DNF in '63 due to engine failure. PETER PROCTER

The 1962 Le Mans start. Number 33 is the Hopkirk/Jopp car and number 32 is the Procter/Harper car. Hopkirk and Procter were first off.

PETER PROCTER

1962 RAC Rally – A weary Rosemary Smith and Rosemary Sears, in the ex-Harper/Procter Le Mans Alpine, arrive at the Peebles breakfast spot on 14 November. COVENTRY ARCHIVES

tics were starting to play more of a part in the day-to-day running of the department, and by the end of '63, amid growing inside and outside pressures, Marcus Chambers, who had at one time been BMC's works competitions department manager, was approached by Brian Rootes to take over competitions. Brian's son, Bill, was aware that his father did not get on well with Garrad, and had wanted to bring in fresh ideas to the department, which Garrad was not happy about. Both characters were stubborn, and Norman Garrad had always been given carte blanche by his old boss Lord Rootes to run the department his way, so probably resented what he saw as interference from Brian.

By all accounts, it was felt by some works drivers that the rather insensitive way in which Norman Garrad's 'retirement' was instigated did not reflect the successes he had brought to the Rootes Competitions Department, or his loyalty to Rootes. Works driver Peter Procter, who had a great deal of respect for Garrad (as did Paddy Hopkirk), has the last word:

> 'Norman was a wonderful team manager and ran a very tight ship and was highly respected in the world of motor sport. He was a great organizer and his attention to detail contributed so much to the success that Rootes teams had over many years.
>
> 'It was his life really ... I would imagine that he probably felt rather disappointed with Rootes, having put so much into the Competitions Department over the years, to then have his nose put out like that ... it must have been upsetting. Norman went from what was a very amateur kind of approach to rallying in those days, to a much more serious and competitive approach, and I think he did it very well.'

1964 – THE LE MANS TIGERS

In the 24 Hour Le Mans events of 1961 and '62, the Rootes Competition Department had achieved a degree of success with the Le Mans Sunbeam Alpines, and with the scent of that success still in the air, Norman Garrad had conceived an idea of taking a race-bred version of the yet-to-be announced Sunbeam Tiger to Le Mans for the 1964 race. The event, however, did not turn out to be a happy one for Rootes.

Several factors were against Rootes from the outset, a principal factor being a lack of time to develop two competitive race cars to compete and hopefully win, but at least finish, in what was one of the motor racing world's most prestigious events. Rootes had barely six months to get the cars ready, when, in reality, at least a year would be needed to design, build and test the cars, in order to do the job properly. This, combined with the fractious political situation within Rootes at the time, and the fact that Norman Garrad was to retire at the end of 1963, having got the project 'rubber-stamped' by Rootes management, only served to compound the problems.

With Garrad's departure, having not been given the opportunity to see his idea through, his position had been taken by Marcus Chambers, who took over in February 1964. Chambers had effectively been given a 'Mission Impossible' task for his first job as Rootes Competitions Department manager. However, with a commitment from Timothy Rootes and with Peter Wilson's backing, there was no turning back, and Marcus Chambers had to make the best job of it he could.

Three cars were built, one 'Mule' prototype and two which were to be entered in the actual race. The drivers were Keith Ballisat and Belgian driver Claude Dubois, in car number 8, and Peter Procter and fellow Yorkshireman, Jimmy Blumer, in car number 9.

The 'Mule' prototype Sunbeam Tiger photographed in April 1964. ROOTES ARCHIVE CENTRE TRUST

**Marcus Chambers – Rootes Competitions
Department manager who replaced
Norman Garrad.**

Early testing at Snetterton showed up some of the faults in the car, in particular the Shelby-tuned 260 cubic inch (4.2 litre) Ford V8. Testing was ongoing, but for some reason, Peter Procter, who was probably the most experienced of all of the four drivers that had been selected, had been kept out of the testing loop. It was only later that he found out that Jimmy Blumer had been doing testing prior to the official test weekend of 18 and 19 April at Le Mans:

'I only found out just before the April practice that the car had been tested at Silverstone [or Snetterton] several times with Jimmy Blumer, who was my co-driver, and they'd never involved me at all. Jimmy Blumer was just a private entry club racer – not that I minded that – but I expected all the drivers to be involved – me and the other two in the other car, but it didn't happen.'

Knowing that Marcus Chambers had a high respect for Peter Procter as a racing driver seems at odds with his attitude to him at the time. Even at the Le Mans test weekend, he did not seem to want to take Procter's advice:

'When we went out in the April, testing, I came in after a couple of laps and said, "The engines aren't going to last… this oil surge on the corners … the pressure's going down to zero!" He [Marcus] said, "Don't worry, you're just the driver; we'll fix it, just you leave it to us."

'Then I came in complaining about the brakes, and he said, "You're driving it too quick!" I told him that was the point of the exercise wasn't it? You drive the car to its limit in practice and … I just realised I was banging my head against a brick wall.'

In Marcus Chambers' defence, Procter was probably reinforcing what Marcus already knew, as Keith Ballisat had also complained about the handling and poor braking of the cars. Mike Parkes, the ex-Rootes designer, now working for Ferrari, took the prototype Tiger out on to the Le Mans circuit, only to confirm that the performance left a lot to be desired. He had lapped in 4 minutes 26.4 seconds against his Ferrari time of 3 minutes 47.1 seconds. The engine oil surge and low oil pressure issues had also come to light during early testing in England. However, Procter felt that more could have been done about the problem: 'I did argue, quite strongly, about doing something about keeping the oil pressure up by placing baffles in the sump – but it never happened.'

During the development of the Le Mans Tigers, constant pressure from the marketing and engineering functions was compromising Marcus Chambers' efforts and therefore the efforts of the competitions department. Despite Carroll Shelby recommending that Rootes use the newer 289 cubic inch (4.7 litre) V8 that was destined for the Mustang, Rootes chose to use the 260 cubic inch (4.2 litre) Ford V8, as they were contractually-bound to do so for the yet-to-be-announced production cars, but also so that the marketing department could say that the race-bred Tigers used the same engine as the one you could buy from your dealer. The marketing involvement did not stop there: Rootes had enlisted the help of Lister to come up with a suitably winning design, capable of competing with the 'big boys' – Ford, Ferrari, Maserati, Porsche, etc. – and preferably winning!

Brian Lister's design called for a light tubular space-frame chassis, with an aluminium body, which was to be produced by Williams and Pritchard. This concept would produce a lightweight race car that could still be entered as a prototype and therefore avoid any homologation requirements. However, Rootes, and probably marketing, who obviously had their own agenda, wanted to base the car on the existing Alpine/Tiger monocoque body/chassis, which would be much heavier than Lister's concept, and ultimately not as competitive, but that's what they wanted, so that's what was built. The aerodynamic body was styled mainly by Ron Wisdom, of the Rootes styling department, and so with less of an involvement from Brian Lister, the project went forth.

Although Brian Lister did see the project to fruition, the Rootes attitude was rather like paying a consultant doctor to sort out a health problem and then telling the doctor he didn't know what he was talking about ... as Peter Procter remembers:

'He [Brian Lister] was always there [while the Le Mans Tiger was being developed] but he was pulling his hair out! I've seen him several times since, and he couldn't believe the attitude. He was a well-known designer, and they were just taking bits of it ... oh we'll have that, but not that ... He was on a hiding to nothing really ... I think Brian was very disappointed he'd got involved.'

As the race weekend of 20 and 21 June got closer, as much testing as possible prior to the race was carried out at either Snetterton or at the MIRA test centre at Nuneaton, but Marcus Chambers now realised that low oil pressure was a problem on not one, but all four of the Shelby-built engines. However, by 14 June it was too late; it was time to ship out and shut up, and hope for the best.

On race weekend, both cars passed pre-race scrutineering, which was good, as this process is generally a stressful one and fraught with petty issues if you are not French, or driving a French car.

In the pre-race practice, number 8 – the Ballisat/Dubois car – ran its engine bearings after only one and a half laps, which meant a hasty overnight engine change with the only spare engine they had. On race day itself, both cars had a good start, and the first hour saw them in twenty-fourth and twenty-sixth positions. After three hours, the first disaster occurred when the engine of

Claude Dubois and Keith Ballisat with their Tiger, at the start of the 1964 Le Mans 24 Hour Race. SUNBEAM TIGER CLUB

Jimmy Blumer in the number 9 Tiger at Le Mans, 1964.
PETER PROCTER

number 8 blew up with a broken piston. Number 9, the Procter/Blumer car, carried on for nine hours and managed to get to eighteenth position, before it too blew up. The car had completed 118 laps and Peter Procter was driving at the time: the incident that put them out of the race is etched on his memory:

'We survived until two in the morning – and then it blew up in a big way ... I was approaching the pits, flat out in top [between 160 and 165mph] when there was an almighty explosion and flames shot out from the back of the bonnet. I stood on the brakes and found that I could not turn the steering wheel.'

Not only had the blast damaged the engine, it had cooked all the knuckle joints and jammed the steering. While braking hard, the car was drifting towards the pit counter and with no way of being able to control the car, Procter slammed it against the pit counter in order to stop it. Thankfully, it scraped along the counter, narrowly missing other cars that were being refuelled until it came to a stop. As the car was tightly wedged against the pit counter, Procter exited via the passenger door, only to be confronted by an angry chief pit-marshal, Procter recalls what happened next:

*'"Pierre", he said, "you are in terrible trouble, you 'av crossed ze line, you cannot do that. But first we must move ze car!" "Okay", I said, "you drive and we will push (as other marshals arrived)." He climbed through the passenger door and said, "She will not steer!" "Now you know why I parked the f***ing thing there in the first place!!" I replied. I then left the scene and made my way to the nearest bar!'*

To place the Rootes' Le Mans result in context, of the fifty-five cars that started the race, only twenty-four

Peter Procter takes his turn in number 9 before slithering to a halt on the pit wall after 118 laps! PETER PROCTER

finished. Many of those cars could be considered highly-competitive machines, and quite capable of winning, were it not for mechanical gremlins that only a race like the 24 Hour Le Mans can find: the Ferrari 330P of Pedro Rodriquez retired after only five hours and fifty-eight laps with blown head gasket; Phil Hill and Bruce McLaren retired after a gruelling 192 laps with a broken gearbox on their Ford Motor Company sponsored GT40 Mark1 (which was running a 4.2 litre V8); and even Mike Parkes' Ferrari 275P retired after seventy-one laps with a broken oil pump.

The race was won by Nino Vaccarella and Jean Guichet in a Ferrari 275P. Graham Hill and Jo Bonnier in a Ferrari 330P came in second place with John Surtees and Lorenzo Bandini in third, also in a 330P. A surprise name would take fourth place and first in class, preventing the Ferrari name from being in the first six places. Dan Gurney and Bob Bondurant in the Shelby Daytona Cobra, powered by the new 289 cubic inch (4.7 litre) Ford V8 ensured that the Ford and Shelby name, which was just starting to chip away at Ferrari dominance at Le Mans, would eclipse that of the famous Italian marque within two years.

For Rootes, there were lessons to be learnt and at least the Tiger's future as a competitive rally car looked good. Carroll Shelby did acknowledge that there were problems with the engines used in the Tigers, and a refund was apparently made to Rootes.

It is also interesting to speculate what the outcome might have been had Norman Garrad been able to see the project through, or if Marcus Chambers had been given the same opportunity, more time and with less management interference. Sadly, we shall never know.

In between the Monte Carlo in January and Le Mans in 1964, Peter Procter had been racing single-seaters for

Ken Tyrell and Colin Chapman. After Le Mans, he left Rootes; he'd had enough! Peter Harper had also departed temporarily – the competition department, during this time was 'in limbo'. Procter then got a call from Alan Mann, who asked him if he was interested in racing for him in one of the new Ford Mustangs.

In August 1964 Procter drove in the Spa-Sofia-Liège Rally with his old sparring partner Peter Harper, but loss of brakes on the Mustang forced them to retire. It was on the next rally that Peter Procter would achieve a hallmark victory for the Ford Mustang with team mate and recent recruit to the Rootes works rally team, Andrew Cowan. Between Procter and Cowan, they would achieve an outright first in the Touring class category in the September 1964 Tour de France Automobile. The victory was notable as being the first competitive victory for the Ford Mustang anywhere in the world!

Andrew Cowan had joined the Rootes Competition Department in 1963, and tells how he got 'noticed' on the 1962 Scottish Rally. He also spent time with some future stars in his local car club – one such star being Jim Clark:

> 'The Berwick and District Motor Club was the best run motor club in Scotland at that time … They had people like Jock McBain, the local tractor dealer. He would buy Jim's cars. The first car he bought was an Aston Martin DB1 for Jim to race. We both joined the club and did road rallies … night rallies. It was a very active little club. We entered our cars and we drove flat out … [There was] little traffic on the roads then.
>
> 'Jim's first car was a Sunbeam-Talbot. He wrote that off coming into Galashiels one night coming home from a dance … a tight left-hand corner. I always think of him when I come

Peter Procter and Andrew Cowan, driving for Alan Mann Racing, achieved the first ever competitive victory for the new Ford Mustang anywhere in the world, when they achieved an outright win in the Touring class category in the 1964 Tour de France Automobile. PETER PROCTER

round that corner. He went through this hedge and was thrown out through the sunroof. The next day his Dad got him a Sunbeam Mark III.

'I got my first Sunbeam Rapier in 1958; my third car … my Dad bought me a new one. He was always keen on motor sport and very supportive, although we didn't have a lot of money. I did the RAC Rally in '60. It was cancelled in '61 and '62. I won the Scottish Rally in '62.

Ian Hall, who was the navigator for Peter Harper, was in Scotland looking after the private entries … and he reported back to Rootes that I had some potential, and they gave me a full works car. Then we crashed in Pickering Forest … and then they asked me to drive the first Imp to be rallied in the '64 Monte Carlo, with Keith Ballisat, who was the then competitions manager for Shell. I was his co-driver. After June '63, Rootes said, "We're going to get this guy Cowan on the books", so they gave me a contract in '63 for '64 and £1,000.'

Another up and coming driver, who had joined just before Andrew Cowan, was Rosemary Smith. From the outset, the Dublin dress designer was full of surprises, and would continue to surprise all who encountered her.

Rosemary had learnt her early driving skills from her father, who ran a small garage at Rathmines, Dublin, but it was while driving in the RAC Rally with a woman named Delphine Bigger, that she was noticed by one Sally Anne Cooper, whose father had bought her an ex-works Rapier, and asked Rosemary Smith if she would accompany her on the Monte Carlo Rally. This was in December 1961. Rosemary described to me in

Rosemary Smith with her Imp. COVENTRY ARCHIVES

2015 that event and the events that led at the age of just twenty-four, to her joining the Rootes works team:

'I thought, Why not? A car is a car and a drive is a drive!! Then of course, never having driven on snow or ice before, I thought it was a bit of a joke. But anyway, I did it and I went over and I was to fly into Heathrow and she said that somebody would meet me there. I arrived with the suit I had on and a small bag and there was a man holding a sign up saying 'Rosemary Smith'. I said, 'I am Rosemary Smith' and he said, 'Miss Cooper has sent me to pick you up' … in a Bentley!

'So we went from there up to her house… I still hadn't met Sally Ann at that stage and then this plain girl came down the stairs in a pale blue taffeta dress, with puff sleeves, and I knew… the minute I saw [her] we were like chalk and cheese, and I thought, make the best of a bad lot. As it turned out, I brought the car up to Glasgow and we parked outside the competition headquarters and Major Tennant-Reid, Bob Tennant-Reid – the head man, welcomed us all. Again, women in trousers weren't allowed into the headquarters… the clubhouse. I don't know what I did about that but…

'The next day she said, 'Of course, we have another girl coming with us – Pat Wright, or Pat Smith as she is now. Well, she turned out to be a darling so I drove and she navigated, and Sally Ann sat in the back in a mink coat with a picnic basket… and that's how we got away from Glasgow. We got to Monte Carlo and we were sitting on the quayside, very early in the morning and Sally Ann said, 'Well, I must be orf now…' The chauffeur was already there and he said, 'I'll be back to pick you girls up in a while'. He arrived back about three hours later… we went up to the mansion where we were staying. I think we were in the servant's quarters, right under the roof!

The 1964 RAC Rally: Andrew Cowan and Brian Coyle, in a works entered Rapier in the Dovey Forest in Merionethshire on 9 November.

'At night, there was a ball in Monte Carlo, so we all went to it and it was there that Norman Garrad entered the scene. I always thought that he was a smoothie, the hair slicked back… and very full of himself indeed. And on the Saturday night he said, 'I have decided that you are going to drive for the Rootes Group!' No… I thought… All I wanted to do was to go home and forget about it, so, in my innocence I said to my Dad, 'This slimy old geezer asked me to join the Rootes Group [works rally team].' Now, my father was the quite the nicest man you ever came across and he was really angry and said, 'You stupid, stupid [girl]… When will you ever get an opportunity to do something like that again – and get paid for it?' Unbeknownst to me, my mother wrote to Norman Garrad at Devonshire House and said that I had had time to reflect on all of this and that I would very much like to drive for him. That got the backs up of quite a few of the girls already rallying because they were all looking for works drives; I was not very popular, I can tell you!'

Rosemary was, however, under no illusions as to why Norman Garrad was so keen to sign her up to Rootes:

'I was nearly 6 foot tall, size 10 and long blonde hair, stuck on eyelashes… great for photographs! So if the cars couldn't win, at least you got publicity. Then, he said, 'You're going to drive the [1962] Le Mans 24 Hour Race – as a reserve driver'. I signed a contract and then the first rally was the Circuit of Ireland.'

Within a short period of time, the name of Rosemary Smith would be synonymous with competition success for Rootes. In the 1962 season, Rosemary won the Ladies Award in the Circuit of Ireland and came second in class and won the Ladies Award in the Acropolis Rally, as well as the Ladies Award and third in class in the Tour de France in September '62.

'Then it came to Le Mans, and you see – 'Innocents abroad' – I didn't know that women weren't allowed to drive at Le Mans! Norman had put me in as 'R. Smith – Ireland'… and you had to go for a medical with this French doctor. I said, 'I'm sorry, but I don't speak French…' and he flipped around and said, 'What are you doing here?' I said, 'I believe I have to have a medical.' and he said, 'But you're not a man!' 'No' I said, 'I'm not.' to which he replied, 'Get out!!

'Then it came out [in the press] and Norman was just [laughing] all the way to the bank because every single newspaper picked up on it … it was on the front [page] of every newspaper… The press never stopped. Norman was

very clever in his own way… he knew exactly what he was doing… They [Rootes] couldn't win, but they got more publicity than the man that did win!'

So, Rosemary decided that working for Garrad wasn't so bad after all, especially with the bonus of

'everything [being] paid for and meeting the most fantastic people… I was still running my [dress design] business, but it took very much of a back seat, so my mother just shut it down…'

Norman Garrad had made a wise choice in Rosemary Smith – as she proved to be a world class driver, regardless of whether she was competing against men or women. The car that she would be associated with during her time with Rootes, and the one that she would make her name with, would be the Hillman Imp. She also has great memories associated with the Imp:

'When we won the Tulip Rally in '65 [with Val Domleo], Elizabeth Taylor and Richard Burton were staying at the Noordwijk hotel and they sent the most amazing bouquet of flowers to us and a lovely letter, but way back, someone asked to borrow it and I never got it back.'

Rosemary followed up her outright victory in the Tulip with class wins and Ladies Awards on the Scottish Rally and the French Alpine, as well as getting the Manufacturers' Team Prize for Rootes with 'Tiny' Lewis and Andrew Cowan, all in Hillman Imps.

THE IMP IN COMPETITION

Former competition successes had proved to be a marketable commodity, and with the Hillman Imp starting to show its ability in rallying and in saloon car racing, Rootes started to see its marketing potential. In 1965, Rootes offered a factory conversion for privateers who wanted to use an Imp in competition – the Rallye Imp. It had a similar 998cc engine to the works cars and gave a useful 65bhp at 6,200 rpm. The Rallye Imp conversion had many of the features of the works cars, such as twin Stromberg carbs, stronger suspension and shock absorbers, a speedometer and rev-counter with additional gauges and an oil cooler and larger radiator.

Competition department engine builder Richard Guy describes some of the efforts that went into making the Imp a competitive car:

Rosemary Smith was the most successful rally driver with an Imp and won many Ladies Cups as well as an outright win in the 1965 Tulip Rally. ROOTES ARCHIVE CENTRE TRUST

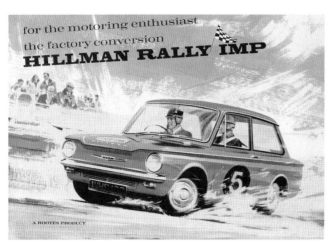

The brochure artwork for the Rallye or Rally Imp, as it was originally christened.

That was the first time we went to 998cc. The maximum you could take the 875cc block out to was +0.30, which would give you 900cc and we would use that as a Group 2 car – just a straight 900cc car with a pair of Strombergs on it. Rosemary Smith used to pick up most of her awards in that category.

'The first time we tried to use a Group 6 car was on the 1966 RAC Rally and we took three of them down to London Airport Holiday Inn, only to find that the event was cancelled due to a "Foot and Mouth" epidemic. They didn't know what to do with the cars, so we took them over to Lydden Hill for the Rallycross, which was televised ... and we actually did quite well. We drove the cars back to Coventry and stripped them down. It was the biggest blessing in disguise that the RAC Rally never started because none of our cars would have finished ... all of them would have suffered

with big-end bearing trouble! We had the wrong bearings and insufficient oil cooling ... We'd taken an engine that was about 70 brake horse [70bhp] on a good day, pushed it up to something like 98 and did little else to try to make it reliable, so we started looking into things ... We improved the oil cooling and went over to a Vandervell bearing, which was a lead indium bearing as opposed to a white metal bearing, and that did solve the problem.

'We had to be far more diligent with our clearances and then the engines were more reliable, but then they started cracking the centre main bearing. The Imp engine only had a 3-bearing crank, so we put a $^3/_8$ in thick steel plate across the bottom of the block and bulked it down, and that seemed to stop the problem. By this time, we were doing wet-liner engines. We'd take the block, bore the middle out, Loctite the four liners in ... but it was a very laborious process because we had to build the engine, run it, then we found that everything had settled ..., so we had to take it all apart again and have the block milled round the outside in order to give the "nip" on the gasket.

'Still it wasn't a great success, but much of it, I think, was due to not getting the cooling right. That's when we investigated [the possibility of using] the "Wills ring", which is a gas-filled ring round the top [where the gasket sits] with a paper gasket around the outside – and that sorted it!

'We had some good engines then. We could run an R17 cam most of the time, which was a 360 lift cam, or an R20 cam, which was a 360 lift cam with a 10-degree dwell on top of it. We got around 100 horsepower, then we increased the inlet valve size to $^{13}/_8$ in [from the standard Imp inlet valve size of $^{15}/_{16}$ in]. The exhaust valve size stayed the same. With Twin 40s [Weber DCOE 40 carburettors] and a Janspeed manifold and all the other little tweaks you needed to keep an Imp going, we had a good car.

'The "Achilles Heel" [of the Imp] was the transaxle. Poor old Brian Wileman tried every trick in the book to get one of those to last a rally. It was very difficult. You couldn't even dream of changing one at a service point.'

By 1966, the Imp had become the Rootes Competitions Department's staple rally car, which was under Marcus Chambers' control, but due to the success Alan Fraser had been obtaining in production car racing with the Imp, it was decided that Rootes would back Alan Fraser Engineering with a three-year agreement to run the Group's racing programme in Britain and abroad. During the 1965 season, Fraser Imps, with drivers such as Ray Calcutt, competed in twenty-five events in Britain and gained nine overall victories, as well as creating new lap records for their class at Brands Hatch, Silverstone and Lydden Hill.

High Jinks in Monte Carlo and Le Mans

If you think that rock groups like Led Zeppelin or The Who hold the exclusive right for giving hotel management stress and sleepless nights, you'd be wrong! Rally drivers virtually invented the practice of alcohol-induced naughtiness in hotels, although never to the level of some of the hotel room wrecking antics of rock bands on tour. However, rally crews certainly set a precedent for rock bands to follow.

During the Alpine Rally, the Rootes team would often stay in Bandol, in the south of France, on the night before the start. The finish was in Cannes, and the 1961 Alpine had seen a great result for Rootes. The following day, a party was held around the hotel swimming pool and it was decided that Paddy Hopkirk and Jack Scott should, by way of celebration, be thrown into the pool. Peter Procter describes the scene:

'As soon as we grabbed them, Paddy pleaded with us to remove his watch and wallet, before throwing him in. This we did, but ... while we were standing laughing at Paddy and Jack, we were pushed in, but still wearing our watches and still with our wallets in our pockets ...'

According to Paddy Hopkirk's account of the proceedings, he and Jack were *'closely followed by Oliver Speight of Dunlop, Tiny Lewis and Tommy Gold...'*, at which point the

The hotel swimming pool in Bandol. Hopkirk and Procter go swimming in full evening dress suits! PETER PROCTOR

hotel swimming pool was full of grown men wearing dinner suits!

One famous occasion which was witnessed by Peter Procter, was in Monaco, when police were called to the Tip-Top bar, situated just between Casino Square and Mirabeau. The bar was full to the brim with rally drivers, who were overflowing on the pavement outside. Whilst the police were busy inside the bar, someone got a wheel brace from one of the parked cars and took the wheel nuts off the Renault police car. When the police came out they were cheered on their way only to have the wheels fall off and roll down the Grand Prix circuit, much to the great amusement of the large crowd.

Rock 'n' roll and the world of rallying did collide one night at Le Mans in 1962, when Peter Jopp decided it would be a great idea to play some practical jokes on some other drivers, who were 'indulging in naughtiness' with young ladies. Following a few drinks, Jopp, aided and abetted by Paddy Hopkirk, had bought some firecrackers and the two *'went round the rooms where some of the crews were "at it"'*. Paddy explains their plan, which was to *'attach these to the door and the frame with drawing pins ... when the "visitors" went back to their own rooms at four o' clock in the morning, there were a number of loud explosions which I think woke up half the hotel and must have embarrassed the culprits! It was so funny!!...'*

Other high jinks stories at Monte Carlo and Le Mans are numerous enough to fill a book, but these really were the golden days of rallying and racing, made even more colourful by a talented bunch of individuals who understood the term 'Work hard – play hard'. Happy Days!

A group shot of the 1961 Alpine Rally team. *Left to right:* **Jack Scott; unknown; Paddy Hopkirk; unknown; Peter Procter; Peter Harper; 'Tiny' Lewis; Keith Ballisat. Seated: Lewis Garrad; Mary Handley-Page.** PETER PROCTOR

CHAPTER 5

BUSINESS AS USUAL – THE MID-SIXTIES

'Rootes – Top of the bill at every show – Hillman Humber Sunbeam'
— 1960s Rootes Group advertising slogan

October 1964 was a tumultuous month in a tumultuous year. In the General Election, Harold Wilson, leader of the Labour Party became Prime Minister and entered number 10, Downing Street, the Beatles were number 1 in the US and UK charts with 'A Hard Day's Night' and Rootes were number 3 in the national car manufacturing charts.

At the Earl's Court Motor Show, held in London during October, the Rootes Group made their presence known with stands showing examples of the latest offerings from Humber, Hillman, Sunbeam and Singer. The Motor Show was an impressive and glitzy display of some of Britain's finest cars and most manufacturers were showing revised versions of models launched at previous shows: Ford had launched their Consul Classic replacement, the Corsair, the previous year and Vauxhall had re-entered the small car market with the 'jet-smooth-whisper quiet' Viva! For the 1964 show, Vauxhall did however launch a new version of the Victor FC model – the Victor 101. Rootes had been able to compete with arch-rival BMC's family saloons very well – the Minx and Rapier had given the Wolseley 1500 and Riley 1.5 a hard time in the marketplace and in rallying. Likewise, the BMC Farina saloons were showing their age against the Super Minx and Vogue saloons from Rootes, but neither BMC nor Rootes were resting on their laurels for the 1965 model year. Rootes had given a very stylish makeover to their Hillman, Singer and Humber saloons, in the form of a smart new, flatter, six-light roofline which effectively got rid of the 1950s-style rounded roofline and wraparound windows. The new look was simple but effective and transformed their four-door saloons, as well as giving improved all-round visibility. But this was a revision of an existing model; BMC were offering a brand new model to compete head on with the Super Minx – the

The launch of the Humber Imperial at the 1964 Earl's Court Motor Show. POST VINTAGE HUMBER CAR CLUB

The big Humbers were given a completely new profile with the new-look roofline in October 1964. Illustrated is the Hawk Series IV.

The brochure front for the new Mark III Hillman Super Minx, launched in 1964.

the luxurious new
HILLMAN SUPER MINX
A ROOTES PRODUCT

A side profile and interior of the new Singer Vogue Mark III model: the six-light design of the new roofline gave the interiors of both Hillman and Singer models a more airy, spacious feel as well as offering improved visibility all round. SINGER OWNERS CLUB

Three Hawk front grille alternatives created by Ted Green in 1960. COVENTRY ARCHIVES

Austin 1800. Designed by Alec Issigonis as additions to the successful Mini and 1100 models, the 1800 was priced exactly the same as the Super Minx Mark III, at £769, including purchase tax.

At least Rootes had a new Imp supplement – the Singer Chamois. This well-executed luxury Imp version from

A more sophisticated approach for a revised dash layout by Ted Green, utilising the trend for recessed dials, similar to those used on Vanden Plas Princess and Rolls-Royce and Bentley models, would have made a big difference to the interior feel of the Super Snipe, but alas, Rootes chose to stick with chrome trim rings. COVENTRY ARCHIVES

Singer was also launched at the 1964 show. The other 'new' model from Rootes was the Imperial, an ultra-upmarket version of the Super Snipe, which brought back an old name into the new line-up. The Imperial also had the new flatter, squarer roofline, but was topped off by a vinyl roof covering and was luxuriously appointed with West of England cloth seats – leather was optional, all trimmed and finished by Thrupp & Maberly. The Imperial bristled with standard power-operated convenience features normally only found on a Rolls-Royce, Bentley or Cadillac. It was to be one of the most luxurious Humbers ever built, and one that Lord Rootes would have been very proud of.

Although the design studio had been looking at various new ideas to update the look of the big Humbers, such as a set of revised grille designs put forward by Ted Green, it was the new roofline that was implemented across the 'Series' Humber saloon car range. Alan Horsfall, who was working for engineering manager Arthur Long, was a design engineer responsible for the feasibility of the new style, which was tried on the big Humbers first. Alan and a colleague did the surfacing and then it was sent to Pressed Steel, who did the production engineering.

'Hawk/Super Snipe stylist Ted Green provided a side elevation and a cross-section of the 'B' post, and from that the surfaces were created... The Super Minx and Vogue followed the same theme.'

The new six-light, flat roof and rear window design for the Super Snipe had been incorporated into some styling renditions, dated 1963, by Humber body stylist Peter

A look at what might have been. New ideas were still being thrown around to re-invigorate the Super Snipe in the early Sixties. These styling mock-ups were built to illustrate the new ideas by Humber body stylist Peter Leeming. POST VINTAGE HUMBER CAR CLUB

Leeming, together with a number of alternative front and rear end offerings. Only the flat roofline made it into production.

THE TIMES THEY ARE A-CHANGING

The youth celebrity market that had started at the beginning of the 1960s was, by the mid-Sixties, in full swing. As a result of the release of the second James Bond film,

Goldfinger in 1964, Aston Martin were about to get the biggest and best product endorsement that any manufacturer could wish for. James Bond's personal mode of transport would turn out to be a very special Aston Martin DB5. Although the Superleggera-bodied super-car from Newport Pagnell was a competitor for the Jaguar E-Type, it is unlikely that Sir William Lyons of Jaguar lost much sleep over it; the E-type, along with the BMC Mini, had already carved out their own super-cool niches in mid-1960s Britain, albeit at opposite ends of the price ladder. However, in an effort to out-glitz the Brits, the mid-Sixties had more offerings from Detroit since before the war, in either right- or left-hand-drive, from any one of the growing number of UK-based concessionaires for North American-built cars. Due to Canada being a Dominion country, many of the right-hand-drive cars destined for the UK market were Canadian-built, as the import tax was significantly less than for US-built cars, thus making the 'Big V8s from across the pond' competitive with British and European prestige cars. Chrysler were marketing their Plymouth Valiant V-200 Saloon and Estate models via Chrysler International, and by 1965, the Plymouth Barracuda was added to the list. But it was the Rambler Classic from American Motors Corporation that would make an impact on sales of vehicles like the Super Snipe Saloon and Estate. The Rambler was a well-built, highly optioned, compact Canadian-built car and it was right-hand drive. If a wood grain dash and leather seating was not an essential, Rambler was another option.

In 1964, an Austin Westminster, Rover 3 Litre or Humber Super Snipe were still considered slightly uncool for aspiring young artists and musicians in mid-Sixties England. Following The Yardbirds pop group's chart success, a new car was a priority for guitarist Jeff Beck – as he remembers:

> *'Rather than put a deposit down on a flat or a house like some of my mates, the first thing I did was go out and buy a '63 split-window Sting Ray.'*

Beck's Chevrolet Corvette Sting Ray came from Lendrum & Hartman in London, as did singer Dusty Springfield's Buick Riviera and actor and comedian Peter Sellers bought a Lincoln Continental from Simpson's of Wembley. There were, of course, celebrity buyers who did choose Humbers over imports: Television comedian Harry Worth bought a new Humber Imperial but England test match cricketer Colin Cowdrey preferred the Humber Super Snipe.

Harry Worth, comedian and star of television comedy programme *Here's Harry* in his new Humber Imperial in February 1966. COVENTRY ARCHIVES

Following their success in the Geneva Rally in October 1964 Rootes decided to show the Tiger, seen here with Rosemary Smith adding some glamour to the occasion, at the 1964 Earls Court Motor Show. SUNBEAM TIGER CLUB

By the spring of 1964, Rootes did have a car to offer that would match the performance and handling characteristics of Corvettes, Mustangs, Pontiac GTOs, and other V8-engined muscle cars that were available on the UK market. The car was the Sunbeam Tiger, a fire-breathing Alpine on steroids powered by a Ford 260 cubic inch (4.2 litre) V8. The Tiger was aimed at the American market and known initially as the Sunbeam Alpine 260; it premiered at the New York Auto Show in April 1964. Although it was shown at the 1964 London show, the Tiger would not be made available in right-hand-drive for the UK market until 1965.

Although the Super Minx 'family' was selling, the profit margins were very slim, and of all of the models built by Rootes during the mid-Sixties, it was still the Hillman Minx that was the bread and butter earner for the Group. Sales volumes for Rootes during 1964 had risen to 138,179 vehicles, which included Rootes' all-important sales to export territories of 17,436 CKD units. Much of the industry had seen increased output, as a result of Chancellor Reginald Maudling's 'dash for growth' between 1962 and 1964, but the increase to Rootes' sales in 1964 came at the expense of some of the other British manufacturers. According to Rootes Group analysis carried out by the marketing team at Ryton, BMC had lost ground in the home market with 39.4 per cent share, after a record 43.3 per cent in 1963. Ford lost some of their share of the market in '64 when it fell from 32.1 per cent in 1961 to 28.4 per cent of British car sales. Standard-Triumph was consistent in its market share and would rise, no doubt due to the introduction of the front wheel-drive Triumph 1300. However, cars like the Rover 2000 were a cause for concern for Rootes. The 2000 had transformed the Rover image to give the company a new impetus.

As it became clear that Maudling's gamble on fast economic growth through spending hadn't worked, it seems he was quite relieved to be handing over the keys to incoming Chancellor of the Exchequer Jim Callaghan. According to political historian Andrew Marr:

'When Callaghan arrived in Downing Street … Maudling is said to have passed him on the way out, stopped with his coat on his arm and said, "Sorry to leave such a mess old cock". He wasn't talking about the furnishings, either.'

It seems that the Tories had been running out of steam during Harold Macmillan's last days in office and by

Sir Alec Douglas Home leaves Buckingham Palace in his Humber Super Snipe as the new Prime Minister, following the resignation of Harold Macmillan in 1963.

1962 his popularity as Prime Minister was waning. With ill health as the reason, he resigned in 1963. His replacement as Prime Minister was Sir Alec Douglas Home. Although it looked like he would continue as Prime Minister, he was pipped at the post by Wilson in the 1964 election.

CHRYSLER GETS A FOOT IN THE DOOR

In the spring of 1964, Rootes were approached by Chrysler International in Geneva, who were actively seeking to invest in a European car manufacturer. Chrysler was the only one of the 'Big Three' manufacturers in America to not have a British manufacturing base in their portfolio. Ford was well-established in Dagenham and Cologne and GM had Vauxhall in Luton and Opel in Russelsheim, as well as an assembly plant in Antwerp. Rootes was not the first company Chrysler were interested in and Chrysler was not the first company with which Rootes were to enter merger talks. In 1956, Chrysler approached Standard with a view to them producing a small car for Chrysler to sell on the European market. That approach and a subsequent attempt in 1961 failed. Chrysler also approached Leyland with an unsuccessful attempt to buy shares in the company in 1962. In France, they were more successful; in 1958, Chrysler Corporation took a fifteen per cent share in Simca, its first foray into future European manufacturing acquisition. They gained control of Simca in 1963. During this period, Chrysler sales were in decline in the US and a European manufacturing base seemed to be a way of increasing profitability. The initial negotiations with Chrysler were made by chairman George Love, someone with whom the Rootes board got on well, but much of the subsequent negotiations between the two companies were conducted by Lynn Townsend, with whom, as Geoffrey Rootes states 'we did not have a happy relationship'.

In 1962, Lynn Townsend was made president, their Desoto range had been culled and a cost reduction programme was instigated across all other model ranges, staff and factory personnel. But Townsend was an accountant – a bean-counter, not a car guy – and although his initiatives during the early Sixties temporarily placed Chrysler in a better financial state, one that would enable them to 'talk turkey' to Rootes, his presence at Chrysler did little to improve their standing as an automaker. Townsend's protégé was John Riccardo, who had worked alongside Townsend when they were both accountants at Touche Ross. Riccardo was made president of the export division in 1960, a post that would bring him into frequent contact with Simca and Rootes.

The other set of discussions that took place with Rootes prior to the approach by Chrysler, was with Ford of Britain. Rootes had attracted the attention of Sir Patrick Hennessy of Ford who, according to historian David Burgess-Wise, 'had a unique rapport with Henry Ford II, [but] even he could not buy a company as big as Rootes without the approval from World Headquarters in America'. So, Ford's top finance man Arjay Miller and his team were sent to London and moved into Ford's company flat in Grosvenor House, Park Lane, prior to a meeting with Lord Rootes and Henry Ford II to conclude a deal. All looked good, but the night before the meeting, Miller realized that buying Rootes, with their mounting debts and problems in Scotland, was not as good a deal as Sir Patrick had envisioned. David Burgess-Wise describes how Miller's gut feeling changed Ford's interest in Rootes: '[Miller] sat outside the door of Henry Ford's apartment until he heard his boss get up. While Ford was shaving, Miller convinced him to call off the deal.'

Ford did call off negotiations and Rootes were then left to consider the approach from Chrysler. Brian and Geoffrey Rootes recommended to Lord Rootes, Sir Reginald and the board, that they should start negotiations with Chrysler, but Brian, according to his son Bill had considered talks with Fiat: 'He was very keen on that … The Agnellis, who we knew, used to say, "We're a family business – we understand – we should work together."'

There followed a long period of negotiation with Chrysler during the run up to the conclusion of the deal. Lord Rootes and Sir Reginald then flew to New York to finalise a formal agreement. The deal reached was that Rootes would sell a portion of its equity shares, but not enough to relinquish complete control. In June 1964, an announcement was made that Rootes Motors Ltd and Chrysler Corporation of America had reached an agreement that Chrysler should acquire thirty per cent of the Ordinary (voting) shares in Rootes Motors Ltd and fifty per cent of 'A' (non-voting) shares. The share purchase was made in September 1964.

Lord Rootes regretted the decision, however, as for the first time in the history of the company, the Rootes family would not have complete control of their business, but at the time it was an inevitable necessity and initially, the deal seemed to work well. Rootes had been saved from the brink; they had investment from one of the 'Big Three' and to all intents and purposes, it was business as usual!

A right-hand drive 1964 Chrysler Valiant V-200 and a '64 Humber Sceptre. Maybe *Autocar* magazine was attempting to illustrate the shape of things to come from the new association between Rootes and Chrysler? AUTOCAR / HAYMARKET ARCHIVES

BIARRITZ BLUE/WINDSOR BLUE

PIPPIN RED/BIRCH GREY

Two of the colour combination examples put together by Rootes Advertising agency Erwin Wasey, seen here on a Humber Super Snipe Series IV and a Hillman Minx Series V, to show a potential Rootes customer what the colour options would look like on their new car. ROOTES ARCHIVE CENTRE TRUST

An historic photograph depicting an historic event: October 1964 at the Paris Motor Show, Lord Rootes is pictured with Chrysler representatives joining the Rootes board. *Left to right*: Robert C. Mitchell, president and managing director of Chrysler International; Sir Reginald Rootes, deputy chairman of the Rootes Group; Louis B. Warren, a director of Chrysler Corporation; Lord Rootes; Irving J. Minett, group vice-president, international operations, Chrysler Corporation and Geoffrey Rootes, chairman of the manufacturing division of the Rootes Group and managing director of Rootes Motors Ltd.

ROOTES MARKETING AND ADVERTISING IN THE 'PRE-CHRYSLER' SIXTIES

During their formative years, the Rootes Group had gained a reputation for skilful product promotion, marketing and selling. The 1960s would prove they hadn't lost their touch.

The Devonshire House publicity and marketing team was functioning much the same as it had done in the late 1950s. John Bullock had been made head of public relations and Bill Elsey was in charge of advertising. Some, new to Rootes, but experienced press and media executives — in the form of John Wilcox and John Rowe – had also joined the team, along with Liam Hunter, and Bill Morris, a seasoned hack from the *Daily Record* in Glasgow. John Bullock invited Morris to join Rootes, as it was felt that a 'local' would best be suited to take on the Imp press and publicity duties, based in Scotland.

Under Bill Elsey's watch, the advertising agencies dealing with Rootes remained the same: Basil Butler Ltd continued with the Hillman and Humber accounts and Erwin Wasey & Co dealt with Singer and Sunbeam. Brian Rootes' son, Bill, was keen to get into advertising and so, with the usual entry conditions for a young pupil, joined Erwin Wasey:

'I went to work at Rootes in 1964. First at Rootes Maidstone, taking Series 5 Hillman Minxes apart and repairing them, then training at the factory for a year, then one of the advertising agencies – Erwin Wasey, as I wanted to go into the marketing and advertising side of the company … under Bill Elsey's advertising department. I wasn't actually in Devonshire House, I had an office in Lord's Court and I handled the ads for Singer and all the London depots'.

Although the agencies handled new model launches, as well as ad copy and design, it was clear that the Rootes family still had the ultimate word as far as marketing was concerned, as Bill Blanch, an account executive at Wasey's found out when the family visited:

'Brian and Tim Rootes and Bill, son of Brian, came to Wasey's … I was arguing about the name of the Chamois and Brian said, "Do you want the account or not?"'

The Chamois name was cast in stone as far as Brian was concerned, so it was not a point for discussion. The London office of Wasey's was a subsidiary of a long-established Chicago-based agency with an office in New York, and had been particularly successful in creating a high media

'IT'S A BEAUT' SAYS JACK BRABHAM
WORLD CHAMPION RACING DRIVER 1959 AND 1960

SUNBEAM ALPINE

now with 1·6 litre engine

'**P**OWER AND GRIP – that's the first impression I had when I tried this great Sunbeam Alpine. Whatever the road was like, you certainly felt that the lively Alpine had things well in hand. This sports car makes you feel good – the road streams away behind you and you know she's got all four corners well down.'

MORE POWER Lively 1592 cc engine develops 85·5 b.h.p., more torque – giving vivid acceleration and ample power.

MORE STABILITY Rear springs are bigger – for greater lateral stability. Larger capacity rear shock absorbers improve ride control and prevent fade.

MORE ROOM There is an extra 1½" between seat and steering wheel, the pedals are adjustable and the seats move farther back.

MORE REFINEMENTS Better weather sealing . . . detachable hood cant rails . . . an extra interior light . . . eight less greasing points . . . quick-action petrol filler cap.

Wire Wheels, White Wall Tyres, Overdrive and Hard-Top are optional extras. You can now choose from *five* colour schemes.

PRICE £695 *plus* P.T. £290.14.2

By appointment to Her Majesty The Queen
Motor Vehicle Manufacturers
Rootes Motors Limited

ROOTES MOTORS LTD
Sunbeam-Talbot Ltd., Coventry, London
Showrooms & Export Div. Rootes Limited,
Devonshire House, Piccadilly, London, W.1.

Rootes and Erwin Wasey used motorsport celebrities such as Jack Brabham to publicise new models like the Sunbeam Rapier and the Alpine. Brabham was a regular contributor to Rootes photo shoots, publicity events and celebrity endorsement.

profile for Sunbeam and now for Singer. Bill Blanch also remembers that they made sure that ad copy of race and rally wins was with the national newspapers on a Monday morning, before all the other agencies,

'even if it meant walking down Fleet Street to the evening newspaper office.'

One of the Wasey magazine advertising campaigns was the 'Zest for living' series for the Rapier. Bill Blanch used various photographers for the photo shoots:

'The photographs were taken by Wasey's in-house photographer Grey Lacey and the art director was Richard Downer. The three of us worked very closely as a team and always went on location together … Several of these were taken on one trip to the New Forest, Buckler's Hard and the Lymington to Isle of Wight ferry.

A mock-up for the 'Zest for living' campaign by Erwin Wasey to promote the Sunbeam Rapier, complete with editors comments about film type and exposure: *'F5.6 @ 1/125. Tri-ex (FP3)?'* BILL BLANCH

'I remember Louis [Klementaski] taking some shots, I think, of a Rapier rather than an Alpine, in Richmond Park. Although he had the full permit, one of the Park Rangers didn't like us being there and tried to chase us away, eventually going off on his bicycle to get reinforcements or a "higher authority", but we had finished well before he returned mob handed! We were trying to get the car in pristine detail while looking as if it was being driven at speed. I remember that for part of it I had to reverse away from Louis and his camera rather than drive towards or past him.'

Both Wasey and Butler continued to utilise the talents of freelance commercial artists for sales brochure artwork, such as Frank Wootton, George Bishop, Terence Cuneo and Vic Carless, despite the industry leaning more towards colour studio photography. It was a gamble that paid off for Rootes, and their trademark look gave them an air of exclusivity that earned them the reputation for creating some memorable and distinctive automotive artwork. During the Sixties, the agencies would commission other talented artistes: Richard Sherrington, for his mid-Sixties Humber Super Snipe and Imperial images and Leslie Wise, who by the Sixties, already had a long association with Rootes, providing graphic artwork for brochures and manuals. Having trained at Harrow Art School, Wise first got a job working as an artist for Rootes as a result of his father, the service manager at the Rootes service depot in Chase Road, Acton, who created an opportunity for him to work for one of the Rootes agencies in 1937. During World War II he worked in the Fire Brigade and in 1945 re-joined Rootes. He left in 1947 to start up his own agency as a freelance artist specialising in car work, but returned once more to Rootes in 1951. Wise was subsequently taken on as a full-time employee and stayed with the advertising team through the 1960s and 1970s.

In April 1964, the Butler agency merged and became Butler & Gardner Ltd. Erwin Wasey would also merge during the Sixties, to become Wasey, Pritchard, Wood & Quadrant but would retain the Sunbeam and Singer accounts until 1967, when Chrysler's agency, Foote Cone and Belding took over. A similar fate awaited Butler & Gardner with the Hillman and Humber accounts in 1967.

The Rootes Group's other principal advertising agency was Walker & Crenshaw Inc, at 500 Fifth Avenue, New York. Conveniently located a few blocks away from the Rootes Group's showroom on Park Avenue, they handled all major ad campaigns for Rootes in the early Sixties, and had a field day when the Alpine was launched. Within weeks of the Series II model being introduced, the agency had placed full-page adverts in *Car & Driver* magazine and

Two of the 'finals' used by Erwin Wasey for the 'Zest for living' campaign. BILL BLANCH

Brochure cover for the 1963 Humber Hawk Series II. The original painting by Frank Wootton is owned by musician and television presenter, Jools Holland, and was used as cover artwork for his 2002 album *Jools Holland & His Rhythm & Blues Orchestra – Small World Big Band, Volume Two – More Friends.*

HILLMAN MINX 1600 DE LUXE SALOON

A bright, simple studio shot worked well for the brochure design for the Hillman Minx Series V.

HUMBER ESTATE CARS

SUPER SNIPE

HAWK

ROOTES PRODUCTS

Rootes commissioned a separate brochure for the Series IV Humber Hawk and Series V Super Snipe Estate Cars, c.1965.

POST VINTAGE HUMBER CAR CLUB

new SINGER GAZELLE

The 'new' Singer Gazelle Series V model was the last Gazelle model to be powered by the 1597cc engine. It is finished in Lake Blue and Foam White and as with most promotional shots of the time is fitted with extra-cost optional whitewall tyres. SINGER OWNERS CLUB

This was one of the images used for the ad campaign by Walker & Crenshaw, Inc for the Alpine, with the strapline *'The prettiest thing that ever kept a man waiting'.* COVENTRY ARCHIVES

Road & Track magazine, appealing not only to the sports car fraternity, but to those wanting a little more sophistication to their choice of sports car. Although we may now wince at some of the strap lines used, it was an effective campaign.

Product placement in films and on television appeared not to be such a priority for Rootes during the Sixties, due to the shift in emphasis to nationals and the specialist automotive magazines, although some memorable television programmes did feature Rootes cars in regular primetime roles. *No Hiding Place* was a popular television series starring Raymond Francis as police Detective Superintendent Tom Lockhart of Scotland Yard. The opening credits featured the car that was Lockhart's personal police vehicle, a Humber Super Snipe Series III Saloon. *No Hiding Place* was produced by Associated-Rediffusion for ITV and provided a primetime plug for the Super Snipe for eight years until 1967.

One of the first high-profile roles for the Alpine came in 1960 with the release of the Hollywood movie, *BUtterfield 8*, starring Elizabeth Taylor and Lawrence Harvey. The red Alpine features as Taylor's daily driver, but it comes to a sticky end when she crashes into a road block and plunges down a steep bank, while being chased by Harvey, in a mid-Fifties Mercedes 300.

Prior to Aston Martin becoming James Bond's daily driver, in October 1962, the first of the Bond movies – *Dr No*, starring Sean Connery as James Bond, secret agent 007 – featured Bond escaping from the bad guys in a blue Series II Sunbeam Alpine.

The Rootes Group's New York advertising agency Walker & Crenshaw Inc. provided some novel straplines for the early Sixties Alpine advertising: 'Our cups runneth over' was a response to the Alpine's competition successes. The same car from the same studio shoot, but with the top up, was used in an advert for the November 1961 edition of a Car and Driver magazine stating, 'How to get a Sunbeam Alpine ready for winter: (1) Roll up the windows – Oh yes… and put in some antifreeze.' COVENTRY ARCHIVES

A still from the 1960 motion picture *BUtterfield 8*, in which actress Elizabeth Taylor removes a parking ticket from her Sunbeam Alpine. COVENTRY ARCHIVES

The sequence did much to enhance the image of the new sports car from Rootes. The Alpine continued to receive cameo roles in many other subsequent films and television programmes. Among them were the 1964 television series *Human Jungle*, starring Herbert Lom and Robert Beatty; Clive Donner's 1965 comedy movie *What's New Pussycat?* and a 1966 episode of the *Batman* television series.

An American television production that was screened on British TV, and which jumped on the popularity of James Bond was *Get Smart*, a hilarious comedy secret agent spoof starring Don Adams, as secret agent 86, Maxwell Smart. Created by Mel Brooks and Buck Henry, the series also featured a red 1965 Sunbeam Tiger, but occasionally a virtually identical Alpine was used. *Get Smart* ran for five years from 1965 and although a Ferrari 250 GT Spider, a Volkswagen Karmann Ghia Convertible or an Opel GT were occasionally used in some episodes as Max Smart's car, it was the red Tiger that most fans of the programme associate with *Get Smart*.

In March 1966, Rootes collaborated in furnishing vehicles for the motion picture *Born Free*, starring Virginia McKenna and Bill Travers. In the film, which depicts the true story of Elsa the lioness, filmed in Kenya, a number of Rootes cars were supplied by Rootes (Kenya) Ltd for use in the movie and as support cars. A Hillman Super Minx

A Series II Alpine similar to the one used in the James Bond film *Dr No*. The girl is there but where's 007? ROOTES ARCHIVE CENTRE TRUST

Estate Car features as well as a Commer pick-up truck. As a quid pro quo for supplying the vehicles for the movie, Rootes received a 16mm colour film showing the movie being made, which they could use for promotional purposes.

Other promotional films and 'shorts' were commissioned for Rootes. The Hillman Imp got its very own 'promo' film, *Young in Heart*. The film was sponsored by 'Films of Scotland' and now features as part of the 'Scotland on Screen' archive. With a voiceover by Brydon Murdoch, the twenty-three minute film starts with shots

German actress Elke Sommer collects her new Sunbeam Alpine Series III Tourer in February 1964. She was in Britain shooting the movie *A Shot in the Dark*. Produced and directed by Blake Edwards, Elke co-starred alongside Peter Sellers in his role as the hapless Inspector Jacques Clouseau, in the second of a series of *Pink Panther* comedy films that would also feature Herbert Lom as the exasperated Commissioner Dreyfus.

Actors Bill Travers and Geoffrey Keen pose with a Hillman Super Minx Estate, while filming on location in Kenya for Carl Foreman's movie *Born Free*. Bill Travers and Virginia McKenna play the real-life husband and wife team of George and Joy Adamson. The film, which is based on Joy Adamson's book about Elsa the lioness, was shot in 1966.
NATIONAL MOTOR MUSEUM

One way of getting effective product promotion on primetime television was to give away a car. A Hillman Imp is the star prize on the ITV-Rediffussion quiz show *Take Your Pick*. Hosted by Michael Miles, the quiz show was one of the most popular shows on television, along with its other ITV rival, *Double Your Money*, hosted by Hughie Green. COVENTRY ARCHIVES

Actor Terence Longdon is seen here as part of the promotion of *The Fast Lady* film, which was released in February 1963. The promotion, a road safety rally at Denham Studios, was hosted by Graham Hill and featured a virtual *Who's Who* of British Film & Television. ROOTES ARCHIVE CENTRE TRUST

of a young couple, played by Bill Simpson and Elizabeth Yuill, driving a Hillman Imp along Scottish coast roads and goes on to document the development and production at Linwood of the new Hillman Imp.

Featured cars in other company's advertisements were a bonus for Rootes, and one such promotional bonus came

Actress Liza Minnelli is seen with her chauffeured Humber Imperial during the filming of *Charlie Bubbles*, in which she co-starred with Albert Finney in 1966, who also directed the film. Much of the filming was done on location in Manchester. The Humber Imperial and Super Snipe were used by many chauffeur firms who were contracted to film and television studios in Britain during the Sixties. COVENTRY ARCHIVES

in 1962, when Shell commissioned a series of television advertisements to augment their 'Keep Going Well, Keep Going Shell' campaign. Initially the ads featured Bing Crosby singing the catchy 'Keep Going Shell' song, while ostensibly driving a Jaguar E-Type Roadster through various parts of England. For the next series, Crosby was replaced by his sound-alike crooner from Britain, Michael Holliday and the Jag was replaced with a Hillman Minx 1600 Convertible. Sammy Davis Jr did one ad in London featuring a Rolls-Royce Silver Cloud. Over a period of a month, four sets of adverts were filmed by TVA – TeleVision Advertising Films Ltd, for each of the Shell England, Wales, Scotland and Ireland regions. The Minx, which was supplied by Warwick Wright Ltd, was seen being driven in various locations all over Britain, and consequently on TVs in millions of homes nationwide.

EXPORT AND OVERSEAS TERRITORIES

On paper, the export territories and overseas locations held by Rootes in the Sixties looked impressive, with around 6,000 dealers and distributors, overseas assembly plants, and regional offices selling cars and trucks to 163 countries. But a change in buyers' tastes and requirements had swept the world, not just Britain, Europe and America. The Japanese car manufacturing industry was also starting to be a force to be reckoned

with. Exporting vehicles had become a much more difficult task than it was in the immediate post-war period.

Rootes management resources were understandably stretched during the early part of the Sixties and they had taken their eye off the ball as far as the exports were concerned. A fundamental misunderstanding of the sophisticated changes that were happening in the world market, allied with quality problems and unsuitability of some Rootes products for certain territories, would start to see an unravelling of the 'empire'. In an effort to address some of these problems, in January 1966 Rootes formed a new company to handle all export merchandising and oversee its overseas distribution and service network. The intention of the new company, which replaced the old export division within Rootes Ltd, would be to provide specialised services to parts supply, after sales service, finance, marketing, advertising, public relations and shipping. As with the old export division, the chairman was Brian Rootes and managing director John Land.

Australasia

One of the quality issues on export products at Rootes Australia was discovered by Tom Cotton, who went to work in the Export Service Department in March 1960, processing warranty claims and giving technical support:

> 'One of the things we were able to do was to nail Pressed Steel as to the quality of their pressings and bodies. I made an analysis of warranty returns and our biggest expenditure was on Pressed Steel items.
>
> 'I had the whole of Australasia, which was interesting because there was a CKD territory in both Australia and New Zealand, but also built up vehicles for other areas. It was busy too because there was a lot going on. They submitted warranty claims for work they had done which had to be vetted and dealt with and reimbursed.'

Tom had identified where the problems were, in order for them to be rectified. Rootes (Australia) Pty Ltd would continue to produce cars and Commer vans at the Port Melbourne plant until 1966, after which it became Chrysler (Australia) Ltd, until 1972. Todd Motors in Wellington, New Zealand, would also continue to be a loyal and successful producer of Rootes cars, and subsequently Chrysler, until 1981, when production was replaced by Mitsubishi.

North America

Another management trainee, who was a pupil at around the same time as Tom Cotton, was Peter Badenoch, who went to work for Rootes Canada as a service technical instructor. As with Tom Cotton, Badenoch had started on his management journey processing warranty claims at the Rootes Export Service Office in Coventry: He quickly found out that Rootes' heady ambitions in Canada were not being met: *'By the time I arrived in Canada in April 1962 we sold virtually no QX trucks or Walk-thru vans, my guess being that they were just not price competitive with GM, Ford or Dodge.'* He also started to witness problems with Rootes products that were simply not being addressed by the factory. This would have considerable repercussions for future sales: *'I watched Rootes and other British manufacturers lose the market they had dominated simply because the cars were chronically unreliable under North American operating conditions.'*

American car buyers had come to expect a level of reliability from their cars that was generally much higher than in some other countries, and due to the extreme weather conditions that American and Canadian cars had to endure, as well as a degree of mis-use and abuse by their owners, the cars had to be tough, reliable, well-engineered and capable vehicles, which most of the American-built products were. British and some European models were not up to the abuse that the North American climate could throw at a car.

As well as Rootes, other British companies were not responding realistically to the demands of the North American market: Vauxhall was a case in point. In 1958, they scored a record export achievement supplying the Victor Saloon to North America. Being a GM product, buyers expected the little car from England to perform with the same reliability as other GM products. It didn't! The Victor was sold and serviced through Pontiac dealers who could not keep up with the issues the car caused, resulting in it being dropped like a hot coal from the GM line-up never to return. Not to be completely put off by the experience, GM did repeat its European export exercise in the mid-Sixties with the German Opel Kadett. Sold through GM Buick dealers, it fared much better, and at least remained on the GM product line-up sheet until the early Seventies. Realising the need for 'smaller' cars, GM, Ford and Chrysler had introduced their compacts into the market in 1960 and '61. Although the Ford Falcon and Chrysler Valiant, which were following the trend for compacts that had been set by the Studebaker Lark and the Rambler Classic, would make a significant dent in the demand for British small-engined saloon cars, the appeal of British cars, especially Rootes cars, was unique. There was one import company, however, that was wiping the floor with the rest of the European industry and that was Volkswagen. Initially with one model, they made sure that the quality of the Beetle would withstand the cold winters and blazing summers of Minnesota, the suburban and city stop-start driving on the East Coast, and the freezing minus 20 degrees F temperatures of Canada. In 1961, Volkswagen introduced the larger 1500 Saloon and 1500 Variant Estate to their product range, which

A Minx Series III Convertible, sold by Sarasota, Florida Rootes dealer Bill Buchman; a Saab; Triumph TR Sports; and a Series 1 Minx Saloon in the background make up this view of imported cars in early Sixties Gulf coast of America. JIM WOODS

Peter Badenoch, about to set off on his tour of Rootes Canada dealerships in January 1964, complete with Commer Walk-Thru van and trailer with Sunbeam Imp demonstrator. He is being bid 'farewell' by Rootes Canada CEO Malcolm Freshney. PETER BADENOCH

already included the now legendary Kombi van range and the Karmann Ghia coupé and cabriolet.

Volvo and Saab were also moving to 'imported car' dominance in North America during the Sixties, but the appeal for a stylish British saloon car was still present. In February 1964, *Car and Driver* magazine road-tested the Hillman Minx 1600. While acknowledging the innovations that had been incorporated into the face-lifted Minx – disc brakes, unit construction, the elimination of grease points and a power boost – they commented that:

> 'Two things are impressive about the Minx. The car makes a very favourable first impression… everything fits and works and seems admirably suited. The impression is somehow of a car four-square and rock-ribbed, business-like yet zestful.'

This poetic media praise, and previous road test reports of this type, no doubt sent willing buyers to Rootes dealers in America and Canada to test drive a Minx or Super Minx. But Peter Badenoch's experiences in the aftermarket tell a worrisome tale of problems such as brake wheel cylinders seizing; starter motors unable to function under cold-start conditions and dynamos that would not be powerful enough to cope with recharging batteries in winter when continuous use of fan, wiper and headlights resulted in flat batteries. Substandard switches and corrosion-prone wiring harness terminals and connectors caused many an electrical fault, and gave rise to subsequent 'Prince of Darkness' jokes aimed at Lucas electrics. Peter explains one example of how a small problem could ruin the impression of an otherwise good car:

> 'Handbrake cables were seizing … they were little problems, but you can understand if somebody buys a Minx or Super Minx as a second car it was probably going to be used by the wife to carry children. She would go out in the morning and try to back the car out of the driveway and the rear brakes would be seized on. It was silly little things like that made owners very angry!
>
> 'The Easidrive transmission was another case where development wasn't adequate – not enough testing was done, particularly in cold climates. The rationale behind Easidrive was that there were very little power losses, unlike a "slush box" with a torque converter.'

Early Super Minx models were available with Easidrive:

> 'The first generation used a control box with electro-mechanical relays which could fail as a result of other problems in the system, and at over $100 in 1960 dollars, the sealed control box was expensive to replace if the 12-month warranty had expired. The second generation Easidrive used a solid-state control box which promised to be better, but in its first winter in Canada it was found to cease operation at sub-zero temperatures.'

On one occasion, when visiting the Vernon Rootes dealership in British Columbia, Badenoch had to endure some banter after abandoning his immobilized Super Minx to return to Vancouver by bus. Rather than let the engineers in Britain drag their feet, Smith's Canadian subsidiary in Don Mills (Toronto) took the initiative and diagnosed the cause, then reworked and cold-tested every control unit in Rootes Canada's parts stock, following which Rootes Canada effected a 100 per cent recall. This was what Badenoch describes as

> 'pro-active customer care, long before the days of mandated recalls'

But dealers had lost confidence in Easidrive; in the mid-1960s Rootes replaced it with the Borg Warner 35 conventional automatic.

> 'The problems we were seeing were almost totally ignored. I remember when I was back in Coventry, after being in Canada for two or three years, for a training session … I was asked to meet with some of the service people to talk about the problems we had in Canada … I mentioned the [impact] Volkswagen were having on the market … At the end of the meeting the fellow who was chairing the discussion said, "Peter, anyone who buys a Volkswagen is a fool!"'

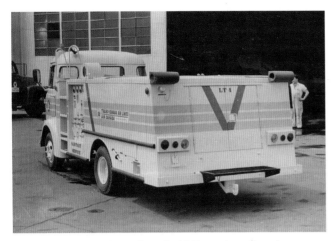

A Karrier Bantam Trans-Canada Airlines aircraft sanitary servicing truck. JOHN MITCHELL, HUNTSVILLE, ONTARIO, CANADA

With that attitude, Badenoch knew he was playing a losing game. Some of the modifications that would make Rootes cars suitable for the North American market were eventually implemented, by which time it was too late – the Japanese had moved in and the market was lost. However, there were some bright glimmers that kept the Rootes Canada spirits up, and this was the winning, against domestic competition, of a huge order from Trans Canada Airlines, later Air Canada, of Karrier Bantams. They were equipped, from the UK, with bodies and

An Air Canada Bantam with an Edghill Autostair aircraft steps body. JOHN MITCHELL, HUNTSVILLE, ONTARIO, CANADA

equipment for mobile stairs, aircraft fresh water supply, and aircraft sewage tank emptying. The order was won by Rootes Canada truck sales people, manager Les Hagell and his assistant, George Blane.

Peter recalls that many of these Karrier Bantams were still operating well into the 1970s but not all had British-built bodies.

> 'Some municipalities across Canada purchased Commer or Karrier trucks equipped with "gully emptier" vacuum equipment, manufactured by Sicard Inc. of Montreal, for cleaning out catch-basins and storm-sewers.'

Venezuela

Another Rootes pupil who would be offered a chance to work in an export territory was Geoff Parr. He had been sent to work at the Rootes dealership George Heath & Company in Birmingham after returning from Suez in 1956. He subsequently left after a year to work for Woolworths, but a chance meeting on the way to the railway station one day with the secretary to Harry Dearns, the director of training programmes at Rootes, resulted in Geoff being asked to go back to Rootes to take on a particular role in exports:

> 'I was sent overseas to do various jobs, but once I'd got established in the parts business, they sent me to Venezuela, because we sold a lot of cars and trucks [there], working with Shell in the Maracaibo oil wells ... [Rootes] found that when Shell sold off their vehicles and ordered more, the old vehicles found their way into the Venezuelan marketplace ... The people liked the product and the company realised they had a good opportunity to build a CKD plant.'

Rootes Venezuela was established in 1962. The plant had two production lines, one for Rootes and the other building Mercedes-Benz cars. Rootes had, by then, opened a depot in Caracas. The assembly plant was in Valencia, but in setting it up, according to Patrick Cook, they made the mistake of putting the same vehicles and spares in stock as the ones Shell was buying:

> 'They had an enormous overstock, so I was sent out to identify the overstock. I then had the job of going round the country to try and sell the spares stocks to the garages who were trying to service the Super Snipes and Commer trucks that Shell had sold off. We got the authority from Devonshire House to scrap a lot of stuff ... I did a similar exercise in Switzerland.'

Rootes Motors assembly plant at Valencia, Venezuela. NICK ROOTES

By 1963, the product line of this new Rootes venture had been decided and personnel were dispatched from Coventry to sell it. Patrick Cook was deemed to be an ideal choice to send to Venezuela to sell Rootes products. His father, Robert W.H. Cook, had been an experienced Rootes export sales manager with the company since 1927. He was assigned to Argentina in 1930 to successfully run the Buenos Aires operation and returned to Devonshire House in 1954. He retired in 1964, just as his son Patrick was getting his feet under the table in Venezuela. The Super Minx and the Imp formed the early product range, as did the Walk-thru van and the occasional Alpine. The Hunter would be a more successful product later on, but with Chrysler involvement, it would be sold alongside Plymouth Valiants and Dodge Polara cars from established Chrysler dealers, such as Zulia Motors, who had dealerships all over western Venezuela, as well as a big GM dealership in Maracaibo. Patrick Cook remembers that *'the Chrysler dealers took on Hillman as an additional product line'*.

In order for Rootes to set up their Venezuela operation in Valencia, a 'local connection' was an important ingredient, as Patrick Cook recalls:

'When they set up Rootes Venezuela in '62, they had a policy that they [would have] a local director and his name was Carlos Kaufmann. He was an Italian/Swiss, who arrived in Venezuela at the tail end of the war, and he was a very dynamic person – a good contact as far as Rootes were concerned. He was the contact who would deal with the government. When the original licence was given to Rootes to set up the plant, in some way he was involved. He was based in Caracas, not in Valencia. He would keep the Rootes image to the government in good order, talk to the right people when we needed licences for a new model [to be built].'

The first managing director was Geoffrey Ellison.

'He was a very good friend to Ellison over the years. He [Kaufmann] had a Volkswagen franchise in Caracas and was the Ferrari agent. He was a close friend of Enzo Ferrari. In those days, in the late Fifties, Venezuela had a Grand Prix [Gran Premio de Venezuela] – Stirling Moss raced there...'

Rootes products would continue to be sold in Venezuela until 1969, by which time Chrysler had taken over. Peter

Rapozo then headed up the Venezuelan operation after Geoffrey Ellison returned to the UK in 1968.

Patrick Cook remembers that Chrysler also used the plant to manufacture aluminium wheels and was manned by some ex-Rootes personnel:

> 'Chrysler offered jobs to all ex-pats who were still there. I went to Caracas and Alan Leach, who was the service manager of Rootes also came to Caracas and two or three stayed in Valencia working with Chrysler, who had built a modern assembly operation.
>
> 'When Chrysler closed in 1980, General Motors bought the Chrysler plant in Valencia, and they turned the Rootes plant into a parts warehouse ... I became MD of Chrysler Peru. 1980 was the end of the Chrysler–Rootes representation in all these markets.'

South Africa

In 1949, Rootes entered into an agreement with Atkinson-Oates Ltd, to build the Hillman Minx from CKD kits at their Paarden Eiland plant in Cape Town. In 1951, Humber and Commer were added and in 1956, assembly was transferred to a new assembly plant at nearby Elsies River, which was also leased to Chrysler.

Rootes had taken advantage, in 1949, of the pound currency being devalued by thirty per cent in relation to the US dollar. This gave a considerable price advantage and a forty-seven per cent market share to small British cars over the big American cars that had dominated the South African marketplace since the Forties. In February 1959, however, Chrysler South Africa (Pty) Ltd was formed and took over the Elsies River plant, forcing Rootes to look elsewhere. Assembly of Rootes cars, and its franchise, was transferred to Stanley Motors Ltd and their Natalspruit plant, near Alberton in the Transvaal.

As well as the Minx, the Hillman Imp was to be part of the CKD operation, and engineer David Lloyd was sent out to Alberton to test the Imp to ensure its suitability to local conditions:

> 'I went to South Africa a couple of times when we were selling the Imp there. They had a lot of dirt roads, but they were very well maintained and you could drive an Imp flat-out from the works at Alberton in the Transvaal, down to Frankfort, in the Free State. There was a 22 mile straight ... the dust was phenomenal. [The Imp air intake system had to be modified to cope with the dusty conditions.] It wasn't acceptable, so they put a pipe through the space between the inner and outer panel, and put an air intake in the door shut, because that was clear of dust.
>
> 'The boss man in South Africa was a 12th Lancer, Arthur Hutchinson. It was a big factory because South African regulations on imports were vastly favourable to CKD, compared with built up imports, and a lot of companies couldn't afford to put in an assembly plant of their own in the 60s. We were building Peugeot, Citroen, Rambler and later Porsche 356 kits, as well as Rootes ...'

Lloyd also developed a close relationship with the Stanley Motors operation, witnessing how Rootes got round the severe apartheid rules of the time:

> 'They weren't allowed to use blacks for skilled jobs because of apartheid, so they had a little school in a discreet corner of the factory and trained the black workers there, and gradually filtered them to the assembly lines. I had one black man working for me; he was a Basotho [from Lesotho]. He was desperate to learn, so it was worth taking the time and trouble to encourage him.'

In 1962, in order to avert a hostile takeover, Stanley Motors management approached Rootes to acquire a majority shareholding of sixty-nine per cent in their company. Brian Rootes was made chairman in 1963. The arrangement with Stanley Motors went well and continued until 1967, when Chrysler gained control of Rootes, and the Natalspruit assembly plant was sold to Peugeot. Assembly of Rootes cars continued until September 1969, moving then to Chrysler's Silverton plant, near Pretoria in 1970.

One of the last Isuzu Hillman Minx Cars, seen on display at the Tokyo Motor Show 1962.

Japan

In an interview with journalist Giles Chapman for *Classic and Sports Car* magazine, Ken Middleton, the Rootes engineering manager who had been sent out to oversee the building of Hillman Minx cars at Isuzu during the Fifties, talked of his disappointment of how Rootes, following his return to Coventry, had ignored the rise of the Japanese product in the early Sixties:

> *'They weren't interested in the Japanese, and cared even less about anything that could be learnt from them. It was all childish jibes about "flied lice" and "slanty eyes" … Some people in Rootes thought they were so clever, and whenever I said anything good about Japan or the Japanese, they said I'd been brainwashed. I'd been looking forward to explaining some of the things I'd learned, but they weren't interested.*
>
> *Rootes pocketed the royalties Isuzu paid for each replica Hillman Minx made until 1963 and then forgot about Japan.'*

This arrogance was not isolated to Rootes; it was an intransigence that had afflicted other sectors of the British motor industry, at a crucial time when the industry should have been responding quickly to the market changes in order to keep ahead of the game.

Europe

However, one export territory that the Rootes Group and other British manufacturers should have made significant sales to, but were prevented from doing so by political differences, was Europe. Not only were British cars more suitable for European ownership, due to similar climatic conditions and customer needs, major car buying nations such as France, West Germany, Holland and Italy were right on Britain's doorstep. British manufacturers such as Rootes, BMC and Triumph were unable to fully exploit any market potential for their products due to one factor – trade tariffs. Despite Britain being a member of the European Free Trade Association, the organisation that was formed to place non-member European countries on a more level playing field with member states, EFTA was inadequate for Britain's purposes in dealing with EEC trade tariffs.

There was one other sticking point to British cars being successful in Europe, and that was service and spares availability. According to Belgian journalist Paul

The new Sunbeam Alpine Series III GT introduction at the 1963 Geneva Motor Show. The 'Gran Turismo' had a new-style hardtop, but no hood. COVENTRY ARCHIVES

Frère, who mounted a scathing attack in an article in *Motor* magazine in December 1962, aimed at the British industry as a whole, but singling out Rootes as having inadequate service and back up facilities that made *'would-be buyers of Hillman Super Minxes usually turn to Peugeot and Renault'*. Frère did not, however, comment on the price disparity between French and British cars being sold in the Common Market, but although Rootes did sell a lot of cars in Switzerland from their concessionaire in Geneva, it is interesting to note that they still only had one main depot in France – in Paris; one in Germany in Dusseldorf and one in Italy, in Milan. This hardly constituted a serious European dealer network. The *Motor* article ended by remarking that *'the most successful exporter in Europe, Volkswagen, has laid down a policy of service before sales are begun in any new field'*.

Historian Ian Nicholls, who has written extensively about BMC and British Leyland, describes the widely held view that British cars were all badly built, badly designed and unsuitable for overseas road conditions as *'palpable nonsense'*. He too is of the opinion, backed up by hard facts, that Britain was *'prevented from competing on price in the larger EEC market by trade tariffs'*. He cites examples where 'budget' cars like the Mini 850 would be sold for 7,000 French francs, while French equivalents such as the Renault 4 sold for 5,000 French francs. Nicholls' comparisons for West Germany tell a similar tale. The price of a premium domestic product such as the BMW 1600 4 door Saloon, when compared with a Hillman Super Minx Saloon, is only 7.7 per cent more expensive than the imported Rootes product.

continued on page 124

LORD ROOTES – 1894–1964

Lord Rootes shares a joke with Prince Philip and future US President, Richard Nixon at the 1960 British Trade Fair in New York. NICK ROOTES

On 12 December 1964, Lord Rootes died at his London home in Shepherd's Close, aged 70. He had been in hospital at the London Clinic, where he was diagnosed with cancer of the liver. His condition deteriorated rapidly and although he was able to be transferred from the London Clinic to home, he died there soon afterwards. His funeral was held a few days later at Highgate Crematorium.

His son Geoffrey always considered that the shock of an accident he had in September 1964, *'accelerated the cancer which was probably latent'*. Lord Rootes had taken a holiday with his wife, Lady Ann. They had chartered a boat to go on a trip in the Mediterranean, during which he had an accident, when he slipped and fell down a companionway and hit his head. Although he appeared to recover, the fall indirectly hastened his death. Sadly Geoffrey and Brian's mother, Nora, who had continued to live at Stype after she and Lord Rootes had divorced, had also recently died. Geoffrey recalls in his memoir his feelings at the time:

> *'My father's death came as a great shock to me, particularly as my mother had also died two months earlier. I had a great affection and admiration for my father and was immensely proud of his great achievements. I missed him very much.'*

Genuine and affectionate tributes followed Lord Rootes' death. Sir William Lyons, chairman of Jaguar Cars, described him as:

> *'... a dynamic worker not only for the British motor industry, but for the country as a whole ... I know many people in many walks of life will be the poorer for his passing. We shall all miss him greatly.'*

> *'A great industrialist has passed from the British scene ... He will be greatly missed in Coventry where his name was so much a part of the industrial scene, but, even more in our national affairs where he was so outstanding a figure.'*
> – Maurice Edelman, Member of Parliament for Coventry North.

> *'Those who knew him personally will miss him because he was a wonderful character, with a sense of fun and an easy approach that endeared him to those who knew him. He has been a great figure in the city in so many ways, and we shall feel his loss.'*
> – Alderman Tom Whiteman, Lord Mayor of Coventry.

On 7 January, a memorial service was given at St Martin-in-the-Fields church in London. As well as the Rootes family, representatives of the Duke of Edinburgh and the Duchess of Kent were present and representatives of the whole of the British motor industry, motor sport personalities, and many of Britain's top industrialists and politicians.

The address was given by the Bishop of Coventry, Dr. Cuthbert Bardsley, who described Lord Rootes'

> *'boundless optimism, rich infectious joie de vivre, immense love of people and dynamic faith in man's intrinsic goodness and capacity to succeed – all combined to make him one of the great leaders of his generation.'*

One of Lord Rootes' proud achievements away from the Rootes Group was supporting the creation of the University of Warwick. He was chancellor-elect at the time of his death and campaigned tirelessly on behalf of the University as chairman of its Promotion Committee. The establishment of the University of Warwick was given approval by the government in 1961 and received its Royal Charter of Incorporation in 1965. Following the death of Lord Rootes, a memorial fund was established to enable students to carry out special projects that would otherwise not be affordable. The fund exists to this day.

DODGE BROTHERS (BRITAIN) LTD

In July 1928, the Dodge Brothers Company was acquired by the Chrysler Corporation. The following year, the Plymouth name was created and used on the Chrysler '50', and subsequently to represent Chrysler's 'low-priced' car lines. Another brand, Desoto, was introduced by Chrysler the same year to fill in the market gaps between Chrysler and Plymouth. The Desoto name was used on trucks for certain export markets, as well as that of Fargo, which was primarily used for heavy duty trucks and coaches.

Dodge had started to build a reputation for innovative and reliable cars, however, long before the Chrysler acquisition. Brothers John and Horace Dodge started building bicycles in 1899, after they left their birthplace in Niles, Michigan, to move to Windsor, Ontario. They then progressed to building car components in Hamtramck, Michigan, prior to going into car production in 1914, where the first Dodge automobile was made. Both brothers died in 1920, but the name of Dodge continued to be associated with rugged, dependable cars and trucks.

In Britain too, the Dodge name was fast gaining a reputation for quality vehicles. In May 1922, Dodge Brothers (Britain) Ltd. was formed as a wholly-owned subsidiary of Dodge Brothers Inc. The company's first factory was at Stevenage Road, Fulham, in south-west London. There, the parent company's cars and chassis were brought in fully assembled. Various chassis imported were fitted with special bodywork, including the 30cwt Graham truck chassis, bodies for these being supplied by various outside coachbuilders. By 1924, Graham Brothers truck chassis, with its Dodge powerplant and

English bodywork was proving to be a popular delivery van, and contributed considerably to Dodge Brothers' total sales to the British market of 1,552 vehicles. In May 1925, Dodge Brothers (Britain) Ltd moved to new premises at Park Royal, north-west London, which had enough space to accommodate a wood mill, body and paint shops and a chassis assembly line.

In the States, largely through the association of Dodge with the Graham Brothers company, based in Evansville, Indiana, the volume of commercial chassis had grown to twenty per cent of total Dodge output. After the death of John and Horace Dodge, the company had been operated by the Dodge heirs until 1925, when Graham Brothers Trucks joined the Dodge company. That same year, Dodge was bought by Dillon, Read & Company, a New York banking firm, for $146 million. On 30 July 1928, the company was purchased by Chrysler Corporation.

With the acquisition by Chrysler, it was decided to move Dodge Brothers to the Chrysler Motors premises at Kew, in order to concentrate on a range of Dodge cars and trucks for the British market. The trucks would be known as the Dodge Kew range.

During the war the factory made Dodge trucks for the Ministry of Supply and components for the Halifax bomber. The post-war period saw more concentration on the production of trucks, such as the 200 and 300 Series. The last trucks to be built at Kew prior to Dodge Brothers (Britain) Ltd becoming part of the Chrysler-backed Rootes Group were a batch of 500 Series tankers for Esso Petroleum.

The Dodge Brothers (Great Britain) stand 104 at the 1933 Olympia Motor Show had two examples of each of the 'Dodge Dependables', the Senior Six and the Victory Six.

CHAS K. BOWERS & SON

The Dodge 500 Series truck range was inherited from the Dodge Kew operation, but it was expanded and improved to be a successful heavy range of vehicles by the chassis engineers at Dunstable. This KT 900 six-wheeler tipper with a Telehoist 'Tel-lite' body is fitted with a Perkins V8-510 diesel engine, tandem drive and two-speed rear axle and power steering. It has a plated GVW range up to 24 tons.

ROOTES MARINE – OUTBOARD MOTORS AND MARINE DIESELS

In 1955, Rootes had formed a subsidiary company, R.L. Engineers Ltd, based in Maidstone, to build a range of marine and industrial diesel engines. Although the efforts at marketing stationary industrial diesel engines was not a success, a number of marinised versions of the TS3 opposed-piston two-stroke diesel engine known as the Rootes-Lister Blackstone TS3 were built and sold through Lister Blackstone Ltd. The Rootes Group's involvement in marine engines seemed short-lived, but was re-invigorated in the early Sixties when Rootes Marine Ltd was formed.

In 1963, Rootes Marine Ltd started to promote a range of outboard motors and inboard marine petrol engines based on the Super Snipe and Alpine car engines. Brian Rootes was always keen to promote new ideas and encourage diversification within Rootes. He had been responsible for instigating the acquisition of Tempair, the air conditioning company, into the Group and had seen the link for Rootes into marine engines, and in particular outboard motors, as a logical progression to their business.

Sianti undergoing sea trials. COVENTRY ARCHIVES

The two Super Snipe 6-cylinder marine engines used to power Sianti. COVENTRY ARCHIVES

The background to the Rootes outboard motor range is a curious one. In the late 1940s, the upmarket American

The Super Snipe Marine 6-cylinder, 3-litre engine had a gross 128bhp output. COVENTRY ARCHIVES

speedboat manufacturer Chris-Craft, based in Grand Rapids, Michigan, decided to go into building outboard motors, but in doing so, upset Mercury, who were one of the leading outboard motor specialists in America. Historian Lawrence Carpenter, writing in *Trailer Boats* magazine in June 1991, states that the animosity between Mercury and Chris-Craft rose when Mercury accused Chris-Craft of copying some of their designs after Chris-Craft had poached some Mercury engineers to help design their range of outboards. There are other stories as to why Chris-Craft decided to get out of the outboard business, but for whatever reasons, they got out. They built their last outboard in 1953 and sold their outboard designs to the Oliver Corporation in nearby Battle Creek, Michigan.

Oliver had been a major manufacturer of farm and industrial equipment, and so not a threat to established outboard builders. Between 1954 and 1957 they built a range of outboards which were gaining a good reputation, with the 35bhp Oliver Olympus model being the latest example of poppet-valve technology. However, a recession in the US in 1959 meant that Oliver did not have the financial clout to stay in business. Competitors such as Mercury, Johnson and Evinrude were building bigger, more powerful engines and pushing Oliver out of the frame, who were unable to meet the development costs of new engines. In order to remain in the outboard business, Oliver struck a deal with Perkins Ltd of Peterborough, England, for them to build their engines and ship them back to the US, as well as to sell re-badged versions in Europe. It was an odd arrangement, but in theory it should have worked. Oliver even stated in their 1960 adverts that their motors were *'American designed – British built…'* but quality control started to slip and so Oliver got out of the business and Perkins took on the range, but it was a very short-lived venture. The Rootes Group, seeing an opportunity to augment their range of inboard marine engines, decided to buy out the Perkins range. In 1963, Rootes was in the outboard motor business.

Ron Roscoe was a divisional sales manager running the Rootes Maidstone and Rochester depots, reporting to Brian Rootes:

> 'During that time, Brian [Rootes] rang me up and asked me to come up to Devonshire House. Brian said, "We're in the marine business. I want you to run it" ... the boat show was on and [he asked me] to go up to the show.
>
> 'Of course, it was just the other company's [engine] with a Rootes name on it. I tried to absorb myself in outboard motors, but I thought, this is not for me, so with my tail between my legs I went back the next week and said "Sorry", I didn't want this business.'

Ron Roscoe was not the only one who failed to gain enthusiasm for outboard motors. As the range was sold through coastal branches of the Robins & Day Group, rather than through specialist boat and marine dealers, car salesmen were expected to sell boat-related products, which they knew little about and had little interest in.

Responsibility for the Rootes Marine Ltd range was left to Desmond Rootes, as the Robins & Day sales manager, but it failed to have any significant impact in the boating world and by the mid-Sixties, the range was sold off to the British Anzani Engineering Co. Ltd. Although British Anzani was an established builder of outboard engines, within a few years, they too would cease to be in the outboard business.

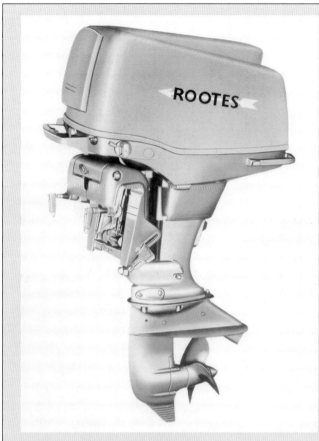

The Rootes 40bhp outboard motor. COVENTRY ARCHIVES

The Rootes Marine 1.6-litre Alpine engine was offered complete with heat exchangers, water-cooled exhaust manifolds, oil cooler in the engine sump, sea water pump, sump emptying pump, carburettor flame trap and flexible mounting feet. COVENTRY ARCHIVES

The Rootes Marine stand at the International Boat Show in 1965. COVENTRY ARCHIVES

999 EMERGENCY! ROOTES FIRE, POLICE AND AMBULANCE CONVERSIONS

A 'Special Equipment Operations' fire tender on a Dodge K850 chassis/cab and fitted with HCB Angus bodywork.
RENAULT VI LTD

From around 1968, Dodge 500 Series 'K' chassis was starting to be specified by more fire brigades as an ideal base for fire-fighting vehicles. This Berkshire Fire Brigade version has bodywork by Carmichael and is fitted with an Orbitor 72 foot (21.94 metres) hydraulic platform by the Swedish company Wibe.

Dodge 500 Series K850 chassis/cab with Carmichael water tender body. The Commercial Vehicle Division at Dunstable had experienced municipal sales managers such as Freddie Best and Sid Cooper and Roland Browne, who formed the Special Equipment Operation at Dunstable, to liaise directly with fire brigades and other municipal customers.

The Dodge 100 Series Commando range was introduced in 1974 as the Commer Commando. As the 500 Series started to be run out in the late Seventies, the 100 Series, seen here in a Carmichael-bodied Dodge fire tender with hydraulic platform, started to be specified by more fire brigades. The car product range also provided the basis for in-house conversions by Rootes Maidstone of Hillman and Humber estate car models to either ambulance or police specification. The police requirements were dealt with by fleet sales manager Peter Dobson.

A Humber Super Snipe Series 2 Estate Metropolitan Police demonstrator. As well as the Met, the Super Snipe Estate was used by many police forces, including Kent County, Sussex and Hampshire. Northamptonshire and Hertfordshire used them as M1 motorway patrol cars to replace the Ford Zephyr Farnham Estates, which had been in service since 1959. POST VINTAGE HUMBER CAR CLUB

As emergency response vehicles, police specification Super Snipes were equipped with the usual blue roof beacon, roof-mounted spotlights, 'Winkworth' bell and heavy-duty suspension. Emergency equipment, road signs, bollards and first-aid boxes could be stored in an interior storage unit in lieu of a rear seat. POST VINTAGE HUMBER CAR CLUB

In the interior of a police specification Super Snipe, a two-way radio was mounted in the glove box, minus lid. Humber also offered three different transmissions – three-speed column-mounted change, Borg-Warner automatic or floor-mounted four-speed, as shown here. Post Vintage Humber Car Club (Thanks to Humber historian Stephen Lewis and ex-police officer turned motoring journalist Ant Anstead for additional information on Humber police cars).

Rootes Maidstone ambulance conversions based on the Commer 1500 and 2500 Series van were primarily built as patient transport vehicles, as well as more specialist conversions by companies such as Lomas or Walker. Illustrated is a Commer-Lomas Junior on a 1500 Series 2 chassis. All could be fitted out with full stretcher equipment and were offered with fitted roller blinds behind driver's seat and rear doors as options.

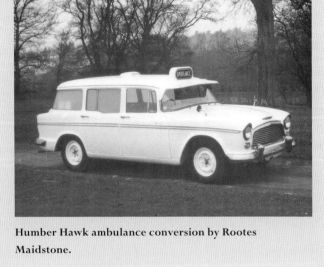

Humber Hawk ambulance conversion by Rootes Maidstone.

A Karrier-Dennis KA30 Walk-thru ambulance. Diesel or petrol engine options were initially available but the Perkins 4.203 diesel became standard following the withdrawal of the 6P.181 in-line six in 1966. The Karrier chassis was built in conjunction with municipal vehicle specialist Dennis of Guildford. The interior was fitted with Lomas stretcher equipment and featured two wide rear doors for easy entry and exit.

Hillman Super Minx Mark 2 ambulance conversion by Rootes Maidstone.

continued from page 117

We could of course argue that the same price disparity is placed on the German import into Britain, once UK import duties and taxes are implemented: in 1965, a BMW 1600 four-door Saloon in Britain was 71.5 per cent more expensive than a Hillman Super Minx Mark III Saloon. These statistics, however, become less relevant set against the backdrop of Britain importing increasingly more cars from Europe than it was exporting to Europe.

Negotiations had started in October 1961, led by Edward Heath, for Britain's entry into the EEC, but in January 1963, President de Gaulle of France held a press conference in Paris, declaring that France would veto Britain's entry into the EEC, and fifteen days later, they did. In 1967, Harold Wilson led a half-hearted attempt to join the EEC again, but failed. It was left to Heath's efforts to secure Britain's entry into the EEC in 1971, by which time it was too late – a whole decade of potential business for Britain's motor manufacturing industry had been lost. Although more conservatively styled than some contemporary counterparts, the Hillman, Singer and Sunbeam ranges had an appeal which was none the less attractive to continental buyers. The challenge of marketing in export territories was one that Rootes were more than up to, and with the right planning and investment, could have made sure the parts and service backup was adequate for the demand. Although it is unlikely that they would have had the production capacity to respond to vastly increased sales to Europe, profitability on car sales in Europe would have been far higher than on sales of cars sent halfway around the globe!

On 19 January 1965, new appointments and organisational changes were announced: Sir Reginald Rootes was appointed chairman, with Geoffrey, now 2nd Lord Rootes, as deputy chairman, continuing as managing director of Rootes Motors Ltd. The Rootes Group was effectively split into three divisions, each with their own managing director. Brian Rootes, managing director of overseas operations and home distributing companies; Timothy Rootes, managing director of passenger car division; and Rex Watson Lee, who continued as managing director of the commercial vehicle division at Luton, which would soon have a new brand incorporated within it – Dodge.

On the export front, John T. Panks, vice-president and managing director of Rootes Motors Inc., New York, was made managing director of the export division of Rootes Ltd, and Malcolm A. Freshney, managing director of Rootes Motors (Canada) Ltd, was made managing director of Rootes Motors Inc. He was replaced by E.J.B. Mackie, who had been an executive at Rootes, New York.

Part of the agreement between Rootes and Chrysler was that Rootes would acquire the Chrysler subsidiary Dodge Brothers (Britain) Ltd. In April 1965, a letter was issued to Rootes shareholders recommending that the share capital to Chrysler be increased to forty-six per cent of Ordinary (voting) shares and sixty-five per cent of 'A' non-voting shares, '*if we are to take full advantage of the opportunities which arise consequent on the acquisition of the Dodge interests and for the normal development of the Group's products and facilities*'.

In February 1965, Rootes issued a press release stating that they had acquired Dodge and its manufacturing facility at Kew. Soon after Dodge was incorporated into the Rootes Group, the board realized that the financial picture was not as good as they had been led to believe. But, as agreed, the Dodge product would be sold alongside Commer and Karrier. As Commer had tended to specialise in the light and medium weight range of vehicles and Dodge had concentrated more on the medium and heavy end of the market, it

seemed sensible to integrate Commer and Dodge dealer networks. Eventually, the Dodge plant at Kew would be closed and Dodge production transferred to Dunstable.

Following the death of Lord Rootes, the responsibilities of the now sprawling Rootes empire were well and truly placed on Geoffrey Rootes' shoulders, but it was a responsibility that he embraced with characteristic enthusiasm and optimism.

In March 1965, the second Lord Rootes took his seat in the House of Lords and, as part of his inheritance, took on North Standen House, near Hungerford, Berkshire, which had 1500 acres of farmland and woodland, and a small part-Georgian farmhouse in semi-derelict condition. It was decided that the house would be extended and renovated with a view to the family relocating from Ladbroke Hall, which was eventually sold.

In the early Sixties, Brian Rootes' family moved from their house in Holland Park, South Kensington, to Flaunden House, Hertfordshire and remained there until 1966, when they moved to Ashington Stud with a view to breeding racehorses. But it was a short stay, as Rootes business took precedence over racehorses and they subsequently moved into a London property that had been leased by Brian's father from the Grosvenor Estate, in Woods Mews. It was decided to split the house into two flats and Brian and Bet had the upstairs flat with Geoffrey and Marian in the downstairs flat. An arrangement between the brothers concerning the late Lord Rootes' estate at Glenalmond in Perthshire was that it too would be split: Geoffrey would take on the main house and the portion of the estate to the east and Brian would take a secondary house on the west called Dallick. Brian '*also had the two best grouse beats, Corriehenzie and West Corrienmuckloch, and I had the remaining grouse ground and all of the low ground, with the exception of a small area adjacent to Dallick.*' It was also arranged that Lord Rootes' estate in Wiltshire, Ramsbury Manor, would be sold. The house and estate was bought by property developer Harry Hyams.

Timothy Rootes had immersed himself in Rootes business during the period following his uncle's death. He still lived in a house he had bought during the late Fifties in Oxfordshire, Barn House at Alkerton. His father, Sir Reginald, had decided to have a house built, with extensive farmland, at Hothfield, near Ashford in Kent, named Polla House. He moved there in the early Sixties, from Rumwood, the house he had lived at since 1936. Sir Reginald also kept up his Scottish estate at Loch Eriboll, near Durness, in what was Sutherland, now Highlands, and was now starting to take more of a non-executive role in the company, leaving the new generation to earn their stripes.

The last Audax Gazelle model was the Series VI. Although it hadn't graduated to alternator charging, it benefited from negative earth electrics, synchromesh gearbox, 1725 power and the usual Singer luxury touches, which made the car an attractive proposition for Singer customers between 1965 and early '67.

The cast-iron head version of the 1725 engine used in Minx and Gazelle Series VI. COVENTRY ARCHIVES

In 1965, Rootes would have 11.9 per cent of the UK market, still slightly ahead of Vauxhall at 11.8 per cent, placing them third behind BMC and Ford, but with a lower output volume in '65 by some 34,000 vehicles, including exports. Meanwhile, imports in 1965 represented 5.1 per cent of the market and were increasing, and not just from North America. The increase in production output and sales in 1964 did see Rootes getting back into the black with a pre-tax profit of £1.8 million, which was wiped out in 1965 as red ink again appeared in the books, with a loss of £200,000. Rootes may have been number three in the charts, but their financial position was still precarious, compared to that of rival BMC, who in 1965 had generated a pre-tax profit of £23.3 million.

Also in 1965, Singer Motors celebrated its sixtieth year as a car maker, and the model line up introduced in September 1965 was considered by some to be the finest ever Singer range; the Chamois Mark 2 and the

Gazelle Series VI and Vogue Mark IV, both now with the new five-bearing 1725 cc engine and a new 4-speed synchromesh gearbox, made the product range highly saleable. The Vogue engine was the same version of the Sunbeam and Humber versions with an aluminium cylinder head, power output of 85bhp at 5,500rpm and a Solex compound twin choke carburettor. But much like the Super Minx Mark IV, with the exception of a small '1725' badge on the front wings, outwardly they looked the same as before. However, the Gazelle now had a new full-width stainless grille, which replaced the oval grille on the Series V model that lifted with the bonnet.

During this period, Singer Motors still had its own dealer network, away from other Rootes brands, although most of the other traditional Rootes dealerships would offer Singer as well as Hillman, Humber and Sunbeam. Some of the main dealers also offered Commer and Karrier. The Singer sales department, under sales manager Jack Caddy and department manager Bill Boss, would remain autonomous until 1967. Doug Field joined the Singer sales department in 1964, and had a lot of success with the range, initially covering the West Country and from 1966 covering the Northern territory of Cheshire, North Wales and Lancashire. He not only dealt with main dealers but also set up new retail dealers, some in remote locations. One such dealer, based in Dorset, who was persuaded by Doug to put a Gazelle on display in their small garage showroom, which at the time had servicing, a petrol forecourt and an accessory shop, ended up becoming one of the biggest car dealership chains in the West Country – the Olds Motor Group in Dorchester. Doug's success in selling Singer cars also gained him the top prize in the sales incentive scheme in 1967, for achieving 167 per cent of his sales target.

Greater power—
higher performance
new SUNBEAM *Alpine*

Alpine brochure announcing 1725 power.

The Sunbeam Rapier still
looked good, eight years
after it was introduced, and
performed even better with
the new 1725 engine.

EXTRA POWER, EXCITING PERFORMANCE
SUNBEAM RAPIER

The new front end styling of the Sceptre Mark 2, featuring Super Minx headlamps, side lights and front wings.

The performance of the '66 Singer range and the other Rootes cars fitted with the new 1725 engine, the Hillman Minx Series VI and Super Minx Mark IV, received some very favourable comments from the press, as did the Sunbeam Rapier Series V and the Alpine Series V. Fitted with twin Stromberg 150 CD carburettors, the Alpine put out 92.5bhp at 5,500rpm and was capable of virtually matching the 0–50mph speed of the Triumph TR4A at 8.5 seconds, and *Autocar* topped off its summing up by stating:

'Compared with its predecessors, this Alpine, with its 1725 cc engine, has noticeably more performance, produced without increase in engine noise and with less harshness at high rpm. It is better appointed than most sports two-seaters ...'

As for the Rapier, the increase in power was:

'... immediately appreciable ... smart and up to date ... [seems to be] one of the strongest cars in its capacity class.'

For a car that had seen no major body style changes for eight years, this was quite an accolade.

The new engine had been a long time in the making, and it wasn't just a lengthened stroke version of the 1592cc engine. Since 1960, when the first castings were made, it had received a lot of input from Rootes engineers. The result was a smoother, five main bearing overhead valve engine that was lighter in weight and of similar outside dimensions to the 1592cc engine it replaced. Most models received alternators, although the Hillman models had to plod on until mid-year before they got rid of their dynamos, and Series VI Minx and Gazelle models continued with dynamos until their runout at the end of '67.

The only member of the class of '66 to get a re-styling of any sort was the Humber Sceptre. Launched at the 42nd Frankfurt Motor Show in Germany, it too received the new engine and transmission as well as a new front end, the aim being that it would not only be less complicated to build, but less expensive. The new Sceptre now proudly lived up to its description of 'Sports saloon'. Design engineer Alan Horsfall and Ron Wisdom from the Styling department consolidated the restyle. In order to rationalise parts in an effort to reduce production costs, Super Minx front wings, headlamps and sidelights were used:

'I did a facelift on the Humber Sceptre and I worked closely with Ron Wisdom at the time. We went from twin 5¾in headlamps to 7in headlamps with inboard 5¾in. lamps. It was probably my first job, that front end.

'I was given a verbal brief: use the front wing of the Super Minx; we mocked up a grille – that was the first concept that the stylists had created and my job was to measure it and then go upstairs into engineering and put it together as closely [as possible to] their ideas.

'The other thing was creating the surfaces for the centre grille and getting people in to see how it could be made, and that presented a huge amount of problems. On reflection, I think it must have been horrendously expensive. At the time, we were influenced by the Rover 2000. They had an extruded aluminium grille with twin headlamps...'

Nearly 12,000 units of the Mark 2 Sceptre were built. According to the Rootes Group production figures, the company built 180,269 cars during the 1966 calendar year and 31,175 trucks. Around 3,759 were Sunbeam Rapier Series V's and 10,329 Mark IV Singer Vogues. Profits however, were non-existent; the Group recording a pre-tax loss of £3.1 million. The loss would have serious consequences for the Rootes Group's future survival. The poignant significance of the 1966 model year line-up was that it would be the last product range offered by the Rootes Group as an independent, wholly British-owned car manufacturer.

CHAPTER 6

KEEPING PACE – TIGER AND HUNTER

'The Tiger was just a fantastic car … fantastic torque from that V8 engine. The Hunter was a very good family car … well engineered … a fine car.'

— Andrew Cowan – Rootes works rally driver

The change in the Rootes senior management structure that had occurred early in 1965 had a knock-on effect throughout the whole group during that year. Peter Wilson was made deputy chief executive engineer at Humber Ltd, responsible to Peter Ware, chief executive engineer. Leo Kuzmicki became chief co-ordinating engineer of Group power units and W.S. (Stan) Taylor was made head of Ryton engineering. Harry Sheron was made head of passenger car design, and would oversee much of the Arrow project and S.W. (Bill) Oliver became head of the experimental department. All of the new appointments were responsible to Peter Wilson.

As well as technical management, sales management within Rootes Ltd, based at Devonshire House, was moved around. George Hartwell, who had been a director of Rootes Ltd (Home Division) since 1962, was made managing director and Geoff Rossiter, who had been a director of Rootes Ltd since 1956, mainly on the service side of the business, joined the headquarters staff as an administrative director.

GRABBING THE TIGER BY ITS TAIL

Initially aimed at the American market, the Sunbeam Tiger was 'unleashed', to quote Rootes advertising parlance, on an unsuspecting British public in March 1965… a Rootes sports car with an American V8 engine, whatever next?

The concept of shoehorning an American V8 engine into a lightweight sports tourer body was not new. In order to obtain maximum performance from a road-going sports car, manufacturers had been doing it for years: in 1952, Sydney Allard came first overall in the Monte Carlo Rally in his Cadillac V8-powered Allard,

beating Stirling Moss into second position in his under-powered Sunbeam-Talbot 90. Jensen Motors went the V8 route in 1962 when they launched their CV-8 Saloon, fitted with a Chrysler small block V8 and Torqueflite transmission, to replace their 6-cylinder 541 models. Perhaps the most famous V8 transformation occurred with the AC Ace, the little Bristol-engined 6-cylinder, two-seater sports from Thames Ditton that became a pavement pounding legend called the Cobra, when it received a Ford 260 cubic inch V8 and a degree of breathing upon by American race car builder Carroll Shelby. It is this car that the Sunbeam Tiger owes much of its bloodline to.

The idea behind the Tiger came from Ian Garrad, the Rootes Group's American-based West Coast sales manager. While talking with Jack Brabham about the Alpine's performance limitations in October 1962 at

The Sunbeam Tiger in right-hand-drive form, at the 1965 Earl's Court Motor Show.

Riverside, California, when Brabham and Stirling Moss came third overall and first in the production car class in an Alpine, Brabham mentioned to Ian Garrad that 'a V8 might fit in the Alpine...' as a possible solution to giving the Alpine more power, without Rootes having to design and build a new engine.

The germ of an idea quickly took on distinct possibilities in Ian's mind. Upon his return to Los Angeles he sent Rootes' Western service manager Walter McKenzie out to measure up small-block V8s to see if any would fit the Alpine. McKenzie visited various GM dealerships – Chevrolet, Buick, Pontiac, Oldsmobile, as well as a Chrysler-Plymouth dealer and finally Ford. To his delight, McKenzie was able to report back to Garrad that Ford's 260 cubic inch small-block V8 that was available on the '62 Fairlane, would fit. The die was cast!

Prior to this, Ian's father, Norman Garrad, the Rootes competitions manager, and his boss Brian Rootes, were also keen to out-source an alternative engine for the Alpine, and had approached Ferrari, following an introduction by racing driver Peter Collins. A 1.9-litre V6 twin-cam engine was apparently discussed and although Enzo Ferrari seemed initially keen on the collaboration, at the last minute he backed out, leaving Norman Garrad and Brian Rootes to high tail it back to Coventry empty-handed.

Back in California, Ian Garrad was endeavouring to prove that his idea would work. He knew there was more than an outside chance that the 260 V8 would do the job – it was powerful, lightweight and it was compact, but he needed to make the idea a reality.

Bill Carroll, the West Coast editor of *Automotive News*, suggested asking Carroll Shelby first. Ian wasted no time and went straight over to the Shelby-American, Inc facility in Venice, California. The two talked about the possibilities, and negotiations sped up with input from Ray Geddes, of Ford Motor Company, who was working with Shelby on the Cobra programme. Shelby was sure that he could make the 260 work in the Alpine as he had with the Cobra. Garrad's next hurdle was to convince his boss, Brian Rootes, that his idea was sound.

In Bill Carroll's account of the story, he tells of Ian's pitch to his boss Brian Rootes, following a Rootes dealer convention in San Francisco in February 1963. In Ian's words:

'Brian was a wonderful man, part executive, part engineer, top salesman and most of all, a man with keen insight of overall automotive marketing strategy.'

Ian carefully outlined his plan, by which time it was near 4 o'clock in the morning. After a few penetrating questions, Brian responded 'It's a bloody good idea!'

Within a few hours and little sleep, the two bleary-eyed hopefuls set off on a flight to see Carroll Shelby. The subsequent meeting resulted in Shelby-American, Inc becoming an unofficial Rootes' engineering consultant, for a budget of $10,000. Brian Rootes would use funds from the Rootes advertising budget to pay Shelby-American. The deal was finalized by March '63, but Brian had to think of a way of keeping the news away from the 'old man' long enough to be able to present Lord Rootes with a workable proposition. He needn't have worried, as Carroll Shelby set to the task with his customary speed and alacrity. Shelby not only had to install an engine, but he also had to modify brakes, suspension and steering to cope with the torque and output of the 260 V8. Work commenced on a white, late-1962 Series II Alpine which was used as the donor car. Shelby promised he would have a car ready in eight weeks. George Boskoff did most of the conversion work and Phil Remington supervised the project.

During the ensuing period, Ian Garrad found it difficult to contain his enthusiasm for a V8 Alpine and decided to approach British race car driver and ace mechanic Ken Miles, and asked Miles if he could also put a 260 V8 in an Alpine if he provided a donor car. Garrad felt that Miles' experience prepping and racing Alpines would be useful, and with a meagre budget of $800, Miles performed the Alpine transplant in just one week, but without some of the 'niceties' that Shelby was installing in his prototype, such as rack and pinion steering. Miles also installed an automatic transmission, whereas the Shelby car had a Borg-Warner T-10 manual box and a Ford Galaxie rear axle.

By the end of April 1963, Ian Garrad was in possession of two V8 Alpines. He had shown the Miles version to Shelby, which proved to be a useful prototype, but it was the Carrol Shelby version which would be the template for the V8 Alpine. Ken Miles subsequently went to work for Shelby-American on the GT40 project. John Panks, the boss of Rootes Motors, Inc was in on the project and witnessed the handover from Shelby-American, but both he and Ian Garrad wanted to be sure that the V8 Alpine was fit to be presented to Rootes 'top brass'. Garrad and Panks subsequently put in excess of 30,000 miles on the prototype during the following two months. In July 1963, they were ready to send the car to England. John Panks gave the car the name 'Thunderbolt', as he thought it suited it. Thunderbolt was duly put aboard a Japanese fruit freighter full of bananas from Central America, bound for Southampton. In order to ensure their additional automotive cargo arrived without being damaged, Ian Garrad apparently slipped the mate $20 to make sure it arrived in perfect condition. It did, and when Ian Garrad and his brother Lewis went to pick up the car, it started first time and was loaded onto a truck and sent up to Coventry, in readiness for its debut appearance for, hopefully, Lord Rootes' approval.

During the development period of the Alpine V8 in California, absolute secrecy had surrounded the car and its true identity, even down to it only having a single exhaust outlet at the rear. Once in England, even greater secrecy was needed, in order to keep inquisitive eyes away from the new car, and this extended to the small circle of people involved in its creation. Ian Garrad, Brian Rootes, John Panks and Ian's father, Norman Garrad, were the only senior Rootes management to be involved with the car during the initial stages of its development. Head of experimental department Peter Wilson drove the car prior to the appointment with Lord Rootes and insisted that chief executive engineer Peter Ware drive the car as well. Both of them loved it and so did all of the other Rootes engineers involved. It was unanimous that this was no 'California knife and fork job'!

So came the day when the V8 Alpine would be shown to Lord Rootes: 8 o'clock on a Monday morning in July 1963, according to Lewis Garrad, who was present. Lord Rootes and his entourage, which included Sir Reginald, Brian Rootes, Timothy Rootes and Peter Ware, came down the main hall and walked into the car park to where the V8 Alpine was parked. Bill Carroll's description of how the event unfolded captures the atmosphere on that Monday morning at Ryton:

> '"They had been talking about the Alpine V8 project upstairs in Lord Rootes' office", Norman [Garrad] commented, "and I believe that's where Brian won his battle to get the old man on his side."'

After carefully and quietly inspecting the car and asking some technical questions, only then did Lord Rootes consider taking a test drive. Norman Garrad:

> 'Lord Rootes was a businessman first and an automotive man second. For us to get him to drive a sports car was as far fetched as getting him to go swimming without a bathing suit.'

Bill Carroll's account of the test drive is as follows:

> 'Lord Rootes started the engine and idled out of the main gate. Not one to take chances, he'd somehow told his chauffeur to follow him in the family's Humber limousine. Though they left the factory in close order, heading towards London, the moment Lord Rootes hit the V8's throttle the Humber was left far behind. In a few minutes the chauffeur returned, parked the limousine and approached the waiting group while shaking his head in amazement. "I've lost the old man", he announced despairingly!'

Lord Rootes had shot off at full speed. He apparently drove straight over a newly grassed roundabout, up a few side roads, before deciding to aim the car back to his offices, returning through a back entrance to the site. Upon arrival back at the Ryton offices, Lord Rootes switched off the engine, and following a meditative pause, turned round and said, 'All right, we'll make it.'

Ian Garrad and father Norman glowed with pride that day and Lord Rootes wasted no time in confirming his commitment to the V8 Alpine. Before even reaching his office, he grabbed the first telephone he saw, and summoned his secretary to get hold of a friend of his – Henry Ford. Bill Carroll's version of how Lord Rootes placed the largest ever order of automotive engines to the Ford Motor Company, by another car maker, is that Ford was eventually tracked down aboard his yacht sailing the Mediterranean off the south of France. Other accounts state that he was sailing in the Bahamas. A radio telephone conversation between the two auto executives resulted in Lord Rootes and Henry Ford sealing the deal, which was initially for 4,000 units. There was apparently much more subsequent effort needed to make the deal a reality. Lord Rootes was referred to Lee Iacocca, vice-president of Ford Motor Company, who, according to Tiger historian Graham Vickery, was not keen on supplying Rootes, fearing competition with his new Mustang. John Panks was apparently brought in to arbitrate and managed to smooth things over with Iacocca.

The 260 V8 was also in full production, being available not only on the Ford Fairlane 500, but on the '63 Falcon Futura Sprint, as well as an option on its sister ship, the Mercury Comet. Although the 260 engine was due to be replaced by the 289 for the 1964 model year, Ford still had some demand for the 260 and kept it in production for the Tiger. Another key point to the power unit's viability was that it was available as a 'crate' engine from Ford's Canadian Windsor plant with an export code.

Tiger AF3, still badged as an Alpine V8, had been sent to Carroll Shelby for SCCA race evaluation. Lew Spencer won the Class B production event in the Pacific Coast Divisional Championship Races at Willow Springs, California in 1964. Spencer finished twelve seconds ahead of the second-place car, a Jaguar XKE, as well as C1 and C2 Corvettes and Cobras.
COVENTRY ARCHIVES

It was Lord Rootes who decided on the name Tiger, after Louis Coatalen's famous Sunbeam Tiger of 1925. John Panks' Thunderbolt name was chosen as an interim name, but once development was under way, it was known internally as 'Sunbeam Alpine 260'. The Tiger had been conceived and would now soon be born.

BUILDING THE TIGERS

As with the Alpine, prototype bodies and eventually production bodies would be assembled and trimmed at Pressed Steel in Cowley. The car would then be sent up to Coventry for final assembly, but it was felt such a specialised job would disrupt normal Alpine production, so an alternative out-sourced final assembly operation had to be found. Jensen Motors, at West Bromwich, who had been assembling Austin-Healey 3000s for BMC and the Volvo P1800, was a good choice for many reasons. In the summer of 1963, the first eight 260 V8 engines were ordered from Ford and fitted into prototype/pre-production Tigers, known as AF cars (Alpine Ford). The first AF car was completed in November 1963. Known as AF1/Project 870, it was the prototype built by Rootes Engineering, and sent to Lister's to be modified as a Le Mans race car. In December 1963, ten Series IV Alpines were sent from Ryton to Jensen, minus engines and transmissions for assembly as AF cars. All were completed around January and February 1964, to start endurance tests, or as

pre-production pilot cars. By March 1964, ten AF cars based on the Alpine Series IV platform had been built, of which two were production cars, plus two Series III Alpines; twelve in total.

Once testing, performance, handling, safety and any quality issues had been addressed and overcome, the job of building the car in the most cost-effective and efficient way came down to production engineering staff at Jensen, but with very close liaison with the Rootes engineering staff. Once production commenced, Pressed Steel would build Alpine bodies with ID plates 'SAL' (Sunbeam Assembly Line), which would be despatched to Ryton and Tigers with 'JAL' plates (Jensen Assembly Line), which would be despatched direct to Jensen.

During this period, the Tiger was tested by the Rootes family, including a comparison test by Geoffrey Rootes, with the E-Type Jaguar, as Nick Rootes remembers:

'My father ordered an E-Type Jaguar, and we took it out on the M1 and it did 145 miles an hour, and then we tried a Tiger – it wasn't as fast, but it was fun!'

Project engineer for the Tiger was Alec Caine, an ideal candidate who had been heavily involved with problem solving as project engineer on the Alpine. He reported to engineering chief executive, Peter Ware, and a small team which included chief test engineer Don Tarbun, would report to Peter Wilson as head of experimental. This was prior to Peter Wilson becoming deputy to Peter Ware.

Tiger development car AF-6, a Series IV GT car, complete with wire wheels, at the Rootes Stoke Humber Road site in 1964. The car was registered on 17 June 1964, and ended up with a Ford 289 V8 engine as an official motorised 'test bed' for Tiger Mark 2 performance figures.

SUNBEAM TIGER CLUB

Tiger development car number AF-7 in March 1964, was also based on a Series IV Alpine. This car was used extensively by Humber Engineering Department and as a Mark 2 mock-up.

SUNBEAM TIGER CLUB

Mike Jones, who had started out as a Rootes pupil in 1955 was the chassis project manager (later to become chief engineer) at Jensen Motors, and proved an ideal technical liaison link between Rootes and Jensen:

'I started at Jensen [in February 1964] when most of the early prototype Tigers had been built. I wasn't involved in the early days ... All the Tiger build was done by Jensen ... I saw the engineering shop full of prototypes. I think we built about eleven of them. They were all called AF1, AF2, 3, 4, etc. ... Rootes took cars to Europe, they took cars to MIRA [Motor Industry Research Association at Nuneaton], they did cold weather testing, hot weather testing ... we didn't do any of that. It's not often realised that Rootes did the majority of the

testing. We merely built the prototypes and did a superficial evaluation of them to sort out minor problems.'

Two of the AF cars were retained by Jensen for evaluation and Mike Jones recalls an impromptu visit to the body shop for AF4 following a crash:

'Two of the AF prototypes were not shipped immediately. These were retained at Jensen for a couple for weeks as "Engineering Reference" cars. My boss, chief engineer Kevin Beattie, and I often used these cars to get to and from our homes, "debugging" them in the process. Unfortunately, the red prototype, I think it was AF 4, was badly damaged in a roll-over accident, in which I was the driver. I expected to be fired, but luckily the accident investigators decided that I was not the cause of the accident. The car was accordingly taken off the prototype test fleet for many months for body repair, eventually coming back to Jensen for installation of a De Dion rear suspension.

'I was involved with the late build and testing in conjunction with Rootes. Jensen essentially did the prototype engineering and prototype build, and finally the setting up of the Jensen factory for volume production.'

Fortunately for Rootes, Jensen had just finished building the Volvo P1800 and so had a ready-made production line.

Mike Jones, who was project manager, was an ideal candidate for the job as he was originally from Rootes, having served his apprenticeship there, so he knew how Rootes operated:

'My main role was to cover all the chassis and mechanical aspects ... but of course I had to work closely with the Rootes people, and one of the reasons I was so closely connected with the Tiger was because I was from Rootes, and I knew the system. When I was at Rootes my immediate boss was Tom Jump – he was chief engineer at Stoke. He was on the point of retiring but I had a couple of years with him, and I had access to all the design and development staff, which was pretty big in those days. It was a fabulous job for a young man and I think it was thanks to the pupilage that I got into that position.

'So, when I went to Jensen, the liaison and personality thing was absolutely ideal. The folks we had to deal with were Alec Caine and Don Tarbun, who was the test man, who did a lot of the testing that Jensen didn't do. Communication was excellent; a lot of it was done on the phone and we had a minimum of paperwork. Rootes were closely involved – Jensen didn't have a free rein. We had to work to the Rootes system of paperwork and releasing of all of the parts and it was closely monitored by the Rootes guys.'

SUNBEAM TIGER MARK I (1964) SPECIFICATIONS

An English seaside publicity shot for the Tiger Mark 1.

ROOTES ARCHIVE CENTRE TRUST

UK Sunbeam Tiger brochure cover from 1965.

Body style
Two-seater sports tourer, unitary construction

Engine
V8 (Ford) (eight cylinders in 90 deg. V) pushrod, overhead valve, lightweight thin-walled cast-iron block design; Five main bearing crankshaft; Hydraulic lifters; Positive crankcase ventilation system. Dual exhaust system

Power output:	260cu in (4261cc) developing 164bhp at 4,400rpm
Bore and Stroke:	3.80 x 2 87in. (96.5 x 73mm)
Compression ratio:	8.8:1
Torque:	258lb ft at 2,200rpm*
Fuel pump type:	S.U. Electric (AUF.301)
Carburettor:	Ford 2-barrel with automatic choke
Cooling system:	Water – centrifugal pump and fan. Crossflow radiator

Transmission
Borg-Warner T-10 four-speed all-synchromesh close-ratio gearbox, short centre floor-change lever (first 56 – later models fitted with Ford HEH-E or HEH-B gearbox)

Clutch:	10in (254mm) diameter single dry plate type. Hydraulic operation.
Gear Ratios:	Top 2.88:1; third 3.715:1; Second 4.867:1; First 6.68:1; Reverse 6.68:1.
Final drive:	Salisbury semi-floating rear axle with hypoid final drive. Axle ratio 2.88:1

A sectioned brochure illustration of the Ford 260 cu in V8.

Electrical and Lighting

Ignition:	Coil and distributor with air-cooled distributor points; centrifugal vacuum advance; dynamo; 18 mm 'turbo-action' spark plugs. 12-volt 67-amp battery.
Lighting:	Two sealed-beam head lamps with floor-mounted dip switch. Combined front side light/ flashing indicator lamp unit. Rear combined tail/stop/ flashing indicator lamp unit and reflector
Instruments:	Speedometer with trip and mileage recorders; rev. counter; oil pressure, water temperature

and fuel gauges. Self-cancelling direction indicators controlled by 'stalk' on steering column incorporating headlamp flasher; dimmable warning lights

Standard equipment: Twin-tone horns; two-speed self-parking windscreen wipers; map light; passenger grab handle; carpeted floor

Suspension and Wheels

Front: Independent coil springs and wishbones with telescopic shock absorbers in each coil. Anti-roll bar

Rear: Semi-elliptic leaf springs and direct acting shock absorbers. Panhard stabiliser bar

Wheels and Tyres: 13in (330.2mm) pressed steel wheels. Chrome hubcaps, stainless trim rings. Dunlop 6.00 x 13 tyres

Steering: Rack and pinion

Brakes: Front: Girling 9.85in (250.2mm) diameter disc brakes. Rear: 9in (250mm) drums. Vacuum servo-assisted. Total swept area 295sq in (1,903cm). Handbrake mounted at the side of the driver's seat operates mechanically on the rear wheels

Dimensions

Overall length: 13ft 0in (3,962mm)
Overall width: 5ft 0½in (1,537mm)
Overall height: 4ft 3½in (1,225mm)
Ground clearance: 4½in (114mm) (laden)
Track:
Front: 51in** (1,295mm)

Rear: 48.5in** (1,232mm)
Wheelbase: 7ft 2in (2,184mm)
Turning circle: 37ft 6in* (11.4m)

Fuel tank capacity: 11¼ gallons – twin tanks housed in rear wings
Unladen weight: 2,525lb (1,145kg) (with fuel and water); 2,407lb (1,092kg) (dry)

Performance:
0–30: 3.1 seconds**
0–60: 9.5 seconds*; 7.8 seconds**
Top speed: 120mph (approx) 118mph**

Colours
Carnival Red with Black upholstery
Midnight Blue with Azure Blue upholstery
Arctic White with Black upholstery
British Racing Green with Black upholstery
Jet Black with Red upholstery
Jet Black with Tan upholstery
Mediterranean Blue with Black upholstery

Optional Extras
Hard top in Black or matching body colour; whitewall tubeless tyres; tonneau cover; clock; Radiomobile radio; cigarette lighter; safety belts; wing mirrors

Price: $3,499 in US; £1,445 in UK, including purchase tax, from 1965

Model Variants: None

Significance: Rootes' one-off model entry into the high performance sports car market

All data Rootes Motors Ltd or Ford Motor Company except *Motor – April 1965 or **Road & Track November 1964

Kevin Beattie, Jensen's chief engineer, oversaw the production processes for the Tiger, but it was down to Jensen's chief design engineer Eric Neale to carry out the implementation of the bulkhead modification, as he explained to historian Mike Taylor:

'We produced a profiled wooden model of the new clutch-cum-gearbox cover pressing ... From this, our experimental panel beaters produced a one-off. At the same time, our development vehicle builders were producing a three-dimensional template for gas cutting the original Alpine structure in order to remove unwanted metal. The new cover [which was made for Jensen by Boulton and Paul in Wolverhampton] was then welded into position, new engine mountings fitted, and the Ford V8 unit installed.'

By March 1964, the first three Tigers to be built were sent to select Rootes dealers for evaluation, and on 3 April

1964, the Tiger, or Sunbeam Alpine 260 as it was still called at that time, made its debut at the prestigious New York Motor Show. By the time the Tiger was introduced to the European market in October 1964, the British motoring press had not had opportunities to test-drive the car, in anticipation of it being available in right-hand-drive form for the UK market. The first UK road tests were conducted in April 1965. The first Tiger to be shown at an Earl's Court Motor Show was in October 1964 and was subsequently shown at Earl's Court in October 1965.

Sunbeam Tigers on the production line at Jensen Motors.

COVENTRY ARCHIVES

From its introduction in the Spring of 1964, on average, 300 Tigers a month were built, and this continued until the Mark 1A, which was introduced in August 1965, when an average of 180 cars a month were built, with Mark 1A production finishing on 9 December 1966. From day one, the Tiger received constant updates, detail changes and small design improvements throughout its production and some of the more noticeable modifications on later Mark 1 and 1A Tigers reflected the changes made on the late model Alpine Series IV and Series V body, such as the rounded trailing door and bonnet corners and lower boot corners being squared off and no leading at seams to the rear wing and valance (rocker panel) in order to reduce production costs.

A number of factors combined during the Tiger's short but distinguished life that would not allow it the success it deserved, not least the fact that it had a Ford engine and transmission and that the Rootes Group had

Chrysler, Ford's arch rival, breathing down its neck. Chrysler's enthusiasm for a powerful sports tourer was clearly a concept they would have liked to continue with, if attempts to put their own small-block V8 into the Tiger had worked. Design briefs were even laid out for future models, but nothing came of them. Some of the Tiger drawings sketched out at the time looked very much like the Barracuda Convertible that Plymouth Division debuted in 1967, and during Tiger production, Chrysler still did not have overall control of Rootes to enable cancelling Tiger production just because it had a Ford V8 powering it, but they did manage to get rid of any reference to 'Ford' in literature and advertising material – referring to the Tiger instead as being 'powered by an American V8'.

The Tiger may not have had the top speed of the Jaguar E-Type, but it was cheaper than an E-Type, although still £339 more expensive than the Austin Healey 3000 Mark 3, which was priced at £1,107 including purchase tax. However, the 120-mile an hour Tiger could match many other British sports cars to 60mph. Unfortunately, the Tiger's looks didn't match its performance! With its steel wheels, hubcaps and trim rings, it didn't

World's Land Speed Record Holder Art Arfons, set the world record of 536.71 mph on Bonneville Salt Flats.

Art Arfons, fastest man on earth, owns the Sunbeam Tiger: world's fastest sports car for $3499*

Britain contributed the racing chassis. America provided the mighty Ford V-8 power plant. The men in England who build the famed Sunbeam sports cars put chassis and engine together to create the hottest car to hit 1965. Test the Tiger's cat-quick reflexes at your Sunbeam dealer. Touch the throttle and get the ride of your life.

'65 Sunbeam Tiger by ROOTES of England   **SUNBEAM**
Ask about our money-saving Overseas Delivery Plan

Check this Tiger's pedigree—write to Rootes Motors, 505 Park Ave., New York or 9830 West Pico Blvd., Los Angeles. *Price POE.

A 1965 Tiger advertisement in Road and Track magazine, featuring World Land Speed record-holder Art Arfons, who set the record of 536.71mph on Bonneville Salt Flats.

1967 Sunbeam Tiger Mark 2, finished in Commodore Blue. Exported to California in 1967, this car was supplied by Hampton Motors in Burbank California to the actor Roddy McDowell, as a gift from his then close friend actress Elizabeth Taylor. The current owner is Andrew Yates.

The 289 cubic inch V8 engine bay of Andrew Yates' Tiger 2, complete with: LAT 73 Stainless Steel Headers; LAT 8 – Finned Rocker Covers; LAT 38 – Aluminium intake Manifold; LAT 39 – 4-barrel Holley Carburettor.

Andrew Yates' Tiger Mark 2, showing off its LAT option wheels. This 289 Tiger is a rare example of a fully LAT (Los Angeles Tiger) optioned car and is fitted with a host of LAT options.

look different enough from the Alpine. One reason steel wheels were used on production models was that wire wheels would not withstand the torque from the Ford V8 engine; Ken Miles proved that point with his prototype. But a set of standard Minilite magnesium alloy wheels, made by Tech Del, which were used on the works rally cars, or the LAT (Los Angeles Tigers) cast aluminium wheels that were offered by Rootes in California, may have swayed more buyers in favour of the Tiger. Safety and emissions legislation was also constantly changing for British cars being exported to America, and Rootes were not in a financially strong enough position to be making the required updates to ensure acceptance in the American market. In the end, it was not Chrysler who was responsible for canning the Tiger, but Rootes themselves. In June 1966, Timothy Rootes, as head of passenger cars division, decreed that by June 1967, the Tiger would cease production.

Reasons given were the rapid changes in Federal vehicle legislation and falling sales.

Figures taken from the Jensen production ledgers by historian Graham Vickery state that 7,088 Tigers in total were built, of which 3,762 were Mark 1 versions, 2,706 Mark 1A versions and 534 were Mark 2 versions. The rest were prototypes, pre-production models, CKD or specials. The Mark 2 was introduced in December 1966. Most of the production went to America and Canada, six became Metropolitan Police cars, a number also went to Europe and four right-hand-drive models were purchased by private buyers. Despite its 289 cubic inch Ford V8 and substantially revised trim, on 27 June 1967 production of the Sunbeam Tiger ceased.

THE TIGER, DES O' DELL AND COMPETITIONS

A few months after Marcus Chambers had joined Rootes as the competitions manager, another name would enter the frame at Rootes Competitions Department who would have an enduring effect on their fortunes and success – Des O'Dell.

According to ex-Rootes employee, aficionado and Rootes Archive Centre trustee, Gordon Jarvis, it was a chance meeting between Peter Wilson and Des O'Dell that brought Des to Rootes. The story goes that Wilson met O'Dell coming out of the toilets at Le Mans, and Peter mentioned to him that they were having much better luck with their Ford-powered GT40s than Rootes were with their Ford-powered Tigers, and if Des ever wanted to join Rootes, he should give Wilson a call. A while later, Wilson's phone did ring and Des explained that he and his wife Jean wanted to buy a house, and property prices were much cheaper in the Midlands than in London or the Home Counties, so yes, he was interested! In November 1964, Des left John Wyer's employ at Ford Advanced Vehicles at Slough and came to work at Rootes Competitions Department. Very soon, it was realized that O'Dell had an intuitive engineering mind, and that he thought virtually anything was possible. He had a catchphrase: 'There's a solution to every problem – it's just a case of finding it in time.'

During the short competition career of the Tiger, Rootes Competitions Department prepared six Tigers for rallying, the first three being ready by September 1964, in preparation for the Geneva Rally in October. Initially, tuned engines were ordered from Shelby-American, but subsequently, after Des arrived, they were ordered direct from Ford in Detroit. Des then had the engines rebuilt, which gave him the opportunity to make sure they were built exactly as he wanted them. Competitions department engine builder Richard Guy remembers some of the tweaks Des suggested, which included a higher lift cam out of the 289 engine, which he procured from Ford Advanced Engineering at Slough:

> 'Because we didn't have any support [from Rootes/Chrysler], we had to do what we could … I remember going down to Ford Advanced Vehicles with Des trying to get bits and pieces for the engines … including a 289 cam. We took the hydraulic lifters out and put in solid lifters and a Holley 4 barrel carb …'

Some of the other modifications that were instigated by Marcus prior to Des O'Dell's involvement were Salisbury Powr-Lok differentials, Ford transmissions with Warner close ratios and of course, the obligatory Minilite Wheels.

The 1964 Geneva Rally had proved to be a success, with the Tigers finishing eleventh, fifteenth and twenti-

Tiger works team at the end of the 1965 Monte Carlo Rally. *Left to right:* **Robin Turvey; Andrew Cowan; Ian Hall and Peter Harper, who came fourth overall with a class win. Cowan came second in class.**

eth overall and Tiny Lewis claiming first in class, with Peter Riley coming second in class. Rosemary Smith won the Ladies award. The next 'official' works Tiger outing was in the 1965 Monte Carlo Rally. It was Peter Harper's turn to demonstrate his mastery of the Monte, this time with the Tiger, a very different Sunbeam to the Rapiers he had been used to pushing to class wins in previous events. With Ian Hall as co-driver, he finished fourth overall and gained the class win. Andrew Cowan, with Robin Turvey, in his first outing with the Tiger, came in eleventh overall and won the driving test at Monte Carlo. Cowan loved driving the Tiger, but realised it had a sting in its tail when he drove it in the next year's Monte Carlo:

> 'In '65 I drove a Tiger with Robin Turvey in the Monte Carlo. It was brilliant. I did it again in '66, but I rolled it at Boulogne – stupid mistake!
>
> 'The Tiger was just a fantastic car – the weight distribution was a wee bit wrong, but if you had the right tyres on it was good … fantastic torque from the V8 engine. Des O'Dell certainly had a lot of input.'

Engine builder Richard Guy is of the same opinion as Cowan as to the handling of the Tiger:

> 'The loading on the limited slip differential was critical on them as they were very light at the back. Get that right and the car handled beautifully; set it up wrong and it was a real dog!'

In the 1965 Tulip Rally, severe snow forced both the Tigers driven by Peter Harper and Peter Riley to retire and although Rosemary Smith was disappointed that she had not been given the opportunity to drive a Tiger again, she won the event outright in an Imp. Peter Harper, driving a 4.7 litre (289 cubic inch) Tiger, came second in the prototype class in the '65 Targo Florio. Privateers John Gott, the Chief Constable of Northamptonshire, with Sgt. D.E. Nicholson won the 1965 International Police Rally at the end of May, in a borrowed works Tiger. In fact, this was the first outright win for the Sunbeam Tiger to date.

Richard Guy remembers the disappointment felt by all concerned with the '65 Alpine Rally: *'The '65 Scottish Rally was quite successful … the Alpine was quite the opposite!'* Peter Harper had won the 1965 Alpine Rally outright, only to be disqualified due to a homologation issue. Tigers registered by Rootes with the FIA had American specification engines which used larger valves than the engines being used in the works Tigers. As the valve sizes used in the engines were smaller than the sizes on the homologation sheet, Rootes were accused of detuning the car for reliability, which was not the case. Richard Guy was one of the mechanics who had to bow to scrutineers' requests following the rally:

'Harper absolutely drove his heart out and it was a good job we lost the other two because we didn't have enough spares to keep those three Tigers going! They were going through spares like wildfire and Harper was doing fantastically, but he was doing brake pads and tyres through one stage. I can remember waiting at the bottom of one Col with Gerry Spencer … We could hear the V8 — a very distinct sound, and you could see the discs glowing through the Minilite wheels as they were coming down the hill. He won the rally and the Alpine Cup [Coupe des Alps] and then the car went into scrutineering. This scrutineer comes out … We were all set up to take one of the cylinder heads off and he walks around the car and says, "I'll have that one" [left – driver's side]. Gerry and I looked at one another and I said, "Can we not do that one [right side]?" "No" he said. He wanted the one on the steering column side and it was much more difficult to get the left off than the right as it was a left-hand-drive car.

'We set to … It was quite hard work, as we'd had a party the night before — with cheap champagne and the headache to go with it! Anyway, we got the head off, put it on the bench and this scrutineer got his paperwork and his calipers out and said, "Too small — valve too small".

Peter Harper and Ian Hall sliding their way around in the snow during the 1966 Monte Carlo Rally, in Tiger AHP 294B.
COVENTRY ARCHIVES

'They threw Harper out because it didn't tally with the homologation papers. He was devastated. It would have been a huge boost and an achievement for the Tiger if they'd won.'

If the 1965 Alpine Rally was a disappointment, the 1966 Monte Carlo was more of an international incident involving the three main British works teams – Rootes, BMC and Ford.

What made the 1966 Monte Carlo Rally go down as the most controversial in its history to date was the introduction of new Appendix J regulations, in particular those concerning lighting. All team managers – Marcus Chambers of Rootes, Stuart Turner of BMC and Henry Taylor of Ford – had sought clarification of the new regulations and thought they had understood what was needed. There was no way that any of them would deliberately infringe regulations – it just wasn't worth it, but by hook or by crook, the French seemed determined that a French car would win the event.

The actual winners were Timo Makinen and Paul Easter, with Rauno Aaltonen and Tony Ambrose in second place and Paddy Hopkirk and Henry Liddon in third – all in BMC Mini-Cooper S works cars. Roger Clark and Brian Melia came fourth in their Ford Cortina Lotus. Rosemary Smith and Val Domleo claimed the *Coupe Des Dames* trophy in an Imp. By the time the scrutineers had found an excuse not to give the British drivers their rightful positions, the first place was given to Toivonen and Mikander, in a Citroën! The *Coupe des Dames* went to a couple, also in a Citroën, who didn't even finish the rally! The disqualification was over alleged lighting infringements, as Paddy Hopkirk, who was aware that the French were 'out to get the British' explained in 2019:

'If you look back, they were trying to get rid of us – they thought we were cheating – they thought we were swapping cars – they took the cars to pieces – they measured the gear wheels in the gearbox … they tried to get us on everything, but couldn't. Then someone realised that in England it was legal to dip on to single filament bulbs – iodine lamps had just come out and we were dipping on to fog lights, which was legal in England but not in France, so they got us disqualified on that.

'We were on Sunday Night at the London Palladium and if anyone had stood up who had been French they would have been shot! I was also interviewed from Monte Carlo at 10 o'clock at night on a current affairs programme by Ludovic Kennedy – and I was terrified as I was just a thick Irish rally driver, and I hoped he didn't use any big words … it was an international incident!'

RICHARD GUY – INSIDE ROOTES COMPETITIONS DEPARTMENT

Richard Guy, Tiger and Imp competition engine builder.

RICHARD GUY

Former Rootes works rally driver Paddy Hopkirk has always had the greatest praise and appreciation for the support and technical know-how of the Rootes Competitions Department. The backroom boys at 'comps' were the unsung heroes of competitive rallying and racing during the 1960s. In 1964, Richard Guy started his competitions apprenticeship to becoming one of them:

'At the end of the Summer [of 1964] I went back into Service [Department] and got immediately transferred up to Competitions, but Jimmy Ashworth had to look after two departments – he was looking after the Transport Department and the Competitions Department. Derek [Hughes] and I went into Transport … We had a fleet of TS3 Commers going backwards and forwards to Linwood with the Imp engines. I used to keep nipping in next door to see what was going on in the "rally" shop. Eventually, I got in on the engine building. I got on well with the job and the people … and a chap who had been there for years, Ernie Beck, was retiring and they gave me

Arthur Bird (left) and Jack Walton with the 'comps' department Super Snipe support car on the 1965 Alpine Rally.

RICHARD GUY

his job. They recognised that I had a bit of a flair for polishing cylinder heads. Ernie Schofield joined about a year after me.

'I went into the Competitions Department in '64 and the first rally I did was the '65 Scottish. I was still [only] 21 and I got the first two rallies – the '65 Scottish and the '65 Alpine. Then I

Rootes Competition Department engine builders Ernie Beck and Ernie Schofield.

RICHARD GUY

did the Monte recce with Des. We were away for Christmas, and in between that I did duty at the Motor Show as well. I was 21 while at the Motor Show and they organised an impromptu party for me at the Regent Palace Hotel. I got a birthday card signed by about 300 people in the lounge of the hotel … We got absolutely slaughtered that night!! We weren't any good for Earl's Court the next day. I was on the Sunbeam stand as well; they put me on there because I knew all about Alpines and Rapiers.'

It wasn't just drivers who risked their all to win a rally – support crews sometimes got themselves into dangerous situations, as a young Richard Guy found out during the Scottish Rally one year when he and Ian Hall set out to rescue a works team car:

'We had a car in Scotland … I can't remember whose it was – maybe Rosemary Smith's – [that had] broken down

a couple of miles before the end of a stage and there was no way of getting to it other than to drive down these unmarked roads and try and find it … so we went hurtling off down these unmarked tracks and the snow was getting deeper and deeper and the Imp bedded itself in a drift. It's snowy, it's cold and we had very little fuel… and we were there for about four hours [by which time] we were getting very, very cold … and nobody knew where we were – there were no mobile phones or anything. To be honest, we didn't know what we were going to do – we had all sorts of discussions… and then blow me, a sheep dog came up and started barking at the car, and a few minutes later the shepherd arrived … he went back to his hut and got some shovels and more muscle and got us out. We were very close to getting hypothermia … we got back to the Perth Hydro Hotel and I was there for about three days!

'Don't get out of the car just yet, Dick…' The 1965 Alpine Rally Super Snipe support car took an unexpected detour over the wall during the event and had to be hauled back onto the road. Richard Guy was a sleeping passenger at the time. The valiant team carried on unfazed by the incident.

RICHARD GUY

The 1968 Scottish Rally team at the Craiglynne Hotel in Grantown-on-Spey. *Left to right*: Andrew Cowan; Jeremy Ferguson of Dunlop; Peter Burgess – technician; Brian Coyle; Gerry Spencer; Arthur Bird; Jack Walton; Brian Wileman; Rosemary Smith; John Brown (Colin Malkin's navigator); Derek Hughes; Des O'Dell; Colin Malkin (behind Des); Margeret McKenzie and Richard Guy.

RICHARD GUY

This farcical situation, far from celebrating the winners, showed the French organisers up for their myopic and unsporting behaviour. The prize-giving on the final Saturday was attended by only a few competitors. Most had boycotted the event. Princess Grace and Prince Rainier of Monaco, who would normally have attended the celebrations and given prizes, also stayed away.

Ex-Rootes team manager Norman Garrad was asked by *Autocar* magazine, as an observer, to comment on the situation. Garrad stated that *'the spirit of adventure and achievement … had gone!'* Never one to mince his words, he aimed his comments straight at the organisers, who

> *'tend to behave like demi-gods and little Hitlers for the duration of the event. Once their tiny hour of self-importance is over, back they go to a humdrum everyday life to reappear the following year as pompous as ever.'*

Autocar published two general classification lists – one being the 'official' list and the other 'How they really finished.' The '66 Monte would go down in motorsport history as the one in which the Brits were knobbled, and everybody knew it.

Although the two Sunbeam Tigers entered for the '66 Monte Carlo did not become part of the lighting controversy, as Andrew Cowan crashed early on and Peter Harper retired due to the fan hitting the radiator and causing the car to boil and blow its engine, Harper did achieve a class win for the Tiger in the 1966 Acropolis Rally. For a car that had received precious little competition development, it had performed remarkably well during its short, but distinguished career.

BACK TO BASICS – DEVELOPING THE ARROW RANGE

In 1963, Rootes started to plan a new model range to replace the Super Minx/Vogue and Minx/Gazelle range of cars, and provide eventual replacements for the big Humbers. The new models were codenamed 'Arrow'.

Prior to the Arrow, or 'A' car, project commencing, around 1961, Peter Ware had tasked ex-ERA engineer David Hodkin with creating a new medium-sized saloon car range. Known as the Swallow project, Ware and Hodkin came up with a four-door saloon with an aluminium, transverse, rear-mounted engine – in effect a big Imp. But costs had started to escalate to unacceptable

A quarter-scale styling model for the Arrow – April 1963.
COVENTRY ARCHIVES

proportions. The range already had inbuilt limitations due to the necessity of having an estate car option. In a rear engine configuration, load space would be severely limited due to having such a high load floor.

A young engineer, still fairly new to Rootes at the time, Anthony Stevens, had been given the task of negotiating with sub-contractors on the project – one of which was Renault, who were involved with high-pressure die casting:

> *'We were using separate liners and I got involved with people who made pipes for the oil industry. They made pipes for us, which we could machine into the liners. Renault were quite good at that so I used to go to Renault quite often, which was interesting. Renault was lovely at the time … At that stage they still had M. Renault's garden shed in the middle of a great park in Billancourt, on an island in the Seine. That's where he started the business ...'*

According to stylist Roy Axe, it was Lord Rootes who realised that Swallow was gobbling up money and ultimately not feasible and stopped the whole project. Bill Papworth, was in charge of product planning within a new Group Operations function with Cyril Weighell as director and remembers the demise of the Swallow project:

> *'The whole Swallow idea [was] another totally new, high unit cost, complex beast. By September, the Swallow had been effectively shelved and the rescue plan was the Arrow. The Swallow was canned in the summer of 1963.'*

Under Bill Papworth, there were three product planning managers, each with their own product line responsibility: C.A. Lynn – Small/Light cars; Graham McBride – Humber Light Car range; and Tony Stevens – Arrow.

The ill fated Swallow prototype.
COVENTRY ARCHIVES

One of the first full-size front end mock-ups for the Arrow, assembled at the Stoke Styling Studio in April 1964.

Tony Stevens had also been working on potential new engines prior to transferring to Product Planning:

> 'The Arrow range was interesting, because I had to cover everything from the Hillman Husky up to the Super Snipe. There was no way you could do that in one range, so the ends "dropped off" because there was a limit to what I could do. Also I couldn't really do two wheel-bases, so I couldn't do a short wheelbase sports, so the Alpine had to go and we ended up with just the fastback Rapier.'

Harry Sheron ran the Arrow project team and Rex Fleming was the project stylist. Ted White was still head of styling, but was very much in the background. He would retire in 1968. The concept behind the Arrow was to create a medium-sized car range using a commonality of parts and platforms, much like Rootes had done in the mid-Fifties with the Audax range. It was aimed directly at the Ford Cortina – so, a conventional rear-wheel-drive, four-door saloon car with an estate car variant formed the template. Arrow would also be the first Rootes car to feature MacPherson strut independent front suspension, the same as the Cortina.

Styling studies commenced in January 1964 with quarter-scale models and a full-size clay model by the end of February. A basic body shape was completed by April '64, during which time a number of changes had been made since the initial styling exercise. Tooling was released to the body toolmakers in April, but numerous changes were made to grilles and frontal treatments for the Hillman and Singer versions, which were not finalised until much later. One of the frustrations of the body styling department was the constant changes that were being asked for by the family, as some contradicted each other as to what was required. Tony Stevens:

Apart from a different grille mesh pattern, little had changed in the front end styling of the Arrow by September 1964.

Rectangular headlamps and squarer profile wings were starting to change the look of the Arrow by December 1964. Note the Sunbeam Rapier fastback styling mock-up at the rear of the studio. ANTHONY STEVENS

A Vogue dash proposal 23 October 1964. ANTHONY STEVENS

A Hunter being crash tested at MIRA during its development.

ROOTES ARCHIVE CENTRE TRUST

A September '64 quarter-scale model of the Estate car.

ANTHONY STEVENS

Vogue front end proposal 13 August 1964. ANTHONY STEVENS

'The guys would work on the clays; a member of the family would wander into the studio and suggest that the roof should be lowered by half an inch, then the next week somebody else would instruct them to raise it up again, so we had this nightmare with members of the family sticking their fingers in. Eventually I started taking Polaroids and asking them to sign them, so I could say "That's what Sir Reginald said last week, so you might like to go and talk to him about it, rather than get the guys re-carving the whole thing." It happened a lot, because they all wanted to have their input.'

Interior seating bucks with full dash layouts were also completed for the Hillman model by April, and although the Singer model interior was started later in 1964, both Hillman and Singer interiors were finalised by mid-1965.

Two estate versions were needed, Hillman and Singer, which had to be produced from the basic saloon models with the minimum of alteration to sheet metal. According to Tony Stevens, *'It was necessary to extend the rear underframe by three inches in order to get a generous load carrying area.'* The specifications for the estate car versions were finalized by the end of 1964.

Clay modellers hard at work on the Arrow project at the design studio at Stoke in May 1964. ANTHONY STEVENS

Interior of the Hillman Hunter Mark I, August 1966.

NIGEL HUGHES / SINGER OWNERS CLUB

Pre-prototype testing started in August 1964 and by March 1965, completed prototype saloons were being extensively road tested and evaluated. Testing continued on pre-production saloons between April 1966 and September '66, with pre-production testing on the estate models being carried out between January 1967 and May '67.

The first production saloon came off the line at Ryton in August 1966, in time to be introduced at the Earl's Court Motor Show in October. The Hillman Hunter, which took its name from the mid-Fifties Singer Hunter, quickly gained high marks from motor-

ing journalists, many of whom were making the obvious comparisons with the Ford Cortina. Motor Sport's Bill Boddy was one, but not necessarily the first, to call the Hunter the 'Coventry Cortina', with cautious praise stating:

'In comparison with the Ford Cortina, it rides a bit better, has perhaps heavier, but more positive steering, and feels, maybe, a bit more stable on corners, until it is driven really hard, when the understeer becomes a bit squidgy.'

He went on to say that:

'the Hunter handles reasonably well in the wet on 5.60 x 13 Dunlop C41 [crossplies] … and with a top speed of 90 mph … is ahead of the Cortina 1500, as it should be with its bigger engine, but is no match for the Cortina GT.'

The Hunter was, of course, not meant to be a match for the Cortina GT – that would come later as the Hillman Hunter range was extended.

Concurrently with the Hillman Hunter launch at Earl's Court, on the Singer stand, was the launch of the Singer Vogue Mark V. The first Vogue to be tested by *Autocar* magazine, in December '66, was an automatic version, fitted with the Borg-Warner 35 transmission: *Autocar* had glowing praise for the new Vogue, stating that the *'automatic transmission is well matched to [an] already smooth engine… [and] low noise level. Light, accurate steering and sure-footed, fade-free braking … good economy for an automatic.'*

The Hunter display at the Paris Motor Show. ANTHONY STEVENS

The new Singer Vogue Mark V, as a 'doors off' version making its debut at the Earls Court Motor Show, 18 October 1966.
NIGEL HUGHES / SINGER OWNERS CLUB

A 1725cc engine installed in a Singer Vogue Mark V.
NIGEL HUGHES / SINGER OWNERS CLUB

The interior of the new Singer Vogue Mark V, together with
a 'doors off' version making their debut at the Earl's Court
Motor Show, 18 October 1966. NIGEL HUGHES / SINGER OWNERS CLUB

Singer *vogue estate car* *big load-carrier with the luxury saloon look*

1007

Call off the search

Here at last! The complete family car

New Hillman Hunter

Complete in every detail. That's Hunter. Safe–for today's crowded roads. Reliable—for today's family motoring. New Hunter is made for more comfort, more economy. Made modern with the long, low line of today. Made to be the complete family car.

Safe Hunter. With tough all-steel unitary construction. With front disc brakes and self-adjusting braking system. With advanced suspension for remarkable roadholding. The new slant engine gives a lower bonnet line and thus better forward vision. All doors are fitted with anti-burst locks; and rear doors have childproof catches. Sunvisors and the stylish facia surround are padded. The steering wheel is dished, the screenwipers two-speed. Front seat belt anchor points are provided.

Reliable Hunter. The new engine is developed directly from the proven Hillman 1725 cc unit. With aluminium cylinder head and constant depression carburettor for better performance. Aluminium sump for more efficient oil-cooling, quiet operation. Five main bearings for smoother running.

Economical Hunter. With excellent fuel economy. Service intervals of 5000 miles—and no greasing points. 35 amp alternator for longer battery life. And no-loss cooling system to save regular topping-up.

Comfortable Hunter. Curved side windows add extra shoulder room. The front seats recline. And the driving position is designed for carefree motoring—controls easy to hand, pedals properly placed. Another useful refinement—the centre console, with a recessed tray and two recessed ashtrays (for front and rear). The boot gives 18 cubic feet of luggage space— thanks to the specially designed spare wheel storage. New controlled fresh air ventilation and heating system.

Powerful Hunter. The power unit is designed for fast economical cruising. For smooth, quiet running. And for swift acceleration: 0-60 m.p.h. in under 15 seconds. Top speed up to 90 m.p.h. The four-speed gearbox is all synchromesh.

The complete family car. That's Hunter. At your Rootes dealer for a recommended price of £837.11.0d. inc. p.t. With automatic transmission or overdrive and whitewall tyres available at extra cost.

HILLMAN ✶ ROOTES

London Showrooms & Overseas Division: Devonshire House, Piccadilly, W1

October 1966 launch advertisement for the Hunter.

1968 Hillman Minx Deluxe.

A Singer Gazelle on a *Motor* magazine road test, 24 January 1967. The 'Arrow' version of the Gazelle was introduced for the 1967 model year. Pitched delicately in price between its Hillman Minx 1498cc iron-head cousin and the Hunter, at £798 including purchase tax, it was only £63 more than the Minx and £103 less than a Hunter. Gazelle did, however, come with the obligatory wood-grain dash, but if you wanted to go the whole hog, the basic 1725 Vogue would cost £911. SINGER OWNERS CLUB

HILLMAN HUNTER (1966) SPECIFICATIONS

Body style
Four-door, four/five-seater saloon. Unitary construction

Engine
4 cylinder, overhead valves pushrod operated, five main
bearing crankshaft. Aluminium cylinder head and sump.
Cast aluminium induction manifold
Power output: 1,725cc (105.2cu in) developing 74bhp
at 5,000rpm
Bore and Stroke: 81.5 x 82.5mm (3.21 x 3.25in)
Compression ratio: 9.2:1
Torque: 96lb ft at 3,000rpm
Fuel pump type: AC-Delco mechanical
Carburettor: Zenith Stromberg 150 CDS side
draught, variable choke
Cooling system: Water – pump and fan

Transmission
Four-speed all synchromesh gearbox. Centre floor change lever
Clutch: Borg and Beck 7½in (190.5mm) diaphragm
spring, hydraulic, single dry plate type
Gear Ratios: Top 1:1; Third 1.39:1; Second 2.14:1; First
3.35:1; Reverse 3.57:1**
Final drive: Semi-floating hypoid bevel type. Final
drive ratio: 3.7:1

Electrical and Lighting
Ignition: Coil and distributor with 35 amp alternator.
12 volt 40 amp battery*

Lighting: Two Lucas sealed-beam 60–45 watt headlamps;
combined side-light and direction indicator light cluster
mounted below front bumper, rear combined stop/tail and
direction indicator light cluster; Reversing lamps
Instruments: Speedometer, fuel and water temperature gauge,
warning lights for ignition, oil pressure, headlamp main beam and
direction indicators. Interior door-operated courtesy light

Standard equipment: Heater with two-speed blower,
ventilation equipment, two padded sunvisors, boot floor mat,
headlamp flasher, reclining front seats, lockable glove box,
two-speed windscreen wipers, screenwasher, overriders,
passenger door armrests, Triplex 'Zebrazone' toughened
windscreen, childproof rear door catches

Suspension and Wheels
Front: Independent coil springs and MacPherson strut,
anti-roll bar, telescopic dampers
Rear: Semi-elliptic leaf springs, telescopic dampers
Wheels and Tyres: 13in (330.2mm) pressed steel wheels.
Chrome hubcaps, stainless slotted trim rings. Dunlop C41
5.60 x 13 tyres*
Steering: Cam Gear, recirculating ball type**
Brakes: Lockheed 9.6in diameter (244mm) front disc brakes;
9in (228.6)mm drums on rear*

Dimensions
Overall length: 14ft 1½in (4,305mm)
Overall width: 5ft 3½in (1,613mm)
Overall height: 4ft 8in (1,422mm)

Publicity shot for the Hillman Hunter Mark I.

Ground clearance: 6¾in (171mm)
Track: Front: 4ft 4in (132 cm)* Rear: 4ft 4in (132cm)*
Wheelbase: 8ft 2½in (2,502mm)
Turning circle: 33½ft (10.2m)
Fuel tank capacity: 10 Imperial gallons (45.5 litres)*
Unladen weight: 2,051lb (930kg) (with half-full petrol
tank, oil and water)*

Performance:
0–60 mph: 14.6 seconds*
30–70 mph (through gears): 16.8 seconds*
Top speed: 90mph*
Fuel consumption: 26.5mpg (Overall)
(10.7litres/100km).*

Colours
Embassy Black with Red upholstery
Storm Grey with Red upholstery
Willow Green with Green upholstery
Tartan Red with Black upholstery
Polar White with Red or Black upholstery
Bermuda Blue with Blue upholstery
Shore Beige with Brown upholstery
Neptune Green with Green upholstery
Oxford Blue with Black upholstery

Optional Extras / Accessories
Laycock-de Normanville type D overdrive (on third and top);
Borg-Warner type 35 automatic transmission; Radiomobile
radio; clock, oil gauge, ammeter; badge bar; wing mirrors;
whitewall tyres; front seat belts; front fog and spot lamps,
mud flaps

Price: £680 (Basic) plus UK Purchase tax*

Model Variants: Estate car (introduced May 1967 as the
Hillman Estate and subsequently Minx Estate)

Significance: First of the new 'Arrow' range of cars to be
launched by Rootes

All data Rootes Motors Ltd except *Autocar*, October 1966;
***Automobile Engineer*, February 1967

A quarter-scale model of the Rapier in August 1964.
At this early stage, a curved one-piece rear window was
still envisaged by Roy Axe, but due to the complexities of
production, and cost, a compromise three-piece rear window
arrangement had to be incorporated into the design.

ANTHONY STEVENS

The Hillman Hunter and Singer Vogue saloon models
were quickly followed up by their estate car versions in
March 1967. In the interim period from introduction of
the Hunter and Vogue, to the estate becoming available,
the Super Minx Estate and Vogue Series IV Estate depu-
tised as estate car options. Early Vogue 'Arrow' Estates
had a 93bhp 1725 cast-iron head engine, but this was
changed to the aluminium head in May. An alternator
also became standard equipment and by 1968, servo-
assisted front disc brakes became standard on Vogue
Estates.

Initially, the Hillman version was simply known as the
Hillman Estate, only to be changed to the Minx Estate
Car in early 1968. This coincided with the introduction

of a Minx Saloon, a basic, no-frills, value-for-money
version of the Hunter. The Minx name had been brought
back into the arena once again, as a reminder of Rootes'
past glories and experience in building family cars. The
Minx had an iron-head 1496cc 5-bearing overhead valve
version of the 1725 engine, but lacked some of the refinements of the Hunter, but was in effect a de-chromed
Hunter. A 'Deluxe' model was also introduced, along
with an 'Arrow' Gazelle version.

The next model to be launched in the Arrow series was
the Rapier – a fastback sports coupé that would replace
all previous Audax Rapiers, and one which would turn
out to be a very different animal to the other Arrow
models. Design studies for the Rapier commenced in
early 1964, with complete design responsibilities being
given to Roy Axe. By August '64, quarter-scale clay
models were well underway, with a full-size clay model
being approved in April 1965. Although the floorpan
and running gear was Arrow, the Rapier had all new
panels throughout, and only the bonnet from the other
Arrow models and rear lights from the Estate were used.
But it turned out to be a successful addition to the Arrow
line-up and a worthy successor to previous Sunbeams.
The Rapier was introduced in October 1967 at the Earl's
Court Motor Show.

In October 1968, the first Rapier variant was
launched. The Rapier H120 was a high-performance
version of the Rapier fastback. The 1725 engine featured
a Holbay modified aluminium cylinder head, two twin-
choke Weber carburettors, wider Rostyle wheels were
fitted with radial ply tyres – and the boot had a spoiler!

2 March 1965 – the full-size Rapier mock-up in the viewing
room at Stoke, with three-piece rear window arrangement.
This version is still showing the Arrow wings, which Roy Axe
was adamant didn't look right. They were dropped for the
unique, but more costly wings that were used in production.

ANTHONY STEVENS

Why go by bus when you can go by Sunbeam Rapier?

COVENTRY ARCHIVES

Initially, the H120 was capable of 120mph and purported to put out 120bhp, but it was felt by engineering to be a bit too hairy, so it was detuned to 110bhp (105bhp gross) at 5,200rpm.

The idea behind the H120 came from Tony Stevens:

'The Holbay Rapier was my personal car, because I married up the Holbay engine they were using for rallying [for the Marathon] and I put it up as a proposal and it made so much money that it went into the range. I saw it through "from soup to nuts", but there was a lot of opposition to that, because when someone controls something from day one to production they can say "that's mine". I put a bit of effort into that. I wanted big tyres on it because that was visually better, rather than the tyres the engineers thought it needed and as a result of them throwing the book at it, the car got more development than it would have got otherwise, which meant it came out a better car.

'The end result was brilliant, but it was a limited edition of 1,000 cars. I went round and interviewed police, fire and ambulance services about the most visible colour, which you'd call "day-glow orange" now, so the intention was that the whole thousand would be produced in orange with black stripes. I then collapsed in a heap, having done all this work and moved aside. Of course, the marketing guys wanted different colours and they didn't stop at a thousand because it made too much money.'

Around the same time, Porsche were introducing a new bright orange colour on their new 912/911 ranges – Bahama Yellow. Great minds think alike?

The Humber Sceptre version was a much simpler car to create than the Rapier from a styling standpoint. Although it utilised all of the sheet metalwork from the Hunter/Vogue Saloons, and mechanicals of the Rapier – 1725 engine, aluminium cylinder head and twin Stromberg carbs – the design team had to make the new Sceptre different enough from the Hillman and Singer models to appeal to previous Sceptre owners, as well as offer a modern take on traditional Humber values. The result was a smart four-door saloon with a luxuriously appointed interior featuring reclining leather front bucket seats, individual leather rear seats and wood veneer finish dashboard, door cappings and centre console.

Outside, a vinyl roof covering, painted coachlines along the reveal strip and twin headlamps flanking a new grille all set the Sceptre apart from other Arrow models. It was the addition, however, of full-width sculpted wheel covers, designed by freelance artist Eric Ball, that sealed the Sceptre's appearance. The same wheel covers

Side reflectors, high-back seats and door mirrors were features of the North American specification Rapier, which was badged as an Alpine. COVENTRY ARCHIVES

If the resources had been available could there have been a convertible version of the Arrow Rapier? COVENTRY ARCHIVES

Export Alpines (i.e. Rapiers) waiting to be loaded onto ships bound for the United States. COVENTRY ARCHIVES

Sunbeam Rapier H120 cockpit.

The Holbay 1725 engine installed in the Rapier H120.

were also used on the Rapier. As with other Arrow models, Sceptre and Rapier models were built up and painted by Pressed Steel. Sceptres also had their vinyl roofs fitted at Pressed Steel and were partly trimmed before being sent to Ryton for final assembly. The Rapier also held the distinction of being the first production car to have bonded-in front screens and rear glass. Painting and trimming of the Singer Vogue saloons and estates, however, was treated differently. The bodies were built at Pressed Steel and then sprayed with the protective coating Astrolan. They were then sent to Stoke to be painted and trimmed before going to Ryton for final

assembly. The rationale behind this exclusive treatment of the Singer models is purely a practical one, as the Singers had exclusive colour ranges to other Rootes models and the Stoke paint plant was capable of spraying up to sixteen different colours. Also, from 1967, capacity of the Stoke paint plant was becoming under-utilised, due to the phasing out of the big Humbers, which had always been painted at Stoke. Seats were made at the nearby Baginton plant, which was used by Rootes as a trim shop, where seat covers and headlinings were also cut, sewn and assembled, and sent to Ryton. Dashboards were assembled and fitted at Ryton. Dashes, armrests

A Sunbeam Rapier H120 dealer showroom poster that harks back to the halcyon days of the 1950s, and the Sunbeam-Talbot Owners Club car shows and social outings. A number of famous restored cars are featured in the photograph.

If ever a car deserved praise, it's the new Humber Sceptre.
Not only for its distinguished styling. Or for the quality and
luxury of its appointments. Or for its smooth, quiet running.
But for the way it combines these features with economy in fuel
and a performance superior to many 2-litre saloons.
Superbly equipped, the new Humber Sceptre is exceptional value.

the astonishing new

HUMBER *SCEPTRE*

4 doors, 1.7 litre engine, overdrive standard

PART OF THE NEW DEAL FROM ROOTES

In 1967, the strapline 'Part of the new deal from Rootes'
appeared across all product ranges, including the new
Humber Sceptre.

The Hillman Super Minx Estate served as the companion estate
car to the Hunter until Hunter Estate production could be
established. One is seen here being tested on the vibration rig
developed by David Hodkin. It was installed at Ryton in June 1966
to evaluate the performance of suspension and steering systems
in-house without having to take cars on rigorous tests abroad.

The luxury, leather and walnut-capped interior of the Arrow
Sceptre.

and other interior mouldings were made at the newly-
created Hills Precision Die Castings plastics division,
housed in the old Singer factory at Canterbury Street. A
4,700 foot long final trim and assembly line at Ryton was
completed in December 1967. A trim stage was added in
the summer of 1968.

Media praise is one aspect of judging how good a car
is, but the acid test is always with the customer. Nigel
Hughes, a long-time fan of Rootes cars and ex-Chrysler
UK employee, puts Singer Vogue ownership into context.
Nigel's Dad traded in a 1966 Super Minx Mark IV for a

An Arrow Minx gets the full 'vibration' treatment on Hodkin's
Parameter rig. ROOTES ARCHIVE CENTRE TRUST

Hills Precision Die Castings main factory at Cateswell Road, Birmingham. COVENTRY ARCHIVES

new Singer Vogue, and the Hughes family were taken to their local Rootes dealership, Parrish's of Longton, near Preston. That day has formed a distinct memory for Nigel, as if it was yesterday:

> 'It [Vogue] looked so much better then the utilitarian look of the Super Minx. We went out for a drive in it – it was a beautiful day and the dashboard was sparkling when the sunlight was on it … We got back to the garage and I think it was about £110 that they [his parents] were short. The car was fractionally under £1,000. It's only now that you realise how expensive cars were then. We actually bought our house two years before we got this car, for £2,500 for a three-bed semi … So it was a big investment, but they found the money somehow …
>
> 'When we took it home, none of our neighbours had a car as posh as this, and they all came out to see it … Our next door neighbour had an MG 1300 – he was amazed at this car [the Vogue]. We felt like we were royalty!'

The Arrow range would find many new other satisfied owners in the years to come. Rootes' new models were off to a good start; a relatively small team had developed a new range of cars – on time and on budget. The Arrow had hit its target in the right place and at the right time for Rootes.

Dispensing polyurethane foam in the moulding of the dash pad at Hills Precision Die Castings plastics division, housed in the old Singer factory at Canterbury Street, Coventry – 1970.

COVENTRY ARCHIVES

1967 Singer Vogue Saloon. Owner Gordon Jarvis.

CHAPTER 7

LIFE UNDER THE PENTASTAR – THE CHRYSLER TAKEOVER

'The Rootes people were gentlemen – Chrysler were animals!'
– Duncan Robertson – Administration Manager, Linwood plant

'They think it's all over!' came the shout from the commentator at the end of the 1966 World Cup final at Wembley Stadium… then England's Geoff Hurst put another goal into the net to score a 4–2 victory against West Germany, to which the commentator replied, *'… It is now!'*

England may have won the World Cup in 1966 and it was all over for West Germany, but towards the winter of '66, it was becoming clear that for the Rootes Group, it was all over for them too. Rootes' financial condition was such that they could no longer continue as a business without a further massive capital injection, which meant one thing – giving financial control to Chrysler. By mid-1967, Chrysler would acquire a majority shareholding, and ultimate control of the Rootes Group. It seemed difficult to comprehend that the company Billy Rootes founded with his father in 1917, fifty years later, would be controlled by Chrysler Corporation of America.

On 24 January 1967, in a letter to shareholders, Sir Reginald Rootes announced:

> *'The accounts for the year ended 31 July 1966 show that year to have been an extremely difficult one and that a loss of approximately £3,000,000 was incurred.'*

He continued, stating that Rootes had been:

> *'in a position to look forward to increased turnover and a return to profitability. In the event, their plans were frustrated by circumstances beyond their control when at the end of July, 1966, the government intensified its deflationary policies which affected not only the economy as a whole but particularly the motor industry.'*

The 'deflationary policies' that Sir Reginald referred to were the measures that had been brought in by the Labour government, which included some of the toughest

Under new ownership… the Pentastar logo in the new sign outside the Ryton plant says it all. ROOTES ARCHIVE CENTRE TRUST

policies of any government since 1949. Hire purchase down-payments on cars, motorcycles and caravans were raised to forty per cent, with higher down-payments on other products and shorter repayment periods. Chancellor of the Exchequer, James Callaghan, also raised tax on oil, petrol and purchase tax. There was a tightening up of foreign exchange controls and a wages freeze. Although the measures also hit other industries, such as construction, it was the motor industry that took the brunt, and it came at the worst possible time for the Rootes Group.

The total domestic new car registrations for the quarter September to November 1966 were about twenty-five per cent down on the same period for 1965. According to SMMT figures, the UK industry built 1,603,679 cars in 1966, as opposed to 1,722,045 in 1965. Rootes were forced to stockpile new cars, which further increased the demands on working capital.

At the end of the 1967 financial year Rootes losses were estimated to be in excess of £10 million, with some estimates as high as £10.7 million. In addition to its original investment in Rootes in 1964, a further increase in Rootes holdings was granted to Chrysler by the government in May 1965, to 45 per cent of the ordinary voting shares and 66 per cent of the 'A' (non-voting) shares. Chrysler had provided £27 million investment and was prepared to invest a further £20 million, of which £10 million was required urgently as working capital, but only if permission was granted from the government to acquire a majority shareholding. Chrysler's proposal was put to the Treasury for approval on 12 December 1966 and granted on 17 January 1967, without reference to the Monopolies Commission being needed. The fact that the government had been presented with a solution to a potentially disastrous industrial situation – that of Rootes ceasing as a company and the knock-on effect that would be felt at component manufacturer level, combined with huge unemployment, made the decision an easy one.

Nationalisation had been rejected by the Labour government, but under the newly-formed Industrial Reorganisation Corporation, 'a kind of government-sponsored merchant bank', as described by Young and Hood in their detailed analysis of the Rootes/Chrysler situation, it would be possible for the government to make Chrysler's control of Rootes conditional, as well as provision of a 48.7 per cent stake in Rootes' total equity capital and the right to nominate one director to the Rootes Board. The Rootes merger with Chrysler also led to the IRC being involved with the merging of British Motor Holdings and Leyland in 1967.

Chrysler's investment in Rootes to date had been used for updating equipment at Coventry and Linwood, as well as enabling the renting of the Baginton plant near Ryton, which was used to produce interior trim, but most of the investment went towards the £14 million acquisition of the Pressed Steel plant at Linwood. Negotiations began in early January and the acquisition was formalised by July 1966. As Rootes Pressings (Scotland) Ltd, the intention was to have pressings and panels made 'in house' for any Rootes models, not just Imps. Although the Pressed Steel plant was not profitable at the time of the acquisition, it was projected that the plant would be in profit within three years.

During 1967, Rootes Motors Ltd, now under the control of Chrysler Corporation, went through a rapid series of changes in management, structure and policy. In February 1967, Sir Reginald Rootes, having reached the age of 70, announced his retirement. His place as chairman was taken by Geoffrey Rootes. On 1 May 1967, Gilbert Hunt was appointed as managing director and chief executive officer of Rootes Motors Ltd. Hunt joined Rootes from Massey-Ferguson in Coventry, where he had been managing director since 1960. In March '67, W.J. Tate joined the board of Rootes Motors Ltd, from Chrysler, as director of finance and legal staff. Also appointed to the board were Erwin H. Graham, vice-president of Chrysler's European operations and Georges Hereil, chairman of Simca. Bernard Boxall and Sir Eric Roll, a former permanent under-secretary to the Department of Economic Affairs, acted as the 'watchdog' from the Industrial Reorganisation Corporation to oversee Chrysler's activities.

CHRYSLER IN BRITAIN

Chrysler's involvement in Britain goes back to 1924, when they acquired the Maxwell Car Company, who built a range of touring cars in the States, and who supplied the British-owned subsidiary Maxwell Motors Ltd in London. Maxwell were already well-established in Britain, having formed a company, in Great Portland Street, London, in 1919. The following year, larger premises at Lupus Street, Pimlico were acquired, and in 1922, Maxwell Motors acquired 14½ acres of land at Kew, Surrey, to build an assembly plant.

In 1924, when Chrysler took over the Maxwell Car Company in the States, and subsequently Maxwell Motors Ltd at Kew, they started to import built-up Chrysler cars from the parent company, and the name was changed to Maxwell-Chrysler Ltd, although the company remained in British hands. In 1925, the name was changed again – to Chrysler Motors Ltd. The acquisition of Maxwell was the beginning

of Walter P. Chrysler's new venture as an independent car maker. With the Maxwell designs he created the Chrysler '70', which was an instant hit on the American market. In 1928, Chrysler Export Corporation acquired the share capital in Chrysler Motors Ltd., and an American, Mr. C.MacAire, was appointed managing director in place of Mr. A. De la Poer, who had run the British concern from the start.

During the Thirties, as well as building Dodge Kew trucks as Dodge Brothers (Britain) Ltd, the Kew factory assembled CKD Dodge cars and Canadian-sourced Desotos for the UK market on adjacent assembly lines as Chrysler Motors Ltd. They were badged as Chrysler Wimbledon, Kew or Richmond.

By 1960, demand was sufficient to set up an assembly line at Kew to assemble Simca cars in SKD condition from France. By May 1962, demand had fallen back to 1950s' levels and

The Chrysler stand at the 1934 Olympia Motor Show, with the Humber stand immediately behind it, displaying a Humber 12 Vogue model. CHAS K. BOWERS & SON

The 1960 Simca Aronde Etoile saloon. COVENTRY ARCHIVES

A Dodge Polara 880 Sedan at the 1965 Earl's Court Motor Show. These right-hand-drive models were available through the London Rootes dealership Warwick Wright Ltd. STEVE MILES COLLECTION.

By 1937, the London motor show had relocated to Earl's Court. Gone was the art-deco elegance of Olympia, but Earl's Court had more space for manufacturers to display their vehicles. Chrysler took full advantage of the new location to show off their right-hand-drive 1938 range. This would be the penultimate pre-war London motor show. CHAS K. BOWERS & SON

One of the first Chrysler North America products to be marketed by Rootes through Warwick Wright Ltd was the Plymouth Barracuda, seen here at the 1967 Earl's Court Motor Show getting a lot of attention. STEVE MILES.

Simca set up their own company in Britain to import and distribute their cars. Throughout the Sixties, Canadian and American-built Chrysler cars were imported through their European offices Chrysler International S.A. in Geneva and distributed from Kew. Prior to this, Chrysler North American products were assembled from CKD kits at Chrysler's Antwerp plant, which was closed down in 1958.

In 1965, Dodge Brothers (Britain) Ltd became part of the Chrysler-backed Rootes Group and American and Canadian cars, such as the Plymouth Barracuda and Dodge Polara continued to be imported through Chrysler Motors Ltd and sold as 'special order' models through the Rootes dealership Warwick Wright Ltd until the mid-1970s. Dodge Brothers (Britain) Ltd at Kew was closed down and sold off to a property company in 1967.

The North London branch of Warwick Wright Ltd, mid-Sixties. NICK ROOTES

In March, 1967, Brian and Timothy Rootes resigned from the Rootes board, although Timothy, Sir Reginald's son, remained divisional managing director of sales and distribution. Brian left the Group after twenty-seven years service to run Prestair Ltd, the air conditioning business which was located on the Isle of Wight. He also had the Nassau Bottling Company, who were Schweppes agents and Central Garage in Nassau, Bahamas (in which Geoffrey and Tim both had shares). Brian's son Bill also resigned as a result of a phone call from his father, when Chrysler's intentions became clear:

'Although we knew that Chrysler were interested in gaining more control, we didn't actually know where things had got to ... He rang me up and said, "I'm resigning, I think that you should do the same too."'

Sadly, Brian's retirement was short – he died on 1 January 1971 of a heart attack. Rupert Hammond, Rootes' financial director, who had reached retiring age, also resigned after thirty-eight years service with Rootes. In 1966, Peter Ware, the Group's chief executive engineer, had also decided to leave Rootes; the American management styles and techniques were not his way of working. He joined Dunlop, where he turned the Wheel Division into a highly profitable part of the Dunlop Group. He also helped develop the Maxaret anti-skid braking system for trucks.

Although Tim Rootes was no longer a board member, as a divisional managing director, he and Lord Rootes

were the only members of the Rootes family to remain in the company. He naturally assumed that by continuing with the company, he would be able to contribute to its future development. Tim recalls those difficult months which led to him leaving Rootes:

'In early 1967, Chrysler had control. Geoffrey remained as non-executive chairman. Brian had left. I was quite prepared to stay, although I had begun to have misgivings about a future attending endless meetings without the family. One Gilbert Hunt had been head-hunted by Chrysler to be chief executive officer. I did not like him much, although Geoffrey had good relations with him. He seemed to me rather pleased with himself and somewhat pedantic.

'About the second or third meeting we had in Devonshire House, he announced plans for further management re-organisation. This involved, amongst others, an appointment of a new sales and marketing executive for the whole Manufacturing Division. Hunt said he would keep us informed of who would be appointed.

'I was in my office in Coventry about a week later when the phone rang. It was Gilbert Hunt's secretary, who informed me that Rex Watson Lee, who was a friend, quite apart from being a colleague, was to be appointed to the position I had imagined I would be offered. It was perfectly reasonable for Rex Watson Lee to be chosen instead of myself, but it was more than likely, in view of subsequent events, that a member of the Rootes family in a senior position would not have been considered desirable.

'The fact that Gilbert Hunt had not had the decency to tell me himself, and that it was left to his secretary, I thought was monstrous and exactly the way not to behave!

'I rang my father, who by then had retired. Naturally, he was in complete agreement and equally appalled, and so I resigned. I took my marvellous secretary, Gladys Taylor, with me and I became involved with Robins & Day. Some of Robins & Day was privately owned by the family, and also the British Leyland dealership in Dartford [Beadles of Dartford], which came into the business when my step-mother's father, John Beadle, died.'

Product Planning director Bill Papworth's opinion of Gilbert Hunt echoes that of Tim Rootes:

'Strange man … hugely ambitious. My impression of him was – very smooth, very polished, very well tailored, but not really very, well, sure of himself … He wasn't relaxed enough to be open to listen. He divorced his wife when he came from Massey Ferguson – he was always straining to keep up with his wife.'

Gilbert Hunt also left an immediate and lasting effect on a young Nick Rootes soon after Hunt was appointed: *'I went with my father and mother to dinner with Gilbert Hunt at a Mayfair restaurant called "Tiberio's". He had such an overly smooth manner that I instinctively mistrusted him.'*

Tim Rootes had helped set up GDR Holdings, a business that he *'ostensibly ran, but with the great help of Dudley Baker, who my father had extracted from Coventry some time before. Dudley did the day-to-day running of the business with exemplary efficiency, and I attended monthly board and finance meetings and any time I was required for a problem'.*

Latterly, Tim's passion and knowledge of horse racing helped him breed a series of successful horses at his Shutford Stud, Oxfordshire farm; the upheaval of the Rootes Group fiasco would, in time, be a distant memory.

RATIONALISATION AND RE-STRUCTURING

Initially, when the 1964 agreement was made, Chrysler sent high-calibre management over to Rootes to help with the integration of the two companies. One of them was Burke Hyde, who joined Rootes, from Chrysler, in 1965 as director of operations. In 1967, he was made director of general manufacturing, responsible for Rootes long-range planning and manufacturing. His credentials on paper were impressive: he had held senior engineering

management posts at six Chrysler plants over the previous fifteen years, having served as an engineering officer in the US Navy during the war. He also brought valuable expertise of overseas manufacturing while at Chrysler Australia. Tom Cotton was assigned to work with Hyde and was immediately impressed with his new boss:

'Burke Hyde had arrived and I went to work for him. They gave me some silly title like Systems and Programming Officer, Long Range Group.

'In June 1966, I was made Head of Long Range Planning. Burke Hyde was a super bloke. He was Group Manufacturing Engineering Director … because his task was to look at Rootes manufacturing and work out a long range plan for it. It was bits and pieces all over the place.

'Initially there were four of us – Burke Hyde and three others – in Halkin Street, one of the Rootes offices near Hyde Park … to try and sift out what sort of manufacturing plan [there should be] for the future. Burke Hyde, apart from being extremely nice, was very good and he excelled himself. He was one of those people who never said anything unless he had something to say. He was great to watch in a meeting; with all the people prattling around … all he had to do was clear his throat and everything went completely silent! In that initial stage they sent top men and they were trying to find out what the hell was going on! They were all well-mannered, nice people and bloody good at their jobs.

'We were on a very tight deadline to go to Detroit and present to the board what the long range plans were looking like. The model plans were fairly well set in stone – with the "B" Car …

'Burke Hyde had to present what the future was for the whole of the manufacturing side. The key points were to use the whole of that enormous area at Ryton for a proper assembly plant … straight from panels, body in white, paint, trim, to final assembly; he'd got all that fairly well sketched out.

'When we went over to Detroit to present the plans we were treated as honoured guests, but Chrysler were getting into trouble …'

Cotton was then tipped to run the Ryton plant, but Linwood was calling:

'George Cattell came to me and said, "Could you go up next Wednesday [in March 1967] and meet Peter Griffiths, who is going to be boss at Linwood? Peter needs someone who can integrate all of the supply, production control, transport" … you name it – all the support services between Pressed Steel and us and run it as a whole.

'Because, by then, Bill Bryant was out … so I went up on the Wednesday and we moved [from Leamington Spa] and I think I was in Linwood the following Monday.

'The Pressed Steel integration was an example of good management communication. That summer [1967], with the usual works closedown looming, there was the usual annual stock take. At first, they [management] said it would be absolutely impossible for the new combined factories at Linwood to do a full-blown stock take, to which we breathed a sigh of relief! … And at the last moment, the Chrysler accountants said, "We need a full physical stock check!!"

'There was a good mixture of Pressed Steel and Rootes people. But we did it and I think it was one of the things that melded them together – the impossible task of counting every nut and bolt in those two bloody great factories over a weekend … there's nothing like stark necessity to help people sort out their relationships. They were good people!

'I remember, just as we were about to get started, I was greeted by a bolshy group of shop stewards … and we just talked it through and said, "Look, we've got to do this … we have to know what we've got and what we haven't got …" And when they knew what it was all about, they went back in and they did a magnificent job – a wonderful job, in fact.'

Peter Griffiths, who had been made the new managing director of Rootes Pressings in 1966 was no stranger to

One of the few management jewels in the Chrysler crown was Burke Hyde, who joined Rootes in 1965 as Director of General Manufacturing. COVENTRY ARCHIVES

Rootes products, having been responsible for production of Rootes Group body shells at Pressed Steel, Cowley. In June 1963 he was put in charge of running Pressed Steel, Linwood. As well as bodies for the Imp range, Pressed Steel was still making bodies for the Ford Thames van, Rover 3-Litre saloon, cabs for BMC's Bathgate commercial vehicle plant and since 1960, the Volvo 1800 Coupé. A variety of railway rolling stock had also been produced at Linwood.

Tom Cotton then finished his time for Rootes at Linwood and left: 'I was at Linwood until June 1968 exactly ten years with Rootes, almost to the hour!'

In May 1967 Cyril Weighell took over the new position of director of product planning and development and on the truck side, A.J. Smith was made engineering-truck director, being responsible for Commer, Karrier and Dodge; Bill Garner returned from Linwood as manufacturing director for the Luton and Dunstable truck manufacturing sites in September 1967. Although Rex Watson Lee became director of the sales division, which also presided over the parts division, he decided that his loyalties were to Rootes and not Chrysler, and resigned in November '67 to run a Rootes car dealership on the Isle of Wight. Cliff Toll, director and general works manager of the truck operations also resigned at the end of November. He had been with Rootes since 1956, and went to join the British Motor Corporation Light Commercial Division in Birmingham.

Scott Glover transferred from Linwood in 1965, to Commer-Karrier as works manager. He was replaced at Linwood by Michael Hancock (son of former works director Bill Hancock). Glover was subsequently made quality and reliability director for car and truck manufacturing and returned to Linwood in 1969 as plant manager.

The transition that had started during 1967 with the Rootes management fallout continued into 1968 and '69. By the end of the decade the management structure and with it the Rootes ethos had completely changed.

In April 1968 Allen Sheppard was brought in from Ford as parts director, becoming director of the parts division in September '68. Sheppard had joined Ford in 1958 and was appointed manager of the Ford parts division in 1966. Geoffrey Ellison was appointed director of sales and marketing for Rootes Motors in August 1968 after returning from Rootes Venezuela. Another experienced Chrysler Corporation manager was James G. Shepherd, who had been a manufacturing facilities and assembly plant manager for Chrysler. In July 1968 he was appointed director of manufacturing for Rootes.

In June 1968 Rootes took a lease on an office block complex, Quadrant House, overlooking Dunstable's main shopping centre, with the intention of centralising the car and truck engineering departments. Subsequently, in March 1969, several hundred Quadrant House technical staff were moved to the newly acquired 'Engineering and Technical Administration Centre' at Whitley, near Coventry. Administration staff would continue to occupy Quadrant House at Dunstable until 1971, when they were moved to the Chrysler International offices at Bowater House in London.

Rootes purchased the 187-acre site at Whitley from Hawker Siddeley Dynamics for £1.8 million in October 1968. In Gilbert Hunt's announcement to the press at the Geneva Motor Show in March, he stated that, *'Whitley will be one of the best equipped technical design centres in the industry'*. Rootes planned to spend £4 million on establishing the new centre, over £2 million

of that investment being spent that year on adapting and equipping the site and the 470,000 square feet of buildings. By the end of 1969, it was intended that the centre would be operational, with 1,600 employees. The product planning function under Cyril Weighell and Bill Papworth was to be centralised at Whitley, but in August 1969, Papworth decided to leave Rootes to join Plessey and then Harland & Wolff in Northern Ireland in the spring of 1973. Papworth could not see a future for himself under Chrysler, headed up by Gilbert Hunt, and confirms a widely held view that the general calibre of management sent over to Britain by Chrysler Corporation was low, and the atmosphere that prevailed at the time prompted him to leave:

'When Chrysler [took over] they did the classic thing of getting rid of people from their HQs that they didn't want to fire. There were one or two that were really good, but there

The 187-acre Engineering Technical Centre at Whitley, photographed in 1976. COVENTRY ARCHIVES

An export Plymouth Cricket being emissions tested in the Chrysler UK technical centre at Whitley.
COVENTRY ARCHIVES

were a lot of second-raters ... They had a guy running the management structure operations for Europe called Bob Cannefax and he was based in Coventry. His title was Director of Management Organisation and Systems – Europe, and I took over from him ... and we were in the process of building a new computer centre at Whitley. That role gave me even more vision as to what was happening in Detroit ... There were some pretty nasty things happening both in Detroit and here ...so I took my leave ... these were murky times!'

By 1968 the rationalisation and re-structuring that had been implemented by Chrysler were starting to turn the business around. For the six months ending 2 February 1968, the company announced an operating profit of £927,000. But... much of the profit had come from the sale of buildings and land at Dunstable and the Dodge plant at Kew, as well as the British Light Steel Pressings plant at Acton and Thrupp and Maberly in Cricklewood, both of which were closed down and sold off during 1967. Even so, by the end of the 1968 financial year, profits had leapt to over £2.7 million. David and Peter Henshaw's higher estimate of £3.05 million also takes into consideration the £3.57 loss from Linwood. However, there remained the question of whether this profitable trend was sustainable or not.

There were many different misconceptions and misunderstandings on Chrysler's part as to exactly what the Chrysler Corporation had acquired in the Rootes organisation, but their myopic view of Rootes only reinforced their flawed opinions about its activities and potential. Rootes' way of doing business may have become outmoded and their way of operating was far from perfect, with many mistakes being made, but exports was one area in which Rootes had been undeniably successful. But that too was trampled upon by Chrysler, as Kit Power witnessed when he returned from Rootes Italia to London, having spent nearly twelve years in Rootes export territories:

'Pretty much all my time with Rootes was taken up with this overseas assembly ... The markets I spent time on were South Africa, Australia and New Zealand, but we also had small-scale CKD operations in Mexico, the Philippines ... and of course Dublin – Buckleys Motors, [later Rootes Motors Ireland Ltd] which was owned by Alec Buckley. They were the main assemblers and distributors for Ireland.

'We closed Rootes Italia and I came home and became the manager of the Overseas Shipping Department, so I was in charge of the outfit that produced all the shipping documentation and got both the CKD and built up cars [for export] down to the docks. That [office] was in Halkin Street.

'I did that for a couple of years ... After the shipping job, we had an office in Portland Street, off of Oxford Street, it was the Gulf Petroleum office, and I went to work for Harry Liebster, in 1967. Harry was an out-and-out Chrysler man, and he

was in charge of Rootes Overseas Sales, and I worked for him looking after the CKD market … but it all became very confused then because Chrysler had a unit called the Far East and Africa Organisation (FEAO) and that basically included Australia and Africa – in fact it was all the export markets except the Americas … and Europe of course. This was the Chrysler International business, and they set up their FEAO in Sydney, Australia and that was run by a man called Bob Worland.

'Within that, was Harry Liebster, who was looking after the Rootes sales in those areas. We went round the world with Harry in '69 and we went to Detroit and met all the people there and then we went across the Pacific to New Zealand, Australia, the Philippines and all the important markets, but we didn't go on to South Africa.

'In mid-'69 I began to wonder if there was going to be much future in all of this. Chrysler was not doing terribly well. One thing that I found depressing was that they had so little understanding of the sort of markets that we'd been working in and the sort of business that we had. I think there was a lot wrong with Rootes, in a way, but there were bits of it that were rather good. Particularly on the overseas side of it, we were doing some very good things and Chrysler had absolutely no understanding of this at all. Some of the people who came over from Detroit, frankly, were fairly second rate – at least that's what I thought. One of the problems is that, seen from the great Chrysler Corporation of the time, Rootes was pretty small beer, so they were not going to send their best people over. Perhaps the better people could have contributed more, but we didn't get them, so I decided that the time had come to move on and I left at the end of '69.'

In October 1969, Rootes did score an export record. Almost fifty per cent of total production went for export.

Of that total, 10,732 vehicles were trucks. A large proportion of the export figure came from one contract with the Sudan worth £2.25 million, to supply 1,420 medium and heavy commercial vehicles and 425 saloon and estate cars. About 1,300 were CKD trucks for assembly at the Sudanese Government's Motor Transport Works, and the remainder, which included coaches, buses and tankers, were supplied with bodies from various other British manufacturers. Much of the praise for obtaining the contract went to the team led by Harry Leibster, which included Roy Tatum, the export sales technical manager, Roger Gordon, Chrysler's African area manager and Toto Barsimian, head of Barsimian Motors, the Rootes agents in the Sudan. What was not clear to the uninitiated was that business like this had been hard fought for and won over many years by the Rootes Group's export division under Brian Rootes. Conflict through duplication of export resources was another area of business that Chrysler seemed unable to resolve easily.

Kit Foster has one abiding memory of working with Brian Rootes following Chrysler's takeover:

'I do remember one occasion which was quite amusing, when the take-over was complete. I was at some meeting in Devonshire House. This new American had come over, Brian Rootes was there. Before the meeting started, the American took out a little box of Chrysler pentastar badges that you wear in your lapel if you're a good corporate man and he went round and put these badges in front of us. Brian, I'm not sure if intentionally or not, came in a bit late to the meeting, saw something on his blotter and just brushed it aside as if it was cigarette ash. It was quite funny at the time.'

A V range Commer re-badged for export as a Dodge, at Dunstable awaiting despatch. Chrysler also used the 'Fargo' brand for certain territories.

By the end of the decade, Rootes was still showing a profit, but only just, at around £600,000. According to their own production figures, although exports were up in 1969, the total for the calendar year was 204,069, down by 12,732 vehicles on the previous year.

THE IMP – CHRYSLER'S 'LITTLE MISS UNDERSTOOD'

To say that Chrysler managers did not understand the Imp is a massive understatement – but the poor souls just didn't get it…!

Management who had spent much of their working lives in the automotive business in and around production plants building cars like the Plymouth Barracuda, Dodge Monaco and the Chrysler New Yorker would have been totally nonplussed by the Imp, especially when the smallest car Chrysler Corporation had built during the previous few years would have been the Dodge Dart or Plymouth Valiant compacts.

But that was only part of the problem. A fundamental inability and unwillingness to understand the ethos behind the Imp, the people building it and the Scottish mentality was a recipe for a bad outcome. They also seemed determined to stamp 'Chrysler' all over anything that was Rootes. At the truck plant in Dunstable, Bill Holmes, who was transferred from Coventry in 1967 to Dunstable as planning manager, remembers one of his first encounters with the Chrysler 'system' when '*a set of Policy and Procedure Manuals were dumped on my desk and I was told, 'This is the way we operate at Chrysler'!*

At Linwood, as well as at the other Rootes plants, Chrysler rapidly imposed American working methods and a top-down management structure which, when they did communicate, was aggressive and very negative. Duncan Robertson, a mild-mannered, polite gentleman, who worked at Linwood from day one to plant closure sums up the difference between his original bosses at Rootes and his new ones:

'The Rootes people were gentlemen – Chrysler were animals! Ron Taylor, a Canadian chief accountant for Chrysler, used to hold a meeting every month and one month we went in and he said, "What about you Duncan?" Point 1 – done, point 2 – done … out of seven points, I'd completed them all, except point 5 and I said, "I must confess, I haven't got round to that yet" and he replied, "Don't come here and confess …

confess in church if you have to!!" That was his attitude, and the American attitude.'

A new Chrysler manager, Bob Irwin, took over the role of manufacturing director in 1967. However, Irwin did not endear himself to the Linwood workforce. Rather than adopt a positive attitude, negativity was his hallmark. When Scott Glover returned to Linwood, Irwin was his boss, but it was '*not an easy relationship … although he was a knowledgeable production engineer, he had a dominating, bullying personality.*' Irwin invented what he called 'The Black Pig Award' and he would award it to what he considered to be the worst performing section in the plant, but, according to Glover, '*it backfired badly on him*'. Irwin used American management techniques which, as Glover remembers, '*undermined the authority of managers working for him*'.

To compound the fragile management/worker relations at Linwood, there was a core of troublemakers and agitators in the workforce too, as toolmaker Stuart Mitchell experienced:

'I started in 1962 [as a toolmaker] at Pressed Steel in the toolroom, then [went] to the press shop making panels for BMC lorries and the Volvo [P1800] … Rootes was OK but Chrysler was bad. A minority of workers during the Chrysler time were causing trouble with the foremen … their nickname was 'The Dirty Dozen' – ex-Clyde shipbuilders … There would be a strike and we'd find ourselves out on the street. A minority of workers closed that plant! I couldn't take anymore, so I left.'

Scott Glover witnessed how a problem at Linwood could affect Coventry and other plants very easily:

'The manufacturing strategy had maximised the utilisation of the assets they had purchased, but it meant that the two major manufacturing sites of Coventry and Linwood were wholly interdependent. As a result, a quite small localised dispute could very quickly have massive knock-on effects.'

The strike record at Linwood escalated under Chrysler. Delays getting supplies or any small stoppage would result in workers being laid off. This, in turn, would fuel the agitators' discontent. Although these types of disputes were short in duration, added up over a year, they proved to be expensive in terms of lost production, and therefore profit. In September 1967, a two-day strike involving

2,650 workers, over an increase in pay for car assembly workers following a revision of production schedules lost 8,000 working days, but the most significant dispute to date came in May 1968, which involved 4,600 workers and lost 79,000 working days. The dispute led to a month long stoppage, before a provisional arrangement was made for a resumption of work on 10 June.

The dispute, over the lack of agreement by all unions to a new pay and productivity deal, eventually became the subject of a court enquiry. Chrysler had been attempting to introduce pay parity with the pressings plant and the main plant. The old Pressed Steel plant had generally paid higher wages than the adjacent Linwood plant and this had led to rivalries between the two plants. In February 1968, the company put forward a proposal to improve productivity and eliminate any differences in the pay structures between the two plants. The deal was agreed upon by the two biggest unions, the National Union of Vehicle Builders and the Transport and General Workers Union, but was rejected by the remaining unions. Meanwhile, management, while attempting to negotiate the deal, implemented the plan without majority union agreement, resulting in a court of inquiry, which found that both unions and management were at fault, pointing out that the unions should have negotiated more fully by responding to management plans, and that management should not have implemented the plan with only the main two unions in agreement and that it *'took a risk which did not work out'* ... and *'had acted with rapidity in a situation requiring patience'*!

This was the only major stoppage at Linwood during this period, but in the first three months of 1969, there were twenty-seven other stoppages, costing nearly 30,000 man hours. In defence of the American management, although it was unacceptable that they pressed ahead with their plans regardless of union approval, in Detroit, manufacturers were used to dealing with one union – the United Auto Workers – not seven or eight, as had existed in the UK since the post-war period. Their attitude, however, showed an arrogance that was to prevail in their future attempts at negotiation. Management had also failed to implement a proper grievance procedure for the company, which would make future pay and conditions negotiations, such as measured day work, very difficult.

Despite production problems at Linwood and Chrysler's lack of interest in the car, Imp development continued with a flurry of new models. The intention from the outset was that a range of Imps and badge-engineered versions for other brands, not just Hillman,

would be offered. Joining the Singer Chamois Mark 2 saloon in October 1966, came the Chamois Sport, a visually similar car but powered by a higher-revving 55bhp version of the standard engine and fitted with twin Stromberg/Zenith carburettors and a new high-efficiency exhaust system made from two individual steel tubes to minimise back pressure; it was a bit noisier though! An identical specification, but different trim level, Sunbeam Imp Sport was also offered. In January 1967, the Hillman Californian was introduced, a fastback version of the Super Imp, but without the very useful opening rear window. It did have a folding split rear seat, which enhanced the luggage carrying ability of the Californian immensely. Singer followed up with a Chamois Coupé version in April 1967, and simultaneously, a new Hillman Husky,

1967 Singer Chamois Coupé. SINGER OWNERS CLUB

The Coventry-based Progressive Group used specialist car transporters to deliver new cars to dealerships. The Commer C Series tractor unit is hauling a consignment of Californians. COVENTRY ARCHIVES

Interior refinement in the new Singer Chamois Sport included reclining front seats. SINGER OWNERS CLUB

Hillman Imp Deluxe Saloon.

'1967 Singer Chamois Sport, photographed during its October 1966 *Motor* road test. SINGER OWBERS CLUB

Hillman Californian.

based on the Commer Imp van, was launched. Hot on the heels of the Chamois and Husky came Sunbeam's coupé, the Stiletto. With a vinyl roof, twin headlamps and a well trimmed interior, it was the most luxurious Imp to date.

In October 1968, Rootes launched a new face-lifted Imp. The new-look Hillman Imp had a cleaner front end with a single stainless bright trim line incorporating a 'Hillman' badge. Super Imps had an aluminium panel on the lower part of the front end, plus a corresponding panel on the rear. Californian and Husky were similarly adorned. Significant changes were made to the interior: newly-styled seats, steering wheel and a dash comprising of two round dials replaced the old Imp binnacle. Some of the changes brought the Imp up-to-date, as well as a few more years in the market place, but in an effort to reduce costs, other changes were just seen by customers as a cheapening of the product. Chamois sales suffered as would-be Singer customers debated whether a stick-on plastic veneer dash was a suitable substitute for the previous model's genuine wood dash and door cappings. A number of cost-cutting suggestions were made that were not practicable and so were dismissed. Others were feasible and did find their way into production, such as an improved synchromesh on the gearbox, which substantially reduced transaxle warranty claims, but others, such as the sealer coat on Imp bodies, which gave the cars their deep shine, was eliminated, and ended up costing the company more money in warranty costs as customers returned their new Imps to dealers, complaining of a poor paint finish.

Sadly, the new-look Imp styling did little to enhance UK sales. In 1967, around 40,858 Imps and variants were sold, according to SMMT figures, of which 2,965 were the new Californian fastback and 9,504 Chamois, which

presumably included Sport and Coupé. In 1968, a total of 35,295 Imps and their variants were sold, of which 7,008 were Chamois models. The Stiletto had its best year in '68 with around 3,000 being sold and virtually half that number the following year, before being discontinued

Hillman Husky.

Sunbeam Imp Sport.

Singer Chamois Sport.

Sunbeam Stiletto. The 'luxury' Imp. COVENTRY ARCHIVES

in 1972. Since its introduction, over 7,900 Stilettos had been sold. In 1969, sales of all fastback models had shrunk to approximately only eight per cent of the total 29,000 Imps sold that year.

Production of the Humber Hawk Series IV and IVA, Super Snipe Series V, VA and Imperial Saloon, Limousine and Estate models ceased in March 1967. Carbodies continued to do the finishing work on the big Humber estates, averaging twenty a week, until the models were run out later in the year. Since the introduction of the 'Series' Humbers in the late 1950s, Rootes had built over 30,000 Humber Hawks and 41,221 Super Snipes and Imperials.

VALIANT – THE IGNOBLE REPLACEMENT

American- or Canadian-built Plymouth Valiants had always been available to the UK since the its introduc-

tion in late 1959, but it was decided that from October 1966, the Australian-built Chrysler Valiant VC range should be made available, and from 1967, that Valiant VE models would form the replacement product range for the discontinued Humber Super Snipe and Imperial models. The idea for the Valiant being a replacement for the big Humbers came from Don Lander, who would later replace Gilbert Hunt as Managing director at Chrysler UK. On the face of it, this was a sensible decision: the Valiant was a well-built, comfortable car, with all the amenities that anyone would expect from a big, luxury family saloon car or station wagon, and being from Australia, it was already right-hand-drive. Standard power plant was Chrysler's excellent 273 cubic inch (4473cc) V8 with a three-speed Torqueflite automatic box. However, to expect the Valiant to replace traditional Humber sales overnight was like expecting a Las Vegas showgirl to take the lead in a Puccini opera at Glyndebourne – either way it would end in tears! The Valiant found favour with very few former Humber

the remarkable new Valiant V8

SALOON & ESTATE CAR
4½-litre Chrysler V8 engine
BUILT IN AUSTRALIA FOR BRITAIN

ROOTES

The official Chrysler UK Valiant sales brochure.

Chrysler Valiant V8 Estate.

customers and played only a brief part in the Rootes/ Chrysler product line-up until the early Seventies, when the Valiant V8 CH Saloon, Valiant Regal Saloon and Estate – both with V6 engines, and the Valiant Charger

Coupé, formed the line up. The range was not marketed effectively, nor was it made available to dealers nationally, being available only through Warwick Wright in London on a shared-commission basis.

The Chrysler Valiant was not the first V8-powered car to be considered for inclusion in the Rootes model line-up. Various attempts to breathe life back into existing Rootes models had been made over the years by utilising V8 engines. Some, like the Tiger, had met with more than a degree of success, but as Chrysler Corporation gradually increased their presence within Rootes, if a V8 power plant was to be used in an existing car, it had to be a Chrysler V8! The first example of an attempt at utilising stock Mopar power came in 1964, when the Experimental Department at Stoke fitted a 273 cubic inch V8 into a Mark 2 Sceptre. The results were astonishing in

Chrysler's excellent 273 cubic inch V8 was mated to a three-speed Torqueflite automatic transmission.

The Chrysler 312 cubic inch V8 installed in an experimental 'SC' Imperial. POST VINTAGE HUMBER CAR CLUB

HUMBER IMPERIAL (1964–67) SPECIFICATIONS

The distinctive profile of a 1966 Humber Imperial cuts quite a dash in any surroundings, whether parked outside a gentleman's club in Mayfair or cruising sedately along a country lane. Owner: Stephen Lewis.

West of England cloth seating was last used in a Humber in 1949 on the Pullman Mark 2 Limousine. The Radiomobile radio had front and rear speakers, with driver controlled sound balance. Owner: Stephen Lewis.

Body style
Four-door, four/five-seater saloon. Unitary construction

Engine
Humber 6-cylinder in-line, overhead valve – pushrod; hemispherical combustion chamber; cast iron cylinder head and block. Four bearing crankshaft; three bearing camshaft with harmonic cams. Fully cushioned engine mounts

Power output:	2965cc (180.8cubic inch) developing maximum 132.5bhp at 5,000rpm
Bore and Stroke:	3.437 x 3.25 in (87.31 x 82.55 mm)
Compression ratio:	7.5:1
Torque:	167lb ft (maximum) at 2,600rpm
Fuel pump type:	AC mechanical
Carburettor(s):	Twin Zenith/Stromberg 175 CD
Cooling system:	Water – pump and fan

Transmission
Borg-Warner DG automatic three-speed transmission with torque converter. (Borg-Warner 35 automatic fitted from 1966)

Gear Ratios:	Top 1:1; Intermediate: 1.435-3.375:1; Low 2.301-5.420:1; Reverse 2.01-4.72:1
Final drive:	Semi-floating with hypoid bevel final drive. 4.22:1

Electrical and Lighting
Ignition: Coil and distributor. 12-volt 57-amp Lucas BT9A battery with Lucas 45 amp alternator
Lighting and Instruments: Twin Lucas sealed-beam headlamps with foot-operated dip switch; separate sidelights with built-in self-cancelling flashing indicators; stop/tail/ flashing indicator lights mounted in rear wing; combined rear number plate/reversing lamp; auxiliary fog and spot lamps; two-speed windscreen wipers – self-parking; screen washer – electric; dual-tone horns; instrument lighting; automatic glove box light; clock; ammeter; boot lamp; two adjustable reading lamps in rear compartment; three cigar lighters; warning lights in edges of all doors

Additional standard equipment exclusive to Imperial: Reutter power-operated individual reclining front seats in West of England cloth or leather upholstery; Radiomobile push-button radio with front/rear speaker control; dipping 'anti-dazzle' rear view mirror; front and rear compartment ventilation and heating system; rear window demister; pile carpeting throughout, nylon rug in rear compartment; two foldaway tables; grab rails in rear compartment

Limousine models with sliding glass partition and adjustable leather trimmed bench type front seat. Fold-away tables in rear compartment omitted

Suspension and Wheels
Front: Independent coil springs with anti-roll bar
Rear: Semi-elliptic leaf springs with anti-roll bar
Armstrong telescopic chock absorbers fitted on front and Armstrong 'Selectaride' electrically controlled variable shock absorbers on rear
Wheels and Tyres: 15-inch disc wheels with chrome hubcaps and stainless trim rings. Dunlop RS5 6.70 x 15 tubeless cross-ply tyres
Steering: 'Hydrosteer' power-assisted
Brakes: Girling 11 3/8in (283mm) disc with vacuum servo

on front. 11in (279mm) drum on rear. Handbrake is operated mechanically on rear wheels. Brake warning light on facia

Dimensions

Overall length:	15ft 7½in (4,762mm)
Overall width:	5ft 10in (1,778mm)
Overall height:	4ft 11¾in (1,517mm)
Ground clearance:	7in (177.8mm)
Track:	Front: 4ft 87/8in (1,445mm) Rear: 4ft 7½in (1409.5mm)
Wheelbase:	9ft 2in (2,793mm)
Turning circle:	38ft (11.58m)
Fuel tank capacity:	16 Imperial gallons (72.7 litres)
Unladen weight:	3,745 lbs. (approx) (1,698 Kgs) (saloon, with petrol and water)

Performance:

30–70 mph:	18.2 seconds*
0–60:	16.2 seconds*
Top speed:	100 mph* (160km/h)
Fuel consumption:	17.5 mpg (overall)*

Colours: Saloon

Embassy Black with Beige West of England cloth or Fawn leather upholstery
Embassy Black with Grey West of England cloth or Grey leather upholstery
Royal Blue Metallic with Grey West of England cloth or Grey leather upholstery
Maroon with Beige West of England cloth or Fawn leather upholstery
Silver Grey Metallic with Grey West of England cloth or Red leather upholstery
Glade Green Metallic with Beige West of England cloth or Fawn leather upholstery

The Imperial was also available as a Touring Limousine with a glass screen division and leather front seats.
POST VINTAGE HUMBER CAR CLUB

Optional Extras: White sidewall tyres; seat belts; rear seat headrests

Price: Saloon: £1,749; Limousine: £1903 (both including Purchase Tax). October 1966

Model Variants: Limousine version
Significance: The last and finest of the big Humbers

All data Rootes Motors Ltd except *Autocar*, 11 June 1965

a straight line, but downright dangerous round corners! The car would have to be completely re-designed to make the V8 Sceptre handle properly, so it was shelved. Next, and more logically, came the 'Snipe Chrysler' project. In August 1965, a project plan was produced for six proto-types and six pre-production Super Snipes. One of the 'SC' cars with a 312 cubic inch, 250bhp V8 with Holley 4-barrel carburettors and a three-speed manual gearbox was taken around MIRA, achieving a remarkable 125 mph, but, according to Humber historian Stephen Lewis, *'it wrecked its standard Dunlop RS5 cross-ply tyres!'*

Returning to Coventry, the car was then fitted with a less powerful 273 cubic inch V8, but was found to be no quicker than the cars with the 6-cylinder engine it was to replace. The V8 Humber very nearly got into produc-tion. Development engineers worked tirelessly on the V8 Snipe-Chrysler project. One of them was Alan Horsfall:

'There had been a proposal to extend the life of the Snipe by putting an American V8 engine in it. I was part of the team … We'd got to the point that we were ready for production – in fact, the first shipment of engines had apparently left the US port, and we'd done all [of] the tooling … It was quite a job testing it. We had terrible problems with the drivelines – wind up of the back axle. There was a hill in Stoneleigh where we used to do standing starts … We had a hole cut in the floor so we could watch the back axle – it was a split prop shaft and it got itself tied up in knots! We had to put a big bracket on to stop the differential kicking up … We used a Ford engine first and then we looked at a Chrysler compact V8 to see if we could make that work … But because they decided to cancel it, we had to put it all back again! You can move for-ward, but it's the devil's own job to move backwards!! We did our best to return the specification back to how it was, before we had to accommodate the V8. That was a miserable job!'

The last Alpine – the Series
V. ROOTES ARCHIVE CENTRE TRUST

Installing the V8 from above, rather than the more conventional method of installing from underneath, was one of the production problems that saw the cancellation of the project, but in the end there were too many factors against the viability of the project and it died, along with the big Humbers.

When it came to the Sunbeam Alpine being axed, there were a few more mitigating circumstances to its discontinuation, but it was sad to see the demise of Rootes' flagship sports car. The Tiger had already bitten the dust but the Alpine continued on to early 1968 before getting the chop. The Alpine had endured nearly a decade, and in its final Series V form, with 1725 power, it was arguably the best Alpine yet, with almost a three-year production run from 1965, with over 19,000 units being built. Since its introduction in 1959, over 69,000 Sunbeam Alpines had been made.

Product rationalisation did not end with Humber and Sunbeam and now the Rootes name was used in conjunction with the Chrysler Pentastar logo on advertising and publicity material. In 1967, Singer Motors lost its autonomy as a standalone sales function and was merged with the other Rootes car brands, as sales manager Doug Field remembers:

'Singer reps either became Rootes representatives or were transferred back to Ryton to work within a new department headed by Bill Boss and Jack Caddy, known as Market Representation. [Its function] was planning the future of the UK and Northern Ireland Rootes dealer network ... to provision the number, size and location of all the future dealerships.'

Market Representation representatives went around the country photographing and analyzing the potential business from existing motor trade outlets and establishing the anticipated growth of towns and cities by visiting the local authorities. These statistics and development information was subsequently used back at Ryton to produce detailed planning reports, known as 'Provisioning Reports' for all Rootes car and commercial vehicle future main and retail dealerships. Duplication of resources, however, became an issue, and Doug Field could see that the Rootes function would not replace the Chrysler function:

'Chrysler had their own marketing organisation and therefore didn't need the work of the Rootes Market Representation Department. The consequence was the closure of the department in 1970 and the redundancy of all the management team and departmental staff. ... So ended my ten years service with the Rootes Group!'

In 1970, Rootes Motors Ltd was renamed Chrysler United Kingdom Ltd. The Singer name and its product range was also discontinued that year and Rootes, as a motor manufacturing business name, would no longer exist.

An Arrow Minx on the track at Ryton, July 1969.

CHAPTER 8

THE LONDON–SYDNEY MARATHON

'I had the confidence of knowing I could drive flat out all the way, and [that] it wouldn't break, so we had a fast tortoise to catch Ford's hare ... that car never missed a beat!'

Andrew Cowan – Outright winner of the London–
Sydney Marathon, 1968 – Hillman Hunter

On Sunday, 24 November 1968, ninety-eight modified family saloon cars left London on a 10,000-mile rally, which would finish twenty-three days later on the other side of the world – in Sydney, Australia. The event would take the cars along some of the world's worst roads, over the most dangerous, inhospitable and arduous terrain, in what would turn out to be the ultimate endurance test for drivers, crews and cars. The event was won by Andrew Cowan, Brian Coyle and Colin Malkin in a Hillman Hunter. Their victory was due to a combination of intense planning and preparation, engineering expertise and highly skilled driving. The event should rank alongside winning a gold medal at the Olympics, climbing Mount Everest, an Antarctic expedition or winning the football World Cup, and therefore be in the history books as part of British folklore! It isn't... but it should be. This is the story:

The idea behind the London–Sydney Marathon came about over a lunch date between Sir Max Aitken, the boss of Beaverbrook Newspapers, Jocelyn (later Sir Jocelyn) Stevens, managing director of the *Daily Express* and racing driver Tommy Sopwith, in late 1967. The *Daily Express* was to sponsor the event, and would be co-sponsored by the *Sydney Daily Telegraph*. Apart from great publicity for the newspapers, it was intended that the rally would give a much-needed boost to British manufacturers, who in this rather doom-laden late Sixties period were struggling with anti-British feelings towards their products and industry generally. In January 1968, Sir Max Aitken made a formal announcement of the rally. A committee was formed which included racing and rally driver Jack Sears, Tommy Sopwith and experienced race and rally personalities such as Tony Ambrose and Jack Kemsley. The winner would receive £10,000 in prize money and a £500 trophy.

Press coverage of the event was undertaken by *Daily Express* motoring correspondent David Benson, with photography by the legendary Fleet Street snapper, Victor Blackman, who, with trusty Nikon 'F' would cover the whole of the rally in black-and-white and colour. Although the organisers had worked out a route for the rally fairly early on, it was clear that some compromises had to be made. It was intended that the greatest possible distance should be covered overland, but entry permits could not be obtained for Singapore and Burma, and Colombo presented big problems in ferrying a hundred cars from India. With the Suez Canal being closed due to the Arab-Israeli war, this reduced the number of ships in Far Eastern waters capable of carrying a hundred cars. Jack Sears consequently negotiated with P&O Line for cars and crews to be carried on the SS *Chusan* from Bombay to Fremantle. Sears and Tony Ambrose were then sent to reconnoitre the route down to Bombay, which included negotiating with local governments to reduce any red tape and paperwork at border crossings to a minimum, and secure the support of local police and motoring organisations. It was not until May that entrants were informed about the whole route, following a survey of the Australian section from Fremantle to Sydney by Sears and Ambrose.

The first that Andrew Cowan heard about the rally was when he was competing, for Rootes, in the 1968 Monte Carlo Rally, shortly after the official announcement. Initially, little notice was taken of the event, but as the word got out, it became all too apparent that no self-respecting manufacturer's competition department would want to miss out on the potential publicity that this event would garner; it therefore seemed that Rootes also had to take the London–Sydney Marathon seriously if it was to maintain its credibility as a major volume car manufacturer. So, at one of the regular Monday morning Rootes Administrative Committee meetings, the decision was made to provisionally enter the rally.

One of the first stumbling blocks was that of budget constraint. The Rootes Competition Department manager, Marcus Chambers, had always managed to get sufficient funds to enable them to run in most of the major rallies – like the Monte Carlo, the RAC Rally and the Alpine – but with Chrysler now calling the financial shots, things were even tighter. Rootes had already committed part of their budget to the 1968 Circuit of Ireland and the International Scottish Rally, so it was decided to not compete in the RAC Rally that year, or the Monte Carlo Rally in January 1969, in order to keep costs down. The decision was also made that Rootes would only enter two cars, although they could bet that their main rivals Ford and British Leyland would enter three, if not more. Marcus Chambers and Rootes team manager, Des O'Dell, really stuck their heads above the parapet in order for Rootes/Chrysler to sanction the Marathon effort, and they would have both certainly got their heads shot off by Chrysler bosses if things had gone wrong. But this was just the kind of event that Des O'Dell had wanted to get his teeth into, and so set about quickly making sure that everything that could be done was done, to make sure it was a success.

EVALUATION, TESTING AND PREPARATION

The first task for Rootes was to choose an appropriate car for the job. Des O'Dell had initially wanted to use a Group 6 Hillman Imp, but they soon realised that a bigger car would be needed to carry the spares and equipment necessary, as well as being able to negotiate the rough pot-holed roads in Turkey, Afghanistan and the all-important Australian section. With these factors in mind, it was decided that the Hillman Hunter would, in theory at least, fit the bill. Early thoughts were for a V-8-engined Hunter, but with too many unknowns and not enough time, this idea was quickly dismissed. Besides, the Hunter had never been designed as a V8-engined car.

Although the Hunter had not been used in any competition events, one car had been prepared for the Alpine Rally for private entrant Harry Skelton and Gerry Birrell to drive, but it was withdrawn at the last minute and used as support vehicle for the Imps instead. Unfortunately, Gerry Birrell crashed on the Col de Galibier, and the car was brought back to the competition department with a lot of front-end damage. However, the Hunter was pulled out again, repaired, and was to prove an ideal test car. Initial testing was done at the Fighting Vehicle Research and Development Establishment's testing ground at Chobham in Surrey. Here, it would be

'London–Sydney prototype'. Des O'Dell, Andrew Cowan and Colin Malkin with the Marathon test car.

possible to simulate the roughest of roads that might be encountered on the rally, and to see what might break! Des O'Dell's plan was to build a car that would be utterly reliable, and be capable of covering the whole 10,000 miles without mechanical failure of any kind. He likened the rally to 'a series of Le Mans events', with which he had had an enormous amount of experience with the GT40s whilst at Ford, so every aspect of the Hunter had to be proven, and every weakness found and modified.

The front suspension layout on the Hunter was very similar to that of the Ford Cortina – i.e. Macpherson struts – and Andrew's brother Willie Cowan had had considerable experience rallying Cortinas, so was a mine of information when it came to strengthening the front struts in order to prevent them from coming through the front wings under the severe pounding they were likely to receive. The rear suspension struts were also plated and strengthened. Further body strengthening was carried out and the testing began. After 100 miles around the Chobham course, the Hunter stood up to the equivalent of covering the whole of the RAC Rally... and it didn't break! But this wasn't enough to satisfy Des O'Dell or Andrew Cowan, so testing with the Hunter continued at another tank testing ground, and sure enough components did start to fail – but not seriously; a bolt fell off the water pump, but they refitted it and carried on. The test car, which became known as 'London-Sydney Prototype', was subjected to every kind of driving condition they were likely to encounter, and eventually they did get the front suspension struts to splay, so they knew that additional strengthening was needed. A special sump guard was also fitted. Fabricated in magnesium, it weighed only 16lb (7.25kg). For additional protection a steel skin was fitted over it. Every minute detail of the car's specification was looked at and constantly revised, and by now the team were starting to get a good idea of what they wanted as a final specification.

Time, and more testing went on, and the jigsaw pieces were starting to be pieced together. In September, Andrew and Brian Coyle would make a reconnaissance trip of the course, after which two decisive modifications would be made: when Andrew returned, a publicity event to show journalists how the testing was progressing, was organised by Jenny Nadin, of Rootes Public Relations Division, and during the event, one of the Dunlop

The number 2 Hunter at Chobham. ROOTES ARCHIVE CENTRE TRUST

Andrew Cowan, in the London–Sydney prototype test car, takes the plunge at the Fighting Vehicle Research and Development Establishment's testing ground at Chobham, Surrey. ROOTES ARCHIVE CENTRE TRUST

A broken Dunlop wheel was the reason why Marcus Chambers decided to go for Minilite wheels for the marathon cars.

alloy wheels shattered into several pieces. This caused the team to re-think the wheel situation. Steel wheels were re-fitted for testing to continue, and a decision was made to abandon the wheels from Dunlop in favour of Minilite alloys. Although Dunlop was sponsoring Rootes by supplying tyres and wheels, the Minilite had to be bought, which put further strain on Marcus Chambers' already tight budget, but it was a very necessary specification change. The second major decision affecting the reliability of the car was the rear axle. During Andrew's recce, a half-shaft broke in Bulgaria; another went on the 'prototype' during testing, which meant that a completely revised rear axle setup would be needed. This is where Des O'Dell's experience while at Aston Martin came in; he suggested using a Salisbury 4HA rear axle with much beefier half-shafts than the standard Hunter axle, which would be, as Andrew put it, *'a belt and braces job, with no chance of any failure!'*

Further body stiffening, including 'A' pillars and roof section were made, as well as a strengthened front cross member to support the Holbay engine that was to be installed. The essential 'belt and braces' aspects to the specification, however, came at a cost – weight! It was consequently decided to use Perspex side and rear windows and an aluminium bonnet to try and save precious weight. By the time the car was fully loaded with crew, spare tyres on the roof, plus a roof-mounted metal tool box, the car was weighing in at nearly 32cwt.

'Rough stuff' testing was one aspect of vehicle evaluation that was essential, but the car would also be running at relatively high speeds over smooth tarmac surfaces, such as the types of roads encountered in France and Italy, so a trip to the Motor Industry Research Association test track near Nuneaton was made to test the car over different road surfaces, and opposite cambers, at high speeds. They were also able to see how the engine stood up to running on low-octane fuel. Shell provided enough 80 octane fuel to enable the team to evaluate the car, which led to a modification to the distributor to enable the advance and retard on the distributor to be adjusted in accordance with the type of fuel being used. In his memoir of the rally, Andrew Cowan explains how it worked:

> 'We realised early on that no matter how much we tried, somewhere, sometime, we would pick up a load of paraffin-type fuel that would start the engine pinking like mad, yet going all the way to Istanbul from London, we would want the ignition timing to be right for normal motoring; which is eight degrees before top dead centre. We built a pointer in the distributor and by using a special spanner made for the job we could turn one screw until it clicked which would retard the ignition. This made the pointer slide along a scooped slot we had cut; until it pointed to two degrees after top dead centre which we knew was ideal for 80 octane fuel. This meant that I turned the screw one way when we went on the bad stuff and turned it back when … we had good fuel … This worked like a treat.'

Immediately after the reconnaissance trip by Andrew and Brian, a suggestion was made by Des O'Dell of having a crew of three, instead of just Andrew and Brian Coyle as originally intended. Although a number of very capable drivers were considered, including Bernard Unett and Gerry Birrell, it was Colin Malkin who was chosen. Brian had highlighted in his report back to Rootes management that a crew of three was essential for the Australian section. Andrew thought it an excellent decision:

> 'The thing was that I had realised we were going to be very, very tired, and going Perth to Sydney non-stop in three days … Des said about going three up with Colin Malkin in the back. Deciding to go three up was our final dotting of the 'I's' and crossing of the 't's'!'

Colin Malkin had proved himself as a tough and capable rally driver, having come second in his class in the 1966 Welsh Rally and third overall in the 1968 Scottish Rally, both in Rallye Imps.

THE RECCE

One of the most important aspects to winning any major international rally event is how well drivers and crew know the course. For an event like the London–Sydney 'the recce' was even more crucial than an established rally like the Monte Carlo, due to the many unknown factors that the teams would encounter.

In mid-September, Andrew Cowan and Brian Coyle set off on their reconnaissance trip in a high-mileage Mark 1 Hunter, that had been used by the Engineering and Transport Department at Stoke and converted to a 'recce car' by the competition department. The car was fairly standard, other than having twin Stromberg carburettors and some of the modifications that testing at Chobham had brought to light. These modifications would enable Andrew and Brian to obtain as accurate as possible a picture of what the various stages would be like for real. It was prepared by the competition department and received a top-end engine overhaul from engine builder Richard Guy prior to the recce. It was intended that they would do the leg down to Bombay together, and then Brian would continue on to do the Australian section on his own. Andrew soon regretted not doing a recce of Australia and felt that it was a mistake, and that things could have gone horribly wrong due to him not having first-hand knowledge of the Australian roads and route.

Everything went well for them on the first leg through France and Italy, until they reached Bulgaria; and about a hundred miles from the Turkish border disaster struck in the form of a broken half-shaft. A catalogue of dramas was about to unfold at this point in order to get the car to Istanbul, where Chrysler Turkey would be able to fix the stricken Hunter. Getting the parts from Coventry to Istanbul would not be a problem; getting the car from Bulgaria to Turkey would be! A phone call to Coventry got the replacement half-shaft out in a day to Istanbul, where it would remain in customs, while Andrew and Brian attempted to organise transport for the car. The driver of a Jeep towed them forty miles to the next town, where they stayed the night. The following morning, a search in vain for one of the Trans-Asia trucks that often passed through ended in the car being hooked up to a breakdown truck to get them as far as the border' where they were able to push the car over the border into Turkey, and hire a truck to get them to Istanbul. With the Hunter still on the back of the truck, they decided to sleep in the car to prevent pilferers getting to it, and so that the impatient truck driver didn't drive off in the middle of the night with their car! A stroke of luck enabled them to make contact with Kenneth Knowlton, the financial adviser to Chrysler Turkey. A taxi driver explained that they were only about twenty yards from his apartment.

Knowlton arranged a hotel for them and for the car to be repaired. Another four or five days passed, along with some discreet changing hands of money, to persuade the Turkish customs officials to let the parts out, before the car could be put back on the road.

Once fixed, the next decision that had to be made was the first of the two route options in the rally. From Sivas in Turkey, there was a choice of taking the longer northern route, which was the main route, to the next check point at Erzincan, or the southern route, which was shorter, but had bad roads, especially in the rainy season. They decided to take the northern route to Erzincan. The southern route in September was a veritable sea of mud due to the heavy rain. The next route decision was between Tehran, in Persia (now Iran), and Kabul in Afghanistan. Time was starting to run out, as Brian was scheduled to catch a plane in Bombay, so they drove non-stop to Tehran. Again, a northern or southern option was on offer. The northern route was a hundred miles longer, over the Elburz Mountains, to Mashhad, but a faster road than the shorter southern route, but held little advantage for a relatively slow car, so the southern route was chosen.

From Mashhad, they drove south-east down to the Afghan border. The customs post was another ten miles over the border into Afghanistan, and from here on the phrase 'sublime to the ridiculous' took on a new meaning as far as roads were concerned. Either smooth tarmac or concreted roads that had been built jointly by the Americans and Russians, stretched for over 700 miles, with virtually no traffic. The only impediment to progress was the many 'tolls' that were put in place by local villagers as an income source. These roads were a stark contrast to the Lataban Pass from Kabul, which was basically a goat track across mountains and *'the roughest road we had ever seen anywhere'*, and ended at Sarobi. Out of Sarobi and into west Pakistan, the roads were mainly surfaced into India and down to Delhi, with a relatively straightforward run into Bombay (now Mumbai) via Lahore.

From Bombay, Andrew flew back to England and left Brian to cover the Australian section. Brian flew to Perth, where he was supposed to pick up a car from the Chrysler agency there, but the car was not available, so he flew on to Adelaide where a Hillman Safari Station Wagon was laid on, together with a driver, Chris de Fraga. From Adelaide, Brian and de Fraga, an experienced Australian rally driver and journalist, would only be able to cover the route through part of South Australia and the section to Sydney. They set off from Adelaide north to Quorn and up through the Flinders Mountain Range as far as Blinman, then south-east to Mingary and on to New South Wales. The route briefly dipped into Victoria before turning north-east to Sydney. Upon arrival in Sydney, Brian then flew back to Perth where he met up with Brian Corey, a service engineer from Chrysler Australia. They then covered the route through Western Australia and the remaining part of South Australia in a Chrysler Valiant Estate.

The recce was valuable for a number of reasons, but two very valuable points came out of it. Firstly, rumours had been circulated by the Australian teams that time lost getting to Bombay did not matter, due to the fact that most entrants would lose a great deal more time on the Australian section. This simply wasn't true, and Brian was able to dispel this myth straight away. Secondly, Andrew and Brian realised they had to be quick in the Turkey and Afghanistan sections, and that the Sivas to Erzincan stage may just well be one of the most important sections in the whole rally. So, Andrew persuaded the 'powers that be' to let him return to Sivas. This time, he took Colin Malkin with him. They flew to Ankara and hired a car, from where they drove both the southern and northern routes, to find that the southern route had completely dried out and consequently were able to knock forty-six minutes off the time it took to cover the northern route. This, for Andrew, made the southern route a definite option, but only if it was dry!

The first recce took twenty-five days and upon his return Andrew was given a ninety-five point questionnaire by Des, in order to highlight problems, solve them, and to give an idea of any other issues that had to be dealt with. The questions ranged from the performance of the car, including fuel and oil consumption, to ambient temperatures and road conditions. One question was about brake pad wear, and Andrew was able to state that, 'The [front] pads will last 6,000 miles, but should be changed at Tehran (approx. 3,500 miles) The [rear] shoes will be OK to Bombay.'

HILLMAN HUNTER – THE FINAL SPECIFICATION

The testing and evaluation of the 'London–Sydney Prototype' test car, plus the 'recce car', as well as the technical modifications that had been made, would act as a template for Andrew Cowan's rally car. Additionally, it had always been Rootes' intention to run two cars, so a second team — in a virtually identical Hillman Hunter — would be entered

The RAF Marathon team: Flt. Lt. David Carrington; Squadron Leader Tony King; and Flt. Lt. John Jones. COVENTRY ARCHIVES

by the RAF Motor Sports Association, driven by Flight Lieutenant David Carrington, Squadron Leader Tony King and Flight Lieutenant John Jones.

Andrew Cowan's car, MKV 15G, was built from new around July/August time. By the time the second car was about to be commissioned, the issue of budget was starting to rear its ugly head again. Funds were being eaten up rapidly, so in order for the second rally car to be run, Des O'Dell literally donated his own company car, LHP 676F, to be stripped and rebuilt as near as possible to the 'rally spec' of Andrew Cowan's car.

The engines for both cars were built by Richard (Dick) Guy; Holbay 1725cc units similar to the ones that Rootes were fitting in the Rapier H120 models:

> 'We took the basic engine, polished the con rods … [built] the Holbay engine [which] had flat-top pistons – the 1500 piston, [from] the short-stroke engine. The normal 1725 engine had a dished piston, even on the Hunter GT. The Marathon engine had the same camshaft and [dual twin-choke Weber 40 DCOE] carburettors, but lower compression ratio. It was probably only 8.5:1 compression when it left us, because of the fuel in Afghanistan which was, at best, 85 octane, and the engine itself was susceptible to burning out valves. Very few of our service cars used to come back from the Alpine Rally or the Monte Carlo Rally without having burnt out an exhaust valve – it was common.'

Due to the problem of having to use potentially poor fuel on the first section to Bombay, and decent high-octane fuel in Australia, Richard Guy then had to build a high-compression head for the Australian section for Andrew Cowan's car, which he had to take out to Bombay. It was essential for them to be as quick as possible on the Australian section if they were to achieve a place in the first five cars to Sydney. Although no official figures seem to exist, Richard Guy reckoned that with the high-compression head the car would be capable of putting out 120bhp @ 6,000rpm, thus squeezing out of it an extra

Competitions Department Engine builder Richard Guy with Cowan's Marathon Hunter outside his father's garage and Rootes service agency in Marnhull, Dorset. RICHARD GUY

10 to 15 brake horsepower over the low-compression head. The second rally car, for the RAF team, ran on a low-compression head all the way.

Dual Bendix electric fuel pumps were fitted in place of a mechanical pump (although a spare mechanical pump was fitted as a back up). Arthur Bird, the competitions department's electrical wizard, was responsible for designing and installing the fuel pumps, which were wired in such a way that the 'off' position on the switch was number one pump and the 'on' position was number two pump, so there was no risk of one or both being accidentally knocked off. A 36-gallon petrol tank was fabricated, covered in fibreglass and positioned behind the rear seat in the boot, in order to get as much weight as possible over the rear wheels. The tank was actually three 12-gallon tanks, with feed lines that could be controlled

Cowan's Hunter receiving final preparations in the workshops of Rootes Competition Department. ANTHONY STEVENS

A smiling Des O'Dell with the Cowan Hunter in the workshops. ANTHONY STEVENS

by Andrew. '*I had taps beside me so I could blend the fuel with 101 octane to lift the 94 up a bit.*'

Arthur Bird put a great deal of thought into the electrics on the car. All cables had to be run inside the car so that maximum protection was afforded in all conditions; cables were cotton covered, not plastic, to prevent the risk of melting. The wiring harness was a three-in-one affair covering the body and rear, the facia and the engine and lamps. A comprehensive set of driving and auxiliary lamps, a Lucas D9 40 ampere/hour battery, and heavy-duty alternator were just part of the array of custom-built electrics.

Arthur Bird couldn't help approaching tasks with a sense of humour, though. At the end of his report, detailing how the electrics were designed, he states:

> '*A host of other circuits, spare coil and normal functional warning light systems are used, but one touch of luxury, a cigar lighter, was asked for by Andrew Cowan, and would you believe it, it was the only fuse that blew. I reckon someone dropped a tanner down the hole!*'

Andrew Cowan also asked for two horns – the normal car horn operated from a horn ring on a Rapier Series V steering wheel and an air horn operated by a button on the passenger side of the steering wheel. Front seats, based on the 'high-back' design used on the American export cars, were fitted to provide better lateral support for driver and navigator. Andrew specified a towelling material to alleviate the obvious perspiration issues that would be encountered with vinyl seats. Andrew's other 'must have' was overdrive – to be fitted on all four forward gears. He was asked, however, not to use it in first gear because the prop shaft would not be turning fast enough to provide the oil pressure in the overdrive to engage it. The transmission guru was Brian Wileman. Brian's skill as a transmission engineer was very important as far as Andrew was concerned, because of the treatment he knew the gearbox and clutch would get. Peter Burgess, Derek Hughes and Jack Walton were the chassis engineers, and Ron Breakwell was the body engineer – the tinsmith. Gerry Spencer was the workshop supervisor who had gained invaluable experience in Rootes rally car preparation, and according to Andrew Cowan, '*knew all the wrinkles to make cars stand up to all conditions*'. Other engineers also had input into the preparation of the car that weren't directly working for the competitions department: Wynne Mitchell acted as a useful link man between Experimental and Competition working on the suspension set up:

A Marathon car is born. Andrew Cowan and Colin Malkin posing for a publicity photo with the Marathon Hunter.

'It was completely unbalanced spring-wise; too stiff at the rear. I remember Des O'Dell saying, "It came towards me like a bloodhound pup!" All we did was reverse the helper springs on the front, [and] that cured it.'

Armstrong shock absorbers helped the now raised suspension, and the 5½-inch wide Minilite alloy wheels were shod with Dunlop SP44 175 x 13 tyres. A Marathon Rally car was born!

FINAL PREPARATIONS

With the rally car for Andrew finished and assembled, all that was needed was road testing. It was now November, and it was getting very close to the start of the rally. It was at this point that the final attention to detail that Des O'Dell had, in Andrew's opinion, helped them win:

'One of the most clever things we did was – we built the rally car, I did 3,000 miles in it … drove it into the factory – took the back axle off, spring carriers off, shock absorbers … brakes … and put them in a box. We took the gearbox and overdrive off – checked it and put it in a box … the two front struts, and put them in a box, and sent them [all] out to Bombay. We knew we had about four and a half hours in Bombay … just dropped the back end and put the new one on … took the gearbox and overdrive, head, front struts off, put the new ones on and the new high-compression head on … and we arrived in Perth with a brand new car!'

Just prior to the start, Des issued a comprehensive set of written instructions to all involved, with highly detailed requirements, from start to finish. The instructions left no doubt as to what was expected of his team. They listed all personnel, addresses and telephone numbers of all controls and contacts, as well as expected weather conditions including ambient temperatures and road surface conditions, which had been collated by Marcus Chambers, with the assistance of his secretary Ann Barnes. The instructions also showed how well Des O'Dell knew the people working with him, as exemplified in these extracts from his notes:

<u>'NOTES TO SERVICE CREWS</u>
Please remember, as I have stated many times, there is <u>always</u> a way. The problem is thinking of it in time. Also remember, in this rally there is no service car 20 miles up the road, and when you let the car go from your service point it has 1,000 miles to do before it will see any of your colleagues. It will therefore affect you personally if the car is lost through mechanical failure between you and the next service point…. Remember, you have earned yourselves a reputation for being the finest service crews in the business. This is your chance to really confirm it.

<u>INSTRUCTIONS [second day – Paris]</u>
Complete check over of cars. Your reason for being so close to the start of a 10,000 mile rally is to ensure that the crews are completely happy with their cars, and to sort out any problems that may have occurred since the start. It is well-known that the moment competition numbers are put on the side of a car, things like alternators, flashers and horns stop working. You are there to beat these gremlins.

<u>INSTRUCTIONS [third day – Belgrade]</u>
<u>DEREK</u> Remember that <u>you</u> and only you are personally responsible for the mechanical condition of both cars leaving your service point. I do not have to tell you that should a sump plug fall out of one of the cars 100 miles from you, you will have to answer to me. So any work carried out on the rally cars by any other person must be physically checked out, to your satisfaction, before the car leaves. I am relying on you; this is why I have sent you here.'

The instructions detailed, on a day-by-day basis, what the service, fuel and spares situation should be at every service point and what needed to be done. A separate and equally comprehensive travel programme was also issued. Much of the detailed weather and climate information put together by Marcus Chambers was provided by the RAF, who had also been very helpful when it came to advising on survival training and vitally important health precautions for the rally crews. Inoculations against various diseases alone would not be sufficient to guarantee against illness. Avoiding contracting dysentery or other bowel infections through contaminated water or unknown food sources and taking precautions against malaria and excessive salt loss were just some of the essential pieces of education to enable the crews to maintain their health throughout their long, arduous journey. Using only trusted food sources from recognised personnel and water that had gone through the appropriate purification process were logical steps to preventing illness. One of the less obvious, but most valuable precautions, was for crew members to avoid touching their mouth, as this was one of the most common ways to allow germs to enter the body!

With the start day looming ever closer, various spares and essentials were loaded into the cars, and a last-minute modification was made to the Kangaroo bars. Wire mesh was fitted behind the 'roo bar', as Andrew had experienced an eagle flying through the bar on the recce, which had broken the windscreen, so he was concerned that anything bigger might hit the radiator. For the Australian section, Des also insisted they carry a spare radiator bolted onto the boot lid of the car.

As well as the two Rootes Hillman Hunters, the service crews would have responsibility for three cars entered by Simca, a privately entered Chrysler Valiant Estate and two cars entered by the British Army Motoring Association. Des had offered assistance to them for the 'unqualified' use of their Land Rover at Kabul!

THE EVENT

On Friday, 22 November, service crews and rally crews left Coventry for London and the start of the Marathon. The previous night, engineer Wynne Mitchell had worked through the night to completely re-write the road book to Bombay, to make it as clear as possible for navigators. Crews and drivers would stay at the Bromley Court Hotel, Bromley, Kent, where a final drivers' meeting would take place that evening. Marcus Chambers and Derek Hughes would set off for Belgrade with a Singer Vogue Estate loaded with spares and Dunlop tyres. At Dover they were to catch the night ferry, to arrive in Dunkirk at 23.30hrs (11.30pm). They were expected to reach Belgrade by Sunday. After an overnight stop in Austria, they actually arrived eighteen hours ahead of the rally.

Enthusiastic crowds surround one of the Simca 1100s at the Crystal Palace start of the London–Sydney Marathon. COVENTRY ARCHIVES

Colin Malkin, Brian Coyle and Andrew Cowan pose for a photograph with the new Miss World, Penelope Plummer, of Australia, at the Crystal Palace start of the London–Sydney Marathon. COVENTRY ARCHIVES

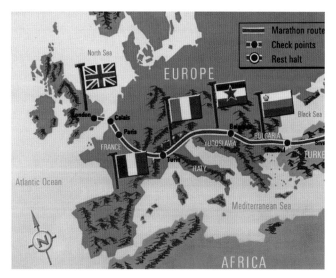

The route – Day 1 to
Day 4 – Europe.

On Saturday 23rd, after scrutineering, the cars would then go into Parc Fermé at Crystal Palace Stadium, until the start the following morning. Andrew Cowan did not get a good draw out of the hat – number 75, which meant he would be about an hour and a quarter behind the first car. But this had little consequence as the rally was, in effect, a series of timed stages, in which cars had to get through each stage within the allotted time, while picking up as few penalty points as possible from being late. The RAF team were drawn number 45. The three Simca 1100s driven by Bernard Heu/M. Harnat, R. Masson/M. Py and Pierre Boucher/M. Houel were drawn 46, 88 and 100 respectively. The Chrysler Valiant was number 5.

DAY ONE – London–Paris

After last-minute checks, on start day, Sunday, 23 November, they were finally ready for the off, but not before a last-minute sponsor was added to the team by Andrew, when he purloined a watch from Seiko after his own had stopped.

At 2pm, amid a packed Crystal Palace Stadium, the first car was flagged away. It was a Ford Cortina GT driven by Bill Bengry. Instead of driving straight down to Dover, the route would take the rally cars back into central London, round Trafalgar Square and across Westminster Bridge, before heading south to Dover. This gave the throngs of people who had packed the start of the route a chance to see rally cars from around the world close up. It also afforded an ideal photo-shoot for press and broadcast media who had turned up en masse. The

rally car drivers responded to the cheers of encouragement from the crowds by blowing their air horns, but after hearing 'Colonel Bogey' for the umpteenth time, a traffic police officer had had enough and stopped one rally car to let the driver know that, *'This is a car rally sir, not a bloody symphony!!'* The incident did not go un-noticed by the press and ended up on the front page of the *Daily Mirror*.

As the Rootes cars made their way to Dover for the crossing to Calais, their service crews were en route to their various service points. Peter Burgess and Brian Wileman were destined for Paris, via Dover and Calais, while Gerry Spencer and Richard Guy were flying out to set up the service points in Turkey. Richard explains that getting from Istanbul to the first service point was not as easy as they had anticipated:

'We flew to Istanbul. We got a taxi [a battered '61 Chevrolet Biscayne Sedan] from the airport to Erzincan, but we kept getting punctures. The driver had three spare wheels in the boot and we had at least two punctures on the way, and Gerry helped him with one. We set up a service point with Chrysler Turkey and went back to Istanbul and got an internal flight to Erzerum [for the next leg of the rally].'

Although the entrants had to drive through fog on the way to Paris, Cowan and team had no problems, and arrived in good time. Some drivers struggled, however. Innes Ireland, in a Mercedes had to drive on side-lights for 150 miles, due to generator trouble. Dave McKay, in a Holden, got lost twice in the fog. The control was at Le Bourget Airport, just outside Paris, where Peter Burgess and Brian Wileman were waiting for the Hunter to give it a check over.

DAY TWO – Paris–Turin–Belgrade

Monday, 25 November. Unbeknown to Andrew Cowan, the French police had put a ban on rally cars using the motorways, and gave the rally cars a police escort through back roads, but Andrew was having none of that and went straight onto the autoroute anyway and down through France. The route would take them through the Mont Blanc tunnel and on to Turin, then through Udino, and into northern Yugoslavia (now Slovenia) to Ljubljana and then Belgrade. Dense fog and icy patches on roads caused problems for some crews, but Andrew and team had an easy run, despite some snow between Switzerland and Italy.

Although less than 48 hours into the rally, some cars had started to develop minor mechanical faults. Peter

Harper's Ford Cortina suffered a broken water pump near Venice and a Russian Moskvitch was delayed by transmission failure. The Swedish Ford team of Bengt Söderström and Gunnar Palm limped into Turin with a broken engine. A cog in the overhead camshaft drive on their Ford Cortina Lotus had collapsed. A few 'phone calls later revealed that there were only three similar cars like that registered in Northern Italy. Eventually, one was tracked down, but the owner wanted £100 for the tiny cog! Söderström made out the cheque. Andrew Cowan witnessed the event. Söderström was philosophical about the incident:

'I would rather pay £100 now than drop out of the rally – and that fellow knew it. I hope he is never in the same kind of trouble himself.'

On arrival in Turin, the Agip motel where the control was situated proved inadequate when it came to catering for seventy or so rally crews, so after a quick wash and brush-up Andrew and crew pressed on for Belgrade, Yugoslavia (now Serbia). The time allowed between Paris and Turin was 13 hours and 20 minutes and Turin to Belgrade 21 hours and 12 minutes, so they were still 'on time'. Most of the teams took less than twelve hours to cover the 720 miles from Turin to Belgrade, where the biggest crowds so far were waiting to welcome the drivers. Andrew's Hunter was met by Marcus Chambers and Derek Hughes, who changed the tyres and oil at the Rootes agent in Belgrade, Unikomerc. Meanwhile back in London, Des O'Dell and Jack Walton had caught a flight from London to Tehran, which was scheduled to arrive at 4am the next morning, to arrange service at Iran National Industrial Manufacturing Co. Ltd. Plenty of Hunter spares would be available, as this is where the Hunter/Paykan was made under licence. Unfortunately, Des and Jack were delayed at Zurich due to engine problems while landing there, and another plane had to be brought from London to Basle in order for them to carry on to their destination. They were taken by coach to Basle, but this delayed them a further ten hours.

DAY THREE – Belgrade–Istanbul

In the early hours of Tuesday, 26 November, came the first serious crash. About 100 miles out of Belgrade, Cecil Woodley's Vauxhall Ventora veered from the road, down a bank, into soft mud and rolled over three times. The crew were pulled out to safety and Woodley

sent off to hospital with a broken collar bone. It could have been worse!

With fifteen and a half hours to get to Istanbul, Andrew Cowan wasted no time getting there, despite having to endure the carefree and wholly unpredictable antics of Turkish lorry drivers. Peter Sargent, who was driving the number 5 Chrysler Valiant Estate, wasn't so lucky and didn't make it to Istanbul. Just outside Istanbul, he moved out to overtake a lorry, and was side-swiped by another lorry coming in the opposite direction. The four-man crew were not hurt but the car was too badly damaged to continue. The investment Bengt Söderström had made the previous day was short-lived. Poor-grade Turkish petrol caused their Cortina Lotus to retire at Istanbul with a burnt-out piston.

DAY FOUR – Istanbul–Sivas–Erzincan

Although the planning and preparation by Des O'Dell and his team had already started to pay off, this was the point in the rally where it would really matter. Wednesday, 27 November – The time allowed to the control at Sivas was 12 hours and 25 minutes, and from there to Erzincan – 2 hours 45 minutes. The route from Istanbul to Ankara was a reasonably good asphalt surface, but from Sivas to Erzincan it was un-surfaced, loose gravel, regardless of whether the southern or northern route option was chosen. Marcus Chambers' weather report warned it would be *'very cold – by the end of November frost almost continuous day and night.'* The crucial Sivas Erzincan stage once again posed the question of whether to take the longer northern route or the shorter, but possibly mud-laden southern route. Although, during the second recce, Andrew had favoured the southern route, and Colin was all for going south this time, he realised that both routes were wet and muddy, so the safer bet was the longer, northern route as it was likely that they would get completely stuck if they went south. Most of the other teams had also realised the perils of the southern route and made the same choice.

One other problem that was to beset them at Sivas, was that there was no 100 octane fuel available, but Gerry Spencer and Richard Guy, who were by now further on at Erzerum, did some remarkable 'blagging' and acquired some 120 octane AVGAS fuel from a local airfield, and sent it the 250 miles back to the control start at Sivas in the spares service truck. Richard Guy's recollection was that: *'We didn't actually buy it … we bartered something … I think we gave away some tyres for it'*. It did the trick, all 40 gallons of it. They left the petrol with Dunlop's

Jeremy Ferguson, who was able to fill up the RAF Hunter when it arrived, as well as helping out the BMC 1800 MkIIs of Tony Fall and Paddy Hopkirk.

Andrew drove flat-out, with Brian reading pace notes to him constantly throughout the whole stage, through rain and sleet, hoping they would not lose too many points at Erzincan. The Sivas to Erzincan 'sprint' also gave Andrew more confidence in how well the car handled, and if they had not been held up by a Holden that he was struggling to get past, would have lost fewer minutes and may have got in front of the BMC 1800s. The Hunter actually managed to pass thirty-one cars on the 170-mile drive up the winding mountain trail to Erzincan, most of it in the dark. They lost twenty-one minutes, just behind the BMC 1800s of Hopkirk and Aaltonen who were seventeen and eighteen minutes down, respectively. Roger Clark in his Cortina Lotus, lost only six minutes, completing the section at an average of sixty miles an hour. Simo Lampinen and Gilbert Staepelaere in the German Ford 20 MRS were only eight minutes behind Clark. The rain, sleet and snow created bad visibility, as well as making the loose gravel roads even more dangerous, but it was not until the next day that the toll of damage to cars became evident. Australian journalist Dave McKay's Holden missed a turn and ended up in a paddock, narrowly missing three other cars which had made the same mistake. One, a Dutch DAF 55 was stuck with a holed sump. The prize for tenacity must go to Bobby Buchanan-Michaelson's team, whose Mercedes 280 SE ran off the road and damaged its gear linkage. To repair it, co-driver Max Stahl lay on his back in three inches of mud while his two colleagues shielded him from the driving sleet at 4,000 feet above sea level. They then discovered that the radiator had been pierced. Bobby hitched a lift on a lorry the forty miles to Erzincan, got

it repaired, came back by taxi and fitted it in a blinding snowstorm.

The car that had caused the biggest stir at the start of the rally was Keith Schellenberg's 1930 Bentley. The huge vintage tourer got to the Sivas–Erzincan stage only to slip down an embankment. The team were forced to retire as one of their crew, Patrick Lindsay, broke his shoulder. Schellenberg and Norman Barclay recovered the big Bentley and would continue valiantly on to Bombay without Lindsay, but effectively out of the rally.

DAY FIVE – Erzincan–Tehran

Thursday, 28 November. After refuelling and a check-over by Chrysler Turkey personnel, the next stop was Tehran (Teheran). Here, at the Iran National Ind. Mfg., Co. factory, the cars were scheduled to have new front struts fitted as a precaution against stub axle failure. Any other parts, as well as routine tyre and wheel checks, could also be fitted if necessary.

Colin drove from here, in order to let Andrew get some rest in the back. The route would take them through Erzerum and on to the border with Persia (now Iran). Once into Iran, with the borders of Armenia and Azerbaijan to the north, they would drive south-east through Tabriz, and along the southern edge of the Elburz Moutains, into Tehran. The time allowed to Tehran was 22 hours. The first car was due to arrive at around 8pm with a stop of four hours. The RAF car arrived first, followed soon after by Andrew, Brian and Colin, who were grateful to Des for arranging a meal of steak and eggs, and for them to be able to get some sleep at Iran National's premises, while their service staff were on hand to do all of the work necessary on the cars.

The route – Day 5 to Day 8 – Middle East and India.

Both team Hunters being serviced at the Iran National workshops in Tehran. ROOTES ARCHIVE CENTRE TRUST

'Large hole 90 miles, Afghan border 292'. **The card index system
used by Cowan's crew to indicate to the driver what lay ahead.**

ROOTES ARCHIVE CENTRE TRUST

**The BMC 1800 team on the Afghan border, refuelling from a
makeshift fuel station on the back of a truck.** PAUL EASTER

Meanwhile, Rootes service personnel had been busy
re-positioning themselves over the previous twenty-
four hours: Richard Guy and Gerry Spencer had flown
from Erzerum to Ankara and the following day would
go from Ankara to Bombay via Istanbul and Athens.
Marcus Chambers and Derek Hughes had driven from
Paris to Athens, where they got a flight to Tehran en
route to Kabul, and to assist with the service at Sarobi on
the border from Afghanistan into West Pakistan. Peter
Burgess and Brian Wileman had flown to Tehran on the
Tuesday to assist with setting up the service requirements at Iran National, and at 07.15 the following day
flew to Mashhad, on the Afghan border of Iran, to set
up the service point there. Despite Des and Jack having
their schedule completely turned upside down, Des still
managed to get the parts that had been sent over from the
UK out of customs and to organise a driver and mechanic
in an Iran National Paykan to 'shadow' Andrew all the
way across the southern desert route to the next service
point at Mashhad, just in case of any problems on what
was, in effect, the more arduous route than the northern
route over the Elburz Mountains.

DAY SIX – Tehran–Kabul

Friday, 29 November. The control point out of Tehran
was located at the Philips factory, Radioelectric Iran Ltd.
The RAF Hunter left first, followed later by Andrew
Cowan, behind a manic driver who was 'guiding' them
through the busy, chaotic traffic of Tehran. Time allowed
to Kabul was 22 hours and 33 minutes, but would be
one of the longest stages in the rally, nearly 1,500 miles.

Not far out of Tehran, they caught up with their service
car, and then saw the RAF car ahead of them. It had hit
a washaway where a river had come across the road, and
bent their front suspension – badly. They had come round
a bend flat out and literally hit a hole in the road. As
luck would have it, the Iran National Paykan was coming
along and so were able to completely rebuild the front
suspension and get them on their way within two hours.

Despite almost missing a fuel service point, Andrew
pushed on to Mashhad, where Brian Wileman and Peter
Burgess were on hand to re-fuel. The border crossing
went smoothly and once into Afghanistan, they came
to the start of the 700-mile Afghanistan Highway. In
order to not put too much strain on the car, Brian had
worked out an optimum engine speed on his slide rule,
at 4,500rpm, and given the time they had to get to the
control, they cruised along at that – for 700 miles. The
next fuel stop was at Kandahar, amid hundreds of excited
people all wanting to see the rally car. Police 'crowd
control' then ensued – big sticks appeared, to disperse
the crowds, so they moved on as quickly as possible and

A fuel dump in a mountain village in Afghanistan. PAUL EASTER

After Landi Kotal, en route to Peshawar. PAUL EASTER

the nearer they got to Kabul, more people appeared, this time in their thousands! David Benson, for *The Daily Express*, reported that:

> 'It was the wildest welcome of the Marathon yet. Around the control point, police repeatedly charged the crowds as they pressed twenty deep round the cars, screaming and hitting the bodywork. Fighting broke out when a uniformed guard at the elegant Spinzar Hotel tried to drive the crowd away from the entrance with a whip.'

By Friday night, only thirty-three cars had reached Kabul within their allotted times. Harry Firth's Ford Falcon GT had come into its own along the fast Afghan roads and came into Kabul first, followed by fellow Australian Dave McKay in his Holden. Both Tony Fall and Ruano Aaltonen with the BMC works 1800s had problems; Fall's suspension collapsed just out of Tehran and Aaltonen, after a front-end shunt, had to drive almost all

View through the windscreen of Aaltonen's BMC 1800 approaching the town of Landi Kotal, Pakistan. PAUL EASTER

the way with the front end of his car held together by a winch rope. Fortunately, the welding kit that was on the Rootes Paykan support car was loaned to the BMC team and enabled them to weld the front end up. Rosemary Smith's Cortina Lotus got to Kabul, but only just; it had suffered a burnt-out piston. Ford service crew removed the offending piston, so she could continue on the rally, but with much reduced power.

At this point, both Des O'Dell and BMC's competitions manager Peter Browning had been worrying about the fate of their cars when they heard that Ford had gone along the northern route. Eventually both the BMC cars and the Cowans' Hunter appeared, much to the team manager's relief. The Hunter had a change of points and plugs, and then the RAF Hunter appeared, twenty minutes late, after their prang outside Tehran. They had new tyres fitted and the car was checked over, but they had broken their jack, so Des sent Derek Hughes out to find one. This would have been difficult enough at night in somewhere like Croydon, south London, but going round Kabul, the capital of Afghanistan, looking for a Hillman Hunter jack – at midnight? Andrew remembers Derek appearing a while later:

> '… grinning from ear to ear clutching an old screw jack. He had bought it from a taxi driver; the twentieth one he had tried, and paid him £5 for it. It was ceremoniously taken up to where the RAF lads were sleeping and laid in the centre of the room.'

DAY SEVEN – Kabul–Sarobi–Delhi

Saturday, 30 November. The next section was to Sarobi over the dreaded Lataban Pass, with only one hour allotted time. This meant Andrew had to drive

The service point at Sarobi. After crashing just after Tehran, the BMC team of Aaltonen, Liddon and Easter found that the only solution to holding the front end their car together was by means of a winch rope. PAUL EASTER

like a man possessed… and he did, giving Colin, in the back seat, more than a few frightening moments as the Hunter hurtled its way up the narrow, rocky road towards the control point, with visibility to the sheer drops either side at a minimum due to the dust the cars were kicking up.

It was at this point that a drama was about to unfold for Des and the service crew, who were waiting for Andrew at Sarobi. Andrew had passed the RAF Hunter, part-way up, who had suffered a puncture and a broken hub, as a result of the hasty tyre change at Kabul. A rear wheel had come loose and some of the studs had snapped off, so they were well and truly stuck up a mountain! This is Andrew's account of the incident:

'At the Sarobi control, Des was waiting for us, and the first he knew was when Roy Fidler and John Sprinzel stopped in their MG and told him a Hunter was stuck on the top of a pass with a puncture. He went on to say that it wasn't me … but the RAF car.

'As the mechanics went over my car with a fine toothcomb, I gave Des the low-down and then set off and left Des to worry about the RAF car. Des knew he had about twelve hours to get the RAF car out and still keep them in the event.'

After trying to persuade Stuart Turner, one of the organisers, to take a service car up, which was refused, they then thought about walking, but it was ten miles! That idea was dismissed. Eventually… after bribing a policeman, Des was allowed to drive into the section after the other cars had gone through. Even so, he was delayed a further one and a half hours by a police car before being

allowed to continue on, and drove right over the pass, but could not find the RAF Hunter anywhere. When they went back to Stuart Turner to ask about its whereabouts, he told them they had passed through two hours before! Derek, meanwhile, had stayed behind with a duplicate set of brake parts, in case they were able to get the car moving again. Andrew:

'What Derek had done was walk into the section, find a policemen with a motorbike and had bribed him to take him to the car. The crew had managed to get the hub off. Because of the spacer, the wheel had collapsed so the back plate was broken and the brake shoes and cylinders had gone. They blanked the brake off and drove out without any, then Derek rebuilt the brakes.'

Des O'Dell's Herculean efforts were in vain, but Derek Hughes saved the day. Des O'Dell must have felt as ragged and tired as the rest of the drivers and crew, if only for the complicated logistical exercises he had had to endure, just to get to service points on time, and keep ahead of the cars – but keep ahead he did. In order to get to Kabul on time, Des and Jack Walton had left Tehran the previous day and flown to Karachi, where they got a flight to Rawalpindi, changed there for another flight to Peshawar, followed by a final half-hour flight to Kabul, arriving at 11.45am the following morning.

At Sarobi, both Paddy Hopkirk in the works BMC 1800 and Roger Clark in the Cortina Lotus had lost five minutes over the section, but with a total of only eleven penalties, Clark was still holding a clear lead. The Lataban Pass proved how quickly it could wreck cars, and how well the Hillman Hunter was standing up to the punishment it was being subjected to. Zasada's Porsche 911S came in with only three tyres and Australian Bob Holden in an 'Amoco' Volvo 142S arrived with rear shock absorbers completely shot, even though they had only been fitted the previous night.

The drive over the Khyber Pass and into west Pakistan was, by comparison to the Lataban, quite tame. Good tarmac roads were the order of the rest of Saturday down through Rawalpindi, across the border into India. By Saturday night, the first cars were coming into Delhi, and most crews had time for a brief rest before the last leg of the Asian section into Bombay. India had opened its heart to the rally. Millions of people lined the route to Delhi, all the way from the Pakistan border. Andrew Cowan was amazed at just how many people there were in Delhi: 'The whole of the centre of the city was crammed full of people, fifty deep. There were police everywhere keeping the crowd in check.'

Cowan's Hunter on the Khyber Pass stage.

ROOTES ARCHIVE CENTRE TRUST

Next it was on to Bombay. Rosemary Smith reversed over the Khyber Pass after the pistons in her Cortina Lotus engine had fried. Being concerned about putting additional strain on the engine going up the steep inclines of the Khyber Pass, she remembered her father's advice '*If a car won't go forward, it'll go in reverse.*'

DAY EIGHT – Delhi–Bombay

Sunday, 1 December. The police had closed the route between Delhi and Bombay to public traffic, which enabled them to get to Bombay in sixteen hours, well inside the allotted time of 22 hours and 41 minutes. Once in Bombay, the car had to be re-prepared to a very high standard. Des reminded service personnel that the car

Intimidating throngs of people crowd round the cars as they enter Bombay. PAUL EASTER

still had to do the equivalent of a rally the length and severity of the East African Safari!

Gerry Spencer and Richard Guy had embarked on an even more convoluted travel schedule in order to get to Bombay: on Thursday afternoon, they had left Erzerum on an internal flight to Ankara. The following day, at 2.30pm, they flew from Ankara to Istanbul, where a flight to Athens got them another flight to Bombay, which arrived at 05.35am on the Saturday. Their principal task was to change the cylinder-head on Andrew's Hunter, which Richard had taken with him:

'I'll never forget the taxi-driver when we got to Bombay. He was ever so keen to look after us and he picked up our cases to put them in the car. The briefcase I took as hand luggage had a complete set of tools in it, and the suitcase had a high-compression head in it. The poor bloke had such a shock when he went to pick them up ... he nearly pulled his arm out of his socket.

'Gerry and I did the cylinder-head job. We only had two hours to do the job. The cylinder-head was held on by seven bolts and three studs, and the bolts are easy enough to undo ... and there are three washers on the studs when you take off the nuts. We lifted up the head and one of the head washers was still on the stud, and it dropped straight down into the engine. We both saw it go ... We looked at each other and Gerry said, "F***ing stays there ... it won't hurt". I don't think Andrew ever found out [until much later]!'

The other mechanics changed the rear axle, shock absorbers, front struts and replaced the windscreen that had been cracked. Andrew then checked the car over and the next day the car was steam cleaned, to comply with Australian import regulations, before being loaded onto the SS *Chusan* for Australia.

When the results were published the following day, Andrew Cowan, Brian Coyle and Colin Malkin, who had started in position number 75, were lying sixth. Seventy-two of the original ninety-eight starters had made it to Bombay. Roger Clark and Ove Anderssen – Ford Cortina Lotus were first; Gilbert Staepalaere and Simo Lampinen – Ford Taunus 20 MRS – second; Lucien Bianchi and Jean Claude Ogier in a Citroën DS 21 – third; Paddy Hopkirk, Tony Nash and Alec Poole in a BMC1800 Mark 2 – fourth; Rauno Aaltonen, Henry Liddon and Paul Easter, also in a BMC1800 Mark 2 were fifth. The big V8 Ford Falcon GT of Harry Firth and Evan Green in a BMC 1800 were lying seventh and eighth respectively.

The compound in Bombay: Saab 96; Ford Taunus 21M of Lampinen; Peugeot 404; the Australian team of Evan Green's BMC 1800. PAUL EASTER

Henry Liddon sits on a wall eating his sandwich while the RAF Hunter and BMC 1800 of Aaltonen, Liddon and Easter are refuelled in Bombay. PAUL EASTER

Bombay street scene taken by Paul Easter from the rear of the 1800 while Aaltonen and Liddon negotiate the traffic.

PAUL EASTER

The SS *Chusan* in Bombay: the ship that would take cars and crew from India to Australia. PAUL EASTER

All cars had to undergo thorough steam cleaning at Bombay prior to being allowed into Australia. PAUL EASTER

A welcome sight! At last the SS *Chusan* arrives at Bombay. A view of the Gateway of India from the Hotel Taj Mahal.

PAUL EASTER

During their wait in Bombay for the SS *Chusan* to arrive, Paul Easter took the opportunity to take his Minolta camera out onto the streets of Bombay to record some day-to-day city life.
PAUL EASTER

On Wednesday, 4 December, the SS *Chusan* sailed out of Bombay with the seventy-two rally cars and crews on board, bound for Fremantle, Australia. The nine-day voyage gave crews a well-earned rest, and after they had recovered from various 'Bombay Belly' stomach bugs, the crews emerged to chat about the rally and what lie ahead... and party! At dawn on

Friday, 13 December, they docked at Fremantle. The cars were unloaded and driven from the quayside, led by Fremantle police, along the twelve-mile road to Perth's Gloucester Park pony-trotting track, where a 35,000 crowd had turned out to welcome them. Another capacity crowd flocked to the arena for the re-start of the Marathon.

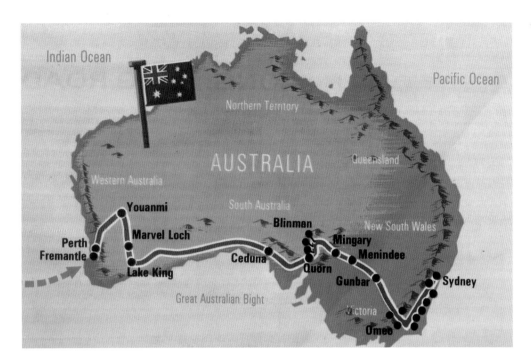

The route – Day 9 to
Day 12 – Australia.

DAY NINE – Perth–Youanmi

The next afternoon, Saturday, 14 December, saw the
re-start of the Marathon. The cars were flagged off in
three-minute intervals by David Brand, Western Australia's Premier. The first leg was the 350-mile stretch out of
Perth up to the mining town of Youanmi. Time allowed
was seven hours. Richard Guy and Gerry Spencer were
waiting there for the Hunter to arrive:

> 'No rally driver likes to be overtaken and I believe the long
> tarmac stretches from Delhi to Bombay illustrated just how
> slow the Hunter was with the low-compression engine as
> Andrew declared that he had lost count of the number of
> people who overtook him on this stretch. I flew to Perth with
> Gerry, and while we awaited the arrival of the cars we had
> time to reflect on what Andrew's attitude would be should the
> Hunter not show a significant improvement in performance.
> However, the first opportunity we had to see the car was at
> the first stop at a place called Youanmi and our fears were
> dispelled as Andrew was now very pleased with the car's per-
> formance. ... What a relief!!!'

From then on, the job of the service crew got more and
more difficult, but not because of problems with the rally
cars. Richard explains:

> 'Then the Australians [Chrysler Australia] let us down quite
> badly with the provision of service vehicles. They had not

taken on board what we wanted to do with regards to chase
cars and such like. We started off with a Singer Vogue Estate,
which lasted about 150 miles before the engine went pop, so
in desperation they looked around and found us a Chrysler
Valiant. That was all right for the first half until the fan
went through the radiator, and that was the end of that! I
think they managed to resurrect one more car because they
were worried we might not get to the other side of Australia.
In the end to ensure that the team got at least one mechanic
to the other side of Australia, I got a seat in the Dunlop plane
and flew to Quorn while poor Gerry and Jack had to drive
the Nullarbor Plain.'

DAY TEN – Youanmi–Marvel Loch–Lake King

Sunday, 15 December. It was now clear who the contenders were in what was becoming a 3,000-mile flat-out
race across Australia. Andrew was well up on time,
having had an hour in hand at Youanmi. Roger Clark was
storming along, but when he pulled into a service area in
the tiny farming area of Southern Cross, on the stretch
from Youanmi to the control at Marvel Loch, he found
he had damaged his steering. Although mechanics took
only eight minutes to fix the damage, in that short time,
second- and third-placed drivers Simo Lampinen in the
German Ford and Lucien Bianchi in the Citroën, hurtled
past. Clark was now in third position, and these three
were the only drivers to get to Lake King ahead of the

time without gaining penalties. On this stage, Andrew had caught up with Paddy Hopkirk, who had had punctures and suspension trouble, and consequently dropped to eighth place. Now in fifth position, Andrew Cowan was also closing in on Aaltonen's 1800. Paul Easter remembers how they lost time:

'Well, I can tell you – there was one section … I was asleep in the back and Rauno and Henry were going along and we should have taken a turning left and we went straight on! With [that] navigational error we lost ten minutes. I woke up when they turned around and were coming back … then for the last twenty-four hours of the rally, the car wouldn't stay in gear, and I spent a lot of the time sitting on the floor holding the thing in gear! That was two [of the] reasons we lost time in Australia, and of course, having the front suspension tied up [with a winch rope] was not helpful on the Lataban.

'We wouldn't have won, but we would've been a lot closer to the front without [that] navigational error and the gearbox throwing us a bit.'

DAY ELEVEN – Lake King–Ceduna–Quorn–Mingary–Brookside

Monday, 16 December. After Lake King came the 900-mile drive eastwards, through the Nullarbor Plain, into South Australia and along to Ceduna, where the Hunter was serviced. For this section the time allowed was 14 hours and 52 minutes. From there, another six-hour slog to Quorn, which was the start of the section through the Flinders Ranges, South Australia's largest mountain range. The Flinders boasts some of the most colourful and spectacular scenery in the world, unless you are in a rally car, and then all you can see is dust... fine red dust! It's the sort of dust that penetrates the best of weather seals.

The stage from Quorn to Moralana Creek was very tough. Roger Clark had limped into Port Augusta, just before the control at Quorn, only firing on three cylinders. Ford officials decided that he had to stay in the rally, regardless, and that the two burnt-out valves in his car should be replaced with those from team mates Eric Jackson and Ken Chambers' car, which effectively forced them to retire from the event. Bianchi was first to arrive at Moralana Creek, followed by Lampinen, then Aaltonen. Between Moralana Creek and the next control, Brachina Gorge, Andrew Cowan had noticed some trouble with the brakes on the Hunter, and just before Brachina, to Andrew's horror, the brake pedal

An exhausted RAF team during the event. COVENTRY ARCHIVES

went straight to the floor at seventy miles an hour going round a bend and they careered into a sand bank. The car was pulled out by onlookers and Andrew clocked in at the control. Des, Jack Walton and Richard Guy were all there, quite prepared to do a major brake rebuild. This would also be the last place on the rally that a service car would be on hand. Richard Guy recalls the circumstances they were faced with:

'The only bit of drama we had [was when] Andrew lost the brakes at the end of a stage and it turned out he'd hit some stones and dislodged one of the pipe nuts on the wheel cylinder. [It was fixed, and within minutes, Andrew and crew were on their way]. Because we were doing so well and because we still had two cars in, it was decided at the last minute to take an extra mechanic to Australia – Jack Walton. He was due to go back home, but it was a good job we did. It was only meant for Gerry and I to go to Australia. We were still scratching around for vehicles and in the end they did the whole of the New South Wales loop [about 800 miles] without service.'

From Brachina, to the end of the Flinders Range section at Blinman, the route went back south-east to Mingary. As the control closed for the night, only sixty-one cars had gone through before passing into New South Wales to Menindee. Shortly after the Flinders section, Andrew, who was by now squeezing everything he possibly could out of the Hunter, ran off the road and into a gully. Fortunately, Evan Green in the BMC 1800 came along, and helped them get the car back on the road.

The next control was at Gunbar, five hours further on, where they were due to meet Des, but he didn't make it,

A local BMC dealer was on hand to provide servicing for the
BMC 1800 team in Australia. PAUL EASTER

due to getting a puncture. Upon arrival, they were to
witness the generous nature, warmth of personality and
sense of humour of the people of Gunbar, which Andrew
recalls in his book:

'When we reached Gunbar … we were in for a surprise. Normally there were thirty-five people in a radius of five miles
but, when we got there, there were thousands of people from
all over. As we were filling up with petrol, an Australian
came up and said he was the Mayor and invited us to a meal.
We went to this big tin shed on which someone had painted
'The Gunbar Hilton' and inside we all sat down at a big
long table with Lucien Bianchi and the BMC boys and had
a fabulous meal. Obviously, they were all farmers' wives and
had cooked the meal themselves. When I asked for the bill,
they said there would be no charge, but I offered to give them

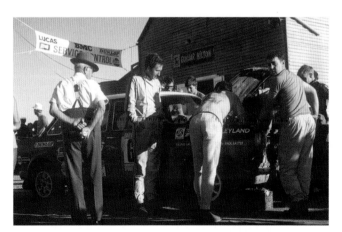

Day 11, Gunbar, New South Wales and the Gunbar Hilton,
where Australian hospitality came into its own; an
opportunity to service cars and enjoy a welcome slap-up
meal provided by the locals. PAUL EASTER

something towards the hall and she asked if 70 cents might
be too much … so I gave her five dollars and that meal was
the most welcome break in the whole of Australia.'

Two more controls at Edi and Brookside would take the
rally briefly into Victoria and up north from Omeo on
the last slog to Sydney. Just before Brookside, they passed
Aaltonen, who had stopped to fill up with petrol. They
were now fourth.

DAY TWELVE – Brookside–Sydney

Tuesday, 17 December is a date that is etched on the
memories of many of the rally drivers on this section of
the London–Sydney Marathon, for a variety of reasons.
The day would see a complete turnaround in the fortunes
of the leaders. Roger Clark experienced serious trouble
with a broken differential shortly after leaving Omeo, but
upon spotting another Cortina by the roadside, he asked
the owner if he could buy his back axle, to which the
owner probably told him to 'Bugger off', but on realising
it was the famous rally driver Roger Clark, offered him
his back axle for nothing! The axles were swapped at a
local garage and Clark continued his relentless blast up to
Sydney, but his catalogue of mechanical failures culminating in the differential trouble had cost him dearly, and
he was no longer a contender for the first five. A series
of sections of between one and two hours each made
up the seven-hour trek to Sydney, through aptly named
places like Slippery Pinch and Dead Timber Hill. Thun-
derstorms then made the going even more treacherous,
turning much of the route into a muddy torrent. From
Murrindal into New South Wales and up to Ingebyrra
to the control at Numerella was where Andrew Cowan
learnt of his changing fortune in the rally, through a
surprise visit: one of his neighbours from Berwickshire,
Billy Hogg, had planned a holiday in Australia and heard
that the rally went through here, so had driven out from
Sydney to greet Andrew. He was able to tell Andrew he
was now officially lying third overall, with only about
250 miles to go to the end.

The Numeralla to Hindemarsh Station section was a
rough, arduous section that had to be covered in forty-
two minutes. Colin had marked a place on his pace notes
with a 'caution' on a bend, and it was here that they
came across Lampinen and Stapalaere, who had crashed
into a ditch. The tie-rod on the steering had broken as
a result of Lampinen pushing just a bit too hard, as he
later admitted to Des O'Dell. They were now out of

Fords and rivers had to be crossed during the epic drive across Australia. COVENTRY ARCHIVES

contention, and would be relegated to sixteenth place overall. At this point, it had not really sunk in to the crew that they were now second. Colin was lying on the back seat fast asleep, the rigours of being thrown around in the back of a Hillman Hunter being driven by a mad Scotsman for thousands of miles, had finally caught up with him, and he was out for the count. It is the next set of events, from the section about twenty miles before the control at Nowra, where Andrew just managed to get into with four minutes to spare, to the finish, 100 miles on, at Warwick Farm, that can only really be told by Andrew Cowan:

'Lucien Bianchi had been leading by quite a margin ... but on the brow of a hill he had collided with a non-competing Mini and when we arrived, shortly after the accident, the road was in an awful mess. ... The road wasn't blocked, for the two cars, which had hit head-on, had obviously rebounded leaving a space between them. We stopped but didn't speak to Bianchi and saw Jean-Claude Ogier [who had been driving at the time] standing about, so we knew he was all right. At this, a man stepped forward and told us just to go ahead and take it easy and we would get through. Bianchi was sitting in the Citroën talking to someone trying to free him from the car so we realised that he wasn't too bad ... Paddy Hopkirk had stopped and gone for help, but this didn't make any difference to him as far as the rally positions were concerned, as [we] both completed the section on time without losing any marks.'

Paddy Hopkirk arrived on the scene just before Cowan:

'I was the next car on the road and it was a special stage, towards the south of Sydney, I think. We came over the brow

... it was a tight section and there was Bianchi's car blocking the road, head on into this Mini. It wasn't Bianchi driving, it was Jean-Claude Ogier who was driving ... The press said it was a "kamikaze" ... the Mini had been sent down to take out the Citroën because Lucien was leading the rally ... Anyway, the road was blocked; Alec [Poole] got out and tried to get Lucien out of the car, but couldn't — his foot was very badly jammed in and he was covered in blood ... Ogier was walking round in circles, just shell-shocked ... and then the Mini started to go on fire, and Alec got the fire extinguisher out of the 1800 and closed the bonnet of the Mini on it ... and it put the fire out.

'We couldn't get the cars apart, so I said I would go back and get help. So I went back a couple of miles and there was a doctor there and I brought him back. In the meantime, the guys had got the cars apart and got the road clear, so we went on.'

Andrew Cowan and crew continued on:

'After this, we were all badly shaken because it was a nasty accident to see and nobody said anything, not even Colin, who had wakened by now. Brian was particularly quiet ... he had to make a physical effort to concentrate on the hundred miles to the finish ... the desperation to get the thing over and done with was almost unbearable. Then we began to come to townships just on the outskirts of Sydney and the people began to start cheering. We didn't know if it was because we were just one of the cars or if they knew we were leading until Brian pointed to a car parked in a driveway outside a house and pinned on the side of the car was a bit of paper with "Andrew Cowan" written on it, and we realised that in fact, we were winning and there was no question about it. Just on Princess Highway at Sydney, where there was a bypass to take us round the city through Liverpool and Warwick Farm, we suddenly noticed two large Chrysler Pentastar signs at the side of the road.... There was a Chrysler Valiant parked with my number on it... and an Australian representative from Chrysler came over and said, "Congratulations, we are here to lead you into Sydney ... Do you want to go now, and how fast do you want to go?" I said I wanted to go immediately and ... to stick to all the speed limits ... we had arrived in Sydney and had only a few miles to go to the finish.'

A few miles on, Paddy Hopkirk, who was in front, pulled over to let them by, and car number 75, a Hillman Hunter, with Andrew Cowan, Brian Coyle and Colin Malkin, drove in to the final checkpoint at Warwick Farm, outright winner of the 1968 London-Sydney Marathon.

Cowan's Hunter crosses the finish line and enters the winners enclosure at Warwick Farm. COVENTRY ARCHIVES

Paddy Hopkirk, Tony Nash and Alec Poole in their BMC1800 were second, getting six more penalty points than Cowan. The Ford Falcon GT of Vaughan, Forsyth and Ellis was third, with the Polish team of Zasada and Wachowski, in a Porsche 911S, fourth; Rauno Aaltonen, Henry Liddon and Paul Easter, in their BMC1800 were proving to be consistent with their fifth position at Bombay, and were fifth overall at Sydney. Hodgeson and Rutherford, for Ford Australia, in a Falcon, were sixth, while Kleint and Klapproth in a Ford Taunus 20MRS scored seventh for Ford Deutschland. Harry Firth's Ford Falcon GT was eighth, and Neyret in a Citroën DS21, ninth. Roger Clark came in a disappointing tenth.

Rosemary Smith's Cortina, three gearboxes later, and still running on three pistons, didn't have enough power to get up the hills at Hindmarsh but achieved 48th position overall. The RAF Hunter, which had come into Bombay in 53rd place, had made a respectable catch-up to finish in Sydney in 32nd place.

THE FINAL ANALYSIS

There are reasons why this victory for Rootes was significant, apart from the commercial advantage for Chrysler, who could have reaped the benefit of the win in more ways than they chose, claiming at the time that there was

Cowan's winning Hunter in the compound at Warwick Farm, Sydney. ROOTES ARCHIVE CENTRE TRUST

The Hunter at journey's end, Warwick Farm, Sydney. ROOTES ARCHIVE CENTRE TRUST

The Holbay engine, still in functioning condition at the end of its gruelling test. ROOTES ARCHIVE CENTRE TRUST

The winning Hunter being unloaded by BOAC cargo staff at Heathrow Airport. ROOTES ARCHIVE CENTRE TRUST

'no budget' to advertise the victory. In human terms it showed what could be achieved by a team of determined and expert people, who, as Des O'Dell pointed out at the very beginning, were the very best in their field, and they proved it during this event. Had these experts like Gerry Spencer, Richard Guy, Brian Wileman, Derek Hughes, Jack Walton, Arthur Bird, Peter Burgess and Ron Breakwell not done their job, Andrew Cowan and Colin Malkin would not have been able to drive the Hunter as hard as they did, and had it not been so well put together, it would not have survived the numerous jumps and bumps they subjected it to. Brian Coyle's cool

head and navigation skills were another essential element to their victory. Without this team effort from start to finish, they would not have come anywhere in the leader board, let alone first! Also, if Des O'Dell had not planned everything like a military operation, they would not have won. The Hunter may not have been the fastest car in the rally, but it did not suffer any major breakdowns in the same way the Ford Cortinas did, and in Andrew Cowan's words, *'would probably have driven the whole way back again!!'*

The victory was also significant because this event was the first of its kind since the Peking to Paris Rally in 1907. This period, at the end of the Sixties, was still,

Colin Malkin, Brian Coyle and Andrew Cowan with the winners trophy, greet the press at Heathrow. COVENTRY ARCHIVES

Outright winners! Time to parade the Marathon heroes: Colin, Brian and Andrew hear congratulations from Fred Peart, Lord Privy Seal and Leader of the House of Commons, and Gilbert Hunt of Rootes Motors Ltd. COVENTRY ARCHIVES

compared with later trans-continental rallies, in the pre-mobile phones, pre-satellite navigation and pre-GPS tracking era. In short, it was 'back of a fag packet' technology and innovation, based on intuition, knowledge and experience – that worked!

The sequence of events that make up this account of the 1968 London–Sydney Marathon are taken from Andrew Cowan's book *Why Finish Last?*, written shortly after the event in 1969, and from interviews by the author with Andrew Cowan in May 2013, Richard Guy in March 2014, Paul Easter in October 2014, Rosemary Smith in November 2015 and Paddy Hopkirk in January 2019. Additional information was taken from Des O'Dell's original rally notes and from a report by *Motor* magazine in December 1968, as well as David Benson's *Daily Express* reports at the time.

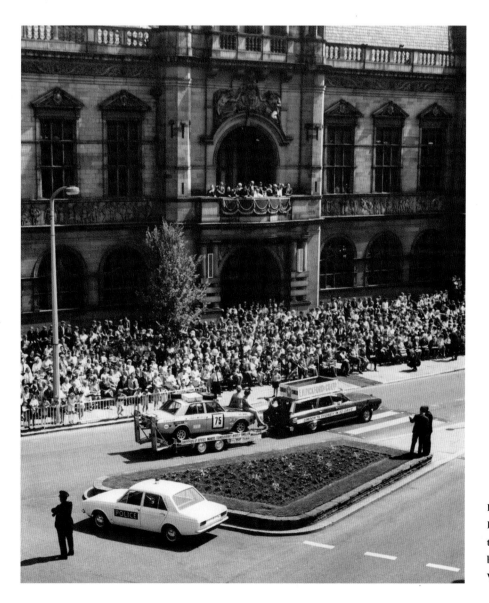

Following the event, the winning Hunter was paraded around Britain to tumultuous crowds. It is seen here being trailered behind its Chrysler Valiant tow car. COVENTRY ARCHIVES

COUNTDOWN TO CRISIS POINT – THE SEVENTIES

'By the time you get to the end of the '60s, Chrysler UK was in as bad an investment situation as Rootes had been.'

– Bill Papworth, Rootes Product Planning Director

The Seventies… wide lapels and flared trousers… Prog rock…Punk rock…Glam rock… Abba… picket lines and the miners' strike… Red Robbo… the three-day week… Mary Whitehouse… the Northern Ireland 'troubles'… these are some of the images that our tabloid brains conjure up whenever the Seventies is mentioned… but it was much more than that. It was an era of extremes and opposites and, whereas the Sixties had been idealistic and optimistic, the Seventies was politically incorrect, turbulent and cynical. The 1970s was an era in which the nation was struggling to find its place in the global hierarchy of the post-war period and it was a roller coaster ride for companies trying to survive in motor manufacturing.

In June 1970, Edward Heath, leader of the Conservative Party, became Prime Minister. The following year, Britain

joined the EEC, and on 15 February 1971, sterling currency was decimalized. Inflation and a recession set in, which was compounded by the OPEC oil embargo crisis of 1973. Unemployment steadily rose as the post-war economic boom started to fizzle out. In 1972, the first miners' strike for fifty years saw coal supplies dwindle to such an extent that power cuts were imposed by the government, which led, two years later, to a three-day week.

But it wasn't all bad. In 1976, Britain had the hottest summer for 350 years, and it was a time in which none of us took ourselves too seriously. Iconic British television comedy tapped into the British sense of the absurd and got us through the dark days of the Seventies: *Monty Python's Flying Circus* took *Goon Show* humour to the next level and TV sitcoms such as *Whatever Happened to the*

For many, the 1970s will be remembered as the age of the cheap package holiday. Airliners like this British Airways Lockheed TriStar would make regular flights from Heathrow to Malaga and other holiday destinations. It is seen being serviced by a stalwart Karrier Bantam baggage truck at Heathrow in 1975. The Bantam had an incredibly long production life which finished at Dunstable in 1978.

Likely Lads typified the changing attitudes and struggles of the period as two working-class lads from Newcastle, Bob and Terry, who regularly got into some amusing scrapes, whilst trying to balance their friendship against Bob's engagement to his snobbish girlfriend Thelma. Mike Leigh's sitcom *Abigail's Party* also took an hilariously cringing swipe at Seventies faux middle-classness, in which actress Alison Steadman insisted on playing her Demis Roussos record to her bored dinner party friends. Let's face it, we all like a bit of Demis Roussos don't we?

Product promotion during the mid-Seventies through television and films did much to push sales of particular car brands and models – Ford in particular, through programmes such as *The Sweeney*, shot between 1975 and '78, which featured a Ford Consul 3000 GT, and Detectives Regan and Carter, played by John Thaw and Dennis Waterman, tyre-screeching their way around London's streets in pursuit of whichever villain they were after that particular week. In the same mould, from 1977, came *The Professionals*, with Martin Shaw and Lewis Collins as agents Bodie and Doyle, who hurled their trademark Ford Capri 3.0 Litre around with at least as much gusto as American TV cops *Starsky & Hutch* in their '76 Ford Gran Torino. However, both British Leyland and Chrysler UK, as Rootes was now known, missed out. British Leyland were allegedly contracted to supply Rover and Triumph cars to London Weekend Television for *The Professionals*, but reliability issues forced the production team to go with Ford instead. Chrysler UK just didn't have the product to offer, as they had firmly nailed their colours to the volume fleet/family saloon car market with the Hillman Hunter and the new Hillman Avenger.

Chrysler's changes to the old Rootes manufacturing infrastructure were based on Burke Hyde's long-range manufacturing plan, which had started in 1965. With the introduction of the Avenger in 1970, the changes that were deemed necessary if Rootes/Chrysler was to be successful as a car manufacturer were starting to come together. To build on that process was what was now needed for recovery, but it would prove a far more complicated and challenging task to sustain.

Chrysler United Kingdom Ltd officially became the new name of Rootes Motors Ltd in July 1970. Rootes Motors Scotland Ltd was changed to Chrysler Linwood Ltd and Rootes Motors Ireland Ltd became Chrysler Ireland Ltd. Chrysler Corporation now held 73 per cent of the total equity in Rootes/Chrysler and 77 per cent of the voting stock. Rootes also undertook a rights issue, underwritten by Chrysler to raise £10.9 million of new capital. In addition, a £5 million loan, guaranteed by

Some of the first B-body quarter-scale models by Rex Fleming and Roy Axe: number 3 and number 5.

COVENTRY ARCHIVES

Some even made it to full-size mock-up, as this 1969 example on the roof of the Styling Studio at Stoke shows.

COVENTRY ARCHIVES

Chrysler, was arranged. This investment represented another shoring up of Chrysler's activities in Britain, as the 1970 half-yearly figures showed a £7.5 million loss and an end of year loss that would again top the £10 million mark.

Geoffrey Rootes, as chairman of Rootes, made a short but stoical and typically positive statement to shareholders and the press regarding the change of name and re-structuring:

'Although my family founded Rootes and has been closely involved in the business, I feel that the change of name is a logical step at this stage in the development of the company. The brand names of the cars and trucks, which are so famous, will remain the same.'

'B' CAR – THE DESIGN AND DEVELOPMENT OF THE AVENGER

Ideas for the Avenger began to take shape around 1965, having been initiated by Rootes management in 1964. The Rootes family were still involved with new products during this period, and during 1965, six quarter-scale models were built and submitted for approval by the family. Of the six, four were selected to be made as full-scale models in clay. Product Planning at Whitley had specified that the new car should have interior proportions of a Minx but have exterior dimensions of a Vauxhall Viva. Ted White was still Head of Styling and would not retire until 1968; his place would be taken by Roy Axe as new Styling Director, much to his surprise, as it had been rumoured that Tim Fry would get the job. In the event, Fry left and went on to form his own successful design consultancy. Much of the early styling exercises were made under the administrative guidance of Rex Fleming, but a lot of influence had come from Chrysler's design studios in Highland Park, Detroit under Elwood Engel, Vice-President of Design. Colin Neal was another senior design manager at Chrysler, responsible for interiors as well as Chrysler International design operations, and he was sent over to Coventry to work with Axe and his team. In his memoir, Axe recalls that the management from Detroit were helpful and supportive and Neal in particular was *'friendly, never overwhelming, considering his role within the organization...'*

By January 1966, an outline specification had been settled on, which included an overhead camshaft engine. An independent rear suspension setup had also been planned but both of these features were canned, follow-

ing a firm cost target laid down by Chrysler. Even after the live axle had become part of the Avenger specification, Mike Jones, who had returned to Rootes from Jensen Motors in April 1968 as a development engineer, campaigned for independent rear suspension:

'It had a live rear axle, which I tried to persuade my elders and betters to change to an independent rear, because it had lots of problems on bumpy surfaces, especially when we went to Europe. We had all sorts of problems on rough roads and the French had pavé, lots of it, and that's why the French were good at [designing] suspension [systems] in those days. They had to make the cars ride and handle well on bad roads, but the Avenger was terrible! It was a very unsophisticated design.'

The four-cylinder pushrod engine was designed by Leo Kuzmicki, *'a fine engineer; very charming and a real gentleman'* was Mike Jones' impression of him. *'Tom Atkinson did the main detail engineering on the engine and Dick Brown designed the gearbox.'* Jones is quite emphatic as to where much of the praise must lie with regard to creation of the Avenger, and that was Harry Sheron, Technical Director:

'Sheron was the guy who was given the job of bringing Rootes down to earth to make normal production cars based on the Cortina ... He was the father of the Avenger.'

With styling and a technical specification fairly well set in stone by 1967, the job of testing and proving the Avenger was given to Peter Wilson's Experimental Department. Don Tarbun was the principal development engineer and a new Road Proving Group was set up by motoring journalist Graham Robson, reporting to Peter Wilson. Mike Jones was part of Robson's team, which included experimental test drivers Bernard Unett and John Harris. It

B car tyre testing in Norway. OWEN SWINERD

was estimated that over 1¼ million miles were covered in testing components and complete cars. Avenger prototypes covered over 500,000 miles, with one car covering nearly 150,000 miles.

Experimental test engineer Owen Swinerd took two Avengers to Norway for cold weather testing. Four other cars, including a Sunbeam Rapier H120 and a prototype 'C' Car coupé, accompanied the Avengers and a team of engineers on tests up to Tynset, just south of Trondheim. Temperatures would go down to minus 20 degrees C and sometimes minus 50 degrees C when doing cold starting and heating system tests. Owen Swinerd remarked that:

'The locals must have thought we were mad – going out in the middle of the night – every eight hours or so to do the

cold start tests! We'd start the car, drive it round and leave it for another few hours and do it all again.'

Tyre and handling tests were also carried out on a frozen lake race track. En route they would meet up with Simca engineers carrying out similar testing programmes. From Norway they continued back through Sweden, Germany, Belgium and France to England, having covered thousands of miles on the journey.

The Plymouth Cricket was the American market version of the Avenger, and covered big distances in America during the testing programme, as Mike Jones remembers:

'The engineers at the Chrysler Proving Ground in the USA had prototype Crickets … At Whitley we received detailed reports

Avengers were taken out to Malta to be photographed for their first brochure and advertising images. The First GL model was available with full-width chrome wheeltrims with exposed lug nut effect centres. The '71 model reverted to conventional hub caps and trim rings.

HILLMAN AVENGER DE LUXE/SUPER (1250) & GL (1500) (1970) SPECIFICATIONS

1970 Hillman Avenger Deluxe. ROOTES ARCHIVE CENTRE TRUST

Body style
Four-door, four-seater saloon. Unitary construction

Engine
4 cylinder, pushrod-operated overhead valves, five-bearing crankshaft, cast-iron cylinder head, high camshaft
Power output:
(1250 engine): 1248cc (77.48cu in) developing 60 gross bhp (53 DIN) at 5,000rpm;
(1500 engine): 1498cc (93.04cu in) developing 72 gross bhp (62 DIN) at 5,000rpm

The Avenger engine was genuinely new and broke the lineage of overhead-valve Hillman engines that was established in 1955.

Bore and Stroke:
1250 engine: 78.6mm x 64.3mm (3.09in x 2.53in)
1500 engine: 86.1mm x 64.3mm (3.39in x 2.53in)
Compression ratio: 9.2:1 **(1250 and 1500)**
Torque: 66lb ft (DIN) at 3,000rpm **(1250)**; 80lb ft at 3,000rpm
Fuel pump type: AC mechanical
Carburettor: Zenith –Stromberg 150CDS side-draught variable-choke carburettor
Cooling system: Water – pump and fan

Transmission
Four-speed, all synchromesh, centre-floor change lever. Aluminium alloy die-cast bellhousing and gearbox casing
Clutch: 7½in (190mm) diameter Borg & Beck diaphragm spring, single dry plate type on 1500 and 7¼in (184mm) on 1250
Gear Ratios: (1250) Top 4.375; Third 5.976:1; Second 8.877:1; First 14.512:1; Reverse 15.094:1. **(1500)** Top 3.89:1; Third 5.312:1; Second 7.891:1; First 12.9:1; Reverse 13.417:1
Final drive: Semi-floating hypoid bevel type. Final drive ratio: 4.375:1 **(1250)**; 3.89:1 **(1500)**

Electrical and Lighting
Ignition: Coil and distributor with dynamo (early models only). 12-volt, 45-amp battery
Lighting: Two rectangular (Lucas 4FR or Cibie) headlamps incorporating separate sidelight bulbs; direction indicators mounted below front bumper (De Luxe & Super); round twin headlamps with main beam on inner lamps. Sidelight bulbs incorporated in outer headlamp. Direction indicator mounted below front bumper (GL). Rear combined direction indicator, tail/stop, reflector and reversing lamp (optional on DL) cluster

Instruments:
(DL and Super): Speedometer, water temperature gauge, fuel gauge, warning lights for ignition, main beam, oil pressure and direction indicators
(GL): Speedometer with trip recorder, water temperature gauge, oil pressure gauge, voltage supply gauge, warning lights for main beam, direction indicators and ignition

Standard equipment: Heater with two-speed blower, ventilation equipment, screen washer, two padded sun visors, headlamp flasher, front and rear ashtrays, Triplex 'Zebra Zone' toughened windscreen, child-proof rear door latches, anti-burst door locks, interior courtesy light, steering column lock

Suspension and Wheels

Front: Independent coil and MacPherson strut type with anti-roll bar and telescopic shock absorbers. No grease points

Rear: Four links and coil springs with telescopic shock absorbers mounted behind axle

Wheels and Tyres: 13in pressed steel wheels with chrome hubcaps. 5.60 x 13in tubeless crossply tyres

Steering: Rack and pinion

Brakes: Girling front 9½in (241mm) diameter disc; rear 8in (203mm) drum; self-adjusting hydraulic operation. Centrally-mounted handbrake operates mechanically on rear wheels

Dimensions

Overall length: 13ft 5¼in (409cm)

Overall width: 5ft 2½in (159cm)

Overall height: 4ft 8in (142cm)

Ground clearance: 5½in (14cm) (laden)

Track: Front: 51in (129.5cm)* Rear: 51.3in (130.3cm)*

Wheelbase: 98in (248.9cm)*

Turning circle: 31ft 9in (9.68m)

Fuel tank capacity: 9 gallons (41 litres)

Unladen (dry) weight: 1,809lb (821kg) **(DL)**; 1,812 lb (822kg) **(Super)**; 1,831lb (830kg) **(GL)**

Performance:

0–60: 13.5 seconds (1500); 16.8 seconds (1250)

Top speed: 87–90mph (1500); 81–84mph (1250)

Fuel consumption: 26 to 30mpg (GL); 27 to 32mpg (DL and Super)*

Colours:

Body colours: Embassy Black, Polar White, Tangerine Metallic, Pewter Metallic, Oasis Green, Tahiti Blue, Firebrand Red, Safari Beige, Baltic Blue, Cedar Green Metallic, Silver Mist Metallic, Sunset Metallic, Aztec Gold Metallic, Golden Olive Metallic, Electric Blue Metallic.

Trim colours: Black, Vellum, Green Opalescent, Red, Pewter Opalescent, Tan Opalescent, Blue Opalescent, Olive Opalescent, Turquoise Opalescent.

Optional Extras / Accessories

DL, Super & GL: Borg Warner automatic transmission with 1500 engine when fitted to DL or Super; metallic paint; radial ply tyres, seat belts, wing mirrors, whitewall tyres, laminated windscreen, electrically heated rear window, push-button radio, underbody protection, servo-assisted brake unit, side repeater flashers

De Luxe and Super: 1500 engine; reclining low-back front seats, reversing lights (DL only)

GL: Full wheeltrims; rev. counter

Prices: De Luxe: £766; Super: £811; GL £903. (All prices ex-works including purchase tax)

Model Variants: Estate Car (introduced 1972)

Significance: The first of the successful 'B' car range and the last true Rootes-designed cars, built under Chrysler ownership

All data Chrysler UK Ltd., except *Car* magazine, March 1970

---

of problems with the prototype cars in the USA. It was a double check on our work in the Rootes Road Proving Department. We picked up some useful feedback from the Americans.'

Mike Jones also remembers that one set of tests nearly didn't happen, due to trade union problems:

'We prepared two Avengers, fully instrumented, for hot weather testing in Italy and Spain. These were prototype Avengers specially prepared for this trip … It was meant to be like the cold weather testing where we had a full team of mechanics and engineers.'

The problems started earlier in the year when some of the development team wanted to keep their cold-weather clothing used in testing, but Chrysler management had told them to hand the gear back as other testers needed it. A strike ensued for the usual reasons of better pay and conditions, but Harry Sheron found a way of getting round the problem, which would otherwise have endangered the progress of Avenger testing. Instead of calling it a 'test programme', and using the original development team, it would be known as a 'Road Evaluation by Management' and the test would be done without any mechanics or technicians. Mike led the two-car evaluation in Southern Europe, together with engineering managers Tom Atkinson – engine, and Mike Simmons – chassis engineering. A report was later written from the 'unofficial' measurements made during the trip.

Other testing at MIRA and Wellesbourne was carried out until the development team was happy that the car was ready for production. The result was a well-conceived, stylish and well-engineered car, designed within a very strict budget, ready to take on the competition. The

Avenger Super interior ROOTES ARCHIVE CENTRE TRUST

In 1971, the twin carburettor Avenger GT version was introduced. As the model illustrated is an export left-hand-drive version, it is badged as a Sunbeam 1500 GT.

ROOTES ARCHIVE CENTRE TRUST

Avenger was available as a four-door saloon with two engine options and three trim levels: Deluxe, Super and Grand Luxe. In February 1970 Chrysler UK introduced the new Hillman Avenger.

Once it had been made available to dealers, Mike Jones was given the job of demonstrating the new car to dealers and the press:

'I was also asked to demonstrate one of the Avenger prototypes to Pathe News at MIRA. The cameraman wanted something spectacular, so he wasn't happy until I had the car airborne! Luckily nothing broke.

'At about the same time, I took an Avenger to the Simca Proving Ground, north of Paris. By then, Chrysler had Rootes and Simca under its wing. The idea was for Rootes and Simca to compare and show off to each other their new models to the Product Planners and the Engineers of both companies. Harry Sheron was there and he asked me to get involved in a rather crude acceleration test from a standing start. My opposition was a FWD Simca; I've sadly forgotten the model name. Luckily, I managed to keep ahead of the Simca, so Harry Sheron, for one, was pleased with the result.'

While the motoring press were not exactly jumping up and down with excitement following the debut of the Avenger, they were positive in their comments about it, *Car* magazine stating that:

'The Avenger strikes us as entirely predictable within the framework of its specification; without showing a real spark of brilliance anywhere, it seems to fulfil its design objectives successfully, has quite attractive road manners and specially good seats, heating and ventilation.'

RE-EQUIPPING RYTON

In order to make way for the projected production of 3,000 Hillman Avengers a week at Ryton, production of the Arrow models was moved to Linwood. The last Arrow model, a Sunbeam Rapier, rolled off the Ryton production line at 3.15pm on Thursday, 20 November 1969. Ryton had produced over 150,000 Arrow models up to June 1969. Phasing of Arrow production to Linwood began in July 1969 with the Hunter, Minx and Vogue models. A new Sunbeam Alpine, an Arrow version based on the fastback Rapier, was launched in the autumn of '69. A Hillman GT version of the Hunter had also been added to the range.

The first phase of re-equipping Ryton came in 1967, with the start of the installation of a new 185,000 square foot paint shop and 'Body In White' section and a 270,000 square foot body assembly area. This was completed in early summer of 1969 and the first Avenger was built in the new plant in June 1969. Car bodies passing through the new Paint Shop would be cleaned, rust-proofed by total immersion in an electro-phoretic dip tank, primed and finally colour sprayed by hand guns. The whole process would take six hours.

Body panels and sub-assemblies were pressed at Linwood for final assembly on Avengers at Ryton; gearboxes, back axles and suspension units built at Linwood were sent to the Stoke Power Train Plant for assembly into transmission and driveline units. All components manufactured at Linwood for Coventry assembly were sent via the Rootes dedicated freight train to Gosford Green, Coventry. Stoke Power Train production included 3,000 Arrow engines and 650 Imp engines a week, as well as

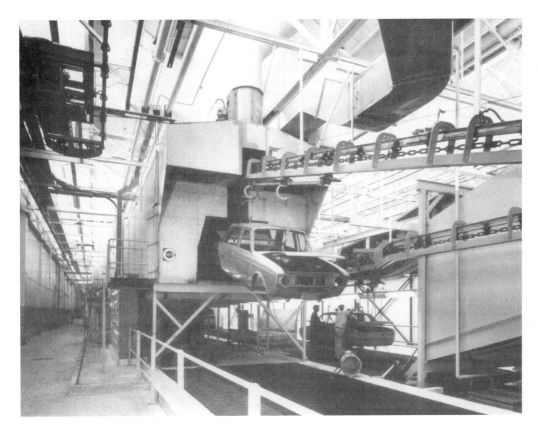

Prior to Arrow production transferring to Linwood, Ryton-built Arrow bodies were being painted in the new state-of-the-art Carrier Engineering paint system. Designed to spray, dip and spray the car bodies in each of seven successive treatments to clean, and passivate the metal before painting, the system could operate at a rate of forty-two bodies per hour. COVENTRY ARCHIVES

A Hunter body gets a final rinse with demineralised water to remove any paint not deposited electrophoretically, and which completes the 'Electrodip' priming process which completely coats the bodies with protective primer inside and out. COVENTRY ARCHIVES

Shop stewards say 'goodbye' to the last Arrow model, a Rapier, to be produced at Ryton, before production moves to Linwood. ROOTES ARCHIVE CENTRE TRUST

An Alpine version of the Arrow Rapier was introduced in late 1969. ROOTES ARCHIVE CENTRE TRUST

gearboxes, axles and front struts, all of which would be sent on return train journeys to Linwood.

In 1967, around 2,500 people worked at Ryton, and by the following year the number had virtually doubled. In December 1968, a final assembly line was completed and engine build commenced at the new 150,000 square foot Stoke 'B' engine shop. Production of 3,600 Avenger engines a week started in late '69. Imp engines continued to be built in 'B' shop. The old '85 Shop' was utilised for machining. Engine blocks were cast in the Stoke foundry at sixty an hour. Chrysler had invested around £12 million in the new engine shop, which was highly automated, employing around 450 people on day and night shifts. The transfer of the old trim operations from Stoke to Baginton had created additional space to enable the expansion of power train manufacture at Stoke.

Once Avenger production had started, quality problems associated with the tooling methodology in the American gate line jig method of body assembly started to rear their head. The gate line method, which had been used in some of the Chrysler plants in the States, seemed fine for full-size Chrysler, Plymouth and Dodge products, and due to its versatility could accommodate different bodies on the same line. However, consistency of quality was proving a problem on early Avengers, as Phil Anslow, who worked in 'B' Shop toolroom explains:

> 'The Avenger was bad, because it was difficult to weld and it didn't fit together well. On the gate line there were sixteen different gates and each one could be slightly different. There were thirty understructure trucks, which then came to the gate line. The two gates came round and married with the understructure and were locked on, and the roof was fitted.'

In the toolroom, a full-size model of the car was used to check for a good fit in a gate, but inconsistency in the gates caused slight variations in panel fit. The panel fit problem on early Avengers was compounded due to inconsistencies in early panels coming from Linwood. Scott Glover, who had been asked by Bob Irwin to come back to Linwood as plant manager in the autumn of 1969, was involved with that scenario:

Avengers receiving their final coat of acrylic paint at Ryton. COVENTRY ARCHIVES

'The mechanical process for assembling the doors, i.e. the inner and outer panel and the window frame, wasn't completed until about six weeks after production had started, so we had to use rather ad hoc and primitive means; a clamping arrangement to assemble the doors, so they weren't as consistent as they should have been.

'It was a real struggle ... Completion and proving of panel tools ran late. There were a total of fifteen major press lines at Linwood. It took two to three months before it got into some degree of sanity, where you could do press runs of sufficient length to be economically viable'

The manufacturing of Arrow panels that was now carried out at Linwood exacerbated the Avenger panel supply problem, as Scott Glover explains:

'There wasn't nearly enough know-how imparted to [our] people before it went into production. It took much more time to resolve problems and the people at Linwood got a lot of criticism ... I'm defending people who worked for me but I very strongly believe that there was not enough interaction between the machine tool suppliers and the setters and maintenance people ahead of time... so the Linwood guys were struggling.'

Despite production problems, the Avenger did sell well and some solutions were found to overcome initial quality issues. On 27 January 1971, Chrysler UK celebrated the 100,000th Avenger off the line at Ryton. The early

Avenger engines being assembled at the new engine 'B' shop at Stoke.

An Avenger body emerges from the dip tank as part of the seven-stage paint treatment process at Ryton. COVENTRY ARCHIVES

The gate line assembly tracks used on 'B' Car were still in use in the late 1970s. This is the Alpine/Solara line at Ryton, at the end of the gate line marriage section showing the understructure jig truck (No. 7). The next station would be where the side jigs were uncoupled from the understructure jig truck. The body side jigs were then returned for the next body side build. The truck would then go round the bend on to the re-spot line which you can see in the background before returning to the understructure build line. This build description by Phil Anslow, 'B' shop tool room manager.

COVENTRY ARCHIVES

Seventies line-up was now rationalised to Hillman, Humber and Sunbeam marques, with the Vogue being sold as a Sunbeam for a short period afterwards. There were now only three different platforms: 'A' Car – Arrow; 'B' Car – Avenger; and Imp. In early 1971, a new car was added on to the UK product line-up – the Chrysler 180.

CHRYSLER EUROPE AND THE 'C' CAR

As Rootes had become Chrysler UK under Chrysler Europe in July 1970, so Simca was renamed Chrysler France. Harry E. Cheseborough became the new head of Simca and Chrysler now held 99.4 per cent of shares in Simca. Philip N. Buckminster was named as vice-president – Europe and president of Chrysler International S.A. in Geneva.

While the Avenger was being developed, a new brief was given to Chrysler UK, to design an executive model that would fill part of the gap left by the Humber Hawk and provide a replacement for some of the Arrow models, namely the Sceptre and Rapier. It had to fit the UK and European market requirements.

In February 1967, styling guidelines were laid down and a market survey and feasibility study by Bill Papworth's Product Planning group commenced. A report was presented to management on 15 March 1967, which set

Avenger final inspection on locks, catches etc., at Ryton, November 1975.

On 27 January 1971, the 100,000th Avenger rolled off the line at Ryton. By 21 April 1972, further celebrations were in order as the 250,000th Avenger was built at Ryton. COVENTRY ARCHIVES

An Avenger Super Estate was added to the line-up in 1972.

A smart new GLS model appeared in September '72. It featured Rostyle wheels and had a vinyl roof covering. Illustrated is the 1974 version. ROOTES ARCHIVE CENTRE TRUST

out a timetable, costings and detailed market analysis for a range of cars that would take Rootes products through the 1970s.

The new car was then simply known as 'C' Car. In basic form it would be offered with an optional bench front seat for export and taxi versions. Initially a four-door, five-seater saloon was planned, followed by a two-door coupé, with the possibility of an estate car model later on. A conventional front engine, rear-wheel drive layout, similar to the Avenger, would be powered by an aluminium head version of the 1725cc 4-cylinder Rootes

engine in basic form, or a new 2.1 litre V6 engine would be offered as an option. A 2.6-litre V6 with automatic transmission would be standard on all premium/performance models, including the coupé, which would be marketed as a Sunbeam and as a possible replacement for the Rapier. Simca's 1.9-litre overhead cam engine was also considered as an optional powerplant. McPherson

A Sceptre-badged full-size clay model in the Viewing Room at the Stoke Styling Studio.

COVENTRY ARCHIVES

strut/coil front suspension was specified, suitably strengthened to carry the extra weight of the V6 and an improved Arrow rear suspension, with coil springs and trailing arms with inboard disc brakes being fitted on premium/performance models. Standard braking systems would be disc brakes up front and drums on the rear.

By December 1967, it was hoped that an endorsement by management would be forthcoming. Indeed, the concept was signed up to and Roy Axe, along with Bob Saward, Curt Gwinn and Ron Wisdom set about styling the new Sceptre and Sunbeam sports models. Much of it was done at Humber Road and finished off when the design department transferred to Whitley and became part of Chrysler Europe. By early 1968, the styling schemes for 'C' Car were complete and body tooling and tooling for the new V6 engine was laid down. By mid-1969, prototype cars were ready and testing commenced. According to experimental tester Ken Foxon, a Ford 3-Litre V6 was installed in the coupé prototype to make sure the chassis and handling would be right for the bigger engine, and when the V6 prototype engines became available test driver Owen Swinerd did extensive testing in a V6 coupé in Britain, Europe and Scandinavia and thought it was '*a fantastic car*'.

A lot of thought and logic based on current and future market trends had been put into 'C' Car, with many of the traditional and potential new customer slots being filled; from a basic version, to a luxury version aimed at buyers of the Vogue; Vauxhall Victor 101; Ford Corsair 2000; Volvo 144; and Renault R16. A premium version to replace Sceptre/Hawk and compete with the Rover 2000; Triumph 2000; BMW 1800; Ford Zodiac; and Vauxhall Cresta, and a performance version to take on the increasingly popular sports coupé models coming in from the Continent and Japan. It was envisaged that a 'B'-derived coupé would be added to the Avenger range in 1971/72 with the launch of the proposed Avenger Estate. Codenamed R429, a stylish offering was created by Axe and co, but it was rejected by Chrysler management. It was a shame, as it could have been a serious competitor to the Ford Capri.

By the time 'Styling' had moved to Whitley, the C Car full-size mock-ups were starting to resemble the final production version. This particular example is still badged as a Humber

POST-VINTAGE HUMBER CAR CLUB

Stylist Mike Moore looks at the rear nearside of a C Car mock-up in the Stoke View Room, while Ron Bazeley works on the roof.

C Car Coupé mock-up at Whitley and another example undergoing wind-tunnel testing. ROOTES ARCHIVE CENTRE TRUST

Chrysler management's plan, under Chrysler Europe, was for Rootes and Simca to co-operate on shared development and so management decided, fairly late on in 'C' Car development, that the 'C' Car could be an ideal project for such collaboration. Simca had been developing their own executive car – Projet 929, with styling exercises being carried out by Simca, by Bertone and by Chrysler's International Design Studio in Detroit – but it was the British design that Chrysler chose as their new European executive car for all seasons and markets. Projet 929 was cancelled and subsequently Chrysler management decided that 'C' Car should be built at the Chrysler France (Simca) factory at Poissy and that the French would finish the job of engineering the car. The upshot was that the project effectively fell between two stools; Poissy didn't want to take proper ownership of it as it was a British design and the British washed their hands of it once it had been taken to France for production.

Two versions of the 'C' Car were introduced at the Paris Show in October 1970 – the Chrysler 160 and the 180. Both were powered by Simca 4-cylinder SOHC engines – the 160, with a 1639cc, 80bhp engine, which conveniently slotted into the 9CV French taxation class and the 180, with a 1912cc, 97bhp engine which fell into the 10CV class.

Britain's version was the 180, introduced in early 1971, which went down like a lead balloon with buyers. Not that it was a bad car. Initially, it wasn't, but it didn't

A 1972/73 version of the Chrysler 180 for the UK market. COVENTRY ARCHIVES

fit any market particularly well and British customers certainly did not identify with anything adorned with a Chrysler badge; that had been proved during the Valiant exercise.

As well as demoralising management and the workforce, in one fell swoop – whether deliberately, or just by plain incompetence – Chrysler had killed potential for any future coherent product line-up that included Hillman, Sunbeam or Humber brands. Chrysler UK would be forced to keep face-lifting existing designs, with a product range that would succumb to price slashing in order to remain competitive. The whimsical egos of Chrysler executives had been satisfied, but little else was achieved. Despite a 2-Litre version with driving lamps, additional bright bodywork trim, a vinyl roof and Torque-Flite automatic being introduced on to the UK market in April 1973, the Chrysler 180/2 Litre was the orphan that no-one wanted.

Although initial development costs were put at nearly £11 million, some estimates for the V6 engine tooling alone were put at nearly £31 million. Rumours were that the V6 tooling was sent to Chrysler Australia for their version, the Chrysler Centura, but when that car debuted, it featured a stock Chrysler 4-litre (245 cubic inch) in-line 6, not a V6. Other rumours were that all Coventry 'C' Car tooling was just scrapped. Either way, Chrysler had wasted an inordinate amount of development money that the Corporation could ill afford. The 'C' Car signalled a pivotal point in the history of Rootes, and a death knell for Rootes car brands.

THE CHRYSLER DEALER NETWORK

In trying to reorganise and rationalise the Rootes dealer network in the early Seventies, Chrysler decided to dispense with the traditional two-tier Rootes network of main and retail dealers and replace them with fewer but larger single-tier dealerships. The new dealerships would order from regional offices rather than deal directly with the factory, as was the case with Rootes Main dealerships. The negative effect of rationalising dealers was to allow Rootes/Chrysler dealers who had lost their franchises to gain an import franchise – of which there were plenty: Citroën, Peugeot, Datsun, Fiat, DAF... thus allowing importers to build up their own franchises and a viable dealer network. In the light of new models still being developed at Chrysler Europe between 1973 and 1976, Chrysler had to rely on an ageing Rootes product range, supplemented by Simca models. This hotchpotch range of cars neither complemented nor highlighted any one model. From 1973, the Imp range was standing in one corner and the Simca 1000 and 1100 models in another, with the Chrysler 180/2 Litre in the middle and the Avenger and Hunter, Sceptre and Rapier hanging on to the ropes, doing their best to survive.

The export picture was a very different one from the old Rootes setup, due to Chrysler already having considerable representation for North American products worldwide. By the 1970s, the only export territories taking any reasonable volumes were North America, with the Avenger/Plymouth Cricket, and Iran, with the

Chrysler Imports Ltd supplied all Poissy-built products for the UK market, which included the Chrysler 180, and had taken over from Simca (Great Britain) Ltd, the company that had been responsible for importing Simca prior to Rootes and Simca being integrated into Chrysler Europe.

Hunter/Paykan. Success in the newly opened-up EEC was minimal. According to Hood and Young, only 663 and 698 Avengers were sold respectively to France and Germany in 1975. One apparent problem for the lack of sales was due to an integration of Simca and Chrysler UK dealerships; instead they overlapped and competed with each other.

The Simca 1100 van provided a useful car-derived van stopgap for dealers during the Seventies. Pick-up and high-top van versions were also available. It was rebranded as Dodge in 1974 along with all other commercial vehicle products.

Initially, sales of the Avenger/Cricket to the United States were successful. According to Ward's Automotive Yearbook, 3,200 vehicles were sold in 1970, rising to 28,000 in 1971; there was no doubt that the Avenger/ Cricket was the sub-compact that American buyers wanted. However, Chrysler UK was unable to meet demand for the Cricket and reliability and build quality issues, combined with long waiting times for delivery, were starting to put Plymouth dealers off of selling it. Chrysler Corporation management's solution to the problem was to import the Mitsubishi Colt, renaming it the Dodge Colt, as a back up to the Cricket. The Colt had a higher build quality, better availability and a wider model range than the Cricket, and had the effect of elbowing the Cricket out of the US market – permanently. In Canada, the Mitsubishi Colt was badged as a Plymouth Cricket and continued as part of the Chrysler Canada line-up until 1975.

Although the Avenger was not built by Chrysler Australia, it was enthusiastically taken on by Todd Motors in New Zealand. Production of the Avenger started in late 1970 at Todd's Petone facility, and in 1972, according to Australian historian Mark Webster, the Todd Group *decided to make a distinctive "New Zealand only" GL version*. It was named the Avenger Alpine and had a 1500cc twin carburettor engine like the Avenger

Guildhall Motors in Grantham, Lincolnshire in March 1973, with three Chrysler 180 police patrol cars which were supplied to Lincolnshire Police. This Chrysler main dealer was a typical example of a town centre dealership selling Avenger, Hunter, Sceptre, Imps and Simca as well as the 180/2 Litre range. ROOTES ARCHIVE CENTRE TRUST

Tiger, and a heavy-duty clutch, but had GLS features such as vinyl roof and a plush interior. It was a success and the Avenger Alpine and other Kiwi versions of the Avenger would continue in production until 1979. Todd Motors

US dealer brochure for the Plymouth Cricket, alias Hillman Avenger.

did assemble a version of the Mitsubishi Galant, but not the Colt. Versions of the Avenger were also built in Brazil and Argentina. Chrysler subsequently sold their Argentinean operation to Volkswagen Group, who continued production of the Dodge 1500, as the Avenger was badged, until 1980.

The early Seventies saw car ownership in Britain increase dramatically; most noticeably in 1972. According to a census carried out by the UK government's Department of Environment, the number of private cars in use rose by 5.3 per cent to 12,700,000, the biggest increase since 1967. The car industry was experiencing a boom, and during 1971, according to SMMT figures, Chrysler UK saw an increase in production to 281,538 and 16.2 per cent of the UK market, which placed them in the number three slot for British manufacturers, behind British Leyland and Ford. This would remain the position until Chrysler's 'crisis point' of 1975.

During this period, industrial relations became more difficult. A disenfranchised workforce combined with an insensitive and impatient management attitude by Chrysler saw the start of one of the worst periods of industrial unrest at Chrysler UK plants. Rootes had persisted with 'piece-work' payment systems long after the rest of the industry had moved to 'measured day work' and Chrysler had made considerable headway with pay and productivity agreements during the latter part of 1969, with the introduction of measured day work over the traditional fixed-day rate system, but a series of relatively small strikes in the early Seventies escalated into serious and financially damaging disputes. Workers at Linwood had always felt that they should have pay parity with the Coventry workforce and this had been a major source of grievance ever since the Chrysler takeover, especially as Pressed Steel workers at Linwood had initially been paid more than Rootes workers at Linwood. But the issue of Linwood inter-plant parity was settled in 1968. In early 1972, however, the issue of parity with Linwood and Coventry workers again raised its head. Linwood workers had always been paid less than their Coventry colleagues due to the Brabloch Agreement of the early 1960s, when William, Lord Rootes, had obtained the consent of the Scottish unions for a regional rate structure as part of the deal to come to Scotland to set up a factory. The 1972 parity dispute was over a demand for an £8 a week increase. The company responded with a £3 a week increase or £4 in return for productivity improvements. Duncan Robertson remembers the dispute, as well as the feeling among the majority of the Linwood workforce:

'There was generally an enthusiastic workforce to get the job done … The thing was, they'd say: "We're not getting the money they're getting in Coventry", and my argument to that was: "Build them to the quality they build them in Coventry!! …"At the time, we were building 60 cars an hour … there were people here that were totally foreign to the car industry. I was one!'

After considerable acrimony the dispute was settled with a £5 a week increase. One particular dispute at Ryton escalated into what became one of the most damaging disputes to date for Chrysler UK. It became known as 'The Shoddy Work' dispute of 1973. Chrysler management had started to overrule decisions made by foremen at Ryton regarding panel quality. Historian Peter Dunnett quotes one Ryton foreman who experienced this undermining of authority:

'I was responsible for the panels coming in from Linwood, and they were not up to scratch. It makes it very difficult for the foreman when he puts a tab on a car for quality and management nips it off. The foreman has no face…'

Dunnett goes on to make the point that, *'foremen are part of management. The chaos caused by strikes had undermined management-management relations as well as labour relations.'*

The spark that lit the 'Shoddy Work' dispute, which would last for five weeks before a solution was found, came, when on 24 May 1973, the Ryton plant manager accused the employees on the A shift of deliberately turning out substandard work because, he alleged, they were disgruntled at being recalled to work after a strike at Linwood. On the day, the whole shift was sent home

Hunter Estate, Imp and Sceptre on the assembly line at Linwood.

[MYTH EXPLODERS]

and the shop stewards contended that the action contravened agreements and that the employees should be paid for the whole shift. The company refused. This example of a seemingly petty grievance not being dealt with, combined with the lack of trust in, or lack of communication by management was not uncommon.

The situation was further aggravated by Gilbert Hunt, who threatened that *'until labour relations improved no further investment in the United Kingdom would be made'*. Hunt regularly made veiled threats to the workforce via the Chrysler in-house newsletter. Unlike Geoffrey, Lord Rootes, and his father, who regularly made a point of acknowledging the efforts and skills of the workforce, Hunt's negative comments only fuelled discontent. His disdain and arrogance towards the shop floor was demonstrated by the second major dispute at Ryton during 1973, the Electricians Staff Status Dispute. Mike Andrews was working for Product Planning during the dispute:

> *'When the electrician's strike was on I went and helped out. They wanted anyone who could work on electrics. After the strike [finished] I was in a position to talk to many on the shop floor to see what they wanted and one chap said, "At least we saw one member of the [Rootes] family every six months" … They really appreciated that.*
>
> *'So I went to Gilbert Hunt and suggested that he and Geoffrey do that … I said, "I think it would be good if you could spend an hour, or half an hour, walking down the production lines …" He just sat back in his chair and said, "I haven't got time for any of that malarkey, Michael!"'*

Geoff Wells was a toolmaker in 'B' Shop toolroom during the early 1970s and confirms Mike Andrews' observations. Geoff had been with Rootes as an apprentice since 1954 and would stay with the company until 1986:

> *'With Rootes, it was great going to work. Those people always seemed to be walking around the plant, but when Chrysler took over, you never saw Chrysler managers – it was the same with Peugeot.'*

Some of the management threats, however, were followed through, as Paul Walden remembers. He worked at the Rootes-owned industrial fastener manufacturer, Auto Machinery in Aldermoor:

> *'We were making UNC/UNF bolts for Rootes and other customers … We were on less money than the main plants. We got unionised – T&G [Transport & General Workers] and*

Toolmaker Geoff Wells, second from right, with colleagues in the 'B' Shop Toolroom at Stoke, with a set of air tools for drilling holes in Peugeot 309 doors. GEOFF WELLS

> *AEU [Amalgamated Engineering Union]. I'm not proud of it, but we went on strike and we got parity and then, within four years they [Don Lander] closed the plant.'*

There is another side to the frustrations that any motor industry management faced during the 1970s, that of 'demarcation'. As unions gained more power, so they laid down more rules, rules that initially were to protect employees and ensure that jobs were carried out correctly, but as experimental tester John Harris remembers, the processes involved could seriously hamper efficiency:

> *'There is a picture to be painted of the Seventies. As an example, we have the development workshop at Whitley, we've got fitters; we've got engineers that write job cards, we've got foremen who control fitters. So you'd say "I want a clutch changing on that Avenger"; you'd write the card out, put the clutch in the boot and it would go on a ramp. First a body man would come along and take the centre console out, then the chassis fitter would drop the back of the gearbox, then the electrician would come along and pull two wires off of the reverse light switch, then the chassis fitter would take the gearbox out, the engine fitter would change the clutch … and the whole thing would take all morning.*
>
> *'There were times when the competitions department was slack and I could have been out of there in twenty-five minutes to get a clutch changed. So this demarcation was an absolute nightmare.*
>
> *'Now when I got to Rover in 1995 at Gaydon, there were certain demarcation lines, but nothing like Rootes/Chrysler. You gave the fitter the job and he did the bloody lot! You only got a specialist in if he wasn't confident in doing that bit. I'm not talking about strikes, I'm talking about process.'*

Bill Papworth, who had witnessed the deterioration of industrial relations at Rootes and Chrysler over a decade, was of the firm opinion that management should take the overall responsibility for motivating a workforce, but often didn't:

'I never perceived during my time in the '60s … discussions with Bill Garner running the Stoke operation that industrial relations were an issue, because the old school — the Bill Garners — actually they had grown up with their union opposite numbers and they spoke the same language … I think it started to become really toxic in the Seventies.

'Once you get people to get away from their separate sides … Once people understand that you're not playing a partisan game they start to trust you, and if they trust you, they start becoming trustworthy themselves. And I don't think the Gilbert Hunts of this world ever had the confidence to do that!

'The reality is — you talk to, not just the toolmakers in Rootes, or Ford, or British Leyland, but the semi-skilled guys working on the line, or the girls in the trim shop. They are absolutely interested in their job. They like their job. They want to do a good job. So if you've got a company that employs 100,000 people and 90,000 are enthusiastic — what can go wrong?

'Much is expected of those to whom much is given. It's the job of management … you have the tools and skills at your disposal … you have a responsibility to do that in a way that will not just serve your own ends, but to try and find a solution that as far as possible serves everybody's ends, because

if you just serve your own ends, you end up just destroying yourself. So, if you have an industrial dispute, you can't "win" it, because [eventually] you will lose.

'What you have to do is find a solution — a coping strategy that is good enough and can lead you to do something slightly better. The adversarial approach may be necessary momentarily, but we have to continue talking … How are we going to move forward? The responsibility of the management at whatever level is to take responsibility for leadership.'

By 1973, Chrysler had acquired 100 per cent of the shareholding in Chrysler United Kingdom Ltd and on 22 May 1973, Lord Rootes announced his retirement, to take effect on 1 July 1973. It was timely, as the transition from Rootes to Chrysler was clear for all to see and he no doubt felt that there was little he could do to support a company that no longer carried his family name. He had spent thirty-seven years with Rootes.

Chrysler took the opportunity to place deputy managing director Don Lander into Gilbert Hunt's role of managing director. Hunt replaced Lord Rootes as chairman. Peter Griffiths, who had risen to director of industrial relations and personnel and Geoffrey Ellison, director of sales and marketing, were both appointed to the main board of Chrysler United Kingdom Ltd. Griffiths would subsequently become a joint deputy managing director with Canadian George Lacy.

Ever the expert after-dinner speaker, Geoffrey Rootes at his retirement dinner at London's Dorchester Hotel in 1973. Don Lander is sitting on Lord Rootes' right and to his left, Gilbert Hunt. NICK ROOTES

THE MYTH EXPLODERS
FROM CHRYSLER

The late Sixties and early Seventies saw some novel advertising campaigns from Chrysler, mostly aimed at the value-for-money family car market sector occupied by the Morris Marina and Ford Escort, in which the Avenger was a main contender. The 'Myth Exploders from Chrysler' campaign was different, in that it utilised a similar theme over the whole product range.

In an attempt to draw younger buyers in to consider a Humber as a new purchase, the strap line ran: *Myth: Humbers are big old cars the rich are driven around in. The young Humber Sceptre £1,259 (chauffeur extra).* Similarly, one for the Rapier proclaimed: *Myth: The British can't make a genuine GT for under £2,000. Sunbeam Rapier £1,352.*

Another campaign, released in October 1973, for the 1974 brochures, featured cars being photographed in various well-known tourist locations in Britain, such as *The '74 Sceptres – photographed in York* or *The '74*

The Avenger Tiger prototype. ROOTES ARCHIVE CENTRE TRUST

Myth: The Hillman Hunter is a stay-at-home family car.

The Hunter's just as at home away from home. That's why Rootes and the R.A.F. are each taking one down under on the London-Sydney Marathon. Over deserts, mountains, swamps, continents and the rest.
Without a rest.
Something of a test for the pilots.
At least they'll be saying goodbye to the cold with the hot Hillman Hunter.

The myth exploders.
HILLMAN ✦ ROOTES

The Hot Hillman Hunter-
you'll be amazed how far it goes.

This 'Marathon' advert was run while the event was on. Andrew Cowan is in the Marathon test car at Chobham, and the 'co-driver' is racing driver and Rootes publicist Jenny Nadin, or Jenny Nadin-Birrell, as she became.

The Avenger range gained a new 'rally-bred' model in March 1972 – the Avenger Tiger – a one-colour only (Sundance Yellow) hot-shoe special to counter Ford's Escort Mexico. The Avenger Tiger featured the same 1500 engine as the other models, but with twin Weber 40 DCOE twin choke carburettors that gave the car 107 gross (92.5 DIN) bhp at 6,100rpm and enabled a standing quarter mile of just over 17 seconds and a top speed of 105 mph. Minilite alloys were fitted with Dunlop SP Sport 185/70 x 13 low profile radial tyres and a rear spoiler and comprehensive instrumentation gave the Avenger Tiger its competition credentials. Gordon Jarvis is seen pushing his Reading Motors Avenger Tiger to its limit. Gordon was a regular rally competitor in Rootes cars prepared by Reading Motors, which included a Rapier H120.

ROOTES ARCHIVE CENTRE TRUST

In October 1972, the Avenger Tiger 2 was introduced, with an uprated 1600 engine; it was available in Wardance Red.

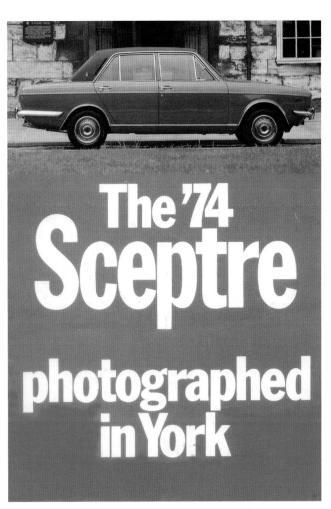

The 1974 Chrysler UK brochure campaign featured cars across the whole range from Imp to Sceptre.

From 1973, the Avenger range featured a two-door version, available in all trim levels, including this GT model on the cover of the 1974 Avenger range brochure.

In 1974, the Humber Sceptre gained a very well-equipped and plush Estate Car version. A Humber Estate hadn't featured in the line-up since 1967 and the days of the Hawk and Super Snipe.

A year after the Hunter was launched came the Mark 2 version, with revised interior trim and grille treatment featuring oblong headlamps and matt black grille, as shown on this 1971 Hunter Super.

A 1973/74 **Hillman Hunter GL Estate.** ROOTES ARCHIVE CENTRE TRUST

A 1975 Hunter Deluxe. This front-end treatment would be the last 'face' the Hunter would wear, but would continue until 1978, when assembly in Ireland finished. The final attempt to sell more Hunters, came in the form of a 'throw everything at it, including a radio, vinyl roof and sports wheels' model called the Hunter Topaz. It was finished in Copperbeech **Metallic.** ROOTES ARCHIVE CENTRE TRUST

Hunters – photographed in Stratford. They were bright, well-themed and attention grabbing.

In 1970, the Hunter Mark 2 model range had been broadened to create a range of four models: a de Luxe 'basic' model fitted with the 1500cc 64bhp engine and aimed at the fleet/rental market, which had started life as the Minx 1500; a Hunter Super, with the 1725cc, 71bhp power unit and a Hunter GL, with an aluminium alloy cylinder head 77bhp version of the 1725 engine, which gave it a top speed of 90mph, and of course, thick pile carpet and wood grain dash like the Vogue to help it earn its status as the 'Grand Luxe' version. The Hillman GT was now the Hunter GT, still fitted with the 94bhp version of the alloy head, twin carburettor 1725cc engine which made it a genuine 100mph saloon. Estate versions were available in all trim levels except GT. Facelifted versions appeared in 1972 with a revised grille, which was further revised for the 1974 models. The Whitley styling department became very adept at freshening up the appearance of the Hunter.

All Imp models received a further cost-cutting exercise in 1970, which saw the gauge of 'body in white' material decreased, according to a specification change directive issued by Whitley. The exercise did save costs, and whether it was as a result of this or not, but Imp panel fit was never quite as good again.

April 1976 – the last Imp off the line at Linwood – a Super Imp. The last Imp model to be conceived was a special-edition version called the Imp Caledonian. Finished in Cherry Red paint, it featured cloth Tartan-patterned seats and was considered to be the best-built and best-finished Imp to date. COVENTRY ARCHIVES

VARIATIONS ON A THEME OF IMP

Soon after the Imp had been introduced, the Imp engine was made available to low-volume specialist car producers who found its light weight and power ideal for their needs. This trend continued into the Seventies. Some of the more notable Imp-based kit-cars were low-volume sports cars such as the **Clan Crusader**, one of the more successful Imp-powered 'specials'. The Clan not only utilised the Imp Sport engine and transaxle but complete Imp drivetrain including suspension. The Clan Motor Company was set up in Washington, County Durham in the spring of 1971 by ex-Lotus employees Paul Haussauer and Brian Luff, and was designed by John Frayling. Production of the GRP monocoque Crusader sports car was limited to five vehicles a week, and at £1,361 (or £1,125 in kit form) in 1972, found buyers for every car built during the first months of production. The onset of the industrial problems that beset the country in the early Seventies was, however, enough to force the company to cease production in late 1973. Just 358 Clan Crusaders were built, of which 18 were competition versions, with a number of successes: second place to Andy Dawson in the 1972 Manx Rally; first place for Alan Conley on the 1972 Tour of Mull and 1973 Derwent Star Rally; first overall for Mike Hinde in the 1973 BARC Production Car Trials and first overall for Donald Heggie in the 1973 Jim Clark Memorial Rally.

After the closure of the Clan factory in County Durham, some of the assets were sold to Andreas Kaisis, a truck builder in Cyprus; but the invasion of Northern Cyprus prevented the resumption of Clan production until 1982, when Brian McCanless started Clan Cars Ltd in Newtownards, Northern Ireland. The company continued until 1987 and despite the use of an Alfa Romeo 1.5 litre 'Boxer' engine to replace the Imp unit in a new model called the Clover, Clan Cars Ltd experienced financial difficulties and after building around 130 road cars and 10 competition cars, ceased trading in 1987.

Davrian was a successful low-volume producer of kit cars utilising Imp power train. Designed in the mid-Sixties by Adrian Evans, it was an entirely glass-fibre construction, which might be considered technically difficult to build, but in prototype form it perfomed so well that Evans decided to build it commercially in 1967. Its success was such that production lasted until 1983, after which over 500 examples had been built.

The Sunbeam Imp Sport-powered **Ginetta G15** first appeared at the 1967 Earl's Court Motor Show. At that time Ginetta were based in Witham in Essex, and the G15 holds the accolade of being the best-selling Imp-based kit car ever. Production of the G15 finished in 1974. The company went on to build other models, such as the bigger G21 model, which was initially powered by a Rootes 1725 engine, but was later offered with a Ford 1600 GT cross-flow engine or a Ford 3 Litre V6 engine. The Walkett brothers, who started the company in 1958, sold the business in 1989. The business has since had several different owners, but Ginetta is still thriving as an independent sports and racing car manufacturer.

The **Zimp** was an Imp-based aluminium-bodied sports coupé model that was another example of right car – wrong time. The Zimp was a Hillman Imp with a body designed by Ercole Spada for Italian coachbuilders Zagato, but rather than suffer the cost of import duties on cars bodied abroad, it was to be built in the UK by British Zagato Ltd, in Dorchester, Dorset, which was run by Englishman Peter Thomas. Only three prototypes were built and a Zimp was exhibited at the 1964 Earl's Court Motor Show under the Zagato banner. Although Rootes had given approval for it to be marketed by them, things didn't work out, as Chrysler,

The Clan Crusader was the ideal sports car to get the best out of Imp Sport mechanicals. ROOTES ARCHIVE CENTRE TRUST

Ginetta G15.

The Zagato-based Zimp.
Senior Rootes/Chrysler test
driver Morris Evans is seen
seated in one of the three Zimp
prototypes that were built.
RICHARD SOZANSKI/THE IMP CLUB

by late '64, were starting to dictate terms and according to historian and journalist, Mike Worthington-Williams: *'Peter Thomas confirms that at no time during their negotiations with Rootes were they ever told of the Chrysler involvement and its subsequent involvement took them all by surprise.'*

Another stillborn Imp derivative that had been seriously considered by Rootes for development was the **Hillman Asp**, a two-seater sports version of the Imp. During the development of the Hillman Imp, Tim Fry, along with Bob Saward and Ron Wisdom, had designed a very attractive little two-seater sports car to run with Imp mechanicals. As with the Zimp, lack of money and an unsympathetic view of the car from Chrysler, Rootes' new paymasters in 1964, forced what could have been a winner into the loser's corner. Another opportunity lost.

The **Bond 875** three-wheeler saloon and Ranger van had a glassfibre body mounted directly onto a complete Imp transaxle and suspension layout. Both the Bond 875 Saloon and the Ranger van could boast over 50 miles per gallon and the uniqueness of being the only three-wheeler on the market to have independent suspension all round! Bond Cars Ltd, of Preston, stated in their publicity material that their Ranger van was as 'Thrifty as a Scots banker' and 'Sure-footed as a ballerina'. It never made it into the fleet of Trotter's Independent Trading though!

Many other Imp-based derivatives and variations were built, including the **Nymph**, a glassfibre-bodied beach buggy-cum-Mini Moke which was introduced in 1976, but only seven were sold; the **Scorpion** of 1974, a relatively sophisticated and expensive sports car built by Innes Lee of Telford; the **TVR Tina**, styled by Trevor Fiore, was a stylish sports car destined to be built by Fissore of Italy, but it didn't get as far as production. The **Gillie** was an off-road mini farm truck developed by Rootes, but which again, never progressed beyond prototype stage.

Modified competition versions of the Imp engine also found their way into a variety of other more unusual applications, and not just cars, as Richard Guy, who was building the Imp engines for the works rally cars remembers:

'They were going into Andy Chesman's hydroplanes, Jim Teagle's sidecar outfit ... You could be building three engines for rally cars, and only one was for a rally car – the others were for a hydroplane or a motor-cycle...'

Prior to moving over to Product Planning, while on engine development for Rootes, Anthony Stevens got entangled with what could have been a tricky situation when trying to respond to an enquiry from the Russian maker of the rear-engined Zaporozhets car. The little NSU Prinz lookalike was one of the cars that accompanied Moskvitch and Volga models as part of a Russian delegation show of Soviet cars that were to be made available in the UK. From the early 1960s, for the next few years, there would be a Russian exhibit at Earl's Court, as Stevens remembers:

The Hillman Asp mock-up did make it to prototype stage and was road tested thoroughly, but did not make it to production. Bob Saward (left) and Ron Wisdom, with their creation. RICHARD SOZANSKI/THE IMP CLUB

Colin Valentine explaining the finer points of his glass fibre-bodied Nymph, at the Imp fiftieth anniversary celebrations at Linwood in 2013.

'The engine in the Zaporozhets was no good, so the chief engine designer was in serious danger of ending up in Siberia. He made contact with the Rootes Group, so I was trying to sell him Imp engines. Then we had the big Soviet show at Earl's Court and there was a Zaporozhets on top of a plinth about 12 feet high. After the show I got a phone call asking for their car back – it had been stolen, somehow! ... I suggested that he talked to some of his staff!'

The Imp, and its derivatives, would soldier on until April 1976 when Imp production at Linwood finally ceased.

The Gillie. ROOTES ARCHIVE CENTRE TRUST

**Alan Fraser (centre) with Impetus, an Imp-based motorcycle
sidecar outfit built by Vic Phillips (left) and Mike Pearce for
the World Motorcycle and Sidecar Sprint record attempt.**

COVENTRY ARCHIVES

PAYKAN – THE TEHRAN ARROW

In 1967, Rootes had started supplying Hillman Hunters in
CKD form to the Iran National Industrial Manufacturing
Company (INIM), based in Tehran. INIM was run by
two Iranian industrialists, the Khayami brothers. Rootes
export manager John Land had much to do with setting
up the deal and Rootes engineers had helped design the
assembly facilities in Tehran for building the Iranian
version of the Hunter. It wasn't until January 1972 that
a formal manufacturing and licence agreement was
signed between Chrysler UK and Iran National to build
CKD cars, with a sales and distribution agreement being
signed in January 1972. Subsequently, Avengers were
also supplied in built-up and KD form. In 1974, around
80,000 kits were supplied to Iran National, which was
later renamed Iran Khodro. By 1979, the figure was
nearer to 100,000.

The Iranian Hunter was known as the 'Paykan',
meaning Arrow in Persian. The contract would turn
out to be one of the largest export orders, not only for
Rootes/Chrysler, but for any British motor manufacturer. It survived the Iranian revolution, and the failure
of Chrysler, but there was always the question of how
profitable the contract was? Throughout the contract
with Chrysler UK it was alleged that a 'commission' of
five per cent was always paid to a company in Germany

called Exporters Forwarding Company, Inc. on sales
of CKD units to Iran. According to Young and Hood,
in their analysis of Chrysler UK, the allegation was
'investigated inconclusively' by the Trade and Industry
Sub-Committee investigating Public Expenditure on
Chrysler UK Ltd.

David Lloyd was manager of engine and transmission
development in the early Seventies, before becoming
chief engineer at Ryton. He was involved with the technical supply side of the contract from the beginning and
remembers how Rootes got the deal:

> 'The Iranian brothers Mahmoud and Ali Khayami had
> been building a few Mercedes buses … and they thought
> they could build a car, so they invited all the reputable
> car companies in Britain, if not in Europe, to meet with
> them in Beirut to discuss CKD operations for cars, and
> reputedly, Rootes were the only company that took them
> seriously! Out of it came hundreds and thousands of [CKD]
> packs … before and after the revolution. I went there once
> before the revolution and three times after the revolution,
> which was in 1979. It was a very different place after the
> revolution.'

The Rootes family continued as friends of Mahmoud
Khayami. Nick Rootes says that his sister, Sally,

> '…distinctly remembers that the Rootes Iranian agent,
> Mahmoud Khayami used to visit us annually for lunch at
> our family home North Standen House. She says he was a
> charming man with a big smile and that he always brought
> with him a huge tub of caviar as a gift.'

Mahmoud Khayami was exiled from Iran after the
revolution and lived in Britain, but production of the
Paykan continued until the Iranian government reput-
edly offered Iran Khodro a large cash incentive to end
Paykan production in 2005, citing the car as an environmental hazard because of its high fuel consumption.
During its production it had become part of Iranian life
and culture and had found a place in the hearts and minds
of the Iranian public, bringing low-cost car ownership
to many.

In 1975, Chrysler Europe reached its 'crisis point'.
Chrysler United Kingdom had lost £16 million in the
first six months of the financial year in 1975, but that
was peanuts compared with the massive losses from
Chrysler's US operations – $231 million in nine months.
On 29 October 1975, Chrysler's chairman John Riccardo held a press conference in Detroit to announce that

Avengers awaiting shipment to Tehran. COVENTRY ARCHIVES

The Shah of Iran visits Coventry. *Left to right:* Mr Ali Khayami; Brian Rootes; His Excellency; the Iranian Ambassador; John Land – Rootes Export Manager; Mr R.H.E. Marks – Stoke production director. COVENTRY ARCHIVES

Roy Axe being shown the newly revamped Paykan design at Whitley. Much of the restyle was carried out by Whitley stylist Keith Cockell. In 1978, it was fitted with a Peugeot engine. COVENTRY ARCHIVES

A weather-beaten 1971 Paykan Deluxe. WIKIPEDIA

Chrysler Corporation could no longer afford its loss-making overseas plants and was considering disposing of them. In November, Riccardo came to London to have talks with re-elected Prime Minister Harold Wilson and his new Industry Chairman – Eric Varley. Riccardo's proposal was blunt – either the government take over Chrysler UK or they would close it! Eric Varley was not inclined towards Riccardo's ultimatum, but apparently

Wilson took a different view. What followed was a period of intense negotiation that resulted in the government agreeing to back a rescue plan for Chrysler United Kingdom. Figures for the year end 31 December 1976 showed Chrysler UK had incurred a loss of £42.8 million.

Chrysler United Kingdom was a political conundrum – it was too small to be profitable, and too big to close down!

COMPETITIONS UNDER THE PENTASTAR

Both the Hunter GLS and the Avenger, when developed for serious competition, would prove to be class leaders in racing and in rallying in the hands of drivers such as Bernard Unett and Colin Malkin.

The 1970 World Cup Rally was to prove disappointing for the Hillman GT privateers. The J.C. Bamford team (yellow roof) of Anthony Bamford, John Bloxham and Peter Brown, retired in South America with mechanical problems. The car finished the rally the day after the event finished, but didn't qualify. The Berry Magicoal entry of Rod Badham, Bernard Banning and Rob Lyall, also failed to qualify. Bad luck was in store for Bernard Unett, also in a Hunter, who crashed into a truck in Yugoslavia.

The gruelling 16,000-mile event from London to Mexico City was won by Hannu Mikkola and Gunar Palm, driving a Ford Escort. GORDON JARVIS

Des O'Dell talks tactics with Colin Malkin, seen here with his Avenger during the 1972 Daily Mirror International Rally.

Chris Sclater and Paul White in a Chrysler Dealer Team Avenger, competing in the 1976 RAC Rally.

The Chrysler Avenger of Will Sparrow and Paul White in the Mintex International Rally, February 1977.

Colin Malkin sliding his Imp around in dramatic fashion on the 1971 RSAC International Scottish Rally.
FOSTER & SKEFFINGTON/ROOTES ARCHIVE CENTRE TRUST

On his way to victory: Bernard Unett, in his Group 1 Avenger 1300 GT at the RAC British Touring Car Championships at Brands Hatch, 1976. COVENTRY ARCHIVES

Bernard Unett was a force to be reckoned with behind the wheel of his Hunter GLS. In 1976, he became British Touring Car Champion, adding to his impressive list of victories to date. ROOTES ARCHIVE CENTRE TRUST

Robin Eyre-Maunsell and Neil Wilson in their Avenger 1600 GT competing in the 1976 International Welsh Rally in which they finished eleventh overall. COVENTRY ARCHIVES

In characteristic style, Bill McGovern raises a front wheel while cornering hard in privateer George Bevan's Sunbeam Imp. The Bevan/McGovern combination gave the Imp some impressive victories between 1970 and 1972 in the British Saloon Car Championship 1,000cc class.

ROOTES ARCHIVE CENTRE TRUST

Chrysler Sunbeam Lotus driven by Jenny Birrell (Nadin) in the Scottish Rally, June 1978. ROOTES ARCHIVE CENTRE TRUST

Chrysler press call. In the lead-up to and beyond Chrysler's 'crisis point' of 1975 and the government rescue plan of 1976, press conferences were necessary tasks that senior management had to engage in. *Left to right:* Gordon Pfeiffer; George Lacy; Don Lander; Marc Honoré and two unidentified.
COVENTRY ARCHIVES

1976 – THE CHRYSLER PLANNING AGREEMENT

On 5 January 1976, Chrysler UK Ltd entered into a financial agreement and rescue plan with the UK government. A Planning Agreement was signed and conditions agreed on, and a report issued by Chrysler UK's managing director Don Lander outlining the details of the £162 million rescue plan. The government agreed to lend Chrysler £55 million up to the end of 1979, half of which was to be guaranteed by Chrysler Corporation, and bank loans of £35 million to reduce the usage of other short-term borrowings, which would also be guaranteed by Chrysler. New investment would be made at Ryton, so that the new Alpine could be produced there. Chrysler Corporation also agreed to write-off loans to Chrysler UK for £19.5 million. In 1977, the agreement was ratified and on 9 November Chrysler UK Ltd. became the

Gilbert Hunt, second left standing next to Chrysler Corporation chairman John Riccardo, during one of the Chrysler boss's visits to Ryton in the early Seventies. COVENTRY ARCHIVES

The workforce says 'goodbye' to the last Avenger to be produced at Ryton in June 1976, to make way for Chrysler Alpine production. COVENTRY ARCHIVES

Chrysler Avenger models, with the new-look Series 6 front end, coming off the line at Linwood.

COVENTRY ARCHIVES

first company ever to sign a planning agreement with the government.

Don Lander subsequently went on to become vice-president for Chrysler Europe. His place as managing director and chief executive officer was taken by George Lacy in October 1976. Car and truck marketing was separated and Gordon Pfeiffer replaced Geoffrey Ellison as sales and marketing director.

In July 1976, Avenger production would be discontinued at Ryton, to make way for the new Chrysler Alpine, and move to Linwood to replace not only Imp, but also Hunter, Sceptre, Rapier and Alpine 'Arrow' production. Since it was introduced, 627,126 Hillman Avengers had been built at Ryton. All cars were now badged Chrysler, including the Hunter, production of which was transferred to Chrysler Ireland under managing director Michael Rowe, who had replaced Malcolm Freshney, the previous head of Chrysler Canada. Freshney was appointed the new Linwood director, replacing Scott Glover, who left to pursue a successful career as manufacturing director of Massey Ferguson tractors in Coventry.

On the truck side, all commercial vehicles, such as the successful Commer Commando, introduced in 1974, were now called Dodge. Commer and Karrier would no longer be brand names and the PB van was given a new front-end treatment and renamed the Dodge Spacevan. One casualty, in terms of factory facilities, was the old Tilling-Stevens plant at Maidstone, which was closed down and work moved to Luton and Stoke.

C6 – the Chrysler Alpine

Development of a new medium-sized car had begun in 1972, and was a genuine joint effort from the outset between Chrysler UK and Chrysler France. Design responsibility was given to Roy Axe and his team at Whit-

Roy Axe (seated) and Marc Honoré inspect a styling rendition for the C6 Alpine.

The Whitley Styling team c. mid-1970s:
Back row: Jeff Davies; John Bint; George Barr; John Jeenes; Robin Austin; Ron Bazeley; Bill Brown; Matt Muncaster; George Morris; unidentified.
Middle row: Handyman; Handyman; Cliff Pickering; Ian Hancox; Dennis Hill; Geoff Matthews; Keith Taylor; John Malyan; Harry Tranter; Gordon Henderson; Tom Mosey; Sid Hall; Dennis Bell; Bob Hipkins; John Teasdale; John Patterson; Ray Downes; Graham Rose.
Front row: Bob Matthews; John Brady; David Franks; Bob Claire; Helen ?; Bob Eidshen; Roy Axe; Curt Gwinn; Norman Terry; Ted Howard; Fred Barrett; Ted Green.

ARTHUR LONG

A Kodachrome tranny for the original brochure cover for the 1976 Car of the Year, the Chrysler Alpine, taken at Biggin Hill with the Red Arrows flying over.

ley, which had become the design centre for Chrysler Europe, and engineering to Chrysler France. Although Product Planning, now under Marc Honoré, had initially considered a conventional three-box rear-wheel-drive saloon car to compete with the Ford Cortina, Vauxhall Victor and Fiat 124 Saloon, as well as being suitable replacements for the ageing Simca 1301/1501 and the Hunter, it was the trend towards the front-wheel-drive hatchback format like the Renault 16 that intrigued them, and this was what they opted for. The other advantage of the hatchback style was that it negated the need for a saloon and an estate version. Buyers of the Simca 1100 certainly favoured a hatchback style and so that became the starting block for the C6. By 1973, Roy Axe had come up with a longer wheelbase version of the Simca 1100 and Poissy had increased the 1100 engine to 1442cc. Product Planning mandated a five-door saloon and the result was the Chrysler-Simca 1307/8 in continental Europe and the Chrysler Alpine in Britain.

The Simca version was launched at the Paris Motor Show in October 1975, and by the end of the year over 46,000 cars had been built. The UK version – the Chrysler Alpine was launched in January 1976. The car was a resounding success in France, but only a moderate

success in Britain, but in 1976 it won no fewer than five major awards, including 'European Car of the Year' and 'Car of the Year' at the Brussels Motor Show.

Due to its popularity, Poissy could not keep up with demand, and so in August 1976, Alpine assembly commenced at Ryton, with around fifty per cent of the parts being shipped in from Poissy.

When it was introduced to the British public, the Alpine was available in two different trim and specification levels: a GL, with the Simca 1294cc tranverse-mounted 4-cylinder engine developing 68 DIN bhp, and an S, which had the 1442cc 85 DIN bhp engine. A GLS was added in September '76, which was basically a GL but with a headlamp wash/wipe system, tinted window glass, front seat head restraints, electric front windows and a radio.

All models had a four-speed gearbox and all featured transistorised ignition. Energy-absorbing plastic bumpers provided adequate protection from low-speed knocks and plush velour seating in all models ensured a comfortable ride for driver and passengers.

The Alpine was a good, well-executed design, and it was a sales success in Europe, but how much of a success as far as the UK market was concerned, is debatable. It was the right car for the rest of Europe, but in 1976, was it the right car for Britain? Maybe it was just ahead of its time.

Project 424 – Chrysler Sunbeam

Part of the government loan conditions was that the investment should fund a new model programme. Project 424, which was aimed at the 'mini-hatchback' market dominated by the Renault 5, Ford Fiesta and the Volkswagen Polo, was the first new model in what was a hoped-for complete Chrysler line-up, which included the new Alpine.

Project 424 Short Avenger. This full-size mock-up at Whitley is from February 1974.

Project 424 started out as the 'Short Avenger'. A shorter wheelbase hatchback version of the Avenger was envisaged and, as with the Alpine, the Whitley design team was given responsibility for creating the new 424. The senior designers on the project were Norman Terry and Bob Matthews. The job of interior design was given to Derek Cockell, an ex-Armstrong Siddeley man who had been with Rootes since 1958. His experience on Avenger, Imp and the Chrysler 180 would prove invaluable. Around this time, Roy Axe had been given a new job as Director of Interior Design at Chrysler's Highland Park studios in Detroit. Art Blakeslee, from the International Studio in Detroit, replaced him. He would prove to be more than a worthy successor to Axe, as a young Keith Cockell (no relation to Derek), then a designer at Whitley, found out:

> 'Art came in – he was a fabulous guy. He saw something in me and gave me a lot of opportunities. He was just so laid back, yet he motivated people – that was his skill.'

As there were considerable constraints on budget, there were a lot of 'carry over' panels from the Avenger, such as the floor pan as far back as the heel board, the dash valances, but also the doors from an Avenger two-door model, which were so skilfully integrated into the design that it would take a very observant person to tell their origin.

All planning, engineering and design staff threw their joint efforts at 424. From January 1976, when the project started, it took just nineteen months to complete, including launch. Graham Deeming, at Product Planning in Whitley, produced a plan for the car, based on marketing and feasibility studies carried out by Bill Padley at the marketing department in Ryton.

Styling sketches by Bob Matthews for the 424 from 1975, plus one unidentified.

Project 424, back at Stoke, after being thrown at a concrete block for its 30mph frontal impact crash test.

Chrysler Sunbeam 1.6S model.

Chrysler Sunbeam 1.3LS.

Chrysler Sunbeam ti.

1981 Plymouth Horizon Euro Sedan in Graphic Red.

Arthur Long, who had started with Rootes in 1950, was one of the first industry design engineers and a design department manager at Chrysler and under Peugeot:

'I was commissioned to take a drawing to America [during Chrysler period – 424] to be digitised. I had to go in case there were any questions, but there was no need for any clarification, it was so good!'

By February 1976, official styling approval had been given and trim approval by March, with 'surface release' also being completed in March. The final shape was approved in June 1976. The first prototypes hit the roads of the world for hot and cold weather testing in October and by January 1977 a pilot assembly line was built at Linwood. Part of its function was to train foremen and supervisors in preparation for actual production. They were determined not to make the same mistakes when the Imp was launched. In July 1977, the 424 was announced to the public as the new Chrysler Sunbeam. Along with the Series 7 Avengers which were now being built at Linwood, the first Sunbeam rolled off the line on 16 August 1977.

Three trim levels (LS, GL and S) were offered and three engine options: a 930 and 1300 on LS and GL and 1600 on GL and S. The 930 was the Imp unit, but a modified and revised version, as David Lloyd, manager of engine and transmission development at the time remembers:

'We knew about most of the troubles [with the Imp engine] and when the engine was revised and used in the 424 project – the Chrysler Sunbeam – we had all the problems ironed out. We had a conventional water pump, not that dreadful thing in two halves … We had a seal on the rear crankshaft, better crankshaft breathing, but [on the Imp] we did make the crankshaft breathing work better by putting it on the downstream side of the air filter … We had a heated inlet manifold, which most Imps didn't.'

The 1300 (1295cc) engine fitted the 7CV tax category in France and the 1600 (1598 cc) was offered in the S model as a 'hot hatch' version. A Sunbeam 1.6ti model was introduced in 1979 as a potent Golf GTi alternative with twin Weber carburettors, special pistons and manifolds; the Chrysler Sunbeam clearly had competition potential, but quite how much potential would not be seen until it came to wear a Talbot badge soon after. Considering how quickly the Sunbeam was developed, the result of Chrysler UK's efforts produced a range of mini-hatchbacks that were fit to take on competition in this growing sector. Given more time, it would have been an even better car, but it sold well and kept Linwood very busy.

During 1977, production of the Chrysler 180 and 2 Litre was transferred to the Barrieros plant in Spain and four months after the first Sunbeam rolled off the Linwood production line, another new model was introduced. C2, the Chrysler Horizon, was a well-packaged five-door hatchback aimed at the Volkswagen Golf. It was launched in France in December 1977, along with its two counterparts in America, the Plymouth Horizon and Dodge Omni. Although the French version and the American versions looked very similar in appearance, under the skin the Plymouth/Dodge versions had uniquely American content that set them apart from the European models. The styling was a Roy Axe effort, and his last before taking up his new job at Chrysler in Detroit.

Chrysler UK may have turned the corner in 1976, but two years on, the road it was on had turned out to be a cul de sac. In 1978, Chrysler threw in the towel. The losses from the American operation were unsustainable and Chrysler had effectively gone bust! The launch of a UK version of the Horizon would have to wait until another company badge could be placed on it.

SIR REGINALD ROOTES 1896–1977

On 20 December 1977, Sir Reginald Rootes died at King Edward VII Hospital in Midhurst, Sussex. The younger brother of William Rootes, later Lord Rootes, he was born in Goudhurst, Kent on 20 October 1896.

The Rootes brothers proved to be an ideal combination of opposites in character; Billy being described as 'the engine' and Reggie as the 'steering and brakes' of the relationship and between them they created an automotive empire that spanned nearly sixty years.

During his career with Rootes Motors Ltd, he took a keen interest in the British motor manufacturing industry as a whole, being President of the Society of Motor Manufacturers and Traders in 1946 and '47, Deputy President from 1946 until 1950 and President of the Motor Industry Research Association in 1952 and '53. He was also Vice-President of the Engineering and Allied Employers National Federation.

Sir Reginald's son, Timothy, died in 2020.

Sir Reginald Rootes talking with Peter Ware, early 1960s.

CHAPTER 10

EPILOGUE FOR A BRITISH MOTORING DYNASTY

'Everyone was quite happy to have a job. We still called it Rootes,
even after it became Chrysler and Peugeot.'
William Stuart – Toolsetter – Rootes Linwood plant, 1962–81

In 1978, both Chrysler Corporation of America and Chrysler Europe needed saviours. Chrysler Corporation got its saviour in the form of a new chairman, Lee Iacocca, and Chrysler Europe got PSA Peugeot-Citroën.

When Iacocca moved into the hot seat at Chrysler, he was aghast at just how dysfunctional the Corporation had become. It was clear that there had been nobody at Chrysler who had the vision to create a viable product range for Chrysler Europe, and that Chrysler's ineptitudes ran deep. Iacocca later commented in his biography:

'Chrysler didn't really function like a company at all. Chrysler in 1978 was like Italy in the 1860s – the company consisted of a cluster of little duchies, each one run by a prima donna. It was a bunch of mini-empires, with nobody giving a damn about what anyone else was doing … Nobody at Chrysler seemed to understand that interaction among the different functions in a company is absolutely critical. People in engineering and manufacturing almost have to be sleeping together. These guys weren't even flirting!

'They were babes in the wood when it came to international operations. I began to think that there were Chrysler people who didn't even know that the British drove on the left-hand side of the street!'

It is ironic that it was to companies such as Chrysler Corporation and General Motors that the Rootes brothers went for inspiration during their formative years, and it was the American product segment model that Rootes had carefully based their car and commercial vehicle product ranges upon. Fifty years later, the bean-counters from Chrysler had taken a wrecking ball to the once proud names of Humber, Hillman, Singer and Sunbeam.

However, during 1978, PSA Peugeot-Citroën had made a bid for Chrysler's European operations. In 1974,

they had bought Citroën, who were in financial trouble, and Peugeot had successfully turned them around. In 1973, Citroën employed 73,000 people and by 1978 the number had risen to 82,000, and Citroën was profitable. Peugeot were looking to expand.

CHRYSLER UK BECOMES PEUGEOT-TALBOT

On 10 August 1978, an announcement was made of an agreement between PSA Peugeot-Citroen and Chrysler Corporation, that subject to Government and other approvals, PSA would take over the principal European operations of Chrysler, in a bid worth £117 million. On 16 August, Chrysler UK issued a statement to employees about the take-over, the main points being that PSA intended to *'carry on the government/Chrysler Corporation agreement of 5 January 1976'*, and that there would be *'no major changes in management'*. On 31 August, the President of PSA Peugeot-Citroën, M. Jean-Paul Parayre, held a press conference in Paris outlining the agreement and the reasons behind the takeover. By 28 September, the UK Government had approved the takeover. On 1 January 1979, PSA Peugeot-Citroen took over the European operations of Chrysler Corporation and on 1 January 1980, the registered name of Chrysler United Kingdom Ltd was changed to the Talbot Motor Company Ltd. On 10 July 1979, Chrysler Europe became Talbot Groupe and all Chrysler UK cars were re-badged Talbot and Chrysler-Simca models became Talbot-Simca.

In June 1979, a new CEO and managing director, George Turnbull, was appointed to run the Talbot Motor Company. Meanwhile, Don Lander had left and in 1980

Talbot Avenger GLS Estate. ROOTES ARCHIVE CENTRE TRUST

1980 Talbot Sunbeam 1.3 GL. COVENTRY ARCHIVES

would join ex-GM maverick John DeLorean as the new managing director at DMC in Dunmurry, Northern Ireland. Lander would be followed six months later by George Lacy, as engineering manager.

Talbot – an old name on a new brand

The UK version of the C2, the Talbot Horizon, was launched in October 1979. It was an instant success, both in terms of media acceptance and public appeal, receiving the prestigious Car of the Year award for 1979. The Sunbeam also received its Talbot badge. The new Sunbeam Ti model was introduced in 1979 and spawned the Talbot Sunbeam-Lotus, which would turn out to be a potent Group 4 rally car, and be homologated for sale to the public.

The car started out as a Chrysler Sunbeam Lotus and according to historian Graham Robson, was Des O'Dell's 'better Avenger'. Des could see the potential in the Sunbeam and backed by Experimental Department manager Peter Wilson, installed a Lotus 907 2.2-litre 16-valve engine from the Lotus Elite, Eclat and Esprit, into the Sunbeam. With twin Dellorto DHLA 45E twin-choke carburettors, the engine developed 150bhp DIN at 5750rpm and 150lb ft of torque at 4,500rpm. A ZF 5-speed gearbox was standard in the Sunbeam-Lotus, which was announced in February 1979. It was produced jointly by Lotus in Norfolk and by Chrysler at Linwood.

Experimental test driver John Harris had the job of putting the Sunbeam Lotus through its homologation process:

'There were only two of us on that, my manager and me, because it was a Lotus project, but we were overseeing the

1980 Talbot Lotus Sunbeam. ROOTES ARCHIVE CENTRE TRUST

Lotus development. We took the job of seeing that the cars complied with everything in the blue book: brakes, transmission, and durability – everything that changed from the standard Sunbeam – a long list of stuff. [We had] six prototypes down at Whitley. Five guys doing the testing and the driving [who] were not meant to get involved to any great degree, because there was no money in the budget … but all sorts of things were done at Whitley that Harry Sheron never knew about when we had problems with it…'

As with the rest of the Sunbeam range, the Sunbeam Lotus was built at Linwood. Painted, modified body-shells complete with suspension, axles, wheels and tyres, would be sent to Lotus in Norfolk for the engine and gearbox to be fitted. The finished cars were then shipped to Stoke for final quality checks, rectification and striping, and sent out to dealers.

In April 1980, the Talbot Solara was introduced as a booted 'notchback' saloon version of the Alpine, built on the same Simca platform as the Alpine. In October 1980, a new flagship saloon model, the Talbot Tagora, was announced for a spring 1981 launch as a replacement for the Chrysler 180 and 2-Litre models. Apart from the Solara, it would be the only other new model to be launched as a Talbot, for inclusion in a Talbot model programme.

C9 Tagora had been conceived during the Chrysler period. Development started in late 1976 and by April 1977, a basic shape and concept was agreed. In August 1978, as many PSA mechanical components as it was possible to utilise were being incorporated into the design, to include engines, suspension and steering. Style approval was given in late 1978. The Tagora was intended as a luxury executive saloon and had some radical design features. Art Blakeslee was head of design but much of the overall design work was done by Keith Cockell:

'I designed it and when the design was put up to Peugeot management they asked for the rear wheel arches to be made to look the same as the front … but that didn't work, so I put an identical wheel arch on the front and rear, i.e. large with an "eyebrow".

'Art Blakeslee asked me to do it and I said I'd done it by making the front look like the back, rather than the back look like the front! I was using levity.'

The Tagora was offered in three versions: a GL, with a 2.2-litre engine developing 115 DIN bhp at 5,400rpm mated to a four- or five-speed manual or a three-speed automatic transmission; a 2.6-litre 90-degree V6 developing 170 DIN bhp at 5,000rpm was also available in the GLS, with a five-speed manual or auto box. A DT turbocharged diesel version was offered later and a super-prestige SX version to replace the GLS, in an effort to boost sales, but only a meagre 200 Tagoras had been sold by 1983 and it was soon put out to grass. It is interesting to note that both the petrol engines had output similarities to the two units originally designed by Rootes engineers for the Chrysler 180, but that's where the similarities ended. The Peugeot V6, known as the 'Douvrin', or PRV engine, was a successful joint development by Peugeot, Renault and Volvo to build a family of V6 power units, and was also used in the Volvo 760 and the Renault 25.

The commercial vehicle side of the business was an element that Peugeot did not want; their business was in cars, so in 1981, Renault Truck Industries Ltd and PSA combined to create Karrier Motors Ltd. Dodge commercial vehicles would continue to be built at Dunstable and eventually the Dodge name would be phased out and in

Talbot Tagora 2.6 GLS.

The third full-size mock-up for the Tagora, styled by Keith Cockell. KEITH COCKELL

Some of the design renditions for the Tagora. KEITH COCKELL

1993 all commercial vehicles would be badged Renault. In October 1977, a new version of the PB van was launched; now designated Dodge Spacevan. It would continue in production until 1983. In March 1993, production of Renault trucks at Dunstable ceased and the company became a truck importer.

Linwood No More

Following the introduction of the Chrysler Sunbeam, a survival plan for Linwood was laid down that would enable the plant to at least pay for itself through co-operation by management and workforce and by achieving more efficient component supply, a factor that had always been a sticking point as far as production efficiency was concerned, only for it to be scuppered four years later. On 11 February 1981, Talbot Motor Company boss George Turnbull decided that the plant was not viable and closed it, with the loss of 4,800 jobs. It devastated the town and its inhabitants. It has never recovered.

With the closure came the discontinuation of Series 8 Avenger and Talbot Sunbeam production. During 1978, Chrysler Hunter assembly in Ireland had ceased and by 1980, Alpine, Solara and Horizon models were being built at Ryton. A further restructuring of assembly plants had affected Poissy, with the loss of 4,000 employees, by which time it was becoming clear to PSA that the retention of three separate brands, Peugeot, Citroën and Talbot made no sense; the Talbot brand had lost credibility in France, as well as in England. A last-ditch attempt to sell Horizons, Solaras and Alpines was made

Talbot Alpine GLS. ROOTES ARCHIVE CENTRE TRUST

Talbot Solara GLS. ROOTES ARCHIVE CENTRE TRUST

1982 Talbot models

Talbot Horizon LD. ROOTES ARCHIVE CENTRE TRUST

Talbot-Matra Rancho. Based on the Simca 1100 platform, it was the first of its kind as a multi-purpose compact SUV.

ROOTES ARCHIVE CENTRE TRUST

by offering special edition models that harked back to the Rootes days by using familiar old names like Pullman, Vogue, Minx and Rapier, but all failed to attract enough sales and by 1985 the Talbot brand was dead in the water and Alpine, Solara and Horizon production ceased. All cars built in Britain would now be badged as Peugeot.

PEUGEOT'S 'NIGHT OF THE LONG KNIVES'

When Peugeot took over Chrysler, there was an initial sigh of relief by management because of a seemingly more positive attitude towards British management, but it was short-lived, as design manager Keith Cockell found out:

> 'The good thing about Peugeot was the empowering of management to take control of things and manage things properly and be responsible ... That was a uniquely good aspect of Peugeot.'

Cockell's enthusiasm for the French way of doing things quickly became tarnished as they gained more control and ultimately more confidence in carrying out their own agenda. It soon became clear that the only way was the French way! In summing up the French attitude, engineer Paul Walden echoes the feelings of many Ryton employees:

> 'Peugeot didn't respect British management, as the French went to the "Grande Ecole" for engineering. They didn't recognize British engineering qualifications. They were ruthless, and you had to do what they asked, otherwise you were put on a "nothing" job. One bloke was asked to go to Nigeria, but he didn't want to uproot his family...'

With Peugeot now the premier brand in Britain and France, Peugeot management saw an opportunity to centralise design in Paris. On a cold winter's evening in 1985, designer Keith Cockell got the news of Peugeot's plans. He explains the so-called reasoning behind the closure of Whitley:

> 'The French always used to throw at us the "English disease", which was strikes and working to rule ... and whenever we had a programme to deliver, you had to deliver your models on the day, or all hell would let loose. The French engineers, product planners and management would all say that we

would not meet the date – that we'd always fail to deliver the final drawings and wouldn't be signed off on time ... but of course, we did deliver on time, we did it out of sheer bloody grit ... but the politics in France was super-sensitive to the fact that all the design work was going on in Whitley. The French engineers didn't want to go to England and have English people telling them what to do, they wanted it in France!

> 'The night of the long knives came to me when I flew back from Paris into Baginton Airport. I got off the plane and Art Blakeslee was on the tarmac with Claude Dubertes and I said something like "What are you two doing here, are you going on holiday?" and Claude said, "You are coming back to Paris with us" and I said "No, I'm going home to Kenilworth!" It was about 8 o'clock at night and then, straight out of the blue, he said, "We are closing Whitley and moving all engineers and all designers to Paris" and I said "You must be barking mad!"

> 'I predicted that out of the ninety personnel we had in the studio, which was made up of engineers, clay modellers, trimmers, designers, only nine will move to Paris!

> 'That was the beginning of my end at Peugeot ... They presumed I would mastermind the move to France ... but I felt there was a brain-drain going on and I said "No!" About nine months later Whitley closed.'

Cockell left Peugeot in 1985 to pursue a successful business career outside of the motor manufacturing industry. The Whitley complex was sold to Jaguar Cars.

BRITISH-BUILT PEUGEOTS

With the Talbot brand gone, Ryton became the focus of Peugeot's UK manufacturing attention. The first of a successful line of British-built Peugeots was the 309 range, which replaced the Horizon. The first 309s were left-hand-drive models for export, which included a diesel version. In 1987, the 405 range of medium-sized four-door saloon cars was introduced for assembly at Ryton. By 1988, Ryton was back on to full two-shift working. This gave Peugeot confidence to bring in the 405 Mi16 model in September, followed in February 1989 by the 405 X4 and the 309 GTi and Turbo Diesel models. The following year, a 405 Turbo Diesel model was launched, which proved to be very successful. Both 309 and 405 models continued in production until 1993, when the 306 was launched. This coincided with the first robot assembly methods to be put into Ryton.

1987 Peugeot 405 Mi16. ROOTES ARCHIVE CENTRE TRUST

Peugeot 309 SR. Peugeot brought new welding technology to ensure a more consistent build quality. The 309 was the first vehicle at Ryton to be assembled with a framing buck. The geometry was set by the buck with automatic clamping but the welding of the body sides and later, the roof, was all manual apart from the welds along the sill which were carried out with a multiwelder. COVENTRY ARCHIVES

In 1997, a new 6,000m² Body-In-White extension was built at Ryton for a new model – the 206. Launched in October 1998, the 206 would be one of Ryton and Peugeot's most successful models. With the introduction of a new 206 CC (cabriolet) model, Ryton had built more than 400,000 cars by 2000, and over 200,000 were produced during the following year alone. Peugeot was proving to be the most popular car brand with private buyers in the UK and number two best-seller overall in 2001.

As 306 production ended, a new 206 SW (station wagon) was introduced in 2002 and Ryton became the favoured assembly plant for 206, over France, Brazil and Argentina. In February 2004, the one millionth 206 came off the line, which included the new 206 GTi 180 model. Speculation as to what the future held for Ryton had always been at the forefront of workers' minds during this period. Would the plant get the chance of producing another model, and if not, how long would 206 remain in production?

In an interview with Peugeot's in-house magazine in 2003, PSA manufacturing director, Frédéric Fabré commented, *'Although we planned to replace the 206 in 2005, the car's success means that PSA now has no plans to stop production at that point. The more likely timescale is 2008.'*

No commitment beyond that date was forthcoming, but a cause of concern had always been with the Ryton paintshop and its ability to meet future government and local council environmental standards. PSA claimed that they were investing in Ryton and that the future for Ryton was not dependent on getting a new paint plant. Others disagreed. There had been proposals for a new paint plant and although Peugeot did invest a considerable amount of money in the plant, it wasn't for 'new' plant to replace the old system, only for essential upgrading and renovation, i.e. where health and safety was a legislative requirement.

Andy Bye was Director of Quality and Customer Relations at PSA and remembers some of the other paintshop-related difficulties:

> *'Part of the problem with the paintshop was the smell from the factory which wasn't liked by Ryton village residents, and which did not help any planning applications the company put in for.'*

Peugeot were also running out of space at Ryton and there was nowhere else to expand. Andy Bye remembers *'the old research building was too difficult to knock down due to the thickness of the walls'.*

In 2005, despite the success of the 206 and Ryton maintaining a consistent finish and high build quality under less than ideal technical conditions, the writing was on the wall as to the fate of the plant, especially when the production figures of 129,618 for 2005 were compared with 209,607 for 2003. It was becoming clear to Ryton personnel that their days were numbered.

1998 – Ryton builds the first British-built Peugeot 206.

THE END OF THE LINE – THE CLOSURE OF RYTON

On Tuesday 18 April 2006, the announcement came that the Peugeot plant at Ryton would close by the end of the year. For some employees, the news was not unexpected, but it was the short timescale and rapidity with which the plant was closing that angered many employees. It wasn't just the loss of Coventry's last major car production plant; it was the loss of thousands of people's livelihoods.

Only weeks before, at the Geneva Motor Show, there had been no hint of any such closure, according to Christine Buckley, industrial editor of *The Times*. Instead, Jean-Marc Nicolle, head of product and strategy was reported to say, '*We will ask ourselves about the evolution of*

Ryton when we have to'. That time came quicker than everyone expected and, on 12 December 2006, Ryton closed, with the loss of 2,300 employees. The site was sold to an industrial development company for warehousing and distribution and the plant was demolished in 2007.

There were many reasons, and opinions, as to why the plant closed when it did. Ray Davies was a metallurgist and works chemist specialising in paint finishes, who had worked on virtually every paint system at Ryton since his apprenticeship in 1965 and was well-placed to give an opinion:

> '*Peugeot built a plant for the 107 in Slovakia, hence they had over-capacity. We were also one of the oldest plants … The death knell for the plant was the paint shop … They got as much out of the place as they could and then closed it!*'

To place Ryton in context with other plants in the Peugeot group, the Poissy plant was not only one of the most modern assembly plants in Europe, it had production capacity which was more than fifty per cent larger than the combined capacity of Ryton and Linwood! To extend the life of Ryton would only have been a stay of execution. Ryton was not only the oldest; it was also less mechanised than many other newer plants. Due to a more labour-intensive production process at Ryton, when labour costs were measured Ryton was, in some cases, costing twice that of other plants, as Paul Walden remembers:

'Peugeot had their industrial engineers comparing times for jobs between UK and France. In some cases we were using

The former Rootes Maidstone buildings were still being used as a Peugeot main dealer premises in 2014. Peugeot have subsequently moved out and the Grade II listed buildings are now destined to become luxury apartments and shops.

In days gone by, specialist bespoke conversions would have been carried out on a variety of Hillman cars, Commer vans and Humber estate cars at the Rootes Maidstone bodyshop in Mill Street. Peugeot cars of all shapes and sizes are the focus of attention in the bodyshop in 2014.

twice the labour. For example, at Ryton, eight people were used to do door glass drops. In France, it was less than half. Peugeot also had cheap labour...'

Sadly, Ryton had just come to the end of its useful time. Andy Kirkman, who was a facilities engineer at Stoke, BIW planned maintenance engineer and production engineer at Ryton from 1981 until 2006, sums up Ryton's dilemma: *'Ryton did not have the space to accommodate the footprint of modern robot assembly stations...'*

The decision to close Ryton was purely a cold, business decision. It's a shame that it was done in such an unsympathetic way... but that's business!

More than a decade later, the motor manufacturing industry has changed beyond recognition. Peugeot and Citroën, having acquired Vauxhall and Opel along the way, are now part of one of the world's largest automotive groups – Stellantis – sharing platforms and technology with world leaders in car manufacturing. The site of the old Humber factory at Stoke Aldermoor is now the headquarters of Peugeot UK.

THE ROOTES LEGACY

There is a document held by Coventry Archives that lists the current usage of former British motor vehicle factories. Most of the sites are pre-war, some were built during the Second World War, like Ryton; all have the same fate attached to them: 'Sold for housing development' or 'Sold for industrial development use'. Ryton-on-Dunsmore has the latter designation. The Rootes Group shares that status with a lot of other prestigious British motor vehicle names: Austin, Morris, Wolseley, Riley, Daimler, Armstrong Siddeley, Triumph, Jensen and Rover... to name but a few of the immortal names in British motor manufacturing.

Rootes was a company from a bygone period, and the Rootes Group, from when it was founded in the late 1940s, to quote historian Graham Robson, *'never put a foot wrong up to the 1960s'*, and then struggled to find its way in the rapidly changing consumer-driven postwar market for motor cars. Perhaps it punched above its weight by trying to compete with major corporations like General Motors and Ford, or even British Leyland, and although there is little evidence of the Rootes legacy in terms of buildings or production plants, there are still hundreds of examples of their cars and trucks, now in classic status, being proudly driven around by their owners.

WILLIAM GEOFFREY ROOTES, SECOND LORD ROOTES (1917–1992)

On 16 January 1992, the second Lord Rootes died. He was 75. Geoffrey Rootes was brother to Brian Rootes and both he and Brian and their cousin Timothy played major roles in the running of the Rootes Group. Although his father, the first Lord Rootes and his uncle, Sir Reginald Rootes, built the Rootes Group and developed the business in its formative years, it was Geoffrey Rootes who kept the company going, through extreme difficulties and challenges, during the 1960s, until he retired in 1973.

He had always been keen on field sports, and in his retirement served as chairman of the Game Conservancy Council and as vice-president of the British Field Sports Society. He was married in 1946 to Marian Slater, widow of Wing Cdr J.H. Slater. They had a daughter, Sally and a son, Nicholas, who succeeded to the barony as the third Lord Rootes.

Geoffrey Rootes with his favourite Springer Spaniel, Bervie, on the moors at Glenalmond. NICK ROOTES

The Hillman Imp is a case in point, and few people are more qualified to comment on Linwood and the Imp than Scott Glover:

'The Imp and the subsequent developments at Linwood generated upwards of 10,000 jobs in a severely deprived area for some twenty years, so the UK government's strategy of dispersing industry perhaps was not a failure.

'Could it all have been different? Despite the Rootes family's protestations, I am quite sure they did not have the money to invest to produce the Imp in Coventry. Going to Linwood opened the door to government grants and loans which funded some seventy per cent of the investment. The Imp was so nearly a winner ...'

Brian Rootes was of the opinion that much of the decision making behind the BLSP dispute and Linwood were down to personal promises made by Harold Macmillan. Bill Rootes, son of Brian Rootes and grandson to Lord Rootes had conversations with his father on the subject:

'He [Macmillan] made promises to the company and I think it was done on a personal basis, because Macmillan and my grandfather knew each other ... In both cases [BLSP and Linwood] government funding that was promised never came – that's what I remember from my father at the time.'

During his life, Lord Rootes engendered a remarkable degree of respect, especially from employees. Alan Turner was an indentured pupil from October 1948 to 1952, and went to work in the Sunbeam-Talbot sales office. He worked right through to the early Peugeot days in 1980, and remembers that 'the pay wasn't that good, but it was a jolly nice place to work! ... When my father died in 1955, I had a personal letter from Lord [then Sir William] Rootes – I always appreciated that.'

When Lord Rootes died in 1964, Sir Miles Thomas, managing director of Morris Motors in the Forties and then of BOAC said: 'His death leaves a gap that can never be filled ... While acknowledging the importance of mechanisation; he knew instinctively that men were more important than machines.'

Over the years, Rootes became expert collaborators. It was a talent that Billy and Reggie Rootes acquired, and honed, in order to achieve their manufacturing ambitions, as they turned to other manufacturers to augment their limited production capacity: Armstrong Siddeley for the Sunbeam Alpine; Jensen Motors for the Sunbeam Tiger and Carbodies for the Humber and Singer estates and early Hillman convertibles. Most important of all was Lord Rootes' intuitive ability for decision making. There were few automotive executives of his level in the early 1960s, who could make a major decision on a product, based on gut instinct, without having to defer to a committee or board, and know that the decision was right!

The hallmark of Rootes engineering and design talent was being able to think 'outside the box' and that talent produced some remarkable and fascinating cars. So, how should we think about Rootes in the future and what they contributed to the past? They created an automotive empire that endured for nearly ninety years, they made vehicles that enhanced our lives, built aircraft to defend our skies during wartime, their Commer and Karrier trucks helped us deliver goods for industry, empty our refuse bins and helped us fight fires. Humber cars took the Queen, heads of state and dignitaries to and from momentous historical occasions all over Britain and the Commonwealth; the Hillman Hunter came first outright in one of the world's most arduous international car rallies – the London–Sydney Marathon; the Hillman Minx and the Singer Gazelle took families on holidays to the seaside and abroad and the Sunbeam Rapier won cups in international rallies against world competition. Rootes factories employed thousands of people, providing homes and incomes for families for many decades ...

... Not bad for two brothers and their father, who started out mending punctures and renting out bicycles for sixpence a week?

ROOTES/CHRYSLER CAR AND TRUCK LISTINGS

Rootes Passenger Car Models (Home Market) 1960–1967

From	To	Make/Model	Variants 1	Variants 2	Variants 3
		Year			
1959	1960	Hillman Minx Series III A	Deluxe & Special Saloon	Estate Car	Convertible
1959	1960	Humber Hawk Series IA	Saloon	Touring Limousine	Estate Car
1959	1960	Humber Super Snipe Series II	Saloon	Touring Limousine	Estate Car
1959	1960	Sunbeam Alpine Series 1	Sports		
1959	1961	Sunbeam Rapier Series III	Saloon	Convertible	
1959	1960	Singer Gazelle Series III A	Saloon	Estate Car	Convertible
1960	1961	Hillman Minx Series III3	Deluxe & Special Saloon	Estate Car	Convertible
1960	1963	Hillman Husky Series II	Estate Car		
1960	1962	Humber Hawk Series II	Saloon	Touring Limousine	Estate Car
1960	1962	Humber Super Snipe Series III	Saloon	Touring Limousine	Estate Car
1960	1963	Sunbeam Alpine Series II	Sports		
1960	1961	Singer Gazelle Series III 8	Saloon	Estate Car	Convertible
1961	1962	Hillman Minx 1600 Series HKD	Estate Car	Convertible	
1961	1963	Hillman Minx 1603 Series IltC	Deluxe Saloon		
1961	1962	Hillman Super MnxMark 1	Saloon		
1961	1963	Sunbeam Rapier Series IIIA	Saloon	Convertible	
1961	1963	Sunbeam Harrington Le Mans	Filed Head Coupe		
1961	1963	Singer Gazelle Series IIIC	Saloon	Estate Car	Convertible (to '62)
1961	1962	Singer Vogue Mark l	Saloon	Estate Car	
1962		Hillman Super Minx Mark 1	Saloon	Estate Car (from mid 62)	Converge (from mid 132}
1962	1964	Hillman Super Minx Mark II	Saloon	Estate Car	Convertible
1962	1964	Humber Hawk Series III	Saloon	Touring Limousine	Estate Car
1962	1964	Humber Super Snipe Series IV	Saloon	Touring Limousine	Estate Car
1962	1964	Singer Vogue Mark l	Saloon	Estate Car	

1963	1965	Hillman Imp Mark 1	Saloon			
1963	1965	Hillman Minx Series V	Saloon			
1963	1965	Hillman Husky Series III	Estate Car			
1963	1965	Humber Sceptre Mark l	Saloon			
1963	1964	Sunbeam Apine Series III	Sports	GT Hardtop		
1963	1965	Sunbeam Rapier Series V	Saloon			
1963	1965	Sunbeam Venezia	Coupe			
1963	1965	Singer Gazelle Series V	Saloon			
1964	1965	Hillman Super MinxMark III	Saloon	Estate Car		
1964	1967	Humber Hawk Series IV& IVA	Saloon	Touring Limousine	Estate Car	
1964	1967	Humber Super Snipe Series V&VA	Saloon	Touring Limousine	Estate Car	
1964	1967	Humber Imperial	Saloon	Touring Limousine		
1964	1965	Sunbeam Alpine Series rv	Sports	GT Hardtop		
1964	1966	Sunbeam Tiger (VIA) 260	Sports			
1964	1965	Singer Chamois Mark l	Saloon			
1964	1965	Singer Vogue Mark III	Saloon	Estate Car		
1965	1976	Hillman Imp Deluxe Mark II	Saloon (facelifted B8}			
1965	1967	Hillman Rallye Imp	Saloon			
1965	1976	Hillman Super Imp	Saloon (facelifted *88;			
1965	1967	Hillman Super Minx Mark fV	Saloon ('66 oriy)	Estate Car		
1965	1967	H umber Sceptre Mark II	Saloon			
1965	1968	Sunbeam Alpine Series V	Sports	GT Hardtop		
1965	1967	Sunbeam Rapier Series V	Sports Saloon			
1965	1969	Sunbeam Rallye Imp	Saloon			
1965	1968	Singer Chamois Mark II	Saloon			
1965	1967	Singer Gazelle Series VI	Saloon			
1965	1966	Singer Vogue Mark IV	Saloon	Estate Car		
1966	1967	Hillman Hunter	Saloon			
1966	1970	Sunbeam Imp Sport	Saloon			
1966	1970	Singer Chamois Sport	Saloon			
1966	1970	Vogue MarkV (Arrow)	Saloon	Estate Car('67)		
1967	1970	Hillman Husky (Imp version)	Estate Car			
1967	1970	Hillman Imp Californian	Saloon			
1967	1970	Hillman Minx (Arrow)	Saloon	Hillman Estate		

1967	1970	Hillman Minx Deluxe (Arrow)	Saloon	
1967	1970	Hillman Hunter MarkU	Saloon	
1967	1976	Humber Sceptre Mark III (Arrow)	Saloon	EstateCar (1974, '76)
1967	1973	Sunbeam Stiletto	Coupe	
1967	1976	Sunbeam Rapier (Arrow)	Coupe	
1967		Sunbeam Tiger II 289	Sports	
1967	1970	Singer Chamois Coupe	Coupe	
1967	1970	Singer Gazelle (Arrow)	Saloon	

Chrysler UK Passenger Car Models (Home Market) 1968–1978

Year				
From	To	Make/Model	Variants 1	Variants 2
1968	1976	Sunbeam Rapier H120	Coupe	
1968	1969	Chrysler Valiant V8	Saloon	Estate Car
1969	1971	Hillman GT	Saloon	
1969	1975	Sunbeam Alpine (Arrow)	Coupe	
1970	1976	Hillman Avenger De Luxe (DL)	Saloon	Estate Car (from 1972)
1970	1976	Hillman Avenger Super	Saloon	Estate Car (from 1972)
1970	1976	Hillman Avenger GL	Saloon	
1970	1977	Hillman Hunter GL	Saloon	Estate Car
1970	1977	Hillman Hunter Super	Saloon	
1970	1977	Hillman Hunter De Luxe	Saloon	Estate Car
1971	1975	Hillman Hunter GT	Saloon	
1971	1972	Hillman Avenger Tiger	Saloon	
1971	1978	Chrysler 180	Saloon	
1972	1976	Hillman Avenger GLS	Saloon	
1972	1973	Hillman Avenger Tiger II	Saloon	
1972	1973	Hillman Hunter GLS	Saloon	
1972	1978	Chrysler 2 Litre	Saloon	
1972	1973	Hillman Avenger GT	Saloon	
1973	1978	Simca 1000 LS	Saloon	
1973	1978	Simca 1000 GLS	Saloon	
1973	1978	Simca 1000 Special	Saloon	
1973	1978	Simca Rallye 1	Saloon	
1973	1978	Simca 1100 LS	Saloon	

1973	1978	Simca 1100 GLS	Saloon		
1973	1978	Simca 1100	Estate		
1973	1978	Dodge 1100	Van	Pickup	
1973	1978	Simca 1301 S	Saloon	Estate	
1973	1978	Simca 1501 S	Saloon	Estate	

1974

1975 (Oct)	1976	Chrysler Imp Caledonian	Saloon		
1976	1977	Chrysler Avenger DL	Saloon	Estate Car	
1976	1977	Chrysler Avenger Super	Saloon	Estate Car	
1976	1980	Chrysler Alpine GL	Hatchback Saloon		79-80 as Talbot
1976	1978	Chrysler Alpine S	Hatchback Saloon		
1977	1981	Chrysler Avenger LS	Saloon	Estate Car	79-81 as Talbot
1977	1981	Chrysler Avenger GL	Saloon	Estate Car	79-81 as Talbot
1977	1981	Chrysler Avenger GLS	Saloon	Estate Car	79-81 as Talbot
1977	1979	Chrysler Hunter	Saloon		
1977	1981	Chrysler Sunbeam	Hatchback Saloon		79-81 as Talbot
1977	1985	Chrysler Alpine GLS (SX to 85) Hatchback Saloon			79-85 as Talbot
1977	1985	Chrysler Horizon	Hatchback Saloon		79-85 as Talbot
1978	1980	Chrysler Alpine LS	Hatchback Saloon		79-80 as Talbot
1978	1981	Chrysler Lotus Sunbeam	Hatchback Saloon		79-81 as Talbot

Commer Commercial Vehicle Models (1960-1969)

Year of manufacture		Model
From	**To**	
1954	1962	7 ton Mk.III Forward Control 9ft 7in w/b; 11ft 9in w/b
1954	1962	10–12 ton Forward Control 'Hands' Tractor Unit
1956	1964	Avenger Passenger chassis Mk.IV
1957	1962	7 ton Mk.III Forward Control 13ft 6in w/b
1957	1962	10 and 12 ton Mk. IIIA Tractor Unit
1957	1963	4, 5, 6 ton Forward Control 11ft 9in w/b

1957	1966	30 cwt Mk. V (B) Superpoise Van and chassis range
1959	1966	1 ton Mk. V (BF) Forward Control Van and chassis range
1960	1962	Cob Series II Light Van
1960	1962	1500 (¾ ton) Series 1 Forward Control Van range
1960	1962	Express Delivery Van
1960	1962	¾ ton Superpoise 9ft 4in w/b
1961	1965	Walk-Thru 11/2 ton Forward Control Van range
1961	1965	Walk-Thru 2 ton Forward Control Van range
1961	1965	Walk-Thru 3 ton Forward Control Van range
1962	1964	1500 Series II Forward Control Van range
1962	1963	CA 71/2 ton Forward Control 9ft 7in w/b (Tipper); 11ft 9in; 13ft 6in w/b
1962	1963	CA 8 ton Forward Control 9ft 7in w/b (Tipper); 15ft 7in w/b
1962	1963	CA 10-11 ton Forward Control Tractor 7ft 10in w/b
1962	1963	CA 12 ton Forward Control Tractor 9ft 7in w/b; 11ft 9in w/b; 13ft 6in w/b
1962	1966	VA 7 ton Forward Control 9ft 7in w/b; 11ft 9in w/b; 13ft 6in w/b
1962	1966	VA 4 ton Forward Control 11ft 9in w/b
1962	1966	VA 5 ton Forward Control 9ft 7in w/b; 11ft 9in w/b
1962	1966	VA 6 ton Forward Control 11ft 9in w/b
1962		Water Tender 11ft 9in w/b
1963	1965	Cob Series III Light Van
1963	1965	CB 7 ton Forward Control 9ft 7in w/b; 11ft 9in w/b; 13ft 6in w/b
1963	1965	CB 8 ton Forward Control 9ft 7in w/b; 11ft 9in w/b; 13ft 6in w/b; 15ft 7in w/b
1963	1965	CB 12 ton Tractor Unit 7ft 10in w/b
1964	1965	1500 Series IIA Forward Control Van range
1964	1965	2500 Series IIA Forward Control Van range
1964	1967	CC.14 ton Forward Control 17ft 11in w/b; 12ft 11in w/b; 14ft 8in w/b
1964	1967	CC.16 ton Forward Control 17ft 11in w/b; 12ft 11in w/b; 14ft 8in w/b
1965	1969	Imp Van
1965	1967	1500 Series III (PA) Forward Control range
1965	1967	2500 Series III (PA) Forward Control range
1965	1967	2500 Series III (PBCM) Forward Control range
1965		CC.7 ton Forward Control 9ft 7in w/b; 11ft 9in w/b; 13ft 6in w/b
1965	1967	CC.8 ton Forward Control 9ft 7in w/b; 11ft 9in w/b; 13ft 6in w/b;15ft 7in w/b
1965	1967	CC.12 ton Tractor Unit 7ft 10in w/b
1965	1967	CC.15 ton Tractor Unit 8ft 5in w/b
1965		VA 8 ton Forward Control 9ft 7in w/b; 11ft 9in w/b; 13ft 6in w/b;15ft 7in w/b
1965		VA 12 ton Tractor Unit 9ft 7in w/b
1966	1974	Walk-Thru KC.30 1.5–1.75 ton Forward Control Van range
1966	1974	Walk-Thru KC.40 2.45 ton Forward Control Van range

1966	1974	Walk-Thru KC.60 3 ton Forward Control Van range
1966	1968	VB.4 ton Forward Control 11ft 9in w/b
1966	1968	VB.5 ton Forward Control 9ft 7in w/b; 11ft 9in w/b
1966		VB.6 ton Forward Control 11ft 9in w/b
1966	1968	VB.7 ton Forward Control 9ft 7in w/b; 11ft 9in w/b; 13ft 6in w/b
1966	1968	VB.8 ton Forward Control 9ft 7in w/b; 11ft 9in w/b; 13ft 6in w/b;15ft 7in w/b
1966	1968	VB.12 ton Tractor 7ft 10in w/b
1967	1971	1500 (PB) Forward Control Van range
1967	1971	2500 (PB) Forward Control Van range
1968	1973	CE.8 Heavy Duty 13 tons 2-axle rigid 115in w/b; 141in w/b; 162in w/b; 187in w/b
1968	1973	CE.8 Commer-Unipower and Commer-York 3-axle rigid G.V.W. range 18–22 tons
1968	1969	CE.12 2-axle 18–18.75 tons tractor unit 94in w/b
1968	1969	Maxiload CE.16 Heavy Duty 2-axle rigid 16 tons 155in w/b; 176in w/b; 215in w/b
1968	1969	LB.6 Low Loader 10.3 tons 140in w/b; 156in w/b; 180in w/b
1968	1973	VC.4 Forward Control Medium Duty 2-axle rigid 7.9 tons 141in w/b
1968	1973	VC.5 Forward Control Medium Duty 2-axle rigid 9.5 tons 115in w/b; 141in w/b; 162in w/b
1968	1973	VC.7 Forward Control Medium Duty 2-axle rigid 10.7 to 12 tons 115 in w/b; 141in w/b; 162in w/b
1968	1973	VC.8 Forward Control Heavy Duty 2-axle rigid 13 tons 115in w/b; 141in w/b; 162in w/b
1968	1973	VC.8 Commer-Unipower & Commer-York 3-axle rigid G.V.W. range 18–22 tons
1968	1973	VC.12 2-axle 18–18.75 tons tractor unit
1969	1971	2000 (PB) Forward Control Van range

All data taken from Commer Cars Ltd Engineering Dept chassis allocation lists and vehicle identification lists.

Karrier Commercial Vehicle Models (1960-1977).

Year of manufacture		Model
From	To	
1958	1963	Gamecock 3 ton 9ft 7in w/b
1958	1960	Gamecock 3 ton 11ft 9in w/b
1956	1966	Bantam 'BK' & 'J' Mark V tractor
1957	1963	Bantam 3 ton Mark V 8ft 2in & 10ft 2in w/b
1963	1974	Bantam Mark V 10ft 2in & 8ft 2in w/b (British Rail)
1962	1966	Karrier 4 ton Forward Control 9ft 7in; 11ft 9in & 13ft 6in w/b
1962	1966	Karrier 5 ton Forward Control 9ft 7in & 11ft 9in w/b
1966	1967	Karrier 4, 5, 6 ton Forward Control 9ft 7in & 11ft 9in w/b

All data from Rootes Vehicle Identification schedules 1974.

Dodge Commercial Vehicle Models (1968-1970)

Year of manufacture		Model (Light and medium duty van range)
From	To	
1968	1974	Walk-Thru KB200 1.5-1.75 ton Forward Control Van range
1968	1974	Walk-Thru KB300 2.45 ton Forward Control Van range
1968	1974	Walk-Thru KB400 3 ton Forward Control Van range
1971	1976	K.120 1500 (PB) Forward Control Van range
1971	1976	K.140 2000 (PB) Forward Control Van range
1971	1976	K.160 2500 (PB) Forward Control Van range
1976	1983	2000 Spacevan Forward Control Van range
1976	1983	2500 Spacevan Forward Control Van range
Dodge 500 Series Medium and Heavy truck 1968 range		
1968		KL600 Low-loader two-axle rigid 10.3 tons GVW
1968		L850 two-axle rigid 13 tons GVW
1968		1050 two-axle rigid 16 tons GVW
1968		K1100 two-axle rigid (Premium Duty) 16 tons GVW
1968		KP700 two-axle tractor (fifth wheel coupling) 20 tons GTW
1968		KP850 two-axle tractor (fifth wheel coupling) 22 tons GTW
1968		KP950 two-axle tractor (fifth wheel coupling) 24 tons GTW
1968		KR900 three-axle rigid (trailing third) 22 tons GVW
1968		KR900 three-axle rigid (tandem drive) 22 tons GVW
Dodge 100 Series Commando Forward Control truck range		
1974	1978	DRG 08 Series 4 7.38 ton
1974	1978	DRG 09 Series 4 8.5 ton
1974	1978	DRG 10 Series 4 9.7 ton
1974	1978	DRG 11 Series 4 11.2 ton
1974	1978	DRG 13 Series 5 13 ton
1974	1978	DRG 15 Series 5 14.5 ton
1974	1978	DRG 16 Series 5 16 ton
Dodge 100 Series Two-axle tractor range		
1974	1978	DRG 18 Series 5 18 ton
1978		DRG 20 Series 5 19.68 ton

The above data is taken from Dodge Vehicle Identification Schedule to show the range of the 500 Series when produced at Dunstable in 1968 only. The 100 Series data is an abridged listing of the range which was initially introduced as the Commer 100 Series Commando in 1974 and re-branded as Dodge later that year. The 50 series van and light duty truck range are not included. All Dodge commercial vehicles subsequently were re-branded as Renault.

BIBLIOGRAPHY

Allan, Robert J. *Geoffrey Rootes' dream for Linwood* (Book-marque Publishing, 1991)

Axe, Roy, *A Life in Style* (A R Publishing, 2010)

Burgess-Wise, David, *Ford at Dagenham – The Rise and Fall of Detroit in Europe* (The Breedon Books Publishing Company, 2001)

Carroll, William, *Tiger – An Exceptional Motorcar* (Auto Book Press, 1978)

Carverhill, Geoff, *The Commer Story* (The Crowood Press, 2002; reprinted 2013)

Carverhill, Geoff, *The Rootes Story – The Making of a Global Automotive Empire* (The Crowood Press, 2018)

Childs, David, 'Britain Since 1945 – A Political History' (Routledge)

Dunnett, Peter J.S., *The Decline of the British Motor Industry* (Routledge, 1980)

Henshaw, David & Peter, *Apex – The Inside Story of the Hillman Imp* (Bookmarque Publishing, 2002)

Kimberley, Damien, *Coventry's Motorcar Heritage* (The History Press, 2012)

Lewis, Stephen, *Humber Cars – The Post-War Years* (Amberley Publishing, 2021)

Munro, Bill, *Carbodies – The Complete Story* (The Crowood Press, 1998)

Nicholls, Ian – *Essay – the decline of BMC – the European dimension* (AROnline www.aronline.co.uk 2016)

Procter, Peter – *Pedals and Pistons* (Mercian Manuals)

Robson, Graham, *The Cars of the Rootes Group* (MRP Publications, 1990)

Robson, Graham, *Rootes Maestros* (Mercian Manuals, 2008)

Taylor, Mike, *Tiger – The Making of a Sports Car* (Gentry Books Ltd, 1979)

Thoms, David & Donnelly, Tom, *The Motor Car Industry in Coventry Since the 1890s* (Croom Helm, 1985)

Van Damm, Sheila, *No Excuses* (Putnam, 1957)

Watts, Martin, *Classic Camper Vans – The Inside Story – A Guide to Classic British Campers 1956–1979* (The Crowood Press, 2007)

Webster, Mark, *Assembly – New Zealand Car Production 1921–98* (Reed Publishing (NZ) Ltd, 2002)

Wood, Jonathan, *Wheels of Misfortune* (Sidgwick & Jackson, 1988)

Young, Stephen & Hood, Neil *Chrysler UK – A Corporation in Transition* (Praeger Publishers 1977)

Autocar magazine
Car magazine
Classic and Sports Car magazine
Motor magazine

Chrysler Bulletin, Chrysler Challenge newspaper
Rootes Review, Rootes Gazette, Arrow newspaper

AROnline (aronline.co.uk) various articles by Ian Nicholls and Keith Adams

INDEX